Plato's Democratic Entanglements

Plato's Democratic Entanglements

ATHENIAN POLITICS AND
THE PRACTICE OF PHILOSOPHY

S. Sara Monoson

PRINCETON UNIVERSITY PRESS
PRINCETON, NEW JERSEY

Copyright © 2000 by Princeton University Press
Published by Princeton University Press, 41 William Street,
Princeton, New Jersey 08540
In the United Kingdom: Princeton University Press,
Chichester, West Sussex

Library of Congress Cataloging-in-Publication Data

Monoson, Susan Sara, 1960–
Plato's democratic entanglements : Athenian politics and the practice
of philosophy / S. Sara Monoson
p.   cm.
Includes bibliographical references and index.
ISBN 0-691-04366-3 (cloth : alk. paper)
1. Democracy—Greece—Athens—History. 2. Plato—
Views on democracy. I. Title
JC75.D36 M65 2000
320.438′5—dc21   99-054924

This book has been composed in Adobe Galliard

The paper used in this publication meets the minimum requirements
of ANSI/NISO Z39.48-1992 (R1997) (*Permanence of Paper*)

www.pup.princeton.edu

Printed in the United States of America

3   5   7   9   10   8   6   4   2

For Mimi and David Monoson,
my wonderful parents

———————————

CONTENTS

ACKNOWLEDGMENTS

I OFFER an interpretation of Plato that aims to expose his forging of a serious, though limited, alliance between the practice of philosophy and Athenian democratic politics. This project may seem preposterous to some, intriguing to others, long overdue to others still. I have tried to write with this diverse and multidisciplinary readership in mind.

My approach is contextual. I juxtapose Plato's depictions of intellectual labor with contemporaneous demotic forms of civic discourse and the democratic ideals celebrated therein. In so doing, I engage work in Greek historiography and literature by classicists as well as recent scholarship on Plato's political thought by theorists and philosophers.

I have relied on Oxford Classical Texts (Oxford: Clarendon) for the Greek text of material cited. I have also regularly consulted the following commentaries: James Adam, *The Republic of Plato, Edited with Critical Notes, Commentary and Appendices*, 2 vols., 2d ed. (Cambridge: Cambridge University Press, 1963); E. R. Dodds, *Plato. Gorgias. A Revised Text with Introduction and Commentary* (Oxford: Clarendon, 1959); A. W. Gomme, *A Historical Commentary on Thucydides*, 5 vols. (vols. 4 and 5 by A. W. Gomme, A. Andrewes, and K. J. Dover) (Oxford: Clarendon, 1950–81); and P. J. Rhodes, *Thucydides Book 2, Edited Greek Text, Translation and Commentary* (Warmister: Aris and Philips, 1988). All Greek cited has been transliterated. Note that I have employed *ch* for *chi, x* for *xi, ph* for *phi, u* for *upsilon, ē* for *eta, ō* for *omega*, and *i* for *iota* subscript. In the case of well-known names, however, I have retained the customary Latinized spelling (e.g., Socrates, not Sokrates). Unless otherwise noted, translations cited are or derive from the following editions: Allan Bloom, *The Republic of Plato. Translation with Notes and Interpretive Essay* (New York: Basic, 1968); Terence Irwin, *Plato. Gorgias* (Oxford: Clarendon, 1979); R. E. Allen, "Plato's *Menexenus*," in his *The Dialogues of Plato*, vol. 1 (New Haven: Yale University Press, 1985), pp. 315–43; Thomas Pangle, *The Laws of Plato. Translated, with Notes and an Interpretive Essay* (New York: Basic, 1980). The remaining texts of Plato cited are from, or are adapted from, those collected in John M. Cooper, ed., *Plato: Complete Works*, (Indianapolis, Ind.: Hackett, 1997). Translations from Thucydides are from Robert B. Strassler, ed., *The Landmark Thucydides: A Revised Edition of the Richard Crawley Translation* (New York: Free Press, 1996). Translations from Aristotle's *Constitution of Athens* are from Kurt von Fritz and Ernst Kapp, *Aristotle's Constitution of Athens and Re-*

lated Texts. Translated with an Introduction and Notes (New York: Haffner, 1974). Editions of other texts are identified in the notes.

This book began as a doctoral dissertation in the Program in Political Philosophy and Department of Politics at Princeton University. It was my great good fortune to work under the supervision of W. Robert Connor, George Kateb, and Alan Ryan, and to have J. Peter Euben as my outside reader. These teachers, now also friends, have shaped my thinking with probing questions and insightful comments. Each one has my enduring gratitude for his generosity and many kindnesses.

Many other individuals have helped me develop the ideas presented here by offering candid comments on earlier drafts of portions of this work. I have benefited from the exacting standards of Richard Dagger, Tracy Davis, Jill Frank, Bonnie Honig, Richard Kraut, Jenny Mansbridge, Gerald Mara, Susan Moller Okin, Arlene Saxonhouse, Stephen Salkever, Keith Topper, Pierre Vidal-Naquet, and Robert Wallace. Panelists and audiences at meetings of the American Political Science Association, Western Political Science Association, and Northeastern Political Science Association, where I presented various portions of this book over the past few years, were also helpful, as were fellow participants at the conference "Democracy and Tyranny in Archaic and Classical Greece" at Northwestern University in April 1999. My thanks also to my research assistant, Ella Myers, for her help in proofreading the entire manuscript.

It has also been a pleasure to work with Princeton University Press. For their thoughtful and gracious help at various stages in the preparation of this book, my warm thanks to my editor, Ann Wald, to her assistants, and to Sherry Wert, Jeffrey Carnes, Ian Malcolm, and Karen Verde.

Many colleagues and friends in and out of the Department of Political Science at Northwestern University have been a delight as I have labored to get the book out. My warm thanks in particular to Susan Herbst and the network of women colleagues on whom I have come to rely for frank talk and good cheer. I also recall with pleasure my two years on the faculty in the Department of Political Science at Arizona State University.

Two fellowships provided support at crucial moments in the development of this project. Most recently, I was a Junior Faculty Fellow in the Alice Berline Kaplan Center for the Humanities in Northwestern University. Some years earlier I received a Charlotte Newcombe Dissertation Year Fellowship.

Parts of various chapters have appeared in print: "Frank Speech, Democracy and Philosophy: Plato's Debt to a Democratic Strategy of Civic Discourse," in *Athenian Political Thought and the Reconstruction of American Democracy*, ed. J. Peter Euben, Josiah Ober, and John Wallach (Ithaca: Cornell University Press, 1994), pp. 172–97, copyright (c) 1994 by Cornell University; "Citizen as *Erastēs*: Erotic Imagery and the Idea of

Reciprocity in the Periclean Funeral Oration," *Political Theory* 22, no. 2 (1994): 253–76, copyright (c) 1994 by Sage Publications; "Remembering Pericles: The Political and Theoretical Import of Plato's *Menexenus*," *Political Theory* 26, no. 4 (1998): 489–513, copyright (c) 1998 by Sage Publications, reprinted by permission.

I have lived with this book for some time and, though in a different way, so has my extended family. All the Monosons, Hochmans, and Grossmans—and in particular, Seth, Jill and Pauline—have displayed an infectious confidence in me that has been a key source of strength. Old friends, too, have sustained me in my labors. In particular, Barrie Place and Vicky Stone have my warmest thanks. To my beloved Michael Berns, whom I met as I was preparing to move to Evanston and who joined me there a few months later, thank you for your patience. To my adored Alexander, know that you inspired my choice of cover art. I have reserved expression of my greatest debt for the dedication.

Plato's Democratic Entanglements

Introduction

SITING PLATO

IN THIS BOOK I argue for a fundamental rethinking of the relationship between Plato's thought and the practice of democracy. I propose that the canonical view of Plato as a virulent antidemocrat is not sound.[1] Rather, in his work, a searching consideration of the possibilities raised by some democratic ideals and institutions coexists alongside severe criticisms of democratic life and politics. Plato finds the lived experience and ideology of Athenian democracy repulsive and fascinating, troubling and intriguing. He not only assails democratic practice but also weaves hesitations about the reach of that attack into the very presentation of his thought. A substantial measure of ambivalence, not unequivocal hostility, marks his attitude toward democracy as he knew it.

This dimension of Plato's thought has remained largely unexplored for some time. This is in part because Plato has for centuries been cast as a founding figure in what has been called the "antidemocratic tradition in Western thought."[2] But even when commentators have noted that state-

---

[1] This view is longstanding and widely held, and thus I call it canonical. Typical are passages such as the following: "Plato's antipathy to democracy as he knew it thus emerges clearly in this section [the simile of the ship at *Republic* 487b–497a]. No doubt his antidemocratic attitude is a product of various complex factors, but what should interest us here is the philosophical ground for his condemnation of democracy" (R. C. Cross and A. D. Woozley, *Plato's Republic: A Philosophical Commentary* [London: Macmillan, 1964], p. 198); "The very notion of democracy has always provided a field day for critics. Critics are roughly of three kinds: those fundamentally opposed to democracy because, like Plato, they believe that while it may be possible it is inherently undesirable . . ." (Robert Dahl, *Democracy and Its Critics* [New Haven: Yale University Press, 1989], p. 2); and, "Plato was antidemocratic in the highest degree" (G.E.M. de Ste. Croix, *The Class Struggle in the Ancient Greek World* [London: Duckworth, 1981], p. 71). A notable exception is Ernest Barker, *Greek Political Theory: Plato and His Predecessors* (New York: Methuen, 1918). He writes that although Plato is a "bitter critic of Periclean democracy . . . he can also do justice to its better side even in the *Republic*" (p. 126, see also p. 299).

[2] Jennifer Tolbert Roberts, *Athens on Trial: The Antidemocratic Tradition in Western Thought* (Princeton: Princeton University Press, 1994). Roberts finds that "the subtleties [of Plato's thought on democracy] have not been incorporated into the tradition on Plato, Socrates and Athenian democracy" (p. 75), noting that the "indictment of democracy that appears in Plato's dialogues . . . was to become an integral part of the antidemocratic tradition and was to be cited by later writers as evidence of the insufficiency both of Athenian government in particular and of democracy in general. In this tradition, Plato's forceful attacks on oligarchy were generally ignored" (p. 82). Nevertheless, and despite expressing these words of caution, Roberts herself goes on to speak of Plato's clear "opposition

ments sympathetic to democracy appear in the dialogues, they typically treat them as anomalous. The most well-known is the passage in the *Statesman* where Socrates is made to identify democracy as preferable to any other regime likely to exist (303a–c), a view Plato repeats in *Letter 7* (342d8–10).[3] But such passages are not momentary irregularities. They are part of a sustained pattern of interest in democracy that runs through the entire corpus. To see this, however, we need to read Plato in the context of contemporaneous understandings of democratic political ideals and practices.[4] We need, that is, to be alert to the way Plato mobilizes the language, imagery, and principles that the Athenians themselves used to fashion their orthodox civic self-understanding. Familiarity with the variety of images and topics that were culturally available to Plato as he crafted his written works is crucial to understanding his commentary on democracy. Once we gain such familiarity, we can more readily see that he does not mount an enemy attack on Athenian democracy, nor does he oppose it totally. Instead, we see that Plato's dialogues contain explicit, albeit qualified, expressions of acceptance of the wide dispersal of political power characteristic of democracy, enlist certain celebrated Athenian democratic principles in the design of his critique of democratic politics, and depict the practice of philosophy as indebted to Athenian democratic culture. Plato indicates that philosophy needs to appropriate some, though certainly not all, of democracy's values.

Situating Plato in the context of the Athenian civic self-image raises some theoretical and methodological issues. The literary record of classical Greece does not include a systematic discussion of the merits and nature of Athenian democracy composed by someone of democratic sympathies. Substantial narrative accounts of "what the democrats think" are embedded in the work of Plato and other critics (e.g., Aristotle, the "Old Oligarch"). We obviously cannot use Plato's account of democratic thought as evidence for a new context within which to situate a reading of his treatment of democracy. Nor can we rely on accounts present in the work of other critics without independent evidence from less problematic sources. In addition, though there are explicit, favorable reviews of demo-

---

to democracy" (e.g., p. 84) and does not hesitate labeling him an "antidemocratic thinker" (p. 95).

[3] Commenting on *Statesman* 303a, for example, George Klosko writes, "This sort of reasoning is alien to Plato's earlier works." See *The Development of Plato's Political Thought* (New York: Methuen, 1986), p. 196.

[4] On the terminology of "practices" and practice theory, see Sherry B. Ortner, *Making Gender: The Politics and Erotics of Culture* (Boston: Beacon Press, 1996). Also see Pierre Bourdieu, *Outline of a Theory of Practice*, trans. Richard Nice (Cambridge: Cambridge University Press, 1978 [1972]).

cratic ideas in drama, oratory, and historical writings, these amount only to occasional, brief arguments in support of particular institutions or practices, or the expression of certain generalizations and maxims about the benefits of democracy. Some scholars have made exceptional use of this evidence to add texture to our understanding of the functioning of particular Athenian political institutions, including the courts and Assembly.[5] Others have focused on examining such things as the emergence of the term *dēmokratia* and the peculiar meanings of Athenian ideas of freedom, equality, and law (*eleutheria, isonomia,* and *nomos*).[6] Others still have attempted to reconstruct a lost systematic democratic theory from this disparate evidence.[7] These scholars are motivated by an admirable concern to demonstrate that among the intellectual products of Greek antiquity was not only fierce criticism of democracy but a sound defense of its basic structure and principles. Unfortunately, these works are often marred by

[5] For example, Moses Finley, *Democracy Ancient and Modern* (New Brunswick, N.J.: Rutgers University Press, 1973), *Politics in the Ancient World* (New York: Cambridge University Press, 1983). Arlene Saxonhouse in *Athenian Democracy: Modern Mythmakers and Ancient Theorists* (Notre Dame, Ind.: University of Notre Dame Press, 1996), turns to the work of historical and philosophical writers of antiquity to improve our understanding of the institutions of Athenian democracy. On the structure and mechanics of Athenian institutions, see Mogens Herman Hansen, *The Athenian Democracy in the Age of Demosthenes: Structure, Principles and Ideology* (Oxford: Blackwell, 1991), which also contains a useful bibliography.

[6] For a representative selection of recent work in this area, see the essays collected as Part One in "Liberty, Equality and Law," in *Dēmokratia: A Conversation on Democracies, Ancient and Modern,* ed. Josiah Ober and Charles Hedrick (Princeton: Princeton University Press, 1996), which also contains a useful bibliography. Also see L. Foxhall and A.D.E. Lewis, eds., *Greek Law in Its Political Setting: Justification Not Justice* (Oxford: Clarendon, 1996); John A. Koumoulides, ed., *The Good Idea: Democracy and Ancient Greece* (New Rochelle, N.Y.: Aristide D. Caratzas, 1995); Martin Ostwald, *From Popular Sovereignty to the Sovereignty of Law: Law, Society and Politics in Fifth-Century Athens* (Berkeley: University of California Press, 1986); Martin Ostwald, *Nomos and the Beginnings of Athenian Democracy* (Oxford: Clarendon, 1969); John Dunn, ed., *Democracy: The Unfinished Journey, 508 B.C. to A.D. 1993* (Oxford: Oxford University Press, 1992); Orlando Patterson, *Freedom: Freedom in the Making of Western Culture* (New York: Basic, 1991); and David Stockton, *The Classical Athenian Democracy* (New York: Oxford University Press, 1990); Lisa Kallet-Marx, "Institutions, Ideology, and Political Consciousness in Ancient Greece: Some Recent Books on Athenian Democracy," *Journal of the History of Ideas* 55 (1994): 309–35; V. Ehrenberg, "Origins of Democracy," *Historia* 1 (1950): 515–48; M. H. Hansen, "The Origin of the Term *Dēmokratia,*" *Liverpool Classical Monthly* 11 (1986): 35–36; G. Vlastos, "*Isonomia,*" *American Journal of Philology* 74 (1954): 333–66, and "*Isonomia Politikē,*" in his *Platonic Studies,* 2d ed. (Princeton: Princeton University Press, 1981), pp. 164–203.

[7] A.H.M. Jones, *Athenian Democracy* (Baltimore: The Johns Hopkins University Press, 1957); Eric Havelock, *The Liberal Temper in Greek Politics* (New Haven, Conn.: Yale University Press, 1957); Cynthia Farrar, *The Origins of Democratic Thinking* (New York: Cambridge University Press, 1989).

an overinterpretation of fragmentary and dubiously situated evidence that is finally unacceptable, regardless of how clever—even ingenious—these analyses may be at times.[8]

I turn to wider cultural resources for expressions of Athenian democratic thought. Specifically, I look to civic ritual performances, oral traditions, popular legends, and other Athenian cultural practices. It is wrong to assume that the absence of a systematic work of democratic theory in the extant literary record of ancient Athens is just our bad luck and to consider our project today to be the recovery of the tenets of such a lost treatise. Rather, it is important to recognize that it is quite possible that the Athenians did not write an elaborate statement of democratic theory but "enacted it."[9] Our challenge is to identify the occasions on which the Athenians experientially engaged important aspects of their civic self-understanding and to develop methods of analysis capable of drawing accounts of that civic self-image out of our sources.

Investigating the Athenian civic self-image involves some reconceptualization of what we ordinarily mean by "Athenian democracy." The Athenians did not consider "democracy" to be a matter of the polis having in place certain governing institutions (though of course it was certainly this in part). For the Athenians, democratic citizenship not only involved participating in some capacity in the work of the Assembly, courts, Council, and military, it was also a matter of the ritualized performance of a cluster of cultural practices that reach into both private and public life. It included the way in which the city ordered the tending of sacred matters, physical exercise, athletic competition, poetic production and experience, burial of the dead, possession and distribution of property, acquisition and maintenance of prestige, education of children, sexual behavior, military training and service, and deliberation on public affairs. Commentators routinely acknowledge this expanded understanding of Athenian democracy when they note how inadequately the Greek word *politeia* translates "constitution." A city's politeia encompasses not only its organization of legislative, judicial, and administrative authority but also the

[8] On the unreliability of these studies, see Josiah Ober, *Mass and Elite in Democratic Athens: Rhetoric, Ideology and the Power of the People* (Princeton: Princeton University Press, 1989), p. 38.

[9] W. Robert Connor, "Civil Society, Dionysiac Festival and the Athenian Democracy," in Ober and Hedrick, eds., *Dēmokratia*, p. 224. On the conspicuous absence of any record of formal democratic theorizing in ancient Athens, also see Josiah Ober, *The Athenian Revolution: Essays on Ancient Greek Democracy and Political Theory* (Princeton: Princeton University Press, 1996), pp. 147–48. He stresses that "in Athens democratic ideology so dominated the political landscape that formal democratic theory was otiose" (p. 148). On democratic thought (in contrast to systematic theorizing) of the period, see Kurt A. Raaflaub, "Contemporary Perceptions of Democracy in Fifth-Century Athens," *Classica et mediaevalia* 40 (1989): 33–70.

patterns of life and ideology that distinguish its civic culture.[10] This is abundantly clear in our sources. For instance, Pericles in his funeral oration attributes Athens' greatness to its democracy, which, he goes on to explain, refers not only to the city's form of government but also to its pervasive patterns of life.[11]

We might think the democratic significance of these cultural activities lies in their capacity to equip citizens for the more straightforwardly political work they perform in such arenas as the Assembly, courts, and Council. For example, the production of tragedy on a grand civic festival occasion provided theater-going citizens with an opportunity to hone intellectual skills that would be valuable when conducting policy deliberations and making decisions in the Assembly, courts, and Council.[12] But while we observe this connection, we must also recognize that to the Athenians, such cultural practices were in themselves part of the conduct of democratic life and not strictly ways to prepare oneself for the (more) real work of governing. Traversing civic space, participating in particular ways in a procession or public sacrifice, attending the theater, heading a household, performing the dithyramb, acting in a chorus, as well as many other activities were all strands of a web of practices through which eligible individuals experienced their Athenian democratic citizenship.[13]

These practices as well as more traditionally political forms of participation in civic life involved citizens in enacting a sort of official public perception of Athenian democracy's character and excellence. This perception was certainly not neutral toward the various citizen and noncitizen populations of the Athenian polis. Rather, it presented the city as a unity, wishfully ignoring or fancifully resolving serious social tensions that plagued the polis. Alert to this dimension of the self-image the Athenian projected

[10] Josiah Ober argues that *politeia* must include ideology, offering a persuasive reading of passages from Aristotle in the process. See *The Athenian Revolution*, p. 173. On Aristotle and a broader, practice-based understanding of democracy, see Jill Frank, "Democracy and Distribution: Aristotle on Just Desert," *Political Theory* 26, no. 6 (1998): 784–802. For discussion of politeia and "forms of society," see Claude Lefort, *Democracy and Political Theory* (Minneapolis: University of Minnesota Press, 1988), pp. 2–3.

[11] Thucydides 2.36.4–42.1. Thucydides develops a critique of this typically Athenian, expansive way of conceiving the scope of collective activities that can properly be considered "political." His account of the war employs a narrower conception of the boundaries of the political. Indeed, his text is one of the first to identify political activity exclusively with governing and military matters.

[12] See, for example, J. Peter Euben, "Introduction," in *Greek Tragedy and Political Theory* (Princeton: Princeton University Press, 1986); and Christian Meier, *The Political Art of Greek Tragedy* (Baltimore: The Johns Hopkins University Press, 1993).

[13] See Pauline Schmidt-Pantel, "Collective Activities and the Political in the Greek City," in *The Greek City*, ed. Oswyn Murray and Simon Price (Oxford: Clarendon, 1990), pp. 199–214.

in the context of performing these activities, I call attention to its partial and at times oppressive character. But my central concern is to interpret a set of practices through which the Athenian *dēmos*, itself an exclusive group, fashioned a public presentation of its own understanding of the "fragment of reality" in which its members lived.[14] I examine what the dominant elements in the democratic polis found politically useful to publicize about itself. The dominant elements were citizens—freeborn native males of mature age who could participate fully in political life. But the demos was not a homogenous group. It was beset by class, regional, age, and clan conflicts, and so sometimes dominant elements will be subsets of the citizen population.

We must, of course, recognize that the Athenian democratic order practiced—and celebrated—gender inequality, xenophobia, imperialism, and slavery. But doing so does not require us to deny that the idea and practice of democracy was an invention of the Greek polis. It was at this historical moment that there emerged both the idea that all citizens, regardless of differences of wealth, birth, talents, trade, or profession, should be political equals and a stable set of practices that effectively placed power in the hands of the common (nonelite) mass of citizens. Despite its many shortcomings, it is the case that, as Geoffrey de Ste. Croix stressed, democracy is "the brilliant achievement of the Greek polis: the Greek polis . . . had to build it up from the very bottom; . . . had both to devise the necessary institutions and to construct an appropriate ideology."[15] My focus in the chapters on Athenian democratic thought is not the extent to which the Athenian democratic order materially depended upon the more disturbing features of Athenian life that accompanied it but how the dominant ele-

---

[14] I have borrowed this phrasing from Lydia Cochrane's translation of Roger Chartier, *Cultural History: Between Practices and Representations* (Ithaca: Cornell University Press, 1988), p. 5.

[15] Ste. Croix, *The Class Struggle in the Ancient World*, p. 281. See also Pierre Vidal-Naquet, Cornelius Castoriadis, and Pierre Lévêque, "On the Invention of Democracy," in Lévêque and Vidal-Naquet, *Cleisthenes the Athenian*, trans. David Ames Curtis (Atlantic Highlands, N.J.: Humanities Press, 1996 [1964]), pp. 100–135; Ober and Hedrick, eds., *Dēmokratia*; Euben, Ober, and Wallach, eds., *Athenian Political Thought and the Reconstitution of American Democracy*; Morris and Raaflaub, eds., *Democracy 2500?*; Bernard Gofmann, Sheldon S. Wolin, J. Peter Euben, Josiah Ober, Arlene Saxonhouse, and Michael T. Clark, "The 2500th Anniversary of Democracy: Lessons of Athenian Democracy," *PS: Political Science and Politics* 26, no. 3 (Sept. 1993): 471–94. On the nature of democracy at Athens, see Ober, who argues that Athenians sustained rule by the people because "the ordinary citizen . . . was a participant in maintaining a political culture and a value system that constituted him the political equal of his elite neighbor" (*The Athenian Revolution*, p. 154). On the manner in which the ordinary citizen wielded power and the nature of the democratic hegemony at Athens, see Ober, *Mass and Elite*, and the useful summary in *Political Dissent in Democratic Athens: Intellectual Critics of Popular Rule* (Princeton: Princeton University Press, 1998), p. 31.

ments in the polis mobilized the available meanings associated with various groups and practices to craft a patriotic civic self-image, that is, to celebrate the achievement of democracy.[16]

This book has two parts. Part One examines aspects of Athenian democratic thought, focusing on the structure of the Athenian democratic imaginary (wishful self-image). Part Two turns to the interpretation of the dialogues of Plato. This strategy of presentation stresses that a new reading of Plato's treatment of democracy becomes possible only once features of the Athenian civic self-image are juxtaposed with Plato's account of philosophical practice.

In Part One, I employ an approach to Athenian democratic thought that builds on a growing literature in classics and political theory that considers Athenian political life fluidly to reach beyond the functioning of specific traditional political institutions. For example, I draw on the extensive work on such topics as the civic context of Athenian drama, the civic ideals that animate festival events and ritual practices unique to Athens (City Dionysia, funeral oration), the meanings of the myths that pervade Athenian political discourse, the character and reach of the power of the ordinary people in the Athenian polis, the gendered nature of Athenian political life, and the political dimension of Athenian erotic life. These chapters contribute to the literature on Athenian politics from the vantage point of political theory. That is, these chapters extend the findings of classicists in theoretical directions and, in doing so, raise the possibility that we can track Plato's interest in Athenian politics at the level of theory—the task to which I turn in Part Two.

The strategy of reading Plato I develop in Part Two builds upon five strands of recent Plato scholarship. First, work tracing the roots of the new genre of writing Plato develops, philosophic dialogue, in Athenian drama (specifically tragedy) supports my efforts to unsettle the common view that Plato's thought is at war with the Athenian democratic tradition. Such work shows, for example, that "Plato's debt to theater is not a debt to some arbitrary aesthetic invention but to the social institutions of his culture, which means that his attitude toward tragedy is a way of locating him in the intellectual traditions and political practices that defined Athenian democracy."[17]

---

[16] For discussion of various recent studies that aim to characterize Athenian democracy, see Lisa Kallet-Marx, "Institutions, Ideology and Political Consciousness." Also see Robert Browning, "How Democratic Was Ancient Athens?" in Koumoulides, ed., *The Good Idea*, pp. 57–70; and Robin Osborne, "Athenian Democracy: Something to Celebrate?" *Dialogos* 1 (1994): 48–58.

[17] J. Peter Euben, *The Tragedy of Political Theory* (Princeton: Princeton University Press, 1990), p. 236. Also Martha Nussbaum, *The Fragility of Goodness: Luck and Ethics in Greek Tragedy and Philosophy* (Cambridge: Cambridge University Press, 1986), pp. 122–35.

Second, the compelling body of literature on why Plato wrote dialogues also supports my view that defining aspects of Plato's thought have roots in Athenian democratic practices. This work demonstrates that the dialogic form has deep philosophic import. It is not simply a clever way to express a doctrine that could have been more easily stated in systematic exposition, but a mode of writing that allows Plato to craft for the reader the unusual experience of philosophic inquiry and dramatize both its departures from and attachments to Athenian traditions.[18]

Third, the few historical studies of Plato that exist have demonstrated that he was deeply engaged with the politics of his city. Glenn Morrow's historical interpretation of the *Laws* shows that Plato was fully conversant with the minutiae of Athenian politics and concerned not simply to denounce democracy but to explore the possibilities that inhere in some specifically democratic structures and practices.[19] Pierre Vidal-Naquet shows how imbedded in Plato's thought are structures of Athenian political discourse. His essays on the myths of Atlantis in the *Timaeus* and *Critias* and of a Golden Age in the *Statesman* detail how Plato's thought not only opposes certain practices of Athenian democracy but also simultaneously explores the possibilities that attend its political life.[20] Most recently, Josiah Ober has placed Plato's philosophical project in the context of Athenian elites' efforts to "reinvent political dissent" at Athens after practical attempts to bring about change failed miserably (i.e., generated the rule of the Thirty).[21] He proposes that a desire to find new grounds for

---

[18] Andrea Nightingale examines "Platonic intertexuality" in relation to Plato's efforts to define the boundaries of philosophy as a discursive and social practice in *Genres in Dialogue: Plato and the Construct of Philosophy* (Cambridge: Cambridge University Press, 1995). Also on the philosophical import of the dialogic form, see Charles Griswold, ed., *Platonic Writings/Platonic Readings* (New York: Routledge, 1988); J. C. Klagge and Nicholas D. Smith, eds., *Methods of Interpreting Plato: Oxford Studies in Ancient Philosophy* (Oxford: Clarendon, 1992); Gerald A. Press, *Plato's Dialogues: New Studies and Interpretations* (Lanham, Md.: Rowman and Littlefield, 1993); and Charles H. Kahn, *Plato and the Socratic Dialogue: The Philosophical Use of a Literary Form* (Cambridge: Cambridge University Press, 1996).

[19] Glenn Morrow, *Plato's Cretan City: An Historical Commentary on the Laws*, (Princeton: Princeton University Press, 1993 [1960]).

[20] Pierre Vidal-Naquet, "Athens and Atlantis: Structure and Meaning of a Platonic Myth," and "Plato's Myth of the Statesman, the Ambiguities of the Golden Age and of History," in *The Black Hunter: Forms of Thought and Forms of Society in the Greek World*, trans. Andrew Szegedy-Maszak (Baltimore: The Johns Hopkins University Press, 1986), pp. 263–301. Also see his "A Study of Ambiguity: Artisans in the Platonic City," in *The Black Hunter*, pp. 224–48.

[21] Ober, *Political Dissent*, p. 5. Other historical studies of Plato include Michael Morgan, *Platonic Piety: Philosophy and Ritual in Fourth-Century Athens* (New Haven: Yale University Press, 1990); and Harvey Yunis, *Taming Democracy: Models of Political Rhetoric in Classical Athens* (Ithaca: Cornell University Press, 1996). Morgan finds important continuities between the practices of the Athenian democratic polis and the structure of Plato's thought.

explaining what was wrong with rule of the people motivates Plato's work. In so doing, he offers an account of Plato's serious critique of democracy, but he also observes that Plato at times utilizes the language and imagery of Athenian democratic practices to articulate these views.[22]

The fourth strand of recent work with which this study stands in conversation are the several efforts to consider the complexities of the relationship between Socrates and Athenian democracy. This work includes assessments of the evidence for the attitudes of the historical Socrates as well as consideration of links between Plato's depiction of Socrates and democratic ideals and practices of his time.[23] In this book I focus squarely

---

Yunis places Plato's critique of democracy in the context of contemporaneous writers' concerns with rhetoric and leadership.

[22] Ober occasionally acknowledges the constructive impact of Athenian political culture on Plato's thought (*Political Dissent*, pp. 49, 158, 247, 281, 370–72), despite characterizing Plato as engaging in an "epic rejection of Athenian political culture" and, he implies, as betraying Socrates, who he takes to have been an "immanent social critic" (p. 213). For example, Ober details how Plato's "imaginative attempt to solve his 'Socrates and Athens' problem . . . [makes use of] exactly the performative, speech-act method characteristic of the democracy: vigorous, open debate conducted according to accepted protocols among persons who regarded one another as equals; followed by a resolution for action by the assembled company" (p. 247). But he seems content for such observations to suggest little more than Plato's recognition of the fact that "to inhabit the public domain of the democratic polis is to be affected by and borrow from the language, procedures, and assumptions of the demos" (p. 214). I find these aspects of Plato's work far more significant. They are part of what I argue is a pattern of interest in the possibilities raised by democratic hegemony and the development of certain practices in democratic Athens. The relation of my project to Ober's assessment of Plato in *Political Dissent* may be clarified further. He refers to his work as an effort to track how theorists, including Plato, describe "alternative visions of consensual and noncoercive—yet nondemocratic—political societies" (p. 5). I focus on the continuity between democratic innovations at Athens and the "consensual and noncoercive" features of the tradition Ober sees Plato embracing. I plot the lingering presence of Athenian democratic traditions in Plato's "alternative vision." I fully agree with Ober that Plato should not be described as a democrat but rather as a dissident voice in democratic Athens chiefly because he so thoroughly rejects "rule of the people" as the Athenians themselves understood that ideal. But Ober's account of the dynamics of Plato's critical attachment to Athens is incomplete. The features of Athenian democratic practice that haunt Plato's imagination are also part of the story of the birth of a tradition of intellectual dissent in Greek antiquity.

[23] J. Peter Euben, *The Tragedy of Political Theory*, and *Corrupting Youth: Political Education, Democratic Culture and Political Theory* (Princeton: Princeton University Press, 1997); Richard Kraut, *Socrates and the State* (Princeton: Princeton University Press, 1984); Gerald Mara, *Socrates' Discursive Democracy* (Albany, N.Y.: SUNY Press, 1997); Gregory Vlastos, "The Historical Socrates and Athenian Democracy," *Political Theory* 11, no. 4 (1983): 495–516; Ellen M. Wood and Neal Wood, "Socrates and Democracy: A Reply to Gregory Vlastos," *Political Theory* vol. 14, no. 1 (1986): 55–82; W. R. Connor, "The Other 399: Religion and the Trial of Socrates," *Georgica: Greek Studies in Honor of George Cawkwell, Bulletin, Institute for Classical Studies* (London), suppl. 58 (1991): 49–56; T. H. Irwin, "Socrates and Athenian Democracy," *Philosophy and Public Affairs* 18, no. 2 (1989): 184–205; I. F. Stone, *The Trial of Socrates* (Boston: Little, Brown, 1988); G. Vlastos, "Why Was

on Plato. I consider what we know of Plato's behavior and personal attitudes, and I examine how the understanding of philosophic labor developed in the dialogues is indebted to Athenian democratic traditions.

The fifth and final strand of recent scholarship on Plato I engage is the work by Arlene Saxonhouse and J. Peter Euben reassessing Plato's treatment of democracy. They attend, as I do, to Plato's interest in the culture of democracy. Saxonhouse explores Plato's interest in the gentleness and variety of democracy, stressing their importance to philosophical investigation. Euben's two books map the affinities between Athenian practices of self-scrutiny (chiefly tragic theater and the pervasive mechanisms of accountability) and key aspects of Plato's portrayal of Socratic philosophy (chiefly rigorous questioning and the explicit demand for an account of one's moral choices and conduct of life).[24] Like these studies, this book explores how far Plato's elaborations of the practice of philosophy not only challenge but also "extend" Athenian democratic traditions.[25] I advance this project by tracking Plato's efforts to combine the practice of philosophy with the "normative imagery" of Athenian democracy.[26]

Socrates Condemned?" in *Socrates: Ironist and Moral Philosopher* (Ithaca: Cornell University Press, 1991), pp. 293–97; and Charles Taylor, "Philosophical Gadfly," *Times Literary Supplement* (June 7, 1991); Alexander Nehamas, "Voices of Silence: On Gregory Vlastos' Socrates," in Nehamas, *Virtues of Authenticity: Essays on Plato and Socrates* (Princeton: Princeton University Press, 1999), pp. 83–107; Roberts, *Athens on Trial*, pp. 71–76; Wallach, "Plato's Socratic Problem, and Ours," *History of Political Thought* 18, no. 3 (1997): 377–98; Ober, *Political Dissent*, pp. 156–213; M. H. Hansen, "The Trial of Sokrates from the Athenian Point of View," in *Démocratie et Culture*, ed. M. Sakellariou (Athens: Academy of Athens, 1996), pp. 137–70. George Kateb, "Socratic Integrity," in *NOMOS XL: Integrity and Conscience*, ed. Ian Shapiro and Robert Adams (New York: New York University Press, 1998), pp. 77–112.

    [24] J. Peter Euben, *The Tragedy of Political Theory*, and *Corrupting Youth*; Arlene Saxonhouse, "Plato and the Problematical Gentleness of Democracy," in her *Athenian Democracy and "Democracy, Equality, and Eidē: A Radical View from Book 8 of Plato's Republic*," *American Political Science Review* 92, no. 2 (June 1998): 273–84. Other recent efforts to reconsider Plato's treatment of democracy are David Cohen, "Law, Autonomy and Political Community in Plato's *Laws*," *Classical Philology* 88, no. 4 (1993): 301–17; and Christopher Rowe, "Democracy and Sokratic-Platonic Philosophy," in *Democracy, Empire, and the Arts in Fifth-Century Athens*, ed. Deborah Boedeker and Kurt A. Raaflaub (Cambridge: Harvard University Press, 1998), pp. 241–53. See also the exchange between Arlene Saxonhouse and Jennifer Roberts on the question of Plato's hostility toward democracy: Arlene Saxonhouse, "Athenian Democracy and Modern Mythmakers: A Lesson from Plato about Democracy, Equality and Gender," *Thamyris* (Amsterdam: Najade) 1, no. 2 (1994): 105–22; Jennifer Tolbert Roberts, "Myths of Democracy and Gender in Plato's *Republic*: A Reply to Arlene Saxonhouse," *Thamyris* 2, no 2. (1995): 259–72; Arlene Saxonhouse, "Response to Jennifer Tolbert Roberts," *Thamyris* 2, no. 2 (1995): 273–76.

    [25] Euben, *Corrupting Youth*, p. 86.

    [26] Simon Goldhill, "The Seductions of the Gaze: Socrates and His Girlfriends," in *Kosmos: Essays in Order, Conflict, and Community in Classical Athens*, ed. Paul Cartledge, Paul Mil-

In my view, Plato decidedly does not assume the posture of an enemy of democratic Athens and does not sustain a thoroughgoing betrayal of the Socratic ideal of committed criticism.[27] An enemy is presumed to have ill will toward his opponent, to be motivated by hatred, to desire vanquishing his foe, and to be enraged by the behavior of his target. The critique of democracy in Plato's dialogues is, of course, radical. But his works deliver just that, a critique. He denounces majority rule, Assembly debate, equality, and the celebration of "living as you like," for example, as disturbing, deeply flawed practices that systematically misdirect citizens to make error upon error regarding what they should consider admirable as well as how they can lead a good life. He indeed resists what Josiah Ober has termed the "democratic hegemony" of his time by bringing into question "the basic assumptions on which democratic knowledge rested; he questioned the validity of mass wisdom as a basis for judgment, the efficacy of public rhetoric as a prelude to decision making."[28] But, I wish to stress, he remains always an Athenian, concerned to identify and publicize what in the local democratic tradition might hold some promise. Plato does not present philosophic practice as a purely other-worldly activity or as a retreat from and opposition to the political world but as a brave and daring effort to call one's community to its own best possible self without romanticizing what a rigorous pursuit of that best self would entail.

Before turning to the analysis of sources in the individual chapters, I must note with dismay the stubborn endurance of the view of Plato as a proto-totalitarian thinker.[29] Readings that link Plato to a totalitarian political agenda not only betray the historical insensitivity of the commentator but also entirely misrepresent the spirit of Plato's works. They also erect impediments to the serious investigation of his assessment of the moral significance of democratic forms of power. Surely we need not adopt such imprecise and highly charged language as well as such anachronistic categories of analysis to give full due to the considerable nondemocratic elements of Plato's thought. Since others have, to my mind, thoroughly dis-

---

lett, and Sitta von Reden (Cambridge: Cambridge University Press, 1998), p. 108. On Athenian normative imagery, also see Nicole Loraux, *The Invention of Athens* (Cambridge, Mass.: Harvard University Press, 1986).

[27] On the language of "immanent" and "connected" social criticism, see Michael Walzer, *Interpretation and Social Criticism* (Cambridge, Mass.: Harvard University Press, 1987), and *The Company of Critics* (New York: Basic, 1988).

[28] Ober, *The Athenian Revolution*, p. 156.

[29] I am referring of course to a view put forward most forcefully by Karl Popper, *The Open Society and Its Enemies*, vol. 1, *The Spell of Plato* (Princeton: Princeton University Press, 1971 [1945]). For evidence of its endurance, see C.C.W. Taylor, "Plato's Totalitarianism," in *Plato's Republic: Critical Essays*, ed. Richard Kraut (New York: Rowan and Littlefield, 1997), pp. 31–48; and D. Dombrowski, "Plato's Noble Lie," *History of Political Thought* 18, no. 4 (1997): 565–78.

credited this approach, I do not take it on explicitly in these pages.[30] Here I wish only to call attention to Quentin Skinner's observation that this reading of Plato provides a fine example of a very serious methodological error he terms "the mythology of prolepsis." He writes: "One such prolepsis which has constantly been exposed, and yet has constantly recurred, has been the attempt to consider Plato's political views in the *Republic* as those of a 'totalitarian party politician.' "[31] My argument in this book applies not merely to the loose way in which such terminology is thrown around. I seek to render problematic the standard view that Plato's texts are unequivocally hostile to democracy. That assumption implicitly informs most work on Plato's political thought and makes such unthinking use of inappropriate terminology possible.

Perhaps paradoxically, I both agree and disagree with the tradition of reading Plato as an antipolitical thinker.[32] I agree that the vision of justice in the *Republic* can be fairly described as one in which a legitimate power "still[s] the unruly conflicts and contests of democratic politics."[33] It is a place of fantastic unity. But I observe that this aspect of Plato's vision actually engages local, democratic structures of political discourse at the

---

[30] Ronald B. Levinson compellingly argued in his *In Defense of Plato* (Cambridge, Mass.: Harvard University Press, 1953) that it is simply not accurate to say that the proposals developed in the *Republic* resemble the institutional structure of modern totalitarianism and that it is simply wrong to suggest that Plato would have approved of fascism. Leo Strauss also cautioned that "Plato, or at any rate Socrates, was not a liberal democrat, or a communist in the sense of Marx or a Fascist" ("Plato," in *History of Political Philosophy*, ed. Leo Strauss and Joseph Cropsey, 3d ed. [Chicago: University of Chicago Press, 1987], p. 35). For useful accounts of the controversy that Popper's work sparked, see Renford Bambrough, ed., *Plato, Popper and Politics: Some Contributions to a Modern Controversy* (New York: Barnes and Noble, 1967); and Thomas Thorson, ed., *Plato: Totalitarian or Democrat?* (Englewood Cliffs, N.J.: Prentice-Hall, 1963). For discussion of the enduring import of these views, see Wallach, "Plato's Socratic Problem." Note that Popper's argument pivots on a reading of Plato's epistemology and its political import. For a valuable recent study of Plato's epistemological critique of democracy that comes to very different conclusions, see Arlene Saxonhouse, "Democracy, Equality and *Eidē*."

[31] Quentin Skinner, "Meaning and Understanding in the History of Ideas," in *Meaning and Context: Quentin Skinner and His Critics*, ed. J. Tully (Princeton: Princeton University Press, 1988), pp. 29–67, at p. 44. A recent example of such an error appears in an otherwise excellent—and indeed, otherwise historically sensitive—essay by M. F. Burnyeat. He writes: "Plato was no democrat, and had no qualms about proposing Soviet-style control from above, by those who know best" ("Art and Mimesis in Plato's *Republic*," *London Review of Books*, 21 May 1998, p. 3). For another account of the pull of this "radically mistaken" interpretation of the *Republic*, see Lefort, *Democracy*, pp. 3–4.

[32] For example, Hannah Arendt, *The Human Condition* (Chicago: University of Chicago Press, 1958); Sheldon Wolin, *Politics and Vision: Continuity and Change in Western Political Thought* (Boston: Little, Brown, 1960).

[33] I borrow this phrasing from Bonnie Honig, *Political Theory and the Displacement of Politics* (Ithaca: Cornell University Press, 1993), p. 14.

level of the imaginary. Embracing the idea of the unified whole as well as some other ideals tracked in the chapters to follow, Plato's vision has some kinship with the city's own patriotic self-image. For example, while clearly taking pleasure in the rough-and-tumble of politics in their material lives, the Athenians did not embrace the messiness of democratic politics in their civic self-image. At the level of the imaginary, they spurned discord and ambition, and embraced instead harmony, responsibility, reciprocity, and respect for "good" arguments. At the level of the imaginary, for instance, the democracy perpetrated the fiction that the view of a majority (even of only one) constitutes the considered view of the whole. This is what the formulaic expression of Assembly decisions suggests ("It seems best to the demos that . . .").[34] To offer another example, when Athens and Athenians appear in tragedy, they are depicted as thoroughly unified.[35] The portrayals of the instability, noise, moral dilemmas, personal conflicts, and costs of politics these texts offer are projected onto other *poleis* and the behavior of members other cities—most strikingly Thebes and Thebans.[36] The Athens of tragedy and the ideal city in the *Republic* appear in this way similar.

I do not doubt that Plato's dialogues make extensive, even systematic, use of the imagery and terminology of elite Athenian discourse. That is, it is indeed likely that Plato also draws upon elements of local aristocratic discourse, a discourse hostile to democracy in the specific sense of being the language of unreconciled foes eager for specific constitutional changes. For example, the language of metals Plato uses to articulate appropriate hierarchies or divisions in the *Republic* is not dreamt up but has a long history in elite discourse.[37] It is also likely that the language of *patrios politeia* to which Plato sometimes alludes was a staple of elite political argument, as was the vocabulary of "better" and "worse" sorts of men. In my view, possible affinities between Plato's thought and the counterhe-

---

[34] Ober terms this element of Athenian civic ideology "the myth of Demos" (*Political Dissent*, pp. 39–40, 69). He notes that some writers at times treat the state as a single organism with one mind (*mia gnōmē; Mass and Elite*, p. 297). For discussion of the relationship between the inscribed record of Assembly decisions and the arguments and activities of the Assembly, see Robin Osborne, "Inscribing Performance," in *Performance Culture and Athenian Democracy*, ed. Simon Goldhill and Robin Osborne (Cambridge: Cambridge University Press, 1999), pp. 341–58.

[35] For example, the portrait of the chorus and relationship between Athenian individuals and Theseus in Sophocles' *Oedipus at Colonus*. The exception is the conflict settled by the intervention of Athena in Aeschylus' *Eumenides*, a play about reconciliation and unity.

[36] See, for example, Froma Zeitlin, "Thebes: Theater of Self and Society in Athenian Drama," in *Nothing to Do with Dionysos? Athenian Drama in Its Social Context*, ed. John J. Winkler and Froma Zeitlin (Princeton: Princeton University Press, 1989), pp. 130–67.

[37] Leslie Kurke, "Herodotus and the Language of Metals," *Helios* 22, no. 1 (1995): 35–64.

gemonic discourse of Athenian elites do not provide evidence of Plato's unmitigated contempt for democracy, his aristocratic bias, his position as a thoroughly conservative foe of Athenian democracy, or, worse, his stance as a partisan of oligarchy any more than his subtle use of the language and imagery of elements of democratic ideology suggests he was a secret partisan of democracy.[38] If Plato works with the imagery and language of both partisans of democracy and elite opponents of democracy, and no doubt he does, interpreters should inquire as to the range of substantive meanings and implications set in motion by such tactics and not assume he is betraying a political bias.

I begin with an examination of aspects of the Athenian civic self-image. My purpose is not to offer a full description of Athenian democratic ideology and practice, but rather to probe those features of that ideology that figure importantly in Plato's thinking in ways that are unexpected and have not been explored extensively in the existing literature. Accordingly, the concepts of freedom and equality do not organize my account, though they are central to the Athenian democratic imaginary and Plato has much to say about them. Much good work already exists on these features of Athenian thought. The structure of this book as a whole highlights that the Athenians also crafted and venerated other, less familiar ideals that Plato's thought engages in highly significant ways.

Taken together, the chapters in Part One show that orthodox Athenian democratic thought strongly identified the achievement of democracy with the accomplishment of social unity, an intellectually capable citizenry, the responsible exercise of power, relations of reciprocity among citizens and between city and individual,[39] and the defeat of tyranny. Chapters One through Four explore various accounts of how these ideals were enacted or represented. Chapter One examines the patriotic story of the historical founding of Athenian democracy that the Athenians told and retold on numerous occasions for generations, that is, the tale of Harmodius and Aristogeiton. Chapter Two examines the Athenian celebration of frank

[38] On the possible affinities between Plato's thought and the counterhegemonic discourse of Athenian elites, especially intellectuals, see Ober, *Political Dissent*.

[39] The centrality of the idea of reciprocity in the Greek moral and political outlook has recently received important attention. See, for example, Paul Millet, *Lending and Borrowing in Ancient Athens* (New York: Cambridge University Press, 1991), esp. pp. 24–52, 109–26, and 148–59; Richard Seaford, *Reciprocity and Ritual: Homer and Tragedy in the Developing City State* (Oxford: Clarendon, 1994); Danielle Allen, *The World of Prometheus: The Politics of Punishing in Democratic Athens* (Princeton: Princeton University Press, 2000); Malcolm Schofield, "Political Friendship and the Ideology of Reciprocity," in Cartledge et al., eds., *Kosmos*, pp. 37–51; Goldhill, "Seductions of the Gaze," pp. 115–24; Paul Millett, "Encounters in the Agora," in Cartledge et al., eds., *Kosmos*, pp. 203–28; and C. Gill, N. Postlethwaite, and R. Seaford, eds., *Reciprocity in Ancient Greece* (Oxford, forthcoming).

speaking (*parrhēsia*) as a specifically democratic ideal as well as a practice of Assembly debate. Chapter Three probes the implications of Pericles' deployment of an erotic metaphor to articulate the demands of democratic citizenship in his funeral oration as presented in Thucydides' *History*. Chapter Four examines the Athenian practice of theater-going as a stage for the performance of democratic citizenship.

Part Two demonstrates that reading Plato in this context raises new questions about the relationship of his thought to the practice of democracy at Athens. In particular, Chapter Five observes a parallel between the imagined excellence of Harmodius and Aristogeiton and Plato's view of the philosopher. The bulk of the chapter questions the canonical view of Plato as a wholesale antidemocrat by showing that each of six factors usually thought to indicate that Plato's dialogues sustain an unrelenting attack on democracy actually are wrong as characterizations of his thought in the first place, or indicate no such thing, or are far less univocal in meaning than is appreciated. The factors I review include Plato's elite personal background, his dismay over the fate of Socrates, his disdain for the common man and consequent opposition to majority rule, his recommendation in the *Republic* of a positive political doctrine marked by autocratic institutions, his actual founding of an elite institution at Athens (the Academy), and the tenor of his personal involvement in Syracusan politics. In Chapters Six, Seven, and Eight, I further show that Plato's understanding of the performance of philosophy draws on aspects of the Athenian civic self-image explored in Part One. These three chapters combine to demonstrate that Plato's depiction of philosophic activity is deeply indebted to three practices of civic discourse developed by the Athenian democratic polis: the pervasive ethic of frank speaking (*parrhēsia*), the performance of the public funeral oration (*epitaphios logos*), and the conduct of theorizing (being an active audience member on the occasion of the dramatic competitions). In Chapter Six I show that Plato represents philosophic activity as a form of frank speaking in the *Laches, Gorgias, Republic*, and *Laws*. In Chapter Seven I demonstrate that in the *Menexenus*, Plato takes on the Athenian tendency to venerate the memory of Pericles, and in so doing explores the links between philosophic practice and a uniquely Athenian democratic form of civic speech at which Pericles is reputed to have excelled—public funeral oratory. In Chapter Eight I show that in both the *Republic* and the *Laws*, Plato models his depiction of philosophic practice on the experience of the intellectual labors of the ordinary theater-going public on the occasion of the City Dionysia, a grand civic festival occasion.

At the most general level, this book is about the relationship between thought and social reality, in particular, between Plato's highly abstract thought and some of the democratic practices of his time. As Vidal-Naquet has stressed, "Even when the disjunction between the textual and the social is at its greatest, as for instance between the philosophical text produced by Plato and what Nicole Loraux calls 'the Athenian history of Athens,' the relation still exists."[40] This book explores some of the complexities of that relation. It is an essay on the presence of specifically Athenian democratic cultural traditions in the structure of Plato's thought. It is an exploration of how intimately connected are two things usually viewed as thoroughly opposed—Plato's thought and Athenian democratic ideals and practices.

[40] *The Black Hunter*, p. xviii.

PART ONE

Aspects of the Athenian Civic Self-Image

Chapter One

THE ALLURE OF HARMODIUS
AND ARISTOGEITON: PUBLIC/PRIVATE
RELATIONS IN THE ATHENIAN
DEMOCRATIC IMAGINARY

ATHENIANS CELEBRATED Harmodius and Aristogeiton as heroic men who slew a tyrant and, though they perished themselves in the process, founded democracy at Athens. That the legend of the tyrannicide forms part of the iconography of the Athenian democratic order is well known. Precisely what it signifies remains little understood. This is largely because mixed in with sharp attention to its resonance as a symbol of Athenian daring as well as general antityrantism is the assumption that Athenians admired the pair centrally for their spirited self-sacrifice.[1] The story is indeed a parable of public-private relations in the democratic city. But it does not celebrate sacrifice. Rather, this tale associates the achievement of freedom, democracy, and steadfast opposition to tyranny with the principle of political equality, the maintenance of unity among citizens, and a vigorous relation of mutual exchange between individuals and the city as a whole—even the accomplishment of the coincidence of individual citizens' personal and private interests. This constellation of meanings is in play whether the myth is being celebrated in song, art, or decrees, appealed to in oratory, or critically evaluated in historical writing such as that of Thucydides.[2]

---

[1] This assumption is pervasive in the literature on Harmodius and Aristogeiton. The following is typical: "Their assassination of Hipparchus came to be seen and celebrated as a decisive act of self-sacrifice that liberated Athens from tyrannical oppression." David Castriota, "Democracy and Art in Late Sixth and Fifth Century B.C. Athens," in *Democracy 2500? Questions and Challenges*, ed., Ian Morris and Kurt Raaflaub, Archaeological Institute of America Colloquia and Conference Papers no. 2 (Dubuque, Iowa: Kendall, 1997), p. 202.

[2] These meanings are also in play in the *Hipparchus*, a little Socratic dialogue of uncertain authorship that contains a digression in which the speaker tells a curious and fanciful version of the story of the murder of Hipparchus. The digression comes in the context of a discussion of the nature of the "lover of gain" (*philokerdēs*) that is highly eudaimonistic. The theoretical interest of this text is the subject of my current research. The case for attributing likely (though not certain) authorship to Plato is forcefully argued by Thomas Pangle in his "Editor's Introduction" to *The Roots of Political Philosophy: Ten Forgotten Socratic Dialogues* (Ithaca: Cornell University Press, 1987), pp. 1–18. See also the interpretative essay by Allan Bloom in Pangle, *Roots*, pp. 32–52; and Paul Friedlander, *Plato 2*, translated from the German by Hans Meyerhoff (New York: Bollingen, 1964), pp. 119–28.

In this chapter I demonstrate that the story of Harmodius and Aristogeiton was the common currency of civic discourse about the character of the relations between the private and public lives of citizens of democratic Athens. I detail how this patriotic tale worked economically to represent Athenian civic ideals, specifically unity and reciprocity. This involves examining the occasions on which an actor or author typically appealed to their story as well as the ways in which this simple story differs from contemporaneously known accounts of the complexity of the events surrounding the liberation from tyranny. I begin with an account of the history of the period, followed by a brief review of the evidence for the Athenians' embrace of the mythic version in civic discourse. I then explore the symbolic resonances of the hygienic version of the founding of democracy at Athens and the critical response to it in Thucydides' *History* and Aristotle's *Constitution of Athens*.[3]

TELLING THE TALE

The story of the liberation of Athens from tyranny and the introduction of democratic institutions as it emerges from the historical writings of Herodotus, Thucydides, and Aristotle is not a flattering tale.[4] On these accounts, the events pivot on bumbling, bribery, foreign intervention, mob action, and the projection of personal, specifically erotic, passions onto the public stage. Pooling the details offered by these writers,[5] we find

---

[3] Aristotle's authorship of this text is contested. There is, however, general consensus that it is a thoroughly Aristotelian text, that is, that even if not the work of Aristotle himself, the text is certainly the work of a member or group of members of Aristotle's school. See P. J. Rhodes, *A Commentary on the Aristotelian Athēnaiōn Politeia* (Oxford: Oxford University Press, 1981); and John J. Keaney, *The Composition of Aristotle's Athenaion Politeia* (Oxford: Oxford University Press, 1992).

[4] Herodotus 5.69–72 and 6.123; Thucydides 1.20.2, 6.54.1–59.4; Aristotle *Constitution of Athens* 18.1–19.2.

[5] The accounts of Herodotus, Thucydides, and Aristotle do not agree in all details. The version I have constructed here collects details from all three sources and focuses on points that, while not independently confirmed by each, are not contested by one another. There are two exceptions. First, I follow Herodotus and Thucydides in reporting that Hippias was tyrant, as opposed to Aristotle, who maintains that Hippias and Hipparchus were joint tyrants. Second, I follow Thucydides that Hipparchus was indeed personally involved in an effort to interfere in the private erotic affairs of Harmodius and Aristogeiton. Herodotus does not mention either that Harmodius and Aristogeiton were lovers or the erotic interference of Hipparchus. He notes only the personal insult Hipparchus aimed at the sister of Harmodius. But Herodotus' silence is not reason to conclude that the erotic component of the story was unknown before being introduced by Thucydides. It is more likely that it was obvious to Herodotus and his readers. I base this view on three observations. First, the group statue of Harmodius and Aristogeiton in the agora that Herodotus and his readers would have known well clearly hinted at the erotic relationship between the two figures. As

the following version of events leading up to the democratic "revolution"[6] at Athens. In the year 527 B.C., the Athenian tyrant Peisistratus died, and his son Hippias assumed power. Thirteen years later, in 514, two Athenian citizens, Harmodius and Aristogeiton, plotted to kill the reigning tyrant and his brother, Hipparchus. Their motive was personal; they aimed neither to create a democracy nor to seize the tyranny for themselves. Rather, Hipparchus, the tyrant's brother, had unsuccessfully approached Harmodius sexually and, rebuffed, had used his position to take revenge by insulting Harmodius' sister sexually. He forbade her to take part in the Panathenaic Procession, a grand civic ritual event, dismissing her as unworthy and, by implication, no longer a virgin or honorable (and thus marriageable).[7] The slander of the sister touched the entire family, but the brother most of all. A response from Harmodius was required for his family to regain honor. Thus the public affront to his family prompted the youthful Harmodius, assisted by his adult lover Aristogeiton, to act, specifically to kill Hipparchus, the source of the insult. They conspired to cut

---

art historian Andrew Stewart notes, the statues invited an eroticized glance by "vigorously promoting the homoerotic relationship that sustained it [the city]" (*Art, Desire and the Body in Ancient Greece* [New York: Cambridge University Press, 1997], p. 73). Second, as Brian Lavelle has argued in detail, Hipparchus' insult was sexual in nature and directed at Harmodius through his sister ("The Nature of Hipparchus' Insult to Harmodios," *American Journal of Philology* 107 [1986]: 318–31). Third, as Fornara has observed, unlike the other details Thucydides claims to introduce, "there is no trace of polemic in his assignment of the role of instigator to Hipparchus." Thucydides never indicates that there was a "competing version of the motivation of Harmodius and Aristogeiton" (C. W. Fornara, "The 'Tradition' about the Murder of Hipparchus," *Historia* 17 [1968]: 402; for an opposing view, see Mabel Lang, "The Murder of Hipparchus," *Historia* 3 [1955]: 395–407). On Aristotle's account, the half-brother of Hipparchus, Thessalus, was involved in the erotic affair, and Hipparchus was killed by accident. The addition of Thessalus is a late "contaminant" (Rhodes, *Commentary on the Aristotelian Athēnaiōn Politeia*, p. 228) or "figment" (Fornara, "The 'Tradition'," p. 411). For discussion of the relationship between the accounts of Herodotus, Thucydides, and Aristotle, see A. W. Gomme, A. Andrewes, and K. J. Dover, *A Historical Commentary on Thucydides* (Oxford: Clarendon, 1972), 4: 320–23; Kurt von Fritz and Ernst Kapp, *Aristotle's Constitution of Athens and Related Texts, Translated with an Introduction and Notes* (New York: Hafner, 1974), pp. 160–61; Rhodes, *Commentary on the Aristotelian Athēnaiōn Politeia*, pp. 226–32; Felix Jacoby, "The Tradition about the Peisistratids," in *Atthis: The Local Chronicles of Ancient Athens* (Oxford: Clarendon, 1949), pp. 152–68; Lang, "The Murder of Hipparchus"; Thomas R. Fitzgerald, "The Murder of Hipparchus: A Reply," *Historia* 6 (1957): 275–86; and Fornara, "The 'Tradition.' " For general discussion of the period of the tyranny, see A. Andrewes, *The Greek Tyrants* (London: Hutchinson and Co., 1969), pp. 100–115; John V. A. Fine, *The Ancient Greeks: A Critical History* (Cambridge, Mass.: Harvard University Press, 1983), pp. 220–26; and Brian Lavelle, *The Sorrow and the Pity: A Prolegomenon to a History of Athens under Peisistratids, c. 560–510 B.C.* (Stuttgart: Steiner, 1993).

[6] Josiah Ober, *The Athenian Revolution* (Princeton: Princeton University Press, 1996).

[7] This interpretation of the sexual implications of the insult directed at the sister draws on Lavelle, "The Nature of Hipparchus' Insult to Harmodios," p. 327.

down the tyrant Hippias and his brother Hipparchus while they presided over the Panathenaic Procession. Yet when the moment arrived, young Harmodius panicked and, believing his plan to have been exposed, frantically attacked Hipparchus. Harmodius killed Hipparchus, but was slain on the spot himself. Aristogeiton, having had no time even to strike at Hippias, was arrested, tortured, and put to death.

The tyranny became much harsher after the murder. Opposition to the tyrant Hippias persisted. Members of a prominent Athenian family (the Alcmaeonids) tried to fortify a base from which to attack the tyrant. Failing in this attempt, they changed their strategy. While at Delphi on a contract to help rebuild the temple, this family bribed the Delphic prophetess, the Pythia, to advise Sparta to free Athens. From then on, in answer to routine queries, the Pythia repeatedly admonished the Spartans to "free Athens first." In 510, four years after the murder of Hipparchus, Sparta intervened militarily, and Hippias was deposed. A rivalry ensued between two elites, Cleisthenes and Isagoras, for power in Athens. Cleisthenes gained the upper hand by allying himself with the demos (Herodotus 5.66, 67). Isagoras then persuaded King Cleomenes of Sparta to intervene to support his faltering aristocratic faction. Cleisthenes, who was not only the leader of the democratic faction but also a member of the family that had bribed the Pythia, fled the city. But even with Cleisthenes out of the city, Isagoras' faction met with popular resistance. The people forced Isagoras and King Cleomenes to withdraw to the Acropolis, where an angry mass of people besieged them. A truce was arranged; the two men were expelled from the city; Cleisthenes was recalled to Athens; and soon after, he set in motion his famous, extensive reforms, which scholars today generally consider the founding of democracy at Athens.[8]

In the years following these events as well as throughout the fourth-century, a very different version of the revolutionary establishment of democracy was promoted and, most importantly, remembered in a variety of contexts. There was an official cult and an annual public sacrifice; songs were sung at private drinking parties and statues prominently displayed in civic spaces; oratory and decrees proclaiming this version were heard on public occasions. The patriotic version of events hails Harmodius

---

[8] On the Cleisthenic reforms, see Mogens H. Hansen, *The Athenian Democracy in the Age of Demosthenes* (New York: Basil Blackwell, 1991), pp. 46–49 and 101–6; J. S. Traill, *The Political Organization of Attica*, Hesperia, suppl. 14 (1975); and David Whitehead, *The Demes of Attica 508/7–ca. 250 b.c.* (Princeton: Princeton University Press, 1986). For theoretical treatment of the democratic import of the reforms, see Josiah Ober, *The Athenian Revolution*; and Pierre Lévêque and Pierre Vidal-Naquet, *Cleisthenes the Athenian*, trans. David Ames Curtis (Atlantic Highlands, N.J.: Humanities Press, 1996 [1964]); and Philip Brooke Manville, *The Origins of Citizenship in Ancient Athens* (Princeton: Princeton University Press, 1990).

and Aristogeiton as heroic men who killed the tyrant, liberated Athens, and founded its democracy. This account reduces the complexity of the events to a tale remarkable for its "utmost simplicity"[9] and striking emotional appeal.

The lean account of the liberation of Athens captured Athenian imaginations in the period after the murder of Hipparchus and for generations to follow. The evidence for this is strong.[10] Very soon after the expulsion of Hippias, possibly as early as 509, the sculptor Antenor made a group statue of Harmodius and Aristogeiton that was placed in the agora, a public space that grew in size and significance with the development of democracy.[11] This was the first political monument in Greek history. The Tyrannicides are the first historical figures so honored, and remained the only such figures for over 100 years.[12] Drinking songs celebrating their heroism also appeared soon after the liberation and remained popular for generations.[13] The particular importance of the statues as "tangible symbols" of

[9] Rosalind Thomas, *Oral Tradition and Written Record in Classical Athens* (New York: Cambridge University Press, 1989), p. 240.

[10] For a full accounting of this evidence, see Jacoby, "The Tradition," pp. 158–60, esp. n. 52 (p. 339); and Michael W. Taylor, *The Tyrant Slayers* (New York: Arno, 1981).

[11] For discussion of the dating of this statue grouping and additional bibliography on this issue, see Castriota, "Democracy and Art," pp. 199–215. For discussion of its location in the agora in the context of other political monuments, see Tonio Hölscher, "The City of Athens: Space, Symbol, Structure," in *City States in Classical Antiquity and Medieval Italy*, ed. Anthony Molho, Kurt A. Raaflaub, and Julia Emlen (Ann Arbor: University of Michigan Press, 1991), pp. 355–80, at p. 371. For discussion of the importance of the agora in the developing democracy, see T. Leslie Shear, Jr., "*Isonomous t'Athēnas epoiēsatēn*: The Agora and the Democracy," in *The Archaeology of Athens and Attica under the Democracy* (proceedings of an international conference celebrating 2,500 years since the birth of democracy in Greece, held at the American School of Classical Studies at Athens, December 4–6, 1992), ed. W. D. Coulson, O. Palagia, T. L. Shear, Jr., H. A. Shapiro, and F. J. Frost, Oxbow Monograph 37 (Oxford: Oxbow, 1994), pp. 225–48.

[12] This is the implication of Demosthenes *Against Leptines* 70. For discussion of Athenian political monuments, especially the statue group of the tyrant-slayers and their import for the developing democratic collective identity, or political self-image, see Tonio Hölscher, "Images and Political Identity: The Case of Athens," in *Democracy, Empire and the Arts in Fifth-Century Athens*, ed. Deborah Boedeker and Kurt A. Raaflaub (Cambridge, Mass.: Harvard University Press, 1998), pp. 153–83; also see Burkhard Fehr, *Die Tyrannentöter Oder: Kann man der Demokratie ein Denkmal setzen?* (Frankfurt: Fischer Taschenbuch Verlag GmbH, 1984). Translation by Margitta Mätzke, "The Assassins of the Tyrant. Or, Is It Possible to Put Up a Monument to Democracy?" (author's files).

[13] An early date for the songs preserved in Athenaeus *The Deipnosophists* 15.69510–13 is argued in Martin Ostwald, *Nomos and the Beginnings of Athenian Democracy* (Oxford: Clarendon, 1969), pp. 121–36, esp. 133–36. The song seems to have been well known in 425, when Aristophanes' *Acharnians* was produced. This play contains the earliest of several references to the singing of "the Harmodius" (line 980, also *Acharnians* 1093, *Wasps* 1225). For discussion of the circumstances of the composition and singing of such songs as well as of the literary references to the singing of the Harmodius, see Taylor, *The Tyrant Slayers*, pp.

Athenian freedom is attested to by the fact that they were stolen by Xerxes during the Persian Wars (480/79).[14] They were quickly replaced by a new statuary group by leading artists, the sculptors Kritios and Nesiotes. The new group was set up in the agora following the defeat of the Persians at the battle of Salamis. The verse attributed to Simonides inscribed on the base of the rededicated statue group reads: "A great light came to the Athenians, when Aristogeiton and Harmodius killed Hipparchus."[15] In the years following the rededication of the new, more impressive statue grouping, the official veneration of Harmodius and Aristogeiton seriously took hold. Soon the Tyrannicides were being represented on vases and coins.[16] They were also honored by a tomb in the Kerameikos[17] and the establishment of a hero cult that included an annual public sacrifice conducted by the chief magistrate overseeing military affairs, the Polemarch.[18]

Later activity also indicates their enduring symbolic resonance. The Athenians awarded special honors to the descendants of Harmodius and Aristogeiton. In the 440s or 430s (the period of Pericles' prominence), the Assembly by specific act gave the descendants of the Tyrannicides the right to take meals at public expense in the Prytaneum (sitēsis).[19] The

---

52–53; and C. M. Bowra, *Greek Lyric Poetry from Alcman to Simonides*, 2d ed. (Oxford: Clarendon, 1961), pp. 391–97.

[14] Taylor, *The Tyrant Slayers*, p. 46. The Tyrannicides' capacity to signal a celebration of freedom is still apparent much later. A law "forbidding the giving of the names Harmodius and Aristogeiton to slaves . . . is mentioned in the 2nd century a.d. by Aulus Gellius (*Noctes Atticae* 9.2.10) and in the 4th by Libanios in his *Apologie Socratis* (5.53)." I owe these references to Taylor, *The Tyrant Slayers*, p. 27.

[15] The couplet is quoted by Hephaestion (*Handbook* 28), who attributes it to Simonides. Translation (slightly modified) is borrowed from Bowra, *Greek Lyric Poetry*, p. 321. For discussion of the inscription, including its attribution, see Bowra, *Greek Lyric Poetry*, pp. 321ff. For the text, see B. D. Meritt, "Greek Inscriptions: Harmodius and Aristogeiton," *Hesperia* 5 (1936): 355–441.

[16] For discussion of and references regarding the specific vase-painters and other artists with whom the tyrannicide myth was popular, see Bowra, *Greek Lyric Poetry*, pp. 394–95; and Taylor, *The Tyrant Slayers*, pp. 78–158. For a list of sources for coins and of Attic vase representations, see Taylor, ibid., p. 209. An iconographic assimilation of Theseus, the mythic founder of Athens, to the Tyrannicides in vase painting and other media is also telling. See Taylor, ibid., pp. 78–146; Castriota, "Democracy and Art," pp. 209–13; C. Kardara, "On Theseus and the Tyrannicides," *American Journal of Archaeology* 55 (1951): 293–300. On Theseus in particular, see Henry Walker, *Theseus and Athens* (New York: Oxford University Press, 1995); and W. R. Connor, "Theseus in Classical Athens," in *The Quest for Theseus*, ed. Anne G. Warde (London: Pall Mall, 1970), pp. 143–74.

[17] Pausanias 1.29.15. This grave may date to several years after their actual death, as it is unlikely that Hippias would have permitted such an honored burial. See Taylor, *The Tyrant Slayers*, p. 23.

[18] Aristotle *Constitution of Athens* 58.1.

[19] Epigraphical evidence makes it "virtually certain" that Pericles himself was mover of the decree (Anthony Podlecki, "The Political Significance of the Athenian Tyrannicide Cult," *Historia* 15 [1966]: 140–41). This epigraphical evidence is the Prytaneion Decree. For dis-

decree lists first priests and then descendants of Harmodius and Aristogeiton. This was the same privilege that Athenian citizens serving as Council members enjoyed during their turn as the presiding tribe and that the city bestowed on victors in the Olympic, Nemean, and Pythian Games. It is also the "punishment" Socrates suggests that he deserves for having lived his life as a gadfly to the body politic (*Apology* 36c–e). Early in the fourth century, after the restoration of the democracy following the defeat of the Thirty, the Athenians extended two additional privileges to descendants of the Tyrannicides—exemption from liturgies (*ateleia*) and front-row seats in the theater (*proedria*).[20] As late as 323, after Athens had lost the critical battle at Chaeronea to the forces of Macedon, orators continued to appeal to their memory. In a speech in support of the prosecution of Demosthenes for bribery, Dinarchus tries to discredit the accused by noting that he had encouraged the city to imprison descendants of Harmodius.[21] Later in the same speech, he complains that the accused did not protest when pro-Macedon elements in the city "share[d] entertainment in the Prytaneum with the descendants of Harmodius and Aristogeiton."[22]

It is impossible to say whether a significant number of Athenians from a variety of walks of life objected to the new and persistent symbolism. It is plausible that the original celebration of the Tyrannicides played a part in the articulation of aristocratic rivalries in Athens, as some scholars have insisted, though our sources do not permit us to settle this question.[23] On the whole, scholarly efforts to fix the partisan origins of the cult of the Tyrannicides miss the great political significance of the myth. What is striking and in need of explanation is that the legend quickly became widely embraced among Athenians and an enduring symbol not of aristo-

---

cussion of this decree, see Martin Ostwald, "The Prytaneion Decree Re-examined," *American Journal of Philology* 72 (1951): 24–46.

[20] For *proedria* and *ateleia* having been granted to the descendants of Harmodius and Aristogeiton, the evidence is a speech of Isaeus, *On the Estate of Dicaeogenes* (46–47). On the privilege of *proedria*, also see Herodotus 1.54 and 9.74; Aristophanes *Knights* 573–76, and *Thesmophoriazusae* 834.

[21] *Against Demosthenes* 63.

[22] 101–2. Translations from Dinarchus are from J. O. Burtt, *Minor Attic Orators* (Cambridge, Mass.: Harvard University Press [Loeb], 1954).

[23] For critical discussion of this literature, see C. W. Fornara, "The Cult of Harmodius and Aristogeiton," *Philologus* 114 (1970): 155–80; and Ostwald, *Nomos*, pp. 121–36. Fornara correctly argues that it is wrong to assume that the legend took hold because some party pushed it as part of its "propaganda." He shows that the debates are problematic in that they have been shaped by the assumption that some party perpetrated "deliberate falsifications" upon the demos. Instead, he proposes, "the tradition about the tyrannicide originated as the accurate reflection of the *sentiments* of those who returned to Athens in 511/510 B.C., that the so-called 'official' version became orthodox, which is to say, popularly believed, because it was heralded by the liberators and because it was *dramatic*" ("Cult," pp. 169–70, my emphasis).

cratic ideals or partisan divisions but of common aspirations. Whatever the circumstances of its initial promotion, it was rapidly transformed into a "national mythos in which all Athenians could take pride."[24]

EMBRACING THE SIMPLIFIED TALE

As a sociologist writing about the cult of George Washington has observed, "People in crisis fortify themselves by embracing their culture's most meaningful experiences."[25] The Athenians' embrace of a cult of Harmodius and Aristogeiton suggests that they found in the sanitized tale an account of the Athenians' self-interpretation of the nourishment they thought would indeed "fortify" them. As Michael Taylor stresses, "That the metamorphosis of the Tyrant Slayers into founding heroes could be said to have an uncertain basis in historical fact was practically irrelevant [to the establishment of a cult]. A need was felt and Harmodius and Aristogeiton were the figures most conveniently situated to supply that need." The religious innovation of creating a cult may, he continues, "smack of expediency" and appear "shocking to modern consciences."[26] But the obviously political circumstances of the origin of the cult and the rapidity of the institution of new founding heroes would have detracted from neither the legitimacy nor the solemnity of the rites in the eyes of the Athenians.[27]

---

[24] Castriota, "Democracy and Art," p. 208. The legend's extraordinary appeal was also immune to attacks from intellectuals like Herodotus, Thucydides, and Aristotle, who found it mendacious. They explicitly object to the legend as a perpetration of a blatant falsehood that leads citizens poorly to understand their circumstances. But even so, the legend flourished. This is despite the fact that the truth of the nondecisive role of Harmodius and Aristogeiton in the liberation was, as Rosalind Thomas observed, well known throughout the fifth century and certainly remained discernible in the fourth (*Oral Tradition*, pp. 242–51). Accounts of details such as the bribing of the Pythia, Spartan military involvement, and the popular uprising against Isagoras and Cleomenes are found in several fifth-century sources in contexts indicating that readers or listeners were being reminded of familiar facts. For example, neither Herodotus nor Thucydides claims to have uncovered much new information. Rather, each one stresses that he is only paying full attention to less savory but known details and is drawing appropriate inferences from this available information. In Aristophanes' *Lysistrata* (1149–56), moreover, Lysistrata bluntly reminds the audience of the Spartan role in the liberation of Athens, and the Chorus recalls the public uprising against Isagoras and Cleomenes.

[25] Barry Schwartz, *George Washington: The Making of an American Symbol* (New York: Free Press, 1987), p. 31. He is drawing on Victor Turner, *Drama, Fields and Metaphors* (Ithaca: Cornell University Press, 1974). I have also found Turner extremely useful in conceptualizing the problem explored in this chapter.

[26] Taylor, *The Tyrant Slayers*, p. 22.

[27] On cult and politics in Athens, see, for example, H. Alan Shapiro, "Religion and Politics in Democratic Athens," in Coulson et al., eds., *Archaeology of Athens*, pp. 123–29; Emily Kearns, "Change and Continuity in Religious Structures after Cleisthenes," in *CRUX: Essays in Greek History Presented to G.E.M. de Ste. Croix on His Seventy-Fifth Birthday*, ed. P. A.

In the Athenian context, religious and political life were intimately linked. Piety was a civic concern, something public as well as private ritual action had to bear out.[28]

What made Harmodius and Aristogeiton "conveniently situated" to supply the religious need Taylor identifies, or to "fortify" the Athenians? How did celebration of these two heroes, and not simply the experience of celebration, somehow "specif[y] the values by which the new collectivity aspired to be known"?[29] Why did the Athenians adopt this tale? More precisely, why did it rapidly become the "official" popularly accepted version and remain so for generations?

THINKING WITH THE TALE

Imagining Unity and Responsible Rule

The tale named the enemy that the diverse Athenian community was undivided in opposing—tyranny. In this way it facilitated the city's efforts to imagine itself a unity.[30] Harmodius and Aristogeiton as a pair were well-suited to the representation of the pervasive sentiment of antityrantism. They had done something dramatic against a tyrant. Many Athenians could easily have found expressed in their act the ideal of passionate resistance to tyrannical overreaching that was itself nicely symbolized by Hipparchus' interference in the erotic relation between Harmodius and Aristogeiton. Also, the two men were well-suited for uninhibited admiration. Venerating Harmodius and Aristogeiton was safe. They were dead. They could not later use their growing status and reputation as a springboard to power, possibly even extralegal power and the return of tyranny.[31] Har-

---

Cartledge and F. D. Harvey (London: Duckworth, 1985), pp. 189–207; Martin Nilsson, *Cults, Myths and Oracles, and Politics in Ancient Greece* (New York: Cooper Square, 1972); Jenifer Neils, "The Panathenaia and Kleisthenic Ideology," in Coulson et al., eds., *Archaeology of Athens*, pp. 151–60.

[28] For discussion of the inappropriateness of the modern distinction between "sacred" and "secular" for the analysis of Greek civic religion, see W. Robert Connor, " 'Sacred' and 'Secular': *Hiera kai Hosia* and the Classical Athenian Concept of the State," *Ancient Society* 19 (1988): 161–88. See also Walter Burkert, *Greek Religion*, trans. John Raffan (Cambridge, Mass.: Harvard University Press, 1985 [1977]).

[29] I borrow this phrasing from Sheldon Wolin, *The Presence of the Past* (Baltimore: The Johns Hopkins University Press, 1989), p. 9. For discussion of Athenian constructions of a usable past, including consideration of the Tyrannicides from this perspective, see Deborah Boedeker, "Presenting the Past in Fifth-Century Athens," in Boedeker and Raaflaub, eds., *Democracy, Empire and the Arts*, pp. 185<->202.

[30] On the city of Athens' determination to imagine itself the embodiment of unity, see Nicole Loraux, "Reflections of the Greek City on Unity and Division," in Molho et al., eds., *City States in Classical Antiquity*, pp. 33–51.

[31] This was key as the Athenians were intensely fearful of the return of tyranny and suspicious of treasonous tyrant-sympathizers among them. On the virulence of Athenian antity-

modius and Aristogeiton were also not remembered as politically ambitious men, nor as skillful pursuers of a political plan. Though ambition and skill were qualities the Athenians enjoyed, they always retained a healthy measure of suspicion toward them. Admiring Harmodius and Aristogeiton did not require negotiating this complexity.

Attributing the liberation of Athens to the Tyrannicides supported Athenian solidarity by making the founding a purely Athenian event. At the very least, it placed at the "head of a sequence" of events a daring act by Athenians unassisted by outsiders.[32] The focus on Harmodius and Aristogeiton concealed the part Spartan military intervention played in the expulsion of the tyrant.[33] A dramatic act by a pair of Athenians captured imaginations more easily than could "the army of Cleomenes or the machinations of Delphi and Cleisthenes."[34]

The tale also helpfully nurtured a forgetting of the severe civil strife that marked the early Cleisthenic period. The tension between the (defeated) aristocratic faction and the (victorious) democratic faction led by Cleisthenes must have been intense in this period. The aristocratic faction had recently committed acts that democrats would have found thoroughly offensive—they had enlisted the help of a foreign power to gain control over the majority (Isagoras had called on the aid of Cleomenes of Sparta). The people, in turn, had recently committed acts that the conservative aristocrats would have found terrifying. In particular, they had mobilized their numbers against a hated individual (a "mob" had taken action against Isagoras). That is, there had been a popular uprising. Untainted by any strong partisan association rooted in these conflicts, Harmodius and Aristogeiton could provide a rallying call that could appeal over the heads of other allegiances in support of the Cleisthenic reforms. The group statue

---

rantism in the fifth century, see Lavelle, *The Sorrow and the Pity*, pp. 27–58. He discusses in particular Hippias' effort to regain his lost power (he joined the Persians in their assault on Marathon in 490) and Athenian suspicions even of Miltiades, the military hero of Marathon.

[32] Castriota, "Democracy and Art," p. 202. As Jacoby is concerned with who promoted the tale, he notes only in passing what I take to be a crucial reason for the tale's continued symbolic importance—it made the liberation a "purely Athenian affair" ("The Athenian Tradition," p. 162). Also noted by Ostwald, *Nomos*, p. 134.

[33] Also noted by Ostwald, *Nomos*, pp. 134–35. I have been helped by Thomas' mapping of the way the tale of liberation was altered to decrease the roles of Sparta and Delphi (*Oral Tradition*, pp. 254ff.). Thomas maintains that these transformations were related to the "patriotic demands of the democratic polis traditions" (p. 256). She does not, however, explore the significance of the alterations that decrease the role of the rivalry between Isagoras and Cleisthenes or of the popular action against Isagoras holed up on the Acropolis. Henry Walker plausibly suggests that the increased attention to Theseus following the Cleisthenic victory may also have been a part of Athenian efforts to minimize—even erase—memory of the Spartan role in the liberation. See *Theseus and Athens*, pp. 51–52.

[34] Ostwald, *Nomos*, pp. 134–35.

commemorating the tyrannicide by Kritios and Nesiotes is telling in this connection.[35] It visually represents the achievement of a sort of solidarity.[36] It engages the viewer in imagining the strength that comes from uniting youthful vigor and boldness with mature, considerate determination. The contrasting individual features of the two men are carefully rendered, as are differences of character. Aristogeiton appears steady and older, positioned slightly behind Harmodius; Harmodius appears young, daring, and eager. Yet their postures are similar, and the composition employs a large number of parallel axes, giving the impression that their movements are choreographed: they are depicted acting in concert, as a unity.[37]

But the tale elicited potentially divisive emotions as well. In doing so, it attached these passions to the greater collective struggle to fashion and come to love the distinctive look of Athenian political life post-tyranny. For example, aristocrats could find in the tale a celebration of the special contribution of the nobly born to the excellence of the newly restructured Athenian polis. The appeal of the tyrannicide story to the demos, on the other hand, could lie in its celebration of an act of supreme boldness, that is, an act that could have recalled for them the daring they themselves had exhibited in the popular uprising against Isagoras. This combination of meanings is present in the cult statue of the Tyrannicides. The confident pose of the figures likely evoked a variety of responses that could have allowed citizens with different partisan convictions to find something in the new political project with which to affiliate. The figures "stride forward boldly."[38] Every gesture suggests self-possession. The facial expressions connote nobility and dedication. The statue suggests the *aretē* to which citizens aspired. But it does so in an inclusive, rather than exclusively aristocratic, manner, as the statue was placed in the agora and was the centerpiece of a public cult.[39] Moreover, the demos, understood as the

[35] I refer here to the second statue group by Kritios and Nesiotes. Photographic reproductions of the surviving Roman copy of this group are available in A. Stewart, *Greek Sculpture: An Exploration*, vol. 2, plates (New Haven: Yale University Press, 1990), p. 227; and in Castriota, "Democracy and Art."

[36] As Andrew Stewart has suggested, "The heroes' similar postures indicate their solidarity in action" (*Greek Sculpture*, 1: 136).

[37] For discussion of how the rendering of contrasting physical features and gestures of the figures signal contrasting human qualities, and how compositional elements in the design of the statue strongly indicate the idea of men acting in concert as a cohesive unit, see Fehr, *Die Tyrannentöter Oder*, pp. 34–41.

[38] I have borrowed some of Castriota's description of the statue ("Democracy and Art," p. 203). I have not borrowed his further description of the statue's representation of selflessness and sacrifice because, as he himself says, these meanings surface only if a viewer is "inclined to see them in this way" (p. 204), and I am arguing that the Athenians were not so inclined.

[39] The Tyrannicides' ability to signal not only ideals but their inclusive reach is also present in an early fourth-century speech of Isaeus. He explicitly downplays their family status: "The

self-conscious collectivity that acted to oppose Isagoras, could have found
in the statue a representation of its own emerging self-confidence—the
pose of Harmodius is of a confident man, arm raised, ready to strike. The
statue served as a visual reminder of the power of the demos to oppose
overly ambitious aristocrats. Stewart finds this meaning apparent: since
Harmodius "stands right in the path" of people coming into the agora,
"the warning is clear: Let future tyrants beware!"[40] As the statue and the
legend appealed to various people in all these ways, the Tyrannicides provided a remarkably dense, multivocal symbol, that is, one capable of eliciting different yet strong feelings from many Athenian groups, thus fostering attachments to the new political order by fostering affections for the
myth. The mythic version of Athens' "founding," reiterated on a number
of public and private ritual occasions, served the development of solidarity
in the absence of a strong consensus.[41] The public commemoration of the
tyrannicide and veneration of Harmodius and Aristogeiton supplied a
common experience through which free citizens of various social and economic positions could develop and sustain affective ties to the idea of a
unified Athenian demos.

Also telling is the tyrannicide's strong association with the embrace at
Athens of political equality (isonomia[42]) in two verses of an Attic drinking
song that was contemporaneous with the upheavals of the Cleisthenic period and that remained popular for generations:

---

great Aristogeiton and Harmodius were honoured not because of their birth but because of
their bravery." Isaeus *On the Estate of Dicaeogenes* 47; translation from Edward Seymour
Forster, *Isaeus* (Cambridge, Mass.: Harvard University Press [Loeb], 1927).

[40] Stewart, *Greek Sculpture*, 1: 136.

[41] For discussion of how the multivocality of symbols is particularly important for rituals
that work to build solidarity in the absence of consensus, see David Kertzer, *Ritual, Politics
and Power* (New Haven: Yale University Press, 1988).

[42] Ostwald argues that isonomia "is not a name for a form of government but for the
principle of political equality" (*Nomos*, p. 97). He stresses that while not a synonym for
democracy, it is the case that this principle is "more closely associated with a democratic
constitution than with any other" (*Nomos*, p. 97). It is the question of precisely why this
was the case—what work it did as a slogan—that I examine here. The meaning of "political
equality" is, however, hard to fix. The Greek, *isonomia*, is based on two elements, each
of which has multiple meanings. *Isos* can mean "equal" or "fair." *Nom*, from *nomos*, can
mean "positive law" or "custom." Whether the term therefore refers exclusively to the
equal role of each in the shaping of the laws or the fair treatment of all under the law is
unclear. It probably refers to both. On the political and legal scope of the idea of isonomia
and its use by Cleisthenes as a slogan, see Gregory Vlastos, "Isonomia," *American Journal
of Philology* 74 (1953): 337–66; and *"Isonomia Politikē*," in Vlastos, *Platonic Studies* (Princeton: Princeton University Press, 1981, 2d ed.), pp. 164–203; Victor Ehrenberg, "The Origins of Democracy," *Historia* (1950): 530–37; Meier, *The Greek Discovery of Politics*, trans.
David McLintock (Cambridge, Mass.: Harvard University Press, 1990), p. 168; and Josiah
Ober, *Mass and Elite in Democratic Athens* (Princeton: Princeton University Press, 1989),
pp. 74–75.

I shall take the myrtle-branch and carry my sword, like Harmodius and Aristo-geiton, when they slew the tyrant and made Athens equal (*isonomous t'Athēnas epoiēsatēn*). . . . Their fame shall live on the earth forever, dearest Harmodius and Aristogeiton, since they slew the tyrant and made Athens equal (*isonomous t'Athēnas epoiēsatēn*).[43]

The line "made Athens equal" is an expression of praise. It names a good that Athens has secured. That good is not only the accomplishment of a decisive break with tyranny (captured in the direct mention of the murder), but also the capacity of the city to sustain this break over time. Invoking isonomia here does the work of signaling the Athenian aspiration to stave off the threat of tyranny into the future and of asserting that the city has developed some means of accomplishing this. To clarify the links I am proposing between antityrantism, isonomia, and democracy in the democratic imaginary, we can look at the praise of isonomia in the argument of Otanes, the advocate for popular rule, in a passage from Herodotus' *Histories* commonly referred to as "The Debate on the Constitutions" (3.80–89).[44]

The setting of this debate in the *Histories* is grisly. Seven Persian nobles have just killed a Magus who had secretly seized power at the Persian court

---

[43] Athenaeus *The Deipnosophists* 15.695.10, 13. Translation (slightly modified) from Bowra, *Greek Lyric Poetry*, p. 392. On the occasions for Attic drinking songs, see Bowra, ibid.,, pp. 373–97.

[44] In this passage Herodotus does not faithfully report an episode in Persian history but rather projects fifth-century Greek thinking about the competing merits of three regimes—monarchy, oligarchy, and popular rule—onto an account of the accession of Darius to the Persian throne. In particular, ideas crisply articulated here, even the terminology utilized, are echoed by Athenian partisans of democracy years later and throughout Plato's lifetime. For philological evidence for the text's connections to the widely attested terminology of Greek politics, see W. R. Connor, *New Politicians of Fifth-Century Athens* (Princeton: Princeton University Press, 1971), pp. 199–206. For discussion of Herodotus' ethnographic sensibility and manner of conveying meaning through his stories, see the articles collected in the special issue of *Arethusa* entitled *Herodotus and the Invention of History*, vol. 20, nos. 1 and 2 (Spring and Fall 1987); Carolyn Dewald, "Introduction," *Herodotus, The Histories*, trans. Robin Waterfield (New York: Oxford University Press, 1998), pp. ix–xli; James Romm, *Herodotus* (New Haven: Yale University Press, 1998); Henry Immerwahr, *Form and Thought in Herodotus* (Cleveland: The Press of Western Reserve University [for the American Philological Association, Philological Monographs no. 23], 1966 [reprinted 1986]); Donald Lateiner, *The Historical Method of Herodotus* (Toronto: University of Toronto Press, 1987); S. Flory, *The Archaic Smile of Herodotus* (Detroit: Wayne State University Press, 1987). For political theorists' consideration of the theoretical sophistication of the passage and of Herodotus in general, see Norma Thompson, *Herodotus and the Origins of Political Community* (New Haven: Yale University Press, 1996); Seth Benardete, *Herodotean Inquiries* (The Hague: Martinus Nijoff, 1969); Stanley Rosen, "Herodotus Reconsidered," in *Herodotus: The Histories* (New York: Norton, 1992), pp. 332–56; and Arlene Saxonhouse, "Herodotus, Democracy and Equality," in *Athenian Democracy: Modern Mythmakers and Ancient Theorists* (Notre Dame, Ind.: University of Notre Dame Press, 1996), pp. 31–58.

after the death of Cambyses. Not only did they kill the pretender to the throne, they also paraded in the streets with his head, as well as those of his aides, eagerly showing the Persians that an imposter had been deposed and urging that they, the Persian people, join the nobles in killing other Magi among them. The constitutional debate takes place five days later, after "the confusion settled"[45] but before any new political authority is in place. The question they take up is, what form of rule should they install in Persia?

Otanes speaks first and boldly. "It is my view," he begins, "that we should put to an end the system whereby one of us is the sole ruler. Monarchy is neither an attractive nor a noble institution." He points out the abuses of power to which a monarch is prone: "You have seen how vicious Cambyses became." Otanes does not attribute the well-known excesses and cruelties of monarchy to the bad character of the man in power. Rather, he faults the practice of concentrating power in the hands of a single man. He faults the very structure of the government: "Make a man a monarch, and even if he is the most moral person in the world (*ton ariston andrōn pantōn*), he will leave his customary ways of thinking. All the advantages of his position breed arrogant abusiveness in him." Worse, the advantage he holds also enables him to act on these thoughts: he ignores law, rapes women, and puts people to death without trial. Majority rule, on the other hand, Otanes asserts, "is entirely free of the vices of monarchy." This is because it is government "by lot, it is accountable government, and it refers all decisions to the common people (*es to konon*)." The multitude (*plēthos*) should rule because "in the majority is the whole."[46]

Otanes' case for popular rule rests on two things: a distinction between responsible and irresponsible ruling,[47] and a deep suspicion of power. Irresponsible rule, exemplified by tyranny, is arbitrary, unaccountable, abusive, self-interested.[48] Responsible ruling is law-abiding, accountable, and concerned with the felt needs and grievances of the public. Otanes' argument is that popular rule is most likely to deliver responsible ruling because it is the only regime that institutionalizes the suspicion of power.[49] The other

---

[45] Translation from *Herodotus, The Histories*, trans. Robin Waterfield, with an introduction and notes by Carolyn Dewald (New York: Oxford University Press, 1998). All subsequent quotes from Herodotus are from this edition unless otherwise noted.

[46] I depart from Waterfield's translation, following instead Christian Meier's rendering of *en gar tōi pollōi eni ta panta* in his *The Greek Discovery of Politics*, p. 164.

[47] Also noted by Kurt Raaflaub, "Contemporary Perceptions of Democracy in Fifth Century Athens," *Classica et mediaevalia* 40 (1989): 33–70.

[48] Compare Aristotle's identification of tyranny with irresponsible rule at *Politics* 1295a20.

[49] Other sources confirm that Otanes is expressing an idea current in Athenian discourse. For example, a link between democracy and the idea of accountable, responsible rule is

speakers in the debate, Darius and Megabyzus, claim that their favored regimes, monarchy and oligarchy, indeed can provide a route to responsible rule and that the mob can act as badly as a dreadful tyrant. The argument of the passage casts doubt on their views. But my concern here is how far Otanes' argument sheds light on the democratic self-understanding, not on Herodotus' own sympathies.[50]

Otanes' praise of popular rule as the best route to responsible government—that is, the best bet against the threat of tyranny—does not involve a defense of the virtue or competence of the common people.[51] Accordingly, Otanes makes no claims regarding the personal qualities of the men in office.[52] Rather, he rejects connecting the possession of virtue with the responsible exercise of power. It is not prudent to rely on the (fragile)

---

present in Aeschylus' *Persians* (lines 210–20). Atossa, queen of Persia, states, "My son, should he succeed, would be admired; / But if he fails, Persia cannot hold him / To account. Whichever comes, safe returned, sovereign / He shall rule" (translation by Seth Benardete in *Aeschylus 2*, ed. David Grene and Richard Lattimore (Chicago: University of Chicago Press, 1991). Also see Aeschines *Against Cteisiphon* 18–22, esp. 22, which explicitly comments on the pervasive Athenian practices of accountability: "There is nothing in the [Athenian democratic] polis that is exempt from audit, investigation and examination" (translation from C. D. Adam, *The Speeches of Aeschines* (Cambridge, Mass.: Harvard University Press [Loeb], 1948).

[50] Even though Darius is victorious in the debate—the Persians choose monarchy and accept Darius as their king—Herodotus' presentation of the arguments spoken and the behavior of the participants signal the author's preference for Otanes' assessment of the best route to responsible rule. Supporting this claim would require more extensive elaboration that I can offer here. There is no consensus in the literature regarding Herodotus' own sympathies. For an example of the approach to the problem I favor, see Lateiner, "Historiographical Patterning: The Constitutional Debate," in his *The Historical Method of Herodotus*, pp. 163–86. For an opposing view, see Flory, *The Archaic Smile of Herodotus*, esp. pp. 128–29.

[51] In this way his view is consistent with Athenian thought. Consider, for example, Aeschines' oration *Against Timarchus* 4–5: "It is acknowledged . . . that there are in the world three forms of *politeiai*, tyranny, oligarchy and democracy: tyrannies and oligarchies are administered according to the tempers of their lords, but democracies according to established laws . . . [democracy is] a *politeia* based upon equality and law (*tēn isēn kai ennomon*)." Translation from Adams, *The Speeches of Aeschines*, modified slightly. See also Thucydides 4.78.3, where *isonomia* is contrasted with *dunasteia*—the irresponsible rule of a few powerful men.

[52] Otanes' effort to shift attention away from the evaluation of the moral qualities of office-holders is apparent in the vocabulary he employs. He does not use the term *dēmos*, which had connotations of "ordinary" and "base." Rather, he uses terms that denote number (*plēthos* and *polloi*). The advocates of oligarchy and monarchy, in contrast, both make liberal use of the term *dēmos*. Megabyzus even speaks as if the *dēmos* were a single actor with determinable moral qualities, like ignorance (*aneu noou*). See also Aristotle's report of democratic principles at the beginning of Book 6 of the *Politics*: "The popular principle of justice is to have equality according to number, not worth" (*kai gar to dikaion to dēmotikon to ison echein esti kat'arithmon alla mē kat'axian*, 1317b3–5). Translation from H. Rackham, *Politics of Aristotle* (Cambridge, Mass.: Harvard University Press [Loeb], 1944). See also *Politics* 1316a5–6.

character of a man to insure that power is exercised responsibly. And it is dangerous to recognize formally any claim to superior competence or knowledge, as such recognition will foster hubris, thereby inviting arbitrary, ill-considered, and self-interested—in a word, irresponsible—ruling. Popular government ensures responsible rule because in relying on the lot, it recognizes no special claims when it invests someone with power,[53] and it counteracts the dangerous effects of even this power by distributing small parcels of power widely, holding officers to account and conducting deliberations in the open. It is in concluding this argument that Otanes praises popular rule as having the "most beautiful name of all, *isonomiē* (*ounoma pantōn kalliston echei isonomiēn*)." Its beauty derives from the healthy political condition of the body politic that its institutions generate.[54]

Otanes' argument for popular rule does not turn on any recognition of a principle of the natural equality of individuals that somehow was gaining credibility and that now needed to be applied to political life. He does not root his argument in any deep philosophical commitment to the inherent moral worth of all individuals and the consequent right of those individuals to participate in politics. Rather, he proposes that a specifically political accomplishment, the political equality of citizen males—a convention self-consciously instituted by the Athenians—best serves the effort to achieve the responsible exercise of power. This point needs stressing, as it is one way in which the ancient way of thinking about political equality differs dramatically from our own. No moral discovery of the natural equality of persons, or even some persons, informed their thinking. Rather, they understood institutions and cultural norms and practices to create equality among a defined group. Being excluded from the work of these institutions meant not being rendered equal by the force of human artifice.[55]

[53] The same idea is expressed in Euripides' *Suppliant Women*. Theseus, responding to the Theban Herald's question, "Who is king here?" states: "Stranger, you began your speech on a false note, / Enquiring for a king absolute. This state is not / Subject to one man's will, but is a free city. / The king here is the people, who by yearly office / Govern in turn. We give no special power to wealth; / The poor man's voice commands equal authority" (lines 403–8). Translation from Philip Vellacott, *Euripides: Orestes and Other Plays* (New York: Penguin, 1972).

[54] On *isonomia*'s use in articulating notions of balance and health, and the health of the body politic, see Ostwald, *Nomos*, pp. 102–6.

[55] Arlene Saxonhouse stresses a similar point. She writes: "The Greek authors were always working from what I shall call a 'constructed equality' rather than the natural equality that we, raised in the language of the Declaration of Independence, consider to be a 'self-evident truth.' It was the assertion of equality among some that lay at the foundation of ancient democracy, not the assumption of equality among all" ("Herodotus, Democracy and Equality," in her *Athenian Democracy*, pp. 33–34).

Being included in the work of these institutions meant participating in the important work of vigorously defending the polis against the ever-present threat of tyranny. To be an active democratic citizen, that is, to exercise one's political equality, was to be a worthy heir of Harmodius and Aristogeiton. The strong link between antityrantism and the enjoyment of political equality in the drinking song discussed above suggests that the Athenians ideally imagined routine acts of public participation—that is, the enjoyment of political equality (jury service, attending meetings, voting, serving as a magistrate, sponsoring a poet, being a Council member)—to have grand significance. Their performance contributed to the collective effort to continue to contain the threat of tyranny over time.

Reciprocity between City and Citizens

The legend was also good to think with in the sense that it supported citizens' efforts vividly to imagine the city and free citizens sustaining a relation of reciprocity. For example, fourth-century orators treat Harmodius and Aristogeiton as model benefactors (*euergetai*) of the city.[56] Of course, the magnitude of the accomplishment attributed to them can explain why orators turned to them as exemplary. But the success of their nomination as model benefactors was due to additional factors.

The story of Harmodius and Aristogeiton placed before the Athenians a model of benefaction that resolved the potential for conflict between a citizen's public and private loyalties. Neither figure in this tale is identified as having willingly neglected personal commitments or sacrificed private goods for the sake of public ones. Rather, the lovers' loyalty to each other and to the familial interest of the kin of Harmodius were all consistent with the best interest of the city, understood as liberation from the tyrant. Making this interpretation particularly compelling is the lack of any effort to conceal the private motive behind the pair's great public act in sources sympathetic to the legend.[57] For example, Aeschines' use of the legend confirms that it was precisely the combination of private motives and public benefit that drew Athenians to it. Warning the jury that his adversary will use the example of Harmodius and Aristogeiton against him, he says: "He will cite those benefactors of yours, Harmodius and Aristogeiton,

[56] See especially Demosthenes *On the False Embassy* 280, and Aeschines *Against Timarchus* 132.

[57] It is possible that fourth-century Athenians exhibit such strong interest in the relation of the public and private motives of the Tyrannicides in part due to Thucydides' stress on their private motives in his critique of the tale (discussed below). But it remains significant that fourth-century thinkers sympathetic to the legend did not respond to Thucydides' attack by denying the pair's private motives. Instead, they embraced Thucydides' focus on their personal concerns in their accounts of the Tyrannicides' political significance.

describing their fidelity to one another, and telling how in their case this relationship proved the salvation of the city."[58] Aeschines here assumes that Harmodius and Aristogeiton typically symbolized the aspiration of citizens to a congruence of their private and public interests.

Another example of a source utilizing the common knowledge of the private motives that lay behind the public act of Harmodius and Aristogeiton is Pausanias' appeal to the memory of Harmodius and Aristogeiton in his speech in Plato's *Symposium.* Pausanias' speech praises conventional Athenian erotic practices in part by asserting that they support the attainment of political excellence. To craft this argument, Plato has Pausanias appeal to the orthodox version of the legend. Pausanias says:

> The Persian empire is absolute; that is why it condemns love as well as philosophy and sport. It is no good for rulers if the people they rule cherish ambitions for themselves or form strong bonds of friendship with one another. That these are precisely the effects of philosophy, sport, and especially of Love is a lesson the tyrants of Athens learned directly from their own experience: Didn't their reign (*archē*) come to a dismal end because of the bonds uniting Harmodius and Aristogeiton in love and affection (*erōs* and *philia*)? (182c)

That this was a conventional attitude much earlier as well is suggested by the ease with which the Kritios and Nesiotes group statue of Harmodius and Aristogeiton that stood in the agora also could convey related ideals. Erected to replace the Antenor group stolen by Xerxes in 480, this statue represents the erotic character of the pair's relation. The statue "acquired a sexual edge" as it presented an "aggressive display of unclothed male bodies" in "striding active poses."[59] Moreover, through a complex visual code, each of the figures conveys the qualities that made up ideal attractiveness in each of the parties—the older erastes and the youthful eromenos. It invites young men to identify with Harmodius and older ones with Aristogeiton, and then for both to "vicariously savor the homoerotic relationship between the two."[60] But the raised arm of Harmodius bearing

---

[58] *Against Timarchus* 132. Translation from Adam, *The Speeches of Aeschines,* slightly modified.

[59] Robin Osborne, "Men without Clothes: Heroic Nakedness and Greek Art," *Gender and History* 9 (1997): 514. On nakedness in this statue group as a signifier of erotic desire and attachment, not elevation to heroic, nonhuman stature, also see Fehr, *Die Tyrannentöter Oder,* p. 30; and Stewart, *Art, Desire and the Body,* p. 73. For discussion of the politics of masculinity in Athens on view in sculpture, see Robin Osborne, "Sculpted Men of Athens: Masculinity and Power in the Field of Vision," in *Thinking Men: Masculinity and Its Self-Representation in the Classical Tradition,* ed. L. Foxhall and J. Salmon (London: Routledge, 1998), pp. 23–42. For discussion of our evidence for the design of the Kritios and Nesiotes group, see Fehr, *Die Tyrannentöter Oder,* pp. 6–9.

[60] Stewart, *Art, Desire and the Body,* p. 73. Citations in the remainder of this paragraph are also from this text, ibid.

a sword and the about-to-pounce postures of both figures also compel the viewer "to stand in for the doomed Hipparchus." In this way we find represented a politicization of their erotic relationship. The liberation depended on the manly virtues that the erotic bond between these men had nurtured. Only similarly manly men could generate confidence that "future aspirants to tyranny would meet a similar fate." The statue may even suggest that the "true guarantor" of Athenian freedom is the homoerotic bonds among citizens, or at least that these bonds can stand for the needed qualities. Mingling citizens' private, erotic attachments with an act of tremendous civic significance, the visual representation of the myth in the Kritios group suggests not only a congruence between a citizen's personal and public responsibilities, but their mutual interdependence.

Another reason late fourth-century orators seized on Harmodius and Aristogeiton as model benefactors was that recalling their act many years later implicitly signaled the city's concrete record of having returned important favors. This implication is present in Hyperides' deployment of the legend in his speech *Against Philippides* (2–4). Hyperides here attacks an Athenian supporter of Macedon in the years immediately following the Athenian defeat at Chaeronea. He heaps scorn not only on the accused but also on the accused's confederate, Democrates, a man who happens to be one of the celebrated descendants of Harmodius. It is shameful, he asserts, that Democrates abuses the demos by day, laughing at her misfortune (that is, her subjection by Macedon), and then dines at her table at night (that is, takes meals in the Prytaneum as is his privilege as a descendant). Further, Hyperides asserts, Democrates should know better than to slander the demos because he is acutely aware of how serious is the city's appreciation of its benefactors: "You needed no one but yourself to show you that the city is grateful to her benefactors, you who now enjoy the honours for services which other men once rendered."[61] Hyperides' appeal to the legend names Democrates' pro-Macedon sympathies not only politically misguided and wrong but also a personal failing.

The myth also provides a referent for a particular interpretation of the most dramatic case of conflict between the interests of an individual and those of the community as a whole—that is, dying in battle. The two heroes were not, technically in any case, war dead themselves. Nevertheless, as their association with the negotiation of the tensions between individual and public interests would lead us to expect, their association with military service was strong. Indeed, they were closely associated with the greatest of war heroes—those of the Persian Wars. Speakers addressing the Athenian demos about impending battles turn to the memory of Harmodius and Aristogeiton. They do so not simply to whip up the citizens'

---

[61] *Against Philippides* 3. Translation from Burtt, *Minor Attic Orators*, vol. 2.

capacity to place a public good (military victory) before their personal interest in safety. Rather, appealing to the memory of these men assimilated the possibility of dying in battle to the individual's capacity to achieve exceptional personal glory. Invoking their memory represented the citizen, even in dying, not only as giving but also as receiving something of great value. Herodotus reports, for example, that Miltiades' exhortation to Callimachus before the battle of Marathon included a challenge to act so as to elicit a reputation for glory that would surpass even that enjoyed by Harmodius and Aristogeiton: "The future of Athens lies in your hands now, Callimachus. You can either cast us down into slavery or win us our freedom—and thereby ensure that you will be remembered as long as there are people alive on this earth, with a higher reputation even than Harmodius and Aristogeiton"(6.109.3). Similarly, in Hyperides' funeral oration spoken over the war dead from the Lamian War in 323 (lines 35–39), the speaker imagines the fallen being welcomed to the underworld by the heroes of the Trojan War, by the heroes of the Persian Wars Miltiades and Themistocles, and by Harmodius and Aristogeiton. Aristotle also indicates that the yearly sacrifice to the Tyrannicides was arranged by the Polemarch and was conducted on the occasion of the state funeral for war dead.[62] The drinking songs also stress the lovers' achievement of extraordinary fame (*kleos*). They not only recall the story of the pair and thereby enact their fame, but they also explicitly comment on their renown. In one the singer proclaims, "Dearest Harmodius, you are not dead. . . ."[63] Harmodius and Aristogeiton represented the Athenian idea that by perishing in battle, one not only dies honorably in defense of home and of great principles like political equality and freedom, but also collects a highly desirous prize: eternal honor and praise.[64] Venerating the memory of Harmodius and Aristogeiton signaled the possibility of achieving even in death a coincidence of a citizen's private and public interests.

The city's record of regularly and publicly recalling the acts of Harmodius and Aristogeiton also conveyed the lasting value of benefits that Athenian war dead receive from the city. The Athenians continued over a

---

[62] *Constitution of Athens* 58.1.

[63] Athenaeus *The Deipnosophists* 15.695.11. Translation modified slightly. Their enduring fame is also stressed in another stanza of the song (15.695.13).

[64] This sentiment is also present in other lines eulogizing Athens or Athenians. For example, Pericles in the funeral oration says that those who die in battle have won "renown that never grows old" (Thucydides 2.43.2). In another example, Simonides frag. 118 (an epitaph for Athenians who fought in the Persian Wars) includes the lines: "We to set Freedom's crown on Hellas' brow, Labored and here in ageless honor lie." Simonides is quoted in C. M. Bowra, *Early Greek Elegists*, Martin Classical Lectures, vol. 7 (Cambridge, Mass.: Harvard University Press, 1938), pp. 196–97. Bowra suggests the comparison with the line from Pericles' speech.

long period of time to commemorate the acts of the pair and took legal action to protect the honor of their memory. For example, a law forbade both speaking ill of (*kakōs legein*) Harmodius and Aristogeiton as well as derogatory singing (*aisai epi ta kakiona*) about them.[65] In addition, as we have already noted, the Athenians granted special privileges to the descendants of Harmodius and Aristogeiton. These privileges allowed the Athenian polis—an abstraction that persists over time, outliving its individual members—to express gratitude to individual men whose acts were important at a given moment in the history of that community. Commemorating their act over a long time highlighted not only its greatness in the eyes of the city but also the reliability of the city to perform the acts necessary to keep their memory alive.

The legend's tie to the idea that the polis owes something to its benefactors and is capable of making good on this promise is strongly articulated in Demosthenes' *Against Leptines*. Speaking of the honors given to Conon after he led an Athenian naval victory that reduced the power of Sparta in the years immediately following the conclusion of the Peloponnesian War, Demosthenes reports that the Athenians "set up his statue in bronze—the first man so honoured since Harmodius and Aristogeiton. For they felt that he too, in breaking up the empire of the Lacedaemonians, had ended no insignificant tyranny."[66] Later in the same speech, Demosthenes again appeals to Harmodius and Aristogeiton to stress the city's performance of great acts of gratitude: "Whoso shall suffer in defence of the democracy shall receive the same reward as Harmodius and Aristogeiton."[67]

This focus on receipt of honor might suggest that the Athenians glossed over citizens' experience of suffering during military campaigns. But the Athenians needed little reminding of the risks to life and health that they endured in military expeditions. These losses were felt immediately and often, as the city normally engaged in military expeditions of one sort or another every year. Athenian poetry and drama address such risks, losses, and glory, often with great intensity and emotional power. The legend of the tyrant-slayers puts a particular cast on such military activity. In appealing to the legend, speakers resisted identifying suffering with a notion of personal sacrifice. The models of benefaction present in the example of Harmodius and Aristogeiton suggest that the Athenians imagined a mutu-

---

[65] Hyperides *Against Philippides* 3. For discussion of this law in relation to Athenian notions of free speech, see S. Halliwell, "Comic Satire and Classical Athens," *Journal of Hellenic Studies* 111 (1991): 48–70, at p. 49.

[66] *Against Leptines* 70. Translation from J. H. Vince, *Demosthenes Olynthiacs, Philippics, Minor Public Speeches, Speech Against Leptines* (Cambridge, Mass.: Harvard University Press [Loeb], 1930).

[67] *Against Leptines* 159. Also see Andocides *On the Mysteries* 98. War orphans were also specially cared for and elevated to privileged status.

ally interdependent relation between the interest of the polis in greatness and glory and the interest of the individual citizen in honor and immortality to animate democratic life.

The Athenians were certainly aware how hard it was to arrange such a coincidence of public and private interests, especially in great matters and in times of great stress such as the Peloponnesian War. Precisely such a conflict is, after all, one of the regular themes of the tragic plays and of Thucydides' *History*. The idealized, simplified version of the relation between the individual and the polis publicized by the legend of the tyrant-slayers helped to counterbalance real experiences of deeply conflicting loyalties.

THUCYDIDES' CRITIQUE

Thucydides' account of the historical errors enshrined in the myth explodes the pleasant fiction lodged at the heart of the story—that is, the imagined coincidence of the private and public interests of individual citizens. Thucydides' account of the events of 514 bluntly reminds readers that Harmodius and Aristogeiton were motivated by *erōs* to carry out an act of unconsidered boldness (*alogistos tolma*) and specifically not by any patriotic commitment. Their daring act, he emphasizes, "was undertaken in consequence of a love affair" (6.54.1), and, as he himself admits, he goes on "at some length" regarding its details. This focus has a dual purpose. First, it establishes that a private motive lay behind the apparently political act. But on this score Thucydides is only recalling for his readers something that was common knowledge and an important building block of its usual meaning. Thucydides' critique amounts to revealing further that this private act issued not in a grand public good but, on the contrary, in serious civic evils. This second purpose is what drives his full accounting of the events of 514. Thucydides attacks the cherished Athenian illusion that a private act can, without difficulty, translate into a public good.[68]

---

[68] Commentators on Thucydides sometimes miss the full significance of Thucydides' attack on the legend because they fail to appreciate the full import of the myth in orthodox Athenian discourse. Thucydides is often depicted as undermining the Athenians' belief in the public-mindedness of the Tyrannicides. For example, Steven Forde proposes that Thucydides' aim is to correct the popular view of the motives of the Tyrannicides, which he takes to be that the Tyrannicides were "public-spirited champions of democratic liberty" (*The Ambition to Rule: Alcibiades and the Politics of Imperialism in Thucydides* [Ithaca: Cornell University Press, 1989], p. 35). But the Athenians did not celebrate the Tyrannicides as self-conscious servants of the public good. Venerating their memory served to glorify the attainment of a coincidence of the private and public concerns of citizens. Once we recognize that this was the Athenian conceit, we can see that Thucydides takes aim at the way this conceit organized Athenian political thinking. It is this conceit that legitimated their erotic attachment to the Sicilian campaign. Forde is right to stress that Thucydides "agrees with

For example, the new facts about the events he claims to have unearthed combine to undermine the tale's capacity to signal a happy coincidence of public and private interests. He insists that the murder of Hipparchus was not even a tyrannicide. He says that he has it on the very best evidence that Hippias, not Hipparchus, was the eldest son of Peisistratus and thus the ruling tyrant in 514 (6.55.1–3, 1.20.2). There is a digression within the digression in which Thucydides grounds this claim in an interpretation of the precise ordering of the names included in the inscription on a presumably well-known "pillar placed in the Athenian Acropolis commemorating the crime of the tyrants" (6.55.1).[69] He also claims that the evidence reveals that the tyranny of Peisistratus and Hippias was quite moderate before the murder. Indeed, Thucydides argues their rule "generally was not grievous to the multitude, or in any way odious in practice" (6.54.5). Hippias taxed the citizens moderately, adorned the city, conducted sacrifices, and left the city "in full enjoyment of the existing laws"

---

the Athenians that the Harmodius and Aristogeiton story somehow captures the essence of the Athenian democracy and character. The story as formulated by Thucydides thus corroborates the view that Athens is characterized by a kind of erotically charged daring" (p. 35). But Forde misidentifies Thucydides' target. Thucydides' aim is not to bring out that the Tyrannicides "aimed at public benefit only incidentally if at all" (p. 35). It is to bring out that this private act (private passion) incidentally issued in a public nightmare instead of a public good. Michael Palmer also takes the "common understanding" of Harmodius and Aristogeiton to have been that they were public-spirited rather than privately motivated (*Love of Glory and the Common Good: Aspects of the Political Thought of Thucydides* [Lanham, Md.: Rowman and Littlefield, 1992], p. 83). Gomme, Andrewes, and Dover also maintain that Attic tradition "treated Harmodius and Aristogeiton as heroes who had sacrificed their lives in the cause of liberty" and, as a result, "saw their act not as an example of fearful jealousy and pride but as an example of a freedom-loving people's reaction against tyranny." They recognize that Thucydides' view is "at odds with" this tradition, indicating that in their view, Thucydides "diminishes the stature of the tyrannicides by emphasizing the element of chance and individual emotion" (*A Historical Commentary on Thucydides*, 4: 322). They miss that the tradition could have been aware of the Tyrannicides' private motives, yet could have seen these not as involving jealousy and pride, but as indicating also a happy link between personal and public goods, and that Thucydides found outrageous the failure to see the role of fear, jealousy, and pride in the events. Thucydides diminishes the pair's stature by stressing that their private acts brought about pain and suffering, tearing apart the pleasant illusion of an easy congruence of public and private goods. Cynthia Farrar and Hunter Rawlings do stress the features of the historians' account on which I focus here, but they do not connect Thucydides' critique of the legend to his effort to challenge the orthodox tale as a parable of public/private relations. Farrar links Thucydides' review of the tale to his account of growing polarization in the city. See Farrar, *The Origins of Democratic Thinking* (Cambridge: Cambridge University Press, 1988), pp. 144–52. Rawlings finds Thucydides maintaining that class and personal hatreds were the root cause of the events of 514. See Rawlings, *The Structure of Thucydides' History* (Princeton: Princeton University Press, 1981), pp. 90–117.

[69] See Gomme, Dover, and Andrewes, *A Historical Commentary on Thucydides*, 4: 324, for discussion of Thucydides' reference to this pillar (*stēlē*).

(6.54.6). Only after the murder of his brother Hipparchus did Hippias became oppressive. The daring act of Harmodius and Aristogeiton, on Thucydides' account, harmed the city by making Hippias fearful and suspicious, ushering in a period of spiraling violence.

Reviewing Thucydides' account of events from Hipparchus' perspective, we again confront a stunning case of the private and public interests failing to be coincident. Thucydides indicates that Hipparchus was twice rebuffed by the lovely Harmodius and felt compelled to strike back. But, Thucydides stresses, he tried to do so in a decidedly moderate way, aiming to secure simultaneously both his own private interest and the public good of peaceable living. He chose to insult Harmodius' sister in the hopes of exacting revenge (satisfying honor) and avoiding violence (6.54.3–4), the implication being that he refrained from committing rape. Instead, as the account of peculiar details of the love affair makes clear, a steady stream of violence ensued. The insult violated the honor of Harmodius and his family, and the sexual advance and the snub of the sister enraged Aristogeiton, triggering a sequence of events that included the conspiracy to murder the insulter, the increasingly violent nature of Hippias' rule (eventually "he put to death many of the citizens," 6.59.2), and, ultimately, Spartan military intervention to depose Hippias.

Thucydides' review of the events of 514 also challenges the orthodox tale's capacity to act as a symbolic vehicle for sustaining civic unity. As Hunter Rawlings has detailed, Thucydides is at pains to identify the central role of class and status antagonisms in the events of 514,[70] specifically the role of class distinctions between Harmodius and Aristogeiton, and between these two and the tyrant's family. This is another reason Thucydides spends so much time on the specifics of the love affair. Harmodius was a lovely youth from a prominent family. Aristogeiton was, Thucydides offers, a man of the "middle rank of life" who had succeeded in becoming his *erastēs*, that is, his recognized partner (6.54.2). This accomplishment was, for Aristogeiton, not simply an erotic victory but an achievement of social status. Hipparchus, brother to the tyrant and a man of obviously higher social status, Thucydides tells us, desired the youth. The youth then revealed to his lover that he had been approached not only by another but by the tyrant's brother. Aristogeiton saw him as no ordinary rival but feared that Hipparchus "might take Harmodius by force" (6.54.3). He immediately began to plot to overthrow the tyranny. The plot, on this account, predates the insult to Harmodius' sister. It was Aristogeiton's

---

[70] Rawlings, *Structure*, pp. 90–117, esp. pp. 101–10. He argues, for example, that Thucydides' account contains slurs on Aristogeiton's status and "makes the [class] distinction between Harmodius and Aristogeiton with confidence, almost delight" (p. 104).

fear of the power of Hipparchus that drove him to scheme and act.[71] In Thucydides' view, the myth nourishes a foolish forgetting of class hatred and its ability to provoke violence, whereas knowledge of the actual events of 514 nurtures attention to precisely this key dynamic.

Thucydides takes on the tale largely because it functioned as a parable. He attacks the symbolic meaning that the perpetration of historical "errors" enable the orthodox story to express. Thucydides also attacks the Athenians' tendency to rely on such myths to guide their thinking about public affairs. To recognize this, it is necessary to attend to the author's placement of the critique of the tyrannicide legend in his narrative as a whole.

Thucydides addresses the Athenians' embrace of the myth in two places. First, he briefly mentions it in Book 1 in the midst of his account of his method. He refers to the story of Harmodius and Aristogeiton as an example of how an uncritical reliance on untested evidence typically results in getting the details of an episode wrong. The Athenian public's (*plēthos*) general belief in this legend is, he says, an example of their troubling eagerness to accept all traditions or hearsay (*tas akoas*) alike. All data, like the legend, he says, are received "without applying any critical test whatsoever" (1.20.1). The lengthier review of the historical inaccuracies perpetrated by the myth comes in the midst of his account of the Sicilian expedition (6.53–60). Thucydides turns to the myth after describing how, in the wake of a huge Athenian naval force having sailed for Sicily, the city is in an uproar over the mutilation of the Herms, over rumors that the Eleusinian mysteries had been parodied, and over implications that Alcibiades—Athens' gifted general and a commander of the forces dispatched to conquer Sicily—had been involved in these events. He pauses to review the tyrannicide myth immediately after recounting the arrival in Sicily of the Athenian ship bearing orders for Alcibiades to relinquish his command and sail

---

[71] Thucydides also depicts Harmodius and Aristogeiton as emboldened by the hope of outside help, that is, by the expectation of assistance from "accomplices" (6.56.2–57.1). This hope not only is dashed but is an important factor in the escalating violence. On Thucydides' account, it is Harmodius' and Aristogeiton's mistaken belief that one of their accomplices had given them away (he was seen "talking familiarly with Hippias," 6.57.1–4) that prompts them to act "recklessly" (6.57.3), setting in motion the spiraling violence. In portraying a pattern of increasing violence that rests on a dynamic of fear of a rival's power combined with hope for reinforcements from outside, Thucydides' depiction of Athens' experience of increasing civil violence and strife during the last years of Hippias' rule recalls his depiction of the events leading up to the full-scale civil war in Corcyra. In that case, each side became increasingly cruel toward the other, not only out of growing fear of the other but also because each was emboldened by the expectation of being reinforced by an outside power— the Corcyrean oligarchs by Sparta and the Corcyrean democrats by Athens as well as by other "outsiders" (e.g., a slave population). See 3.69.1–82.2.

home to answer formal charges.[72] While no one finds Thucydides' interest in debunking the myth to be mysterious—there is general agreement that his aim was, as he himself stresses (6.54.1), to expose the inaccuracy of a commonly held view—for some time the insertion of the extensive critique into the account of the Sicilian campaign puzzled scholars.[73] Why interrupt the narration of this key event in the course of the war? Why impose review of this myth upon readers when they are surely eager for some insight into how Athens got set on what they now know was a disastrous course?

Thucydides wrote the "digression" on Harmodius and Aristogeiton for readers who took seriously the possibility that historical knowledge can guide understanding of the present and future.[74] He wrote it for "those who desire an exact knowledge of the past as an aid to the understanding of the future, which in the course of human things must resemble if it does not reflect it" (1.22.4). Rawlings proposes in particular that "the account of the tyrannicide was written as a paradigmatic model for the events of 415 [the affair of the Herms], designed to bring out the parallelism historiographically."[75] In sum, Rawlings suggests the following links.

> The people . . . suspect Alcibiades of selfish designs on their liberty. They turn to demagogues who, while professing common concerns, wish only to supplant Alcibiades (6.28.2, 29, cf. 2.65.11, 3.82.6, 6.35–40). As Alcibiades has reenacted Hipparchus' error of giving private offense to Harmodius and Aristogeiton (cf. 6.15 with 6.56.1) so the demagogues, in gaining his condemnation, reenact the tyrannicides, with motives as selfish and results as dire.[76]

---

[72] Thucydides' discussion of the Tyrannicides is lodged at the core of a ring composition encircled by mention of the galleys sent to bring Alcibiades to Athens for trial. See W. Robert Connor, *Thucydides* (Princeton: Princeton University Press, 1984), app. 6.

[73] For example, Gomme, Andrewes, and Dover ask, "Why did Thucydides want to correct so carefully misconceptions about the end of the tyranny?" and they suggest that "the most plausible explanation [for the digression] is that [Thucydides] succumbed here to the temptation before which all historians and commentators are by their very nature weak, the temptation to correct historical error wherever they find it, regardless of its relevance to their immediate purpose" (*A Historical Commentary on Thucydides*, 4: 328–29).

[74] It is now generally agreed that pausing to consider the legend at this particular moment in the text as a whole is not an aesthetic flaw but instead an example of Thucydides' consummate artistry. For discussion of the relevance of the Book 6 discussion of Harmodius and Aristogeiton to the account of the Sicilian campaign and the relation between Alcibiades and Athens, see Rawlings, *Structure*, pp. 90–117; Connor, *Thucydides*, pp. 176–80 and app. 6; Forde, *Ambition to Rule*, pp. 34–36; Farrar, *Origins*, pp. 147–48; Palmer, *Love of Glory*, pp. 80–89; Virginia Hunter, *Thucydides: The Artful Reporter* (Toronto: Hakkert, 1973), pp. 173–74; and Clifford Orwin, *The Humanity of Thucydides* (Princeton: Princeton University Press, 1994), pp. 125–26.

[75] Rawlings, *Structure*, p. 116.

[76] I have borrowed Orwin's succinct summary of Rawlings (*Humanity*, pp. 125–26).

W. R. Connor also suggests that Thucydides' discussion of the Tyrannicides is more than a refutation of the popular story. In his view, it is "an
exploration of similarities between Athens' past and present conduct and
at the same time an inquiry into a surprising and paradoxical connection
between them."[77] But while Rawlings stresses that Thucydides' critique
of the legend offers the reader a model for thinking about the precise ways
in which Athenian responses to the mutilation of the Herms, specifically
the treatment of Alcibiades, were inadequate to the emergency at hand
(even tragic), Connor stresses that it offers a model for thinking about
how a combination of daring and erotic attachment drove the Athenians
unwisely to embark on the Sicilian campaign. A goal of Thucydides' digression on Harmodius and Aristogeiton is, Connor urges, to elaborate
the effect on Athens of unconsidered boldness by political actors of all
stripes. Both commentators agree that the critique of the legend offers
an example of the kind of historical thinking Thucydides advocates and,
indeed, hopes future generations will conduct using the material he provides in his own *History*.

Thucydides' critique of the legend and development of parallels between the actual events of 514 (the liberation) and the more recent events
involving Alcibiades elaborates Thucydides' view of precisely how the
knowledge of past events can be useful in the conduct of political affairs.
We can discern this intention from the way he introduces his attention to
the story of the Tyrannicides. The digression is necessary, he says, to identify how it is that references to the events of 514 failed to provide the
Athenians with intelligent guidance during the affair of the Herms.[78] He
explains that the Athenian people's decision to do an extraordinary
thing—dispatch a ship to arrest Alcibiades abroad during a campaign—
was motivated by the fear of the growth of a tyranny (Alcibiades) that they
would not be able to crush on their own if need be (6.53.3, 6.59.4–60.1).
As a result, the Athenians became obsessively suspicious and eager to act
on their worries, that is, they went about arresting and imprisoning
many.[79] How did they come by this reasoning? It derived from thinking

---

[77] Connor, *Thucydides*, pp. 176–77.

[78] While Gomme, Andrewes, and Dover do not see the historical parallels that Rawlings
and others were to detail in later years and thus miss the relevance of the so-called digression,
they do note the relation of the passage to patterns in Athenian political discourse. They
write: "The seed from which the digression grew must have been the use in 415 of the
argument: 'Beware, men of Athens, of the would-be tyrant; for nothing is easier than to give
yourselves into the hands of a tyrant, but nothing harder than to escape him again. Why,
not even the tyrannicides. . . .' " *A Historical Commentary on Thucydides*, 4: 329.

[79] For an account of the extreme political tensions, indeed "inner turmoil," in Athens at
this period, see William Furley, *Andokides and the Herms: A Study of Crisis in Fifth-Century
Athenian Religion* (London: Institute of Classical Studies, School of Advanced Study, University of London, 1996). Furley suggests that Thucydides' account of Athenian politics in

about the example of the Tyrannicides. "The people had heard [got it on hearsay] how oppressive the tyranny of Peisistratus and his sons had become before it ended, and further that tyranny had been put down at last, not by themselves and Harmodius, but by the Spartans, and so were always in fear and took everything suspiciously" (6.53.3). Thucydides reiterates the point at the close of the digression. With the role of Sparta in deposing Hippias "in their minds, and recalling everything they knew by hearsay on the subject [the brutality of the tyrants], the Athenian people grew . . . suspicious of the person charged in the affairs of the Mysteries [chiefly Alcibiades], and thought that all that had taken place was part of an oligarchical and monarchical conspiracy" (6.60.1). Thucydides not only suggests that there is an instructive historical parallel here[80] but also addresses how debilitating getting the details of past events wrong can be. He notes that the Athenians knew more than the myth itself because they are clearly portrayed as knowing of the role of Spartan intervention in the liberation. But the rest of their information is erroneous, and they could have detected this. It was on "hearsay evidence" that the Athenians took Hippias' tyranny to have grown increasingly harsh on its own, that is, absent the murder of Hipparchus. In getting this wrong, they failed to acquire the tools necessary to observe that fear and suspicion triggered the cycle of violence.[81]

Had the Athenians been armed with more accurate information, perhaps the people would not have assumed that those citizens who were crazed about the mutilation of the Herms and eager to condemn Alcibiades were acting out of patriotic zeal. Perhaps they would have probed the zealots' motives and interests as well as the reliability of their sources of data. Perhaps they would have avoided accelerating factionalism. Instead, they accepted fabrications and stories as truth, with disastrous consequences. Thucydides' own unmasking of the tale exemplifies the kind of analysis that the Athenians failed to carry out at a crucial moment. The critique of the tale certainly chides the Athenians for being "no more

---

the wake of the affair of the Herms exhibits the classic pattern of developing stasis that he also illustrates in the cases of Epidamnos, Corcyra, and Mytilene (p. 3).

[80] That Thucydides uses critique of the legend to introduce the problem of Alcibiades further supports my view that it is a myth of public-private relations. It is generally agreed that, for Thucydides, Alcibiades is, as Orwin has put it, "the incarnation of the problem of the 'individual and society' in its peculiarly Athenian manifestation" (*Humanity*, p. 124 n. 15).

[81] Farrar and Hunter have noted similar points but do not connect their insights to Thucydides' interest in the mythic import of the tale of the Tyrannicides. Farrar notes that Thucydides emphasizes "the irony of the Athenian belief that they were acting in awareness of historical precedent (6.60.1)" (*Origins*, p. 147). Hunter also stresses that Thucydides addresses the story of Harmodius and Aristogeiton to "demonstrate just how dangerous it may be for people to be inaccurate or misinformed about the past" (*Artful Reporter*, p. 174).

accurate than the rest of the world in their accounts of . . . the facts of their own history" (6.54.1)—and thus, we might add, in this respect chides Athens for being no "School of Hellas," as Pericles had boasted (2.41.1). But Thucydides' review of the myth demonstrates not only that they got it wrong but also the enduring significance of doing so. Citizens miss the link between increased suspicion and increased oppression (between fear and violence) and fail to take the reality of a sometimes tense relation between personal and public interests of citizens to guide their deliberations.

ARISTOTLE'S CRITIQUE

Aristotle also treats critical review of the tyrannicide myth as a mode of representing unorthodox thoughts about the relationship between public and private concerns of citizens. Aristotle's attack on the legend in the *Constitution of Athens*, like that of Thucydides, proposes that it is a mistake to allow the imagined achievement of a coincidence of one's private and public interests to organize one's thinking about politics. His telling of the circumstances of the tyrannicide confronts the reader with emotional material that points to the conflict between public and private interests of individuals who wield power. In particular, Aristotle makes the tyrannicide into a chapter in his account of developing factional conflicts that drive Athenian constitutional development (*Constitution of Athens* 2).

Aristotole reworks the tyrannicide's role in the liberation, correcting Thucydides' account in some ways, but also preserving central features of Thucydides' representation of the "true significance" of the episode in contrast to the orthodox understanding of it (*Constitution of Athens* 18.1–19.2).[82] Aristotle suggests that Hippias and Hipparchus were joint tyrants. He also reports that Thessalus, the half-brother of Hipparchus, was actually the one who interfered with the lovers, not the tyrant. He further argues that Harmodius and Aristogeiton took their rage out on Thessalus' family, the tyrants, not on the actual perpetrator. Moreover, he indicates that Harmodius and Aristogeiton had many accomplices (Thucydides had suggested they had a few), implying that opposition to the tyranny was brewing and that this issue supplied an opportunity for concerted action. These details stress the private origination of the deed but also suggest that personal concerns fueled factional strife. This dynamic is clearest in Aristotle's attention to the torture of Aristogeiton. There is no recollection of the torture of Aristogeiton in the popular tale. Aristotle dwells on

---

[82] For review of the ways in which Aristotle's version differs in detail from Thucydides and for discussion of the sources Aristotle may have consulted for additional details, see note 5 above.

this issue. He does so not to generate sympathy for the tyrant-slayer or
merely to present a fuller account of the events, but to report more ways
in which Aristogeiton's personally interested behavior harmed the polis.
Specifically, Aristotle indicates that Aristogeiton's efforts to secure his own
private interest in a speedy death not only made the tyrant angrier and
thus more violent but also managed to foment more civil strife. Aristotle
details how Aristogeiton gave up the names of his accomplices. At the
time, Aristotle indicates, some thought he made up names to manipulate
the tyrant into turning on his own real friends. Others thought he be-
trayed true co-conspirators. But the point Aristotle is at pains to make
clear is that Aristogeiton's pursuit of his own personal interest caused an
escalation of violence and harm to the polis. Aristotle's account of Aristogeiton's final achievement of death drives home this point:

> When he was unable to find relief through death, in spite of all his efforts, he
> declared that he would reveal the names of many more persons; and, having
> persuaded Hippias to give him his right hand as a pledge, he reviled him for
> having given his hand to the murderer of his brother. In this way he stirred
> Hippias to such a fit of rage that, unable to control himself, he drew his dagger
> and killed Aristogeiton. Following this, the tyranny became much harsher.
> (18.6–19.1)

The last line recalls Thucydides' language as well as his view.[83]

Whether critically reviewing the popular myth in historical writings or
deploying it in oratory, comedy, or symposia, Athenians and writers concerned with Athens consistently turned to the legend of Harmodius and
Aristogeiton to consider—and reconsider—the complexities of the relationship between individuals and the community and between the private
and public interests of individual members of the democratic city. These
treatments of the legend show Athenians imagining that unity and reciprocity distinguish relations among citizens and between citizens and the
city in the democratic polis, and critics insisting that willful inattention
to the tensions between private and public interests of citizens is politically
dangerous.

---

[83] Thucydides 6.59.1. Also compare Thucydides' mention of confessions and naming
names in his discussion of the affair of the Herms (6.60.2).

Chapter Two

CITIZEN AS *PARRHĒSIASTĒS*
(FRANK SPEAKER)

THE ATHENIANS closely linked the practice of democracy with that of free speech. For example, Assembly meetings opened with the proclamation, "Who wishes to speak?"—a ritual affirmation of the right of all male citizens to address the Assembly (as well as to attend and vote).[1] Much has been written about the formal scope (legal, moral, and artistic) of free speech at Athens as well as about the extent to which the democracy actually tolerated the speech it professed to value.[2] The focus of this work is often the degree to which it is possible to maintain that, despite the absence of explicit talk of rights, the Athenians implicitly did recognize a personal right to free speech and understood the protection of such a right to be among the aims of democracy.[3] But how did the Athenians represent to themselves the connection between free speech and democracy? What made these practices intimately linked in their view?

Strikingly, the Athenians considered democracy to require not only a widespread participatory ethic in the political culture[4] and strict obser-

---

[1] See Demosthenes *On the Crown* 169–73 for a dramatic example.

[2] For discussion of the Athenian understanding and practice of free speech generally, see Robert J. Bonner, "Freedom of Speech," in his *Aspects of Athenian Democracy* (Berkeley: University of California Press, 1933), pp. 67–85; S. Halliwell, "Comic Satire and Freedom of Speech in Classical Athens," *Journal of Hellenic Studies* 111 (1991): 48–70; Robert Wallace, "The Athenian Law against Slander," in *Symposion*, ed. Gerhard Thür (Köln: Böhlau Verlag, 1993), pp. 109–24; Arnaldo Momigliano, "Freedom of Speech in Antiquity," *Dictionary of the History of Ideas*, vol. 2, ed. Philip Weiner (New York: Scribner, 1973), 252–63; Max Radin, "Freedom of Speech in Ancient Athens," *American Journal of Philology* 48 (1927): 215–30. On the idea of freedom of thought, see Robert Wallace, "Private Lives and Public Lives and Public Enemies: Freedom of Thought in Classical Athens," in *Athenian Identity and Civic Ideology*, ed. A. Boegehold and A. Scafuro (Baltimore: The Johns Hopkins University Press, 1994), pp. 127–55. For references to discussion of *isēgoria* in particular, see note 21 below.

[3] E.g., Robert Wallace, "Law, Freedom and the Concept of Citizens' Rights in Democratic Athens," in *Dēmokratia: A Conversation on Democracies, Ancient and Modern*, ed. Josiah Ober and Charles Hedrick (Princeton: Princeton University Press, 1996), pp. 105–19.

[4] On patterns of political participation, see R. K. Sinclair, *Democracy and Participation in Athens* (New York: Cambridge University Press, 1988); and M. I. Finley, "Popular Participation," in his *Politics in the Ancient World* (New York: Cambridge University Press, 1983), pp. 70–97.

vance of the formal, legal privilege of all citizens to address their fellows in the Assembly (*isēgoria*), but also the maintenance in their culture of a pervasiveness ethic of frank speaking (*parrhēsia*).[5] That is, they considered a specific variant of free speaking, namely frank speaking, to be a necessary precondition for the smooth functioning of democratic deliberative and decision-making institutions. In this chapter I explore the key political role the Athenians assigned the practice of frank speaking.

TRUTH-TELLING AND RISK-TAKING

Parrhesia is a complex idea with a long history in ancient Greek thought.[6] Speaking with parrhesia (*meta parrhēsias*) meant, broadly, "saying everything." More specifically, it meant speaking one's own mind, that is, frankly saying what one thinks, and especially uttering a deserved reproach. The Athenians appear to have recognized that the open enjoyment of democratic parrhesia has a dangerous underside in the potential for harmful speech. As Athenian society was highly sensitive in matters of honor, shame, and reputation, it is not surprising that they developed legal restrictions on the scope of free speech. For example, Athenian law included a prohibition against slander.[7] Parrhesia did not mean willfully malicious speech.

Frank speaking could refer to speech in a variety of spheres of life—in personal relations (most importantly friendship), in the theater, and in

---

[5] To stress that speaking with parrhesia suggests a particular set of substantive features of the things spoken and a specific disposition of the speaker, I translate *parrhēsia* as "frank speech" rather than "free speech." This translation keeps in focus the ease with which Greek allows speakers to distinguish between the exercise of a formal right to speak (*isēgoria*) and the practice of speaking freely (*parrhēsia*), a distinction that is less crisp in English, as the term "free speech" conveys both meanings. Jeffrey Henderson has recently chosen this translation. See his "Attic Old Comedy, Frank Speech, and Democracy," in *Democracy, Empire and the Arts in Fifth-Century Athens*, ed. Deborah Boedeker and Kurt A. Raaflaub (Cambridge, Mass.: Harvard University Press, 1998), pp. 255–73. Discussion of the distinction between *isēgoria* and *parrhēsia* follows.

[6] The evolution of the idea and practice of parrhesia in Greek literature was the subject of a remarkable series of lectures by Michel Foucault in 1983 that remains unpublished to date. He showed that parrhesia was linked to truth-telling and argued that tracing its changing meanings in Greek philosophy provides an account of "a genealogy of the critical attitude in Western philosophy." See Foucault, "Discourse on Truth: A Study of Parrhēsia," transcript of lectures given in English at the University of California, Berkeley, 1983, transcribed by Joseph Pearson, Department of Philosophy, Northwestern University, p. 114.

[7] For discussion of the legal scope of free speech at Athens, see Wallace, "The Athenian Law against Slander"; and Halliwell, "Comic Satire."

political deliberations. In personal relations it referred mostly to candid speech among friends and associates.[8] It could also be thought to characterize the openness and easiness of daily life. Demosthenes mentions that slaves at Athens enjoy more parrhesia than citizens of other poleis, an exaggeration, surely, but a telling one.[9] In the theater it referred mostly to comedy, specifically to hurling insults at identifiable individuals and ridiculing Athens.[10] In oratory, speakers also utter blunt, and at times nasty, criticisms of policy and of specific people. In addition, orators explicitly defend such frank speaking as the kind of speech ideally expected of them in their role as advisors to the demos.[11]

In each of these contexts, parrhesia is consistently and closely associated with two things: criticism and truth-telling. To speak with parrhesia was to confront, oppose, or find fault with another individual or a popular view in a spirit of concern for illuminating what is right and best.[12] Parrhesia implied, therefore, a claim on the part of the speaker to be capable of assessing a situation and pronouncing judgment upon it. This implication of intellectual autonomy was so much a part of the word's meaning, moreover, that we find it made quite explicit: speaking with parrhesia is equated with "telling the truth as one sees it." This truth claim did not, it needs to be stressed, entail any assertion of a view's alignment with an absolute, transcendent standard. Rather, it asserted a specific relation between the speaker and his view; that is, it affirmed that the speaker sincerely and strongly held his view to be right. The main work the truth claim did was to assert the honesty and personal integrity of the speaker and the apparently critical import of his logos—not the certain flawlessness of the logos itself.

---

[8] Isocrates uses it to describe a quality of friendship (see *To Demonicus* 34, *To Nicocles* 3 and 28, *To Antipater* 4–5). Aristotle uses it to describe the how one ought to behave with friends (*Nicomachean Ethics* 1165a29).

[9] *Third Philippic* 3.

[10] The Athenians tolerated, perhaps welcomed, an extraordinary measure of frank speaking on the comic stage. As Halliwell has shown, "There existed in classical Athens a climate of attitudes which accepted, permitted, and even encouraged the liberty of comedy to indulge in forms of personal ridicule, denigration, and *aischrologia* [shameful speech], which flagrantly flouted otherwise common standards of public propriety" ("Comic Satire," p. 69). Halliwell suggests that comic parrhesia enjoyed a "privileged status" and that a "distinctive ethos of free speech" guided the comic theater (p. 67).

[11] On the relationship between frank speaking in the Assembly and drama, especially comedy, see Henderson, "Attic Old Comedy," *passim*.

[12] Demosthenes *Third Olynthiac* 32, *Fourth Philippic* 54, *Against Aristocrates* 204; Isocrates *To Nicocles* 3, *Panathenaicus* 96; Euripides *Electra* 1055–60; Aristophanes *Thesmophoriazusae* 540–43.

FRANK SPEAKING AND FREEDOM

That the Athenians claimed the idea and practice of specifically frank speaking as an essentially democratic ideal is very clear from several sources.[13] But why? What work did it do in the construction of a patriotic self-image of democracy?

Frank speaking worked at Athens to assert the excellence of democracy in two significant ways. First, it forcefully articulated some of the meaning of the Athenian conception of freedom (*eleutheria*). Second, it expressed an idealized version of Assembly debate. Frankness could be considered a virtue in a variety of settings or political meetings. But parrhesia conjured up a particular set of associations that the Athenians sought to identify specifically with the conduct of Assembly debate. I map the political concerns that help explain the importance of parrhesia in this context. I find that the idea and practice of parrhesia was thought to be at the very heart of Athenian democracy's coherence as a *politeia*.

The association of unrestrained speech, and specifically the term "parrhesia," with freedom is very strong in Greek literature. Aeschylus' *Persians* names an unguarded tongue a sign of freedom (591–94). Euripides' *Hippolytus* closely links being free with the practice of parrhesia, and joins both with Athenian citizenship (421–23). A fragment of Demokritos also confirms an intimate connection between freedom and parrhesia.[14] It might be tempting to think that the Athenians typically linked these largely because of the intellectual freedom that the practice of parrhesia presupposes. But once we recall that Anaxagoras, Protagoras, Diagoras, and perhaps Diogenes of Apollonia had to run for their lives and that Socrates did not flee and was killed, this account of the root attraction of parrhesia for ordinary Athenian democrats becomes far less appealing.[15] It is more plausible to attribute the prominence of parrhesia in the popular Athenian understanding of freedom to its contribution to the standard representation of a sharp contrast between democratic citizenship and life under a tyranny. The Athenians expressed the excellence of democracy to

---

[13] Plato *Republic* 557b; Demosthenes *Funeral Speech* 25–26; Euripides *Ion* 671–75, *Hippolytus* 420–23. See also "Old Oligarch," *Constitution of the Athenians* 1.12; Demosthenes 9.3; Euripides *Suppliant Women* 433–41; Plato *Gorgias* 461e.

[14] Hermann Diels and Walter Kranz, *Die Fragmente Der Vorsokratiker* (Dublin and Zurich: Weidmann, 1969), 2: 190, frag. 226.

[15] Momigliano, "Freedom of Speech," p. 258. Also see John Stuart Mill's comments on the Athenians' suspiciousness of intellectual life in his essay "Grote's Plato," in *The Collected Works*, vol. 11, *Essays on Philosophy and the Classics*, ed. J. M. Robson (London: Routledge, Kegan Paul, 1963), pp. 377–440, esp. pp. 398–99; and Gregory Vlastos on why Socrates was condemned, in *Socrates: Ironist and Moral Philosopher* (Ithaca: Cornell University Press, 1991), pp. 293–97.

a great extent by contrasting it with the Athenian experience of the tyranny as well as with their knowledge of Persian despotism. The practice of parrhesia in politics and personal life at Athens was treated as a sign, indeed as proof, that the Athenians had defeated tyranny at home, fought off the threat from abroad, and were now in fact living as free citizens.

An intolerance of parrhesia marked tyranny of both the Hellenic and Persian varieties in the Athenian view. A tyrant's arbitrary, unaccountable, and absolute power virtually precluded that individuals would risk saying anything other than what the tyrant wished to hear. When an individual dared to speak his own mind to the tyrant, moreover, it was considered surprising and strange. Aristotle, for example, names Peisistratus' willingness to listen to a common man's parrhesia as evidence of the mildness of his tyranny.[16] Speaking freely among even one's neighbors was dangerous, as the possibility of betrayal to the tyrant was ever present. Silence was normally expected of the subjects of a tyranny. An intolerance of parrhesia was a symptom of the watched character of daily life. A citizen of a democracy, on the other hand, was expected to have and to voice his own critical political opinions.[17] Being free meant being able to hold those who exercise power accountable, that is, at the very least, to expose lies, name abuses, and demand change. The principle of accountability was absolutely central to the Athenian understanding of the distinction between the democratic and the tyrannical exercise of power.[18] The connection between unrestrained speech and being free also celebrated the termination of guarded, suspicious relations among neighbors that had been characteristic of life under tyranny. The coupling of freedom and parrhesia in the democratic self-image therefore functioned to assert two things: the critical attitude appropriate to a democratic citizen, and the open life promised by democracy.

The celebration of parrhesia in democratic politics did not carry any demand for a notion of protected speech. Quite the contrary. Speaking with parrhesia in the democratic political context retained a strong association with risk. The risks did not normally include execution, but they certainly included humiliation and fines. The risks were not thought by the Athenians to undermine or even conflict with the practice of frank speech. Rather, the risks affirmed that the speaker could be held accountable for the advice ventured.

The strong association of political parrhesia with danger illuminates the value of this idea for Athenian democrats. The free democratic citizen

---

[16] *Constitution of Athens* 16.6. See also Plato *Republic* 567b–d; and Euripides *Bacchae* 668–71, for the tyrant's intolerance of parrhesia.

[17] Critical opinions in religious matters were not quite as welcome.

[18] For example, see Aeschylus *Persians* 210–20; and Aristotle *Politics* 1295a20.

presupposed by the ethic of parrhesia is daring and responsible, self-con-
fident and eager to enter the fray—the very antithesis of the slavish subject
of a tyranny.[19] The risks emphasized that participation in democratic politics, forming and expressing an interpretation of the public good, was a
difficult endeavor. Success at it—as an individual leader or a collective
body—commanded praise and admiration. The coupling of freedom and
parrhesia suggested the daring that democratic politics demanded. Praising parrhesia asserted the excellence of democracy by naming one virtue
that democratic practice cultivates in citizens (the virtue of critical intellectual autonomy in political matters) and suggesting the glorious possibilities for citizens of democratic polities.

FRANK SPEAKING AND THE INTEGRITY
OF ASSEMBLY DEBATE

Precisely how, then, does parrhesia figure in the Athenian patriotic representation of good Assembly debate? Good Assembly debate depended first
of all on meeting certain formal conditions necessary for decisions to be
democratically legitimate (e.g., equal access to the Assembly, the right to
speak at the meeting, and majority rule). But the Athenians also worried
about whether democratic debate could produce wise decisions, and it is
in this connection that critical parrhesia takes on its greatest importance.
Demosthenes specifically claimed that a democracy is in grave danger
when no one dares to speak out truthfully and critically in the Assembly.[20]
Precisely what part the concept of parrhesia played in articulating the substantive conditions under which debate could be thought to generate wise
decisions is a complicated story, however, requiring a digression on a related but distinct conception of free speech, isegoria.

Isegoria referred to the equal right of all citizens in good standing to
address the Assembly. It was a central element in Athenian democratic
thought. Herodotus used the word as a synonym for democracy.[21] In it,

---

[19] See Euripides *Phoenician Women* 386–94, where, in the middle of a discussion of the
miseries of an exile's lot, the subject of parrhesia comes up. Polyneices states: "The worst is
this: parrhesia does not exist" (391), to which Iocasta responds, "That's a slave's life—to be
forbidden to speak one's mind" (392). Translation by Philip Vellacott, in *Euripides: Orestes
and Other Plays* (New York: Penguin, 1972).

[20] *On Organization* 15.

[21] Herodotus *Histories* 5.78. See also "Old Oligarch," *Constitution of the Athenians* 1.2.
On isegoria, see G. T. Griffith, "*Isēgoria* in the Assembly of Athens," in *Ancient Society and
Institutions, Studies Presented to Victor Ehrenberg on His Seventy-Fifth Birthday*, ed. E. Badian
(Oxford: Basil Blackwell, 1966), pp. 115–39; J. D. Lewis, "*Isēgoria* at Athens: When Did It
Begin?" *Historia* 20 (1971): 129–40; Yoshio Nakategwa, "*Isēgoria* in Herodotus," *Historia*
37 (1988): 257–75; and A. G. Woodhead, "*Isēgoria* and the Council of 500," *Historia* 16

the twin democratic ideals of freedom and equality merge. Derived from the components *iso-*, meaning "equal," and the verb *agoraomai*, meaning generally "to speak" (especially in the Assembly), it expressed the thought that each citizen has an equal right to conduct his life as a free being, that is, to engage in political activity, where political activity means offering an interpretation of the public interest for consideration by the collectivity.[22] It is therefore a richer formal democratic principle than the equal right to attend and vote in the Assembly for, as Ober has suggested, it enabled citizens to be far more actively engaged in the deliberative process, in effect transforming the ordinary man's experience of political life.[23] Isegoria implied a participatory ethic.[24] Isegoria was, accordingly, especially important for democratic Athens' assertion of the legitimacy of the decisions of the Assembly. The opportunity for active participation in debate was part of the formal apparatus—along with equal access to the Assembly and majority rule—that the Athenians relied on to give credibility to the claim that individual citizens are meaningfully implicated in the decisions of the Assembly and therefore morally obligated to obey them.[25] This claim was ritually affirmed at the opening of each Assembly meeting when, as we noted earlier, the herald asked, "Who wishes to speak?"[26] The language announcing decisions also affirmed the claim. It did not read, "The majority wants . . ." but rather, "It seems [best] to the Demos that . . .,"[27] suggesting that the entire demos was implicated in the decision of the Assembly.

(1967): 129–40. For discussion of the differences between ancient and modern notions of free speech focusing on isegoria, see Ellen Meiksins Wood, "Demos versus 'We the People': Freedom and Democracy Ancient and Modern," in Ober and Hedrick, eds., *Dēmokratia*, pp. 121–37.

[22] See Euripides *Suppliant Women* 438–42, where the equal right to address the Assembly is linked to the positive exercise of freedom.

[23] Josiah Ober, *Mass and Elite in Democratic Athens* (Princeton: Princeton University Press, 1989), p. 79.

[24] This is true in spite of the fact that most citizens did not address the Assembly often, if at all. The experience of the ordinary man was one of feeling the opportunity to speak in the Assembly, but only actually speaking before and after the meeting to his friends and associates in multiple public settings.

[25] The "Old Oligarch" argues that democracy at Athens is in no real danger of attack precisely because it has no significant population of the "disenfranchised" to rise up. He ignores the population of slaves, metics, and women. But his point that citizens are well integrated and implicated in the life of the polis is significant. *Constitution of the Athenians* 3.12–13.

[26] Aristophanes *Acharnians* 45; Demosthenes *On the Crown* 169–73.

[27] Inscriptions might also mention the Council, as in *edoxen tēi boulēi kai tōi dēmōi*. The decision-making authority was, however, the Assembly, represented as the demos. See, for example, E. L. Hicks and G. F. Hill, *Greek Historical Inscriptions* (Oxford: Clarendon, 1901),

The Athenians relied on a celebration of free speech to do more ideological work in the Assembly as well. The general, nontechnical notion of speaking freely (*eleutherōs*) figures importantly in the Athenian view of how it is that democratic deliberations manage to produce wise, as well as legitimate, policy. Some words from Pericles' funeral oration assert this connection. The Hobbes translation captures it with precision: "We Athenians weigh what we undertake and apprehend it perfectly in our minds, not accounting words for a hindrance of action but that it is rather a hindrance to action to come to it without instruction of words before" (Thucydides 2.40)."[28] This passage suggests that the Athenians valued the general practice of free speaking in the Assembly for its role in the education of action, chiefly collective action. But precisely how do the particular concepts of isegoria and parrhesia figure in this process?

Isegoria was understood to do some of the work of educating action, that is, producing wise policy and public confidence. Many uses of the concept affirm that ideas—rather than the status of the speaker or the artistry of his presentation—matter in Assembly debate. Consider the following passage from Demosthenes' *First Olynthiac*:

> Oh Athenians, I believe that you would prefer it to great wealth if it could be made clear to you what would be the best policy in the matters now under discussion. This being the case, it is proper for you to listen intently to all those desirous of giving advice. For not only might someone come forward with a carefully thought out proposal, and you, having heard it, might decide to adopt it, but I consider it part of your good fortune that other speakers may be inspired with suitable suggestions on the spur of the moment, so that from among many proposals it will be easy to choose the one most in your own interest.[29]

Isegoria also implied the airing of various and conflicting proposals, and therefore the expression of differing opinions, before a binding decisions was taken. In this way it could contribute to intelligent debate and thoughtful decision-making.

Isegoria gave rise to the practice of skillful oratory. The right to speak did not guarantee one a hearing. For example, "It is no easy matter to address several thousand people in the open air, even when they are orderly

---

nos. 73, 74, and 75. On the politics of inscriptions, see Robin Osborne, "Inscribing Performance," in *Performance Culture and Athenian Democracy*, ed. Simon Goldhill and Robin Osborne (Cambridge: Cambridge University Press, 1999), pp. 341–58.

[28] *The Peloponnesian War. Thucydides. The Complete Hobbes Translation with Notes and a New Introduction by David Grene* (Chicago: University of Chicago Press, 1989).

[29] *First Olynthiac* 1.1. I have borrowed this crisp translation from Ober, *Mass and Elite*, p. 317. All other translations from Demosthenes in this chapter are from J. H. Vince, *Demosthenes* (Cambridge, Mass.: Harvard University Press [Loeb], 1954).

and attentive, but if, like the Athenian Assembly, they were always volubly critical and often unruly and tumultuous, the difficulty was materially increased."[30] Skill was necessary on most occasions, especially if one wished to offer new, critical, or unusual advice. We know from Plutarch, for instance, that even Demosthenes' first effort at addressing the Assembly was a disaster.[31] Yet the Athenians delighted in excellent oratory, for the most part taking enormous pleasure in hearing competing views argued intensely and beautifully, and expecting the competition among orators for the respect and admiration of the polis to increase the likelihood that the arguments brought before them were clear and informed.

Isegoria did have severe limitations as a guarantor of intelligent debate. It gave rise to what the Athenians themselves perceived to be the greatest threat to the ability of democratic deliberative processes to discern the public interest and produce wise decisions—manipulative and deceptive oratory in the service of an individual speaker's personal ambitions rather than the interpretation of the public interest. By pandering to the whims and desires of the people, a clever orator could elevate himself into a position of leadership. He could also perhaps direct public policy in such a way as to benefit his pocket or to suit his own private purposes. Expert oratory could, then, corrupt the deliberations, leading to the neglect of the public interest and, perhaps, to disastrous decisions and actions. Recognizing this problem, the Athenians were intensely suspicious of expert oratory, even as they expected and enjoyed the display. The "evils of flattery" topos commonly employed by orators provides good evidence for Athenian awareness of the danger and their public willingness to be reminded of their vulnerability.[32] The Athenians attempted to safeguard themselves against the influences of a deceitful orator in a number of practical ways. Meetings of the Assembly opened with the pronouncement of a curse against those who would deceive the people.[33] Individual citizens who had committed certain offenses (prostitution or maltreatment of parents, for example) were considered untrustworthy and stripped of their right of public address.[34] Athenian law also provided for the prosecution of individuals who "deceive the Assembly" and abuse the public confidence. Individuals could be charged, tried, and punished (e.g., through the *graphē paranomōn*) for having offered insincere (perhaps bribe-induced) advice, or even only for what proved later to have been unwise advice. The practice

[30] Bonner, "Freedom of Speech," pp. 74–75.

[31] Plutarch *Life of Demosthenes* 5.

[32] See Ober, *Mass and Elite*, p. 323.

[33] Bonner, "Freedom of Speech," p. 76.

[34] See Aeschines *Against Timarchus* 28ff., where he lists the offenses that would result in the loss of one's right of public address.

of isegoria both raised the possibility of wise democratic decision-making and erected serious obstacles to its realization.

Thus, though the concept of isegoria was of great importance in the Athenian democratic self-image, it could not, on its own, ideologically suggest the positive ability of democratic deliberations to produce wise as well as lawful decisions (that is, to educate action), nor could it adequately confront and allay Athenian suspicion of expert oratory. The efforts of orators to link their critical arguments to the idea and practice of parrhesia, on the other hand, appear to have had precisely these aims in mind. When, on several occasions, Demosthenes identifies his efforts to criticize a common Athenian viewpoint with the ideal of speaking with parrhesia, he explicitly contrasts his speech with flattering, deceitful, or self-promoting oratory. The closing of the *Fourth Philippic* is typical: "There you have the truth spoken with all parrhesia, simply in goodwill and for the best—no speech packed by flattery with mischief and deceit, and intended to put money in the speaker's pocket and control of the polis into our enemies' hands."[35] Such an appeal to the ethic of parrhesia was a central strategy for speakers because it economically affirmed two points absolutely necessary to defend against Athenians' suspiciousness about expert oratory: the personal virtue and integrity of the speaker, and the priority of the public interest over personal pleasures.[36]

The invocation of parrhesia asserted the personal integrity of the speaker in a number of ways. First, it identified the speaker's motivation as a commitment both to truth and to the exposure of truth. There was no claim to have uncovered a timeless truth, but rather a view supremely worthy of confidence given the present circumstances. But just as important as this truth claim was the suggestion that the speaker willingly embraced considerable risks by speaking—risks to his reputation, financial well-being, and personal safety. When one spoke out in the Assembly, one risked being disliked, shouted down, humiliated, fined, or brought up on any one of a variety of charges, some of which could carry stiff penalties. Orators often emphasized this climate of personal risk. The presence of risk made more credible the orator's claim to be saying what he thought was true and right, that is, what he thought was in the best interest of the polis, in

---

[35] *Fourth Philippic* 76. See also *Third Olynthiac* 3, *First Philippic* 51, *On the Chersonese* 32, *Third Philippic* 3–4, and *On Organization* 15. Isocrates, too, cites his commitment to parrhesia to distinguish his speech from mere flattery; see *Antidosis* 43.8–44.1, and *Panathenaicus* 96.

[36] The importance of the integrity of the speaker to the Athenians' consideration of the merit of his proposal is apparent from the extent to which orators attack each other on precisely these grounds. The personal invectives are at times quite extreme. See, for example, Demosthenes *On the Crown* and Aeschines *Against Kteisiphon* as a pair.

contrast to what might benefit him personally. Demosthenes, for example, chose to close his *First Philippic* by reminding his audience of the risks he ran by speaking with parrhesia:

> I have spoken my plain sentiments with parrhesia. Yet, certain as I am that it is to your interest to receive the best advice, I could have wished that I were equally certain that to offer such advice is also to the interest of the speaker. . . . But, as it is, in the uncertainty of what the result of my proposal may be for myself, yet in the conviction that it will be to your interest to adopt it, I have ventured to address you. (*First Philippic* 51)

In this passage, Demosthenes uses an acceptance of risk to bolster his claim to be offering thoughtful, justified criticism, not just wielding a malicious attack, delivering deceitful, manipulative advice, or acting on a bribe. The appeal to parrhesia perhaps even associates his speech with the exercise of a moral obligation.[37]

Linking debate with the practice of parrhesia affirmed the virtue of the hearers as much as it did that of the speaker. The performance of the role of speaking with parrhesia and giving priority to the promotion of the public good required the collaboration of the hearers.[38] To the extent that the hearers willingly suffer criticism, reflect on their opinions, and generally listen to others, *their* public-interestedness (that is, their placement of the public good before that of personal pleasure) is on display as well as that of the speaker. Demosthenes' appeal to parrhesia at the beginning of his *For the Liberty of the Rhodians*, for example, affirms the importance of political parrhesia to debate and good outcomes and indicates that the cooperation of the hearers is essential: "Your duty, men of Athens, when debating important matters, is, I think, to give parrhesia to every one of your counsellors."[39]

In addition to asserting the personal integrity of the speaker and the moral virtue of the hearers, the ideal of speaking with parrhesia in the Assembly affirmed the usefulness of rigorous, critical appraisal of proposals before the Assembly, including, most importantly, the subjection of the apparent will of the demos to interrogation. Athenian democrats believed the proposal or view that could garner the confidence of a large number was likely *actually to be* the best available alternative.[40] But their belief in the truth or accuracy of a majority decision was predicated on certain

---

[37] Cornelius Castoriadis, "The Greek Polis and the Creation of Democracy," *Graduate Faculty Journal* 9, no. 2 (1983): 79–115.

[38] Demosthenes *On Halonnesus* 1.

[39] *For the Liberty of the Rhodians* 1.

[40] See Ober, *Mass and Elite*, pp. 163–65.

expectations regarding the quality of the debate that preceded the vote. The Athenians did not expect the collective desires of the many magically to translate into an intelligent collective will. Rather, they considered a proposal that could gain the confidence of many more likely to be good than one favored by a few, or by only one. They assumed that a proposal that could withstand the separate scrutiny of a large number of individuals would most likely be best. The association of critical parrhesia with Assembly debate helped establish confidence in the collective wisdom of the demos. A vote taken after speeches delivered in a spirit of parrhesia could represent not simply the preferences of the majority, but the considered judgment of the demos. Such a decision could reasonably be thought wise, worthy of the confidence of the demos. Even a common criticism of democracy in the ancient sources indirectly stresses the same point. The complaint is that when things go badly, the people fail to remember that they—and not a solitary individual advisor—had chosen the policy in question, that is, that they had deemed it best. The policy represented the best judgment of the demos at the time. Consider the speech of Diodotus in Thucydides. He pleads with his audience to recognize their share of the responsibility for decisions. Whenever you meet with a reverse, he says to the Assembly, "you visit the disasters into which the whim of the moment may have led you, upon the single person of your advisor, not upon yourselves, his numerous companions in error" (3.43.5).

The ideal of parrhesia celebrated in the Athenian patriotic self-image implied an intimate relation between a speaker and the words spoken. One's critical and bold speech was taken to express—even to expose— something of who one was, what one cared about, how one had chosen to live. One's convictions were on display when one spoke with parrhesia. Such exposure was a risky business. When hearers listened seriously in the spirit of parrhesia, their convictions, too, hung in the balance. Parrhesia must not, therefore, be confused with mere audacious speech,[41] with playing the devil's advocate, or even with bold speculation. That the speaker and the audience had personal and political stakes in the truth values of views uttered was a crucial characteristic of the ideal of democratic parrhesia.

In celebrating frank speaking, the Athenians articulated symbolically some of the substantive qualities of a free citizen, expressed strong opposition to the return of tyranny, and projected an image of both the kind of

---

[41] Parrhesia was sometimes used in a pejorative sense to mean mere audacious or hot-tempered speech. See, for example, Euripides *Orestes* 905; Foucault, "Discourse on Truth," pp. 34ff.; and Isocrates *Panathenaicus* 218. This pejorative sense is not present in the sources that supply some insight into the official, celebrated Athenian patriotic self-image.

risky speech ideally expected of those who chose to step forward to advise the Assembly and the kind of critical attitude ideally to be adopted by all citizens. Representing the ability of democratic institutions to foster inquiries into the public interest as turning on the citizens' capacity and willingness to be frank with one another in highly public settings, Athenians showed themselves cognizant of the interdependence of social norms and governing structures in a robust democracy.

Chapter Three

CITIZEN AS *ERASTĒS* (LOVER): EROTIC IMAGERY AND THE IDEA OF RECIPROCITY IN THE PERICLEAN FUNERAL ORATION

AT A KEY POINT in Pericles' famous funeral oration, Thucydides has him urge his fellow citizens "to gaze, day after day, upon the power of the city and become her lovers (*erastai*)" (2.43.1).[1] In this chapter I investigate the implications and resonances of Pericles' use of this metaphor. I show that, far from being simply a pleasing turn of phrase, this metaphor does some important, substantive work in the speech. The metaphor suggests a way of thinking about the relationship between citizen and city. In particular, here again we find that the idea of democratic citizenship pivots on a notion of reciprocity between individual citizens and the polis.[2]

The manner in which the erastes metaphor stresses the idea of reciprocity is not readily apparent to the modern reader. It emerges only once we restore the historical context sufficiently to recognize that the metaphor alludes to the highly formalized and valorized relations between adult, citizen men (*erastai*) and adolescent, freeborn boys (*erōmenoi*) that were common among Athenians. By appealing to citizens to conceive of themselves as "lovers (*erastai*) of the polis," Pericles is proposing that the Athenians can—*and should*—turn to their ordinary understanding of what it is like to love as well as to the well-known, clearly defined codes of conduct regarding legitimate sexual behavior and the maintenance of an intimate relationship between an adult citizen lover (erastes) and a freeborn boy beloved (eromenos) for some guidance in thinking about the demands of democratic citizenship. I try to do what Pericles asks: use an analogy between an erastes and a citizen, as well as one between the erotic relationship of erastes and eromenos and the political relationship of citizen and polis, to illuminate the Athenians' understanding of the demands

---

[1] Translation modified.

[2] Cynthia Farrar also stresses that reciprocity figures importantly in the Greek conception of citizenship in her "Gyges' Ring: Reflections on the Boundaries of Democratic Citizenship," in *Démocratie Athénienne et Culture*, ed., M. Sakellariou, (Athens: Academy of Athens, 1996), pp. 109–36. Lionel Pearson noted that the Periclean ideal of citizenship pivots on reciprocal benefactions between city and citizens, but he did not elaborate upon this observation. See his *Popular Ethics in Ancient Greece* (Stanford: Stanford University Press, 1962), 181–82

of democratic citizenship.[3] The result is that the metaphor, and indeed the speech, presents a view of democratic citizenship that prizes reciprocal mutual exchange between city and citizens and not, as an anachronistic and romantic reading of the metaphor in translation might suggest, the selfless devotion of the individual citizens to the good of the city. In fact, the metaphor suggests that there is an ever-present danger that relations between city and citizens could deteriorate into domination, dependence, or exploitation.[4] The metaphor implicitly stresses that such possibilities need to be self-consciously and vigorously avoided by both parties.

Pericles' use of the erastes metaphor is unquestionably striking. We must be careful, however, not to attribute this simply to its sexual content. Sexual imagery and metaphors were not unusual in Athenian political dis-

---

[3] The Periclean oration has long been thought to contain some of our most reliable evidence for the ideals that animated the Athenian experiment in democracy, largely for four reasons: (1) the undeniable importance of Pericles in the development of Athenian democratic politics; (2) the high regard in which Pericles is held by ancient commentators from Thucydides to Plutarch as well as by contemporary scholars; (3) the view of most scholars that Thucydides' rendering of the orations is a reasonably authentic representation of Pericles' own ideas, even if not exact words; and (4) the fact that the speech is the most systematic account of the attractions of democracy uttered by (if not "recorded" by) a committed democrat extant from the classical period. To my mind, three additional considerations having to do with the oration's place in Thucydides' work are persuasive: (5) the type of oratory, (6) the practical setting, and (7) the literary context of the speech. These last three elements combine to make it abundantly clear that this speech aims to provide citizens/readers with a powerful expression of a popular idealization of democracy with which the Athenians wished to be identified (and not necessarily an accurate description of day-to-day practice). Praising and displaying a recognizable image of Athens' "best self" was the key aim of funeral oratory. Aristotle notes how encomiastic aims of such oratory constrain a speaker (and would have had to constrain Thucydides' rendering as well) in his discussion of epideictic in *Rhetoric* 1358b2–5; see also Nicole Loraux, *The Invention of Athens: The Funeral Oration in the Classical City*, trans. Alan Sheridan (Cambridge, Mass.: Harvard University Press, 1986). The practical setting for the delivery of the oration was a ritual, public burial of war dead. The occasion, too, placed well-defined expectations on the speaker. Last, the work this speech performs in Thucydides' narrative of the war supports viewing it as a projection of a vision of Athenian democratic ideals that would have indeed appealed to the Athenians themselves. The speech presents a glorious vision of a unified and robust democracy. As the narrative of the war progresses, however, the painful gap between Athens' self-image and reality becomes increasingly apparent. For Thucydides' narrative to have had any serious effect on his contemporary readers, this initial portrait of Athens' best self would have to have been arresting for its attractiveness and familiarity to them. The self-congratulatory image of democratic Athens presented in the speech had to be a clear and compelling account of the Athenians' self-image. It is more important for the coherence of Thucydides' whole narrative that this speech presents popular pretensions or aspirations of the time (albeit in an extraordinarily eloquent way) than it is that the text recreates the letter of Pericles' actual speech. For these several reasons, I accept the speech as good evidence for the ideals that animated Athenian democratic life.

[4] This would include abuse of the city by manipulative citizens as well as abuse of individuals by the collectivity.

course. For example, Dougherty shows that during the archaic period, the discourse of rape and the institution of marriage figure importantly in the popular explanations and justifications of the practice of colonization. She writes, "Within the ideology of colonization—of foreign conquest and overseas settlement—the discourse of rape and the institution of marriage provide models for representing the complicated relationships that Greeks must forge with native populations upon colonizing foreign territory."[5] In addition, while it may be that Pericles first used the erastes/eromenos relation as a political metaphor,[6] this particular erotic metaphor became commonplace in Athenian political debate during the period of the Peloponnesian War. Aristophanes' *Knights*, for example, mocks Cleon's overuse of the image. The meaning conveyed by Cleon's use is, however, very different from that suggested by Pericles'.[7] We can further observe that Thucydides relies on the metaphor in his analysis of the Athenian demos' attitude toward the Sicilian expedition.[8] The point I wish to stress in noting the presence of these metaphors in these different contexts is that we can assume that erotic images resonated with the Athenian citizenry. It is reasonable for us to assume that Pericles could use specific kinds of erotic imagery not only to be dramatic but also to be precise. Accordingly, I am concerned here to recover what is striking about the meaning that Pericles' metaphor conveys.

There are a multitude of resonances and suggestions emanating from Pericles' erastes metaphor, and I try to capture this complexity. It should be noted at the outset that my investigations do not involve consideration of the evidence for actual sexual behavior of individual Athenians.[9] Rather, what concerns me is the social construction at Athens of two public fictions or cultural images: (1) the ideal erastes, and (2) the exemplary, beau-

---

[5] Carol Dougherty, *The Poetics of Colonization: From City to Text in Archaic Greece* (New York: Oxford University Press, 1993), p. 62.

[6] The limitations of our sources make it impossible to settle this question.

[7] *Knights* 732 and 1340–44. These passages are discussed below. On the eroticization of the polis in the Periclean funeral oration and other sources, see Gregory Crane, *Thucydides and the Ancient Simplicity: The Limits of Political Realism* (Berkeley: University of California Press, 1998), pp. 318–21.

[8] See Josiah Ober's discussion of the erotic component of Thucydides' description and analysis of the debate at Athens regarding the Sicilian expedition in "Democratic Ideology and Counter-Hegemonic Discourse: The Case of Thucydides," in *Athenian Identity and Civic Ideology,* ed. A. Boegehold and A. Scafuro (Baltimore: The Johns Hopkins University Press, 1994). See also W. R. Connor, *Thucydides* (Princeton: Princeton University Press, 1984), pp. 178–80. Arlene Saxonhouse discusses the erotic language in Book 6 in its relations to similar themes in Plato in "An Unspoken Theme in Plato's *Gorgias:* War," *Interpretation* 112, no. 2 (1983): 139–69, at 150–51.

[9] For a collection and review of the evidence for some of the actual sexual practices of the Greeks, see K. J. Dover, *Greek Homosexuality, Updated and with a new Postscript* (Cambridge, Mass.: Harvard University Press, 1989).

tiful relationship between an erastes and an eromenos. Pericles' metaphor engages prescriptive cultural ideals and norms, not ordinary behavior.[10] I will first look at the range of suggestions that Pericles conjures up by urging citizens to conceive of themselves as erastai of the polis and their possible political import. This involves consideration of the purely sexual dimension of the metaphor. This also requires a digression on the Greek understanding of the physical and psychological nature of sexual experience. I then move to consider the implications of the relationship suggested by Pericles' metaphor: I probe what is implied by saying citizen is to city as erastes is to eromenos, where the eromenos is an adolescent boy.

CITIZEN AS *ERASTĒS*

The first thing to notice about the citizen-as-lover metaphor is that it is highly erotic. As a recent commentator has stressed, "It should not be diluted in translation, as it is by versions such as 'fall in love with her' (Warner) [and] 'filled with the love of her' (Jowett, similarly Crawley)."[11] The term "lovers" (*erastai*) has very clear erotic and sexual connotations.[12] It is free from the ambiguities inherent in the English word "love." The term explicitly refers to the active, "insertive" partner in a sexual encounter, heterosexual or homosexual. It alludes to the physical act of penetrating. It also alludes to the psychological state of loving, and therefore to the complex web of attitudes an individual may feel toward the object of his eros—affection as well as physical desire.

[10] The entire speech engages idealized images of prescriptive cultural norms, not ordinary behavior. See note 3 above, and Aristotle's discussion of the aims of epideictic oratory at *Rhetoric* 1358b. Of course, we cannot assume that the Athenians did not stray from these norms. See, for example, David Cohen, "Law, Social Control and Homosexuality in Classical Athens," in *Law, Sexuality and Society: The Enforcement of Morals in Classical Athens* (New York: Cambridge University Press, 1991). Cohen observes that Athenian law carefully regulated the contact that older men had with schoolboys (p. 176). This implies, however, that the boys needed protection. In addition, Athenian law seems to have allowed a father to bring an action against an adult man who had erotic relations with his son before the boy had reached the age of consent (p. 177).

[11] Simon Hornblower, *A Commentary on Thucydides*, vol. 1 (Oxford: Clarendon, 1991), p. 311.

[12] See Dover, *Greek Homosexuality*, p. 16. Dover notes the clarity of this point by stressing that this family of words is "so regularly sexual that other uses of it can fairly be regarded as sexual metaphor" (p. 43). Thucydides' use of "gaze" (*theomenous*, 2.43) in the funeral oration also emphasizes the erotic connotations of the metaphor, for, as David Halperin notes, the Greeks "located the source of *eros* in the eyes . . . [and] considered eye-contact between lover and beloved the erotic stimulus par excellence" ("Why Is Diotima a Woman? Platonic Eros and the Figuration of Gender," in *Before Sexuality: The Construction of Erotic Experience in the Ancient Greek World*, ed. David Halperin, John J. Winkler, and Froma Zeitlin [Princeton: Princeton University Press, 1990], 267). The importance of sight to the arousal of erotic

The purely sexual dimension of the image of citizen as erastes strongly associates being a citizen with being an active and, in some respects, dominant, rather than passive and submissive, participant in some affair.[13] To appreciate how this first implication works, however, it is necessary to discuss the Greek conception of sexuality in its differences from modern understandings.[14] For example, the Greeks did not understand a physical act of penetration to be something in which two partners jointly engage for their mutual satisfaction. To the Greek way of thinking, the penetrating/penetrated dimension of sex was not a mutual activity at all. Rather, it was conceived of as "an action performed by one person upon another."[15] Crudely put, one partner was a means to the other's pleasure. As Winkler explains, for the Greeks, "sexual activity [was] symbolic of (or constructed as) zero-sum competition and the relentless conjunction of winners and losers."[16] Winners were dominant, active, and penetrating; losers were submissive, passive, and penetrated.[17] As Athenian society valorized activ-

---

desire is also stressed by Michel Foucault in *The History of Sexuality*, vol. 2, *The Use of Pleasure*, trans. Robert Hurley (New York: Vintage, 1990).

[13] Focusing on the purely sexual character of the role of erastes does reduce the richness of the metaphor's meaning. It is necessary at this point in the discussion only for the purpose of analytic clarity.

[14] There are a number of recent studies on the ancient understanding of the social significance of sexual activity. See David Cohen, "Sexuality, Violence and the Athenian Law of *Hubris*," *Greece and Rome* 38 (1991): 171–88; Dover, *Greek Homosexuality*; Page duBois, *Sowing the Body* (Chicago: University of Chicago Press, 1988); Foucault, *The Use of Pleasure*; David Halperin, *One Hundred Years of Homosexuality and Other Essays on Greek Love* (New York: Routledge, 1990); Halperin, Winkler, and Zeitlin, eds., *Before Sexuality*; Jeffrey Henderson, "Greek Attitudes toward Sex," in *Civilizations of the Ancient Mediterranean: Greece and Rome*, ed. Michael Grant and Rachel Kitzinger (New York: Scribner's, 1988); Eva C. Keuls, *The Reign of the Phallus: Sexual Politics in Ancient Athens* (New York: Harper and Row, 1985); Martha Nussbaum, *The Fragility of Goodness: Luck and Ethics in Greek Tragedy and Philosophy* (New York: Cambridge University Press, 1986), chaps. 6 and 7; A. Schnapp, "Eros the Hunter," in *A City of Images*, trans. Deborah Lyons (Princeton: Princeton University Press, 1989), pp. 71–78; John J. Winkler, *The Constraints of Desire: The Anthropology of Sex and Gender in Ancient Greece* (New York: Routledge, 1990). Studies critical of the perspective developed by Foucault include B. Thornton, *Eros: The Myth of Ancient Greek Sexuality* (Boulder: Westview, 1997); T. K. Hubbard, "Popular Perceptions of Elite Homosexuality in Classical Athens," *Arion* 6 (1998): 48–78; J. Thorp, "The Social Construction of Homosexuality," *Phoenix* 46 (1992): 54–61; and James N. Davidson, *Courtesans and Fishcakes: The Consuming Passions of Classical Athens* (New York: St. Martin's, 1997), pp. 253–54, 313–14.

[15] Halperin, *One Hundred Years of Homosexuality*, p. 29.

[16] Winkler, *Constraints of Desire*, p. 54.

[17] At the extreme, Henderson notes, "Oral and anal rape was a punishment meted out to trespassers, defeated enemies, and adulterers." Henderson continues that this is "part of the significance of phallic boundary-markers, herms, and statues of Priapos (who guarded gardens)" ("Greek Attitudes toward Sex," p. 1260). The social import of penetration is

ity and denigrated passivity, intercourse was always portrayed as something expressive of rigid hierarchies as well as personal feelings. Sex was, as Halperin stresses, a "manifestation of personal status, a declaration of social identity,"[18] not solely an expression of inner feelings. Status categories determined, for example, who could pursue whom.[19] Freeborn Athenian women could actively pursue other women (free, slave, or foreign), but never men. A (male) citizen could pursue an Athenian female only for the purpose of marriage but could pursue unfree or foreign women for any reason. The fact that social standing determined patterns of sexual activity is perhaps most clear when we observe that a citizen male could legitimately pursue other citizen males only under very special circumstances. In fact, such activity was circumscribed by complicated conventions designed to enable the junior, pursued male to evade the social stigma attached to being cast in a submissive, losing sex role as well to enable the adult suitor to evade the suggestion of treating a fellow citizen as a servant. These conventions will be discussed in greater detail below.

It is also important to note explicitly that the Greeks did not classify a person according to the gender of his or her chosen partner, as we do when we describe individuals as "homosexual," "heterosexual," and "bisexual." Rather, they classified acts. Accordingly, as Halperin notes, in sharp contrast to modern understandings of sexuality, to the Greek way of thinking, sexual partners came in two varieties—"not male and female but 'active' and 'passive', dominant and submissive."[20] Accordingly, not only did one's social standing determine the partner one could legitimately choose, such social standing—and not one's "inclination"—also determined the particular role one could legitimately adopt in a sex act. For example, erotic pleasure in being penetrated was thought socially unacceptable for a citizen male. As Winkler notes, this does not mean it was an erotic impossibility. Rather, what seems clear from our sources is that such behavior did not offend eros, but rather honor.[21] Of course, gender intersected with

---

also clear from an illustration on a red-figure oinochoe of 465/64 described by Winkler (*Constraints of Desire*, p. 51): "[It] shows a young, short-bearded Greek man, wearing only a cape and holding his erect penis in his right hand, approaching a Persian soldier in full uniform who is bending over away from the Greek and looks out at the viewer with his hands raised in horror. The inscription identifies the about-to-be-buggered soldier as a representative of the losing side in the Athenian victory over the Persians at the battle of Eurymedon (465 B.C.)."

[18] Halperin, *One Hundred Years of Homosexuality*, p. 32.

[19] Henderson, "Greek Attitudes toward Sex," p. 1256.

[20] Halperin, *One Hundred Years of Homosexuality*, p. 33. See Thorp, "The Social Construction of Homosexuality," and Hubbard, "Popular Perceptions," for critical discussion of Halperin's *One Hundred Years of Homosexuality.*

[21] Winkler, *Constraints of Desire*, p. 54. This is clearest from the text of Aeschines *Against Timarchus.*

these sexual and social roles in complex and significant ways.[22] Women were thought biologically and socially fit for a passive role in sex with men.[23] Of special interest is the way the active/passive opposition not only is mapped onto a male/female opposition but also is made internal to the male gender. Masculinity marked, as Foucault stresses, not only a penetrating sex role but also an attitude toward pleasures in general, including sexual pleasures.[24] Virility required rigorous self-mastery of one's own desires for pleasure. A lewd, lusty hedonist did not fit with the idealized image of a free, virile man. Rather, to be "free" and "virile" in the Athenian view required self-control and temperance (*sōphrosunē*) regarding the allure of pleasures. Femininity, on the other hand, marked the lack of resistance to the lure of pleasure. The very concept of "passivity" was conceived in terms of "nonresistance with regard to the force of pleasures"[25] and was closely bound up with the Athenian view of femininity. In the ancient Greek world, therefore, masculinity was conceived as a "hard-won achievement" and a man as "always in peril of slipping into the servile or the feminine," always in danger of becoming "soft" or "womanish."[26]

When Pericles exhorts citizens to conceive of themselves as lovers, he is thus asserting, first and foremost, that citizens of Athens are not submissive and subordinate to anything—people or passions. The term "erastes" clearly denotes the assertive, superior partner in sexual activity between either same-sex or different-sex partners.[27] Pericles' use of the term un-

[22] See Halperin, *One Hundred Years of Homosexuality*; Winkler, *Constraints of Desire*; du-Bois, *Sowing the Body*, Keuls, *The Reign of the Phallus*; and Sarah Pomeroy, *Goddesses, Whores, Wives and Slaves: Women in Classical Antiquity* (New York: Schocken, 1975).

[23] Accordingly, it was not problematic for women to enjoy (physically and emotionally) their submissive role (Halperin, *One Hundred Years of Homosexuality*, p. 133). Women's roles with other women were, however, more complex. See the discussion of Sappho in Winkler, *Constraints of Desire*, pp. 162–87. For critical discussion of Foucault's view of sexuality in antiquity as it relates to women in antiquity, see Lin Foxhall, "Pandora Unbound: A Feminist Critique of Foucault's *History of Sexuality*," in *Rethinking Sexuality: Foucault and Classical Antiquity*, ed. David Larmour, Paul Allen Miller, and Charles Platter (Princeton: Princeton University Press, 1998), pp. 122–37; and Amy Richlin, "Foucault's *History of Sexuality*: A Useful Theory for Women?" in Larmour et al., eds., *Rethinking Sexuality*, pp. 138–70.

[24] Foucault, *The Use of Pleasure*, p. 84. For critical discussion of Foucault's view of sexuality in the ancient world, see the collection of essays in Larmour et al., eds., *Rethinking Sexuality* (this book also includes a good bibliography to 1996); and Simon Goldhill, *Foucault's Virginity: Ancient Erotic Fiction and the History of Sexuality* (New York: Cambridge University Press, 1995).

[25] Foucault, *The Use of Pleasure*, pp. 84–85.

[26] Winkler, *Constraints of Desire*, p. 50. He continues: "The two sexes are not simply opposite but stand at poles of a continuum which can be traversed. Thus, 'woman' is not only the opposite of a man, she is also a potentially threatening 'internal émigré' of masculine identity."

[27] Dover, *Greek Homosexuality*, p. 16.

questionably evokes an image of the erect, penetrating phallus and asserts the manliness of Athenian citizens. It effectively projects an image of active, energetic, controlling Athenian citizens. It is an easy step to the idea of Athenians as holders of empire and victors in battle. The image of a citizen of Athens as an erastes thus celebrates the individual's status as citizen of a powerful, dominant polis.

The image also celebrates a citizen's control over his own passions and therefore his inner strength. The allusion to penetration does not, for example, exhaust the sense in which the erastai/citizens are conceived of as "active." Insofar as Pericles' metaphor stresses the virility of the citizens, as we have seen above, it emphasizes the self-control they are supposed to exercise with regard to the allure of pleasures.[28] The metaphor thus recalls and implicitly affirms a key assertion of Pericles' speech: Athenian "patterns of life" encourage individual citizens to "live as they like" and pursue all variety of enjoyments and interests, but they also foster a commitment and tendency to moderation. In particular, the "patterns" do not promote a "slipping into" unmanly, servile behavior, but guide individuals toward honor. This point is perhaps nowhere more dramatically articulated than in a passage that has often puzzled commentators: Pericles says, "We are lovers of beauty without extravagance, and of wisdom without softness (*malakias*, 2.40.1).[29] Moreover, the self-control linked to the image of the erastes perhaps can be seen to link up with Pericles' counsel regarding the conduct of the war. The Athenians must show restraint—that is, refrain from trying to expand the empire and stick to fighting a defensive war—if they are to retain their dominant status and its attendant honor and glory. The metaphor expresses the need for citizens to display the inner strength associated with the behavior of exemplary erastai.

Another political implication of the purely sexual resonance of the metaphor concerns the status of citizens inside the polis. It validates the self-definition of the Athenian citizen body as a "vigorous elite."[30] The citizens-as-erastai metaphor recalls the predominant position of citizen males vis-à-vis all other residents of the polis (women, slaves, metics).[31] Further-

---

[28] The erastes metaphor also clarifies Pericles' understanding of "courage." At 2.42.4 Pericles suggests that bravery largely consists in a sort of self-mastery toward the allure of pleasure. Simply put, courage is self-control in the face of the allure of safety. He states that soldiers are to be admired for not succumbing to the temptation to desert in order to enjoy one's private wealth or to pursue its accumulation. Courage is marked by choosing to flee shame rather than danger.

[29] Translation from P. J. Rhodes, *Thucydides Book 2, Edited Greek Text, Translation and Commentary* (Warminster: Aris and Philips Ltd., 1988). "Lovers" here denotes compounds of *philia*, not *erōs*.

[30] Winkler, *Constraints of Desire*, p. 47.

[31] I do not include male minors here because they enjoy the status of potential members of the elite citizen body. I do mean to include all females.

more, insofar as it upholds this divide, it distracts hearers' attention away
from the status differences among members of the (male) citizen group.
In this way, Pericles' use of this metaphor is consistent with his effort in
the earlier part of the speech to identify Athenian democratic politics
with the notion of the collective rule of all (male) citizens rather than the
dominance of a part of the citizenry, the common people, over the rest
(2.37). The metaphor celebrates chiefly the category "(male) citizen." In
appealing to the category "erastes," Pericles found a striking way of praising the whole (male) citizen body with a term that was not steeped in any
partisan meanings. It highlights the distinction between male citizens
and the rest of the populace (female Athenians, resident foreigners, slaves)
but downplays distinctions interior to this group. It had great ideological
potential.

There is, moreover, some precedent in Greek literature for the use of
erotic language to advance this image of a unified demos. In particular, it
is used to stress the possibility of an individual having an attachment to
the polis that is not mediated by membership in a particular family or
faction. As Gomme suggests,[32] a passage from Aeschylus' *Eumenides* probably provided Pericles with the "first impetus" to use erotic language in
discussing political attachments. In this play, Athena, addressing the
Furies, warns, "If you / Now make some other land your home, your
thoughts will turn / With deep desire to Athens" (851–53).[33] Sommerstein, in his commentary on the *Eumenides*, is more direct in his translation of the last line: "You will long for this land like lovers" (*gēs tēsd'
erasthēsesthe*).[34] The *Eumenides* passage continues with an admonition to
avoid civil strife (853–56). As Vellacott remarks, "The whole of this passage is plainly a stern warning against political disunity within Athens."[35]
In the *Eumenides* passage, the erastes metaphor is used to appeal to citizens
as individuals and not as members of any intermediate group or faction.
In both the *Eumenides* and the funeral oration of Pericles, then, the metaphor implicitly rejects the importance of any group identity other than
"Athenian citizen."

Casting the citizens in the role of lovers also carries the strong suggestion that the object of their attentions is alluring and beautiful. Before
moving on to consider what the metaphor suggests about the nature of

[32] A. W. Gomme, *A Historical Commentary on Thucydides*, vol. 2 (Oxford: Clarendon,
1956), p. 137. Connor seems to agree (W. R. Connor, *The New Politicians of Fifth-Century
Athens* [Princeton: Princeton University Press, 1971], p. 96 n. 14).

[33] Translation from Philip Vellacott, *Aeschylus: The Oresteian Trilogy* (New York: Penguin,
1956).

[34] Alan H. Sommerstein, *Aeschylus' Eumenides: Introduction, Greek Text and Notes* (New
York: Cambridge University Press, 1989), p. 250.

[35] Vellacott, *Aeschylus: The Oresteian Trilogy*, p. 194.

the relationship between the citizens and the city, I shall discuss what it suggests about the separate character of the beloved object, that is, the city. What is it about the city that Pericles believes is alluring, that he proposes can arouse erotic feelings? Investigation of this issue requires a short digression on the Greek view of the nature of erotic desire.

As Foucault stresses, the ancient Athenians did not think that individuals experience different "kinds" of erotic desire or competing erotic "drives." He explains, "What made it possible to desire a man or a woman was simply the appetite . . . in man's heart for 'beautiful' human beings, whatever their sex might be."[36] As a result, for the Greeks, "the enjoyment of boys and of women did not constitute two classificatory categories between which individuals could be distributed, a man who preferred *paidika* [boys] did not think of himself as being 'different' from those who pursued women."[37] The perception of beauty, preeminently physical beauty but moral and intellectual beauty as well, was thought to activate the passions of the perceiver. When Pericles suggests that citizens be self-conscious about the fact that they find life at Athens attractive and appealing—that is, that Athens *arouses* them—he is not proposing, nor is he validating, the idea that citizens are "naturally inclined" to love their city. Rather, he suggests that the beauty of Athens is capable of stirring the passions of individual citizens, moving them to choose to seek an intimate relationship with this particular city—not "a city" in general.

Pericles' speech does, moreover, offer an account of the city's exquisite beauty, and Pericles' language at the moment he offers the metaphor recalls that account. Pericles employs two nouns, *dunamis* ("power") and *polis* ("city"), in the first part of the metaphor: "Gaze, day after day, upon the power of the city (*tēn tēs poleōs dunamin*)." In the next sentence, however, he uses a pronoun, "become lovers of her (*autēs*)." With Hornblower[38] and, reportedly, Dover,[39] I accept that *autēs* refers primarily to *polis*. Citizens become lovers of a specific object, the city of Athens, after having perceived that it possesses an exceptionally alluring quality, power. With "power" Pericles is, of course, referring chiefly to Athens' possession of empire. But Pericles also refers to the greatness of the democratic patterns of life that define Athens, patterns that he argued actually amount to the proximate cause of its military successes and acquisition of empire. For example, the likely objects toward which Pericles could have directed the gaze of those assembled with a simple gesture, perhaps a sweep of his

[36] Foucault, *The Use of Pleasure*, p. 188. This appetite is like other appetites, for example, for food (hunger) or drink (thirst).

[37] Ibid., p. 190. For discussion of this point see Morris Kaplan, *Sexual Justice*, (New York: Routledge, 1997), pp. 49–55.

[38] Hornblower, *Commentary*, p. 311.

[39] Reported by Hornblower, ibid.

arm, combined with his words, fit with this view of Pericles' interpretation of the city's arousing beauty. The monuments of the agora, Acropolis, and Pnyx would have been clearly visible from the vantage point of the Kerameikos, the cemetery just outside the city where citizens would have assembled for the funeral rites. The monuments of the Acropolis included, of course, some of the most extraordinary accomplishments of the Athenians under Pericles' leadership and were among the most dramatic physical expressions of the military and financial (imperial) power of the city present in Athens. As Pericles uses a pronoun in the second part of his comment, he allows hearers to make multiple connections—perhaps they might think of the city's patron goddess, Athena, or in particular the cult statue inside the Parthenon (another symbol of the military strength of the city). But gazing at these monuments would also call to mind Athenian "patterns of life." The agora and Acropolis were, between them, the sites of religious rites and grand festivals as well as of the daily activities of politics, commerce, and gymnastics. The Pnyx was the site of Assembly meetings. Pericles' next line implies this connection. It identifies the city's exquisite beauty (its power and greatness) with the general character of Athenian patterns of life. He says: "When it [the city] appears great (*megalē*) to you, you must realize that men have made it great, by daring, by recognising what was needed, and by acting with a sense of honour" (2.43.1).[40] Pericles thus praises Athenian character and patterns of life as much as the city's observable power.

Citizenship as Reciprocity between Lover and Beloved

So far I have argued that the metaphor characterizes the citizen and the city by invoking qualities ideally associated with each party in an erotic relationship: the citizens are conceived of as an active, manly, self-controlled, and vigorous elite, the city as exhibiting alluring, beautiful patterns of life. But the metaphor is more revealing and interesting once we move to consider in more detail what it suggests about the relations these two parties can strive to sustain. This is because the metaphor contains a paradox. On the one hand, it praises the citizens by emphasizing their manhood. It also praises the city by exalting its beauty. These suggestions are, moreover, wholly appropriate to the spirit of the occasion and the encomiastic task of the speech. On the other hand, however, the metaphor implicitly casts the target of citizens' erotic attention—the city—in the role of the sexual object, that is, the passive partner in a sexual relation. In so doing, it might appear to cast the city in a potentially shameful, instead

---

[40] Translation from Rhodes, *Thucydides Book 2.*

of valorized, position. As I stressed above, to the Greek way of thinking, sexual relations were, as Foucault put it, "always conceived of in terms of the model act of penetration, assuming a polarity that opposed activity and passivity." Sexual relations were "seen as being of the same type as the relationship between a superior and a subordinate, an individual who dominates and one who is dominated, one who commands and one who complies."[41] Implying that the city is somehow subordinate and dominated is certainly out of the question. Such an implication would undermine the epideictic, encomiastic mission of the speech. However much we may find the notion of the "state as servant" attractive, to the ancient Greek way of thinking, anything that smacked of servility was unworthy of admiration and honor. For the metaphor to work, that is, for it to deliver praise of both citizens and city, it must successfully avoid suggesting that the city plays this role. It must successfully negotiate Greek views of honorable and shameful sexual behavior.

How does it do so? Here we encounter the brilliance of the metaphor. It does so by evoking the Athenian idealization of one specific type of sexual relation—that between an adult, citizen male and an adolescent, freeborn male, between an erastes and an eromenos. The characteristics linked to the city and praised by Pericles are those appropriate to a free male and potential citizen—not softness, but daring and honorable behavior of the sort that can develop into the production of great power, honor, and glory. Pericles clearly does evoke this particular erotic relation, moreover, because he implicitly praises the masculinity of the citizens and self-control of the city in his portrayal of the citizens and account of the beauty of the city.[42] As this was the most highly valorized of erotic relations in which citizens engaged, and relations of this sort were central to the lives of citizens, Pericles' language would easily have brought this image to the front of the minds of his hearers and Thucydides' readers.[43] We should be

[41] Foucault, *The Use of Pleasure*, p. 215.

[42] This is despite the feminine abstract nouns in play at 2.43.1: power (*dunamis*) and empire or rule (*archē*).

[43] I am not assuming that the practice of pederasty was widespread in classical Athens among all strata of society. It is likely that erastes/eromenos couplings were commonplace only among the elite, though they were certainly not unheard of among others or between elites and young men of more modest status. I am assuming only that erastes/eromenos relations were so well-known and highly valorized that they easily lent themselves to metaphorization in political discourse. On the reach of the valorization of these erotic relations in democratic Athens, see Nick Fisher, "Gymnasia and Democratic Values of Leisure," in *Kosmos: Essays in Order, Conflict and Community in Classical Athens*, ed. Paul Cartledge, Paul Millett, and Sitta von Reden (Cambridge: Cambridge University Press, 1998), pp. 84–104. Fisher argues that, in large part due to the extensive participation in athletics required by the numerous and elaborate festival competitions staged by Athens, nonelite citizens became involved in athletics and, through this, pederastic relationships. He even notes that

clear, moreover, that the metaphor thus signals and affirms the general exclusion of women from participation in politics in the democratic polis. Pericles' use of an image of sex between man and boy suggests the irrelevance of women to politics and public life in his view of democracy, a view made explicit later in the speech (2.45.2), when Pericles virtually ignores the women present, addressing them only to assert that the virtue of a woman is to be seen little and heard even less.[44]

It remains for me to explain how this species of erotic relation manages to negotiate Greek views of honorable and shameful sexual behavior between man and boy in order to show how the metaphor illuminates an Athenian conception of relations between citizen and city.

As Foucault has demonstrated so well,[45] the physical dimension of erotic relations between citizen males was potentially "problematic" for the Athenians, not because of the homoeroticism, but rather because such activity required that one partner assume a passive, inferior role. Any behavior that might cause a citizen to bear the mark of passivity or inferiority, that is, of shame and servitude, would pose enormous problems for the Athenians. Sexual relations between men, while erotically legitimate, were thus the object of considerable cultural concern during the classical period; they were "a problem." But Greek culture did not therefore "disqualify" or prohibit homosexual love. Rather, it developed conventions that stylized it in such a way as to valorize it.[46] Accordingly, sexual relations between men were the object of rigorous "ritualization," which, by imposing certain rules on the mutual behavior of the partners, gave the relation a "beautiful" and honorable form.[47] One form was pederasty.[48] In this relationship there is an obvious asymmetry—there clearly is an older, higher-status "pursuer" and a youthful, lower-status (because as yet only a potential full citizen) "pursued." However, in the idealized cultural image of this relation, there is no suggestion of the domination of one party over another.

---

being particularly beautiful or talented at sport could be a means of social mobility, a process that erotic ties could facilitate (see esp. pp. 94–104).

[44] Compare Joan Scott's comment on the symbols of Islamic political thought: "In medieval Islamic political theory, the symbols of political power alluded most often to sex between man and boy, suggesting not only forms of acceptable sexuality akin to those that Foucault's last work describes in classical Greece but also the irrelevance of women to any notion of politics and public life." "Gender as a Useful Category of Historical Analysis," *American Historical Review* 91 (1986): 1071.

[45] Foucault, *The Use of Pleasure*, pp. 220–25.

[46] Ibid., p. 245.

[47] Ibid., p. 196.

[48] While personally close relations between adult men are well attested and highly valorized in the culture, any sexual dimension to such relations was well hidden, or at least certainly not valorized.

As Foucault helps us to see, it was the observance of certain courtship formalities that enabled the junior partner to evade the social stigma associated with a submissive sexual posture and the senior partner to evade the shame of hubris.[49] In fact, these formalities enabled the participants to establish a relation of mutuality and reciprocity. It remains for me to look closely at these formalities for some insight into precisely how these conventions managed to define the relation as mutual and, by implication, how they illuminate Pericles' view of the political conventions necessary to establish and sustain such mutuality between citizens and city. That is, how does the metaphor help us understand his view of the conditions under which citizens and city assume and discharge legitimate obligations toward each other?

The ideal relationship between erastes and eromenos was not simply a transient erotic encounter. The two parties were expected to develop long-term bonds of mutual affection and special responsibility, bonds that would outlast the sexual dimension of their relationship (which was imagined to cease with the adolescent's physical maturation, induction into the citizen rolls, and adoption of the role of an erastes toward another himself). The interaction between erastes and eromenos is represented in literature and iconography,[50] for example, as a reciprocal game of mutual exchange where both partners are imagined together to create bonds of mutual affection that lead, ultimately, to the bonds of friendship and camaraderie upon which the community of citizens is based. Their initial interaction is a sort of "game" of pursuit and flight conducted in an agonistic context. The (would-be) erastes competes with other suitors in an effort to demonstrate his superior worthiness to be chosen as a lover through the performance of certain acts, including eulogizing the boy, giving appropriate gifts—typically a cockerel, or wild game (hare, rabbit, stag); never money[51]—and generally behaving in exemplary ways in the many arenas of public life. The boy also competes with rivals for the attentions of admirable suitors. The boy's physical beauty, but also his demonstrated skills (athletic, military, musical, etc.), as well as how artfully he plays the game of pursuit and flight, were imagined to make him desirable. Eagerness was, on the other hand, supposed to signal softness and, conse-

---

[49] Intending to cause a sexual partner shame was "hubristic" and legally actionable. The law of *hubris* would cover prosecutions of rape, for example. See Cohen, "Sexuality, Violence and the Athenian Law of *Hubris*."

[50] I am relying on the appraisals of the evidence in Dover, *Greek Homosexuality*; Foucault, *The Use of Pleasure*; Schnapp, "Eros the Hunter"; and Winkler, *Constraints of Desire*.

[51] Gifts of animals were symbolic of the relationship as well as of the traits ideally possessed by desirable eromenoi. See Schnapp, "Eros the Hunter," on the significance of game in particular. A money gift, on the other hand, suggested prostitution, which was always disgraceful for a citizen. See Aeschines *Against Timarchus*.

quently, a lack of self-control and lack of potential for manliness in the youth. In fact, in response to attention, the boy is expected first to flee and refuse, yielding only when satisfied that the lover is "worthy." Dover notes that the yielding eromenos would (ideally) refuse to accept physical penetration, insisting instead on other acts. Iconographic evidence, for example, suggests that an exemplary eromenos would be strong enough to permit only intercrural "penetration" (between the thighs). He is also represented as self-controlled enough to resist becoming aroused himself while with his erastes. The boy is shown as yielding only in gratitude for clearly defined benefits received, not out of sexual appetite or his own erotic madness. These benefits are, in particular, training in the execution of the responsibilities of manhood that he gains through keeping company with honorable and thoughtful adult men experienced in the ways of the polis. His "yielding," that is, his entering into the relation, is thought to advance his education and social standing. The adult erastes, moreover, is also thought to gain more than base pleasure. His bond with his eromenos brings him the honor and status associated with "winning" a desirable youth as well as with cultivating the personal ties that unite citizens and support the creation of a body of manly Athenians.

The courtship formalities thus stress two points necessary to evade the potentially problematic implications of sexual activity between these two parties. First, the boy is portrayed as active, demanding, and self-controlled, even though sexually "obliging." He averts becoming the passive object of the erastes' pleasure by observing the rituals of the relationship. Second, the rituals portray the relationship as one of mutuality and reciprocity between unequals,[52] not one of dominance and subordination.

Iconographic evidence (vase painting) as interpreted by Schnapp also confirms that the Athenians of the fifth-century did not represent the personal relation between an erastes and eromenos as one of dominance and subordination, but rather as one of mutuality.[53] He shows that erotic desires and relations are typically represented by images of a hunt and kill during the earlier archaic period, but that in the fifth-century the imagery changes dramatically. Sixth-century black-figure painting shows the return of the hunter and the presentation of a dead hare (for example) to his beloved, or scenes from the hunt itself. The meaning is, moreover, apparent: lover is to beloved as hunter is to hunted. In fifth-century red-figure painting, however (from the century of the Cleisthenic reforms and the founding of democracy at Athens as well as the period of Pericles' prominence), the imagery begins to suggest a more mutual understanding

[52] They are unequal because of the age difference, but the idea that the boy represents a potential equal is always present.
[53] Schnapp, "Eros the Hunter."

of a sexual relationship. The hare, for example, "becomes less the prey and more the partner in seduction."[54] The animal is now presented to the beloved alive. The scenes depict the animal's taming or its performance in races and games. The boy is, therefore, no longer likened to a trophy; instead, insofar as he is represented by the animal, he is likened to a wild animal entering into an ordered world. The fact that the settings in which the images are placed also change during this period—from that of the brush to clearly defined urban space—reiterates this point. The youthful eromenoi are "clearly installed" in an "urban universe"[55] in the paintings of the fifth century. As for the races and games, as Schnapp plausibly offers, they suggest a mutual and playful understanding of eroticism, one that assumes it to involve an "art of approaches and dodges,"[56] not a violent initiation.

While the game of pursuit and flight is imagined to be enjoyable for both parties in the idealized representation of the relation, the sexual activity between them is not. The mutuality of the personal relation did not imply a "community of pleasure" in sex between erastes and eromenos.[57] The ideal eromenos is imagined not to experience any pleasure during sexual activity; indeed, the cultural norm insists that he refrain from identifying with or defining himself in terms of the submissive role he plays in the sexual part of his relation with an erastes.[58] The ideal eromenos is conceived of as rigorously in control of his passions throughout courtship as well as during its "consummation." Nussbaum describes the cultural image of the boy's behavior as follows:

> He will smile sweetly at the admiring lover; he will show appreciation for the other's friendship, advice, and assistance. He will allow the lover to greet him by touching, affectionately, his genitals and his face, while he looks, himself, demurely at the ground. And, as Dover demonstrates from an exhaustive study of erotic painting, he will even occasionally allow the importune lover to satisfy his desires through intercrural intercourse. The boy may hug him at this point, or otherwise positively indicate affection. But two things he will not allow, if we judge from the evidence of works of art that have come down to us. He will not allow any opening of his body to be penetrated; only hairy satyrs do that. And, he will not allow the arousal of his own desire to penetrate

---

[54] Ibid., p. 82.

[55] Ibid., p. 86.

[56] Ibid., p. 82.

[57] Foucault, *The Use of Pleasure*, p. 223.

[58] In this way, this variant of "mutual exchange" avoids being an elaborate way to validate relations of dominance and subordination. Compare, for example, the traditional terms of a modern marriage contract. See Carole Pateman, *The Sexual Contract* (Stanford: Stanford University Press, 1988).

the lover. In all surviving Greek art, there [is only one example of a boy with an erection]. . . . The inner experience of an eromenos would be characterized, we may imagine, by a feeling of proud self-sufficiency.[59]

Of course, the eromenos is not self-sufficient. He needs and desires the attention and mentoring of an erastes. But now we can perhaps better see how it is that the boy's struggle to behave honorably in his sexual relations with a lover could be thought to be good training for the rigors of citizenship. A citizen needs to be able to rely on his own judgment. He must also be resistant to the lure of pleasures lest they cloud his judgment or entice him into corruption. Insofar as the eromenos might actually identify with the submissive role, his behavior would, in fact, be indicative of the likelihood of "wrong manhood." Behavior such as promiscuity, payment for sexual favors (prostitution), or an eagerness to assume a passive or receptive role was thought to signal "deviant manhood" and was a ground for being stripped of one's rights as a citizen (for example, the right to speak in the Assembly).[60]

Although the mutuality achieved by the erastes and eromenos was not supposed to be sexual, there is some sense in which the erastes and eromenos could achieve "erotic reciprocity."[61] To the extent that mutual appreciation of the beauty and order achieved and displayed by each party characterizes their relationship, it may be marked by some measure of erotic reciprocity. In particular, each party may perceive beauty and order in the other and want to respond by together creating another aesthetically satisfying form—a beautiful relationship.

The ideal image of the relation between erastes and eromenos is thus perhaps best described as an elaborate "gift exchange" that creates a defined set of mutual obligations and that, from an aesthetic point of view (always significant to the Athenians), increases the order and beauty present in the lives of the participants. As such, it is possible to characterize

---

[59] Nussbaum, *Fragility of Goodness*, p. 188, modified to reflect Dover, "Postscript, 1989," in his *Greek Homosexuality.*

[60] On the political import of such sexual behavior and the figuration of the *kinaidos* (one who takes pleasure in being the passive partner in anal intercourse), see John J. Winkler, "Laying Down the Law: The Oversight of Men's Sexual Behavior in Classical Athens," in *Constraints of Desire*, pp. 45–47. The pervasiveness of contempt for the *kinaidos* among the Athenians finds expression in Plato's portrait of Socrates' contest with Callicles in the *Gorgias.* Callicles is inclined to consider all pleasures equally valuable and happiness to be a matter of maximizing satisfactions. Socrates trips him up by challenging him to allow that the life of a *kinaidos* is happy (494d–e). For discussion of this passage, see Nussbaum, *Fragility of Goodness*, pp. 142–43; Josiah Ober, *Political Dissent in Democratic Athens* (Princeton: Princeton University Press, 1998), pp. 204–5; Charles Kahn, *Plato and the Socratic Dialogue* (New York: Cambridge University Press, 1996), pp. 136–37.

[61] Cf. David Halperin, "Plato and Erotic Reciprocity," *Classical Antiquity* 5 (1986): 60–80.

the interaction between these parties as a *charis* relation. Charis typically consisted in gratitude for material benefaction.[62] An erastes would, on this view, ingratiate himself with an intended beloved by bringing the finest offerings it was within his power to provide. These would include the practice and promise of the benefits of companionship and tutelage. The erastes would expect, in return, charis (gratitude), which meant not only companionship but favors as well. Terminology often used to describe the boy's sexual compliance supports this view. Foucault and Dover both note that the verb *charizesthai*, which can be translated "to gratify" or "to grant favor," is used to designate the performance of sexual acts between an erastes and eromenos.[63] But the charis relation does not end here. Charis bonds were thought to endure. It is a relation therefore perhaps modeled on the tradition of "guestfriendship."[64] As such, the exchange between the parties is conceived to inaugurate a potentially lasting mutual bond.[65]

I now turn to making explicit the metaphor's implications regarding the proper relations between citizens and city in a democratic polis. To begin, the metaphor stresses that the bonds between citizens and the city are not "natural," nor do they exist prior to and independent of the conscious choices of the parties involved. The erotic metaphor implies instead that an individual citizen should conceive of his interest in a relationship with the city to be rooted in his own felt desires and willful actions, not as a given or as a result of a mere accident of birth. Correspondingly, the city's interest in the citizen is also not given or "natural," but earned. This point is perhaps made clearest not only by the presence of the erastes metaphor but also by the complete absence of any suggestion on Pericles' part that the relationship between citizens and city is in any way like that between children and parent. In fact, Pericles' speech is unusual among funeral orations for the absence of such a representation. The closest he comes to such a suggestion is to assert that fathers should beget more children not only to repopulate the polis but also because the concerns of a father can sharpen a citizen's judgment on matters of policy that might

[62] Josiah Ober, *Mass and Elite in Democratic Athens* (Princeton: Princeton University Press, 1989), p. 245.

[63] Foucault, *The Use of Pleasure*, p. 209; and Dover, *Greek Homosexuality*, p. 44.

[64] J. T. Hooker, "*Charis* and *Aretē* in Thucydides," *Hermes* 102 (1974): 167.

[65] See Hooker, "*Charis* and *Aretē*," for discussion of the way cities seek to manipulate charis obligations to form alliances in Thucydides' account of the war. We can also note that in the funeral oration, Pericles seems to boast that Athens followed this strategy in building its alliances (2.40.4). Of course, in his last speech he openly declares that Athens' empire amounts, in effect, to a tyranny (2.63.1–2). See W. R. Connor, "*Tyrannis Polis*," in *Ancient and Modern, Essays in Honor of G. F. Else*, ed. J. H. D'Arms and J. Eadie (Ann Arbor: University of Michigan Press, 1977), with critical discussion by Kurt Raaflaub, "Stick and Glue: The Function of Tyranny in Fifth-Century Athenian Democracy," in *Popular Tyranny*, ed. Kathryn Morgan (in preparation).

come up in the Assembly. The funeral orations of Lysias and Demosthenes, in contrast, define Athenian citizens as "the lawful issue of their fatherland."[66] Lysias refers to the country as both mother and father to citizens (*Funeral Oration 17*). In fact, these other orations, as well as the one put forward by Plato in the *Menexenus*, develop the metaphor of city as provider and nurturing parent. They appeal, moreover, to norms regarding how children should honor their parents to illuminate the attitude a citizen should appropriately have toward the city. The treatment of parents was, in addition, a well-defined matter in Athenian society. For example, as Lacey argues:

> The city laid it on children as a legal obligation, not merely a moral duty, to ensure that their parents were looked after when they were old. Maltreatment of parents ranks with maltreatment of orphans and *epiklēroi* as a prosecution in which a prosecutor ran no risk of punishment, and "Do you treat your parents well?" was a question asked at the examination not merely of aspiring archons, but of all public officers, including orators. From other phrases, too, we may gather that expectations did not stop at refraining from maltreatment; positive services were required, especially the provision of food supplies.[67]

The city also assumed, with great fanfare, the role of parent to war orphans in need of guidance and financial support and the role of the dutiful son to dead servicemen in need of honorable burial. The relationship of parent, chiefly father, and male child was a common point of reference for orators' construction of a praiseworthy account of the relations between city and citizens. The exception, of course, is the funeral oration of Pericles, in its effort to articulate an idealization of democratic citizenship.

The erastes metaphor also does not engage the traditional (liberal) problem of political obligation as we know it in the modern era. It does not assume that the problem at the heart of relations between citizens and city is that the liberty of individual citizens and the authority of the "state" can conflict and that, therefore, there is a need to spell out the conditions under which the claim of liberty or of authority should prevail over the other. The striking thing about the metaphor is, in fact, that it does not assume that the problem facing Athenian democratic society is that citizens may be cast in a subordinate position in relation to the city.[68] It is not

---

[66] Noted by Loraux, *The Invention of Athens*, p. 284 n. 119.

[67] W. K. Lacey, *The Family in Classical Greece* (London: Thames and Hudson, 1968), pp. 116–17.

[68] We should note that although the metaphor in particular does not harbor worry about dangers to individual liberty, the speech is by no means silent on this score. Pericles sees the danger to personal liberty (to "living as one likes" in private) originating in the "suspicious attitudes" and intolerance of fellows (neighbors) and not from the watchful eye of the "state." His worry has, in fact, much in common with Tocqueville's concern about the tyr-

fueled by concern that "the state" might abuse its power and exceed the bounds of its authority. Rather, Pericles' metaphor is animated chiefly by a worry that the city might be cast in a subordinate, subservient position in relation to citizens. It harbors a worry that citizens (erastai) might act shamefully and abuse the polis (eromenos) in an effort to service their own desires. At the extreme, this would mean corruption, malicious litigation, demagoguery, factionalism, perhaps even civil war and the rise of a tyrant. Pericles' metaphor thus urges citizens not to think of the city (its institutions) as their servant or plaything, nor of themselves as servants or playthings of the city.

The metaphor suggests, instead, that interactions befitting free citizens and a free city are those of mutual exchange, understood on the pattern of benefaction and gratitude, which tie in with the compulsion of honor, not power.[69] In the conduct of daily affairs, for instance, it suggests that citizens understand that if they act to cultivate the city's virtue, they can expect to receive, in turn, the gratitude or favor (charis) of the city. This means that citizens should view all the things that they actively do in their capacity as citizens—attend meetings, serve on juries, perform ritual obligations, compete in athletic contests, perform military service, pay taxes—as ways in which they ingratiate themselves with the city and which enable them legitimately to expect to receive, in return, certain favors, for example, public recognition, legal protection, the favor of the gods, and the pleasure of living "freely" (2.37.2).

The metaphor implies, moreover, that each citizen is capable of sustaining such an exchange with the city, that is, that each citizen has "something to offer." This is democratically significant, for it was commonplace for a wealthy person to understand his performance of liturgies (for example) to constitute a benefaction for which he could expect to receive charis from the demos, understood as the "common people" and not the "whole community." For example, a wealthy man could approach the performance of liturgies as a way to elicit the favor of the "common people" who would likely populate a jury before which he might be brought.[70] Similarly, a wealthy hoplite might expect his "special service" to beget charis as well. Pericles' metaphor, to the contrary, proposes that benefaction and gratitude is properly a relation between every individual and the whole polis,

---

anny of the majority. Of course, in line with the epideictic mission of the speech, that is, its aim to express aspirations and idealization (not reality), Pericles asserts wishfully that Athenians do not actually conduct themselves in this manner and people are indeed able to "live as they like." On the epideictic mission of the speech, see Aristotle *Rhetoric* 1358b2–5; Loraux, *The Invention of Athens*.

[69] Gerald Else, "Some Implications of Pericles' Funeral Speech," *Classical Journal* 49 (1954): 154.

[70] Ober, *Mass and Elite*, p. 268.

not between a wealthy individual and poorer individuals. In fact, Pericles explicitly insists that poverty is no barrier to an individual's ability to confer a benefit on the city (2.37.2), and therefore to be granted recognition and honor by the collectivity. The metaphor implies that all citizens, not just the wealthy, can and should compete for the charis of the polis, and that all are potentially worthy to receive it.

Pericles' treatment of the relation between fallen soldiers and the city confirms the importance of this notion of mutual exchange in the Athenian understanding of the bonds between citizens and city. Only a few lines after the statement of the erastes metaphor, Pericles proposes that those who die should be understood as having given "the finest contribution (*eranos*) to it [the city]. Together they offered their bodies; individually they received eternal praise and the most distinguished of tombs" (2.43.1–2).[71] The term *eranos* is significant. In Homer it meant a common meal or feast to which each contributes a share.[72] Later it came to mean a "friendly group loan at no interest."[73] In this passage from Thucydides, it is a metaphor meaning simply "favor," but with the "strong implication that the favor is to be returned."[74] It is, as Hewitt notes, "practically a synonym for charis."[75] The verb, as Gomme points out, also stresses that the contribution is "freely" made.[76] The citizens' deaths are thus viewed as gifts intended to elicit a countergift. The polis must meet this expectation, moreover, if the original gifts are to achieve their full meaning. The dead citizens are, therefore, not glorified as having demonstrated selfless devotion to a cause bigger than themselves, but as parties to a mutual exchange that confirms the honor of both citizens and city. Not only are Athenians exemplary for their bravery, but democratic Athens, unique among the Greek cities in its practice of a public funeral rite, is also portrayed as exemplary in its treatment of citizens.

Pericles' dramatic mention of "giving bodies" in the passage quoted above in fact emphasizes the mutual exchange model of relations between citizens and city. Even on the occasion of the public funeral, the city is not seen as acting unilaterally. Rather, this rite is seen as the city's response to the citizens' presentation of their bodies for collective rather than private burial.[77] The funeral rites and oration provide the city, moreover, with a

---

[71] Translation from Rhodes, *Thucydides Book 2*.

[72] *Odyssey* 1.226. See Joseph William Hewitt, "The Terminology of 'Gratitude' in Greek," *Classical Philology* 22 (1927): 160.

[73] Hornblower, *Commentary*, p. 311.

[74] Hewitt, "The Terminology of 'Gratitude' in Greek," p. 160.

[75] Ibid.

[76] Gomme, *A Historical Commentary on Thucydides*, 2.43.1.

[77] I take *koinē* at 2.43.1 to denote the public, collective aspect of the funeral. In addition, we should note that bodies were actually burned on or near the field of battle. Remains

dramatic lesson in and exhortation to excellence. In giving their bodies, even in death citizens perform a role associated with an ideal erastes. They are providing Athens with instruction in virtue. We can also note that the egalitarian treatment of all the dead confirms the ideal that every citizen is capable of bestowing significant benefits on the city and thus of meriting high honors and praise. The remains were grouped according to the tribe to which the dead soldier had belonged, with no special notice given to family, status, or rank. In fact, Thucydides says that the funeral procession included the bearing of eleven coffins: each of the ten tribes had one containing the remains of men from its tribe, and the city added an additional one symbolic of the men whose remains had not been recovered, the missing and presumed dead (2.34). The names inscribed on the memorial also noted only the citizen's deme. Insofar as the metaphor also recalls the resistance that the boy is supposed to exercise toward the granting of sexual favors, it suggests that the city, Athens, is not eager to grant favors (now understood as providing a funeral for dead servicemen). The erastes' presentation of such fine gifts (bodies) elicits the eromenos' (city's) gratitude and respect, but it does not stir the city's appetite for more. The boy, we must remember, was ideally thought to be highly self-controlled and able to resist becoming aroused himself. The city is thus not portrayed as eagerly devouring its citizens in order to service its own pleasures (perhaps its pretensions to glory). On the contrary, the metaphor suggests that a city that fails to exercise control is, in some sense, deviant and shameful. Perhaps it articulates some of the boundaries of the legitimate exercise of political power.[78]

Pericles again stresses the mutual-exchange model of relations between citizens and city in the closing lines of the oration, lines that emphasize the lesson with which the funeral rite and oration provide the Athenians and with which Athens, in turn, provides Hellas. He proclaims, "Where the prizes for valor are the greatest, there the men will be the best citizens" (2.46.1).[79] The relation between citizens and city that sustains both parties' pursuits of excellence and honor is, this closing remark stresses, one of free, mutual exchange, not dominance and subordination or self-less devotion to something larger than oneself or to an abstraction. As

---

were returned to Athens for interment in the cemetery in the Kerameikos on the occasion of the annual public funeral.

[78] We can note that Thucydides portrays the Athenians as being in love with the Sicilian expedition (6.24). The restrained, honorable love conjured up in the funeral oration is, in this case, nowhere to be seen; instead, a furious, raging eros is in control, with disastrous consequences. Twice Thucydides reports that the Athenians became more eager for the expedition (6.19, 24).

[79] Translation from Rhodes, *Thucydides Book 2*.

democracy sustains these relations of mutuality, Pericles suggests, it achieves excellence.

A different understanding of democratic exchange appears in surviving examples of deliberative and forensic oratory. For example, it is commonplace in forensic oratory for the speaker to remind the audience of liturgies and other generous benefactions he performed in the past so as to elicit some goodwill (charis) from the hearers.[80] I have stressed that Pericles' metaphor, in contrast, proposes that benefaction and gratitude is properly a relation between every individual citizen and the whole polis, not between a wealthy individual leader and many poorer individuals. Herein also lies the key difference between Pericles' metaphor and another appearance of the erastes/eromenos metaphor in Athenian political oratory. In Aristophanes' *Knights*, Paphlagon, "the ranting, fraudulent, bombastic servant of old man Demos . . . the character who both in antiquity and in modern times has been recognized as a caricature of Cleon,"[81] professes his devotion to the Athenian people and proclaims, "I adore you, Mr. Demos, and . . . I'm your lover (*erastēs*, 732)."[82] This metaphor does not cast all citizens in the role of lover but only the leader/orator. The speaker is cast in the position of an erastes and the Athenian demos (personified as Demos) in the role of the eromenos. For this metaphor to work, the audience must supply an image of the honorable lover who behaves admirably toward his beloved. No doubt, Cleon would have had this meaning in mind when he used this metaphor in his serious oratory. His use of the metaphor would seek, at its best, to assert the legitimacy of a measure of dependence on the guidance of a leader if Demos is to achieve excellence. Cleon will honorably nurture his beloved into virtue, the metaphor might suggest; the demos needs the orator and the orator can be trusted. But his metaphor casts Demos in a dangerously passive position. It does not call on the conventions that the parties observe in their effort to evade any potentially shameful implications of the submissive sexual role assumed by the eromenos. It does not emphasize the active role of the eromenos or the reciprocity of the relation. Rather, it calls attention to the asymmetry of the relationship. Aristophanes makes the most of this troubling dimension of Cleon's version of the erastes/eromenos metaphor in his caricature of Cleon. Later in the *Knights*, Paphlagon's (Cleon's) rival, the Sausage-seller, criticizes Demos for naively being taken in by speakers in the Assembly who play the role of an adoring erastes only to get Demos to "put out"

---

[80] See Ober, *Mass and Elite*, pp. 226–30; and Paul Millet, *Lending and Borrowing in Ancient Athens* (New York: Cambridge University Press, 1991), pp. 124–25.

[81] Connor, *New Politicians of Fifth-Century Athens*, p. 96.

[82] *Aristophanes. Acharnians. Knights*, trans. Jeffrey Henderson (Cambridge, Mass.: Harvard University Press [Loeb], 1998).

for the leader's personal benefit. He complains, "Whenever someone said in the Assembly, 'Oh Demos, I'm your erastes and I love you and care for you, and I'm the only one who looks after your interests'—whenever someone used these preambles, you crowed like a rooster and proudly shook your head [you were eager]. . . . In return, he cheated and left" (*Knights* 1340–44). The Sausage-seller calls up an image of less-than-ideal behavior on the part of both parties.[83] Pericles' metaphor, on the other hand, does not divide the citizenry into leaders and led. Pericles uses the metaphor to develop a conception of citizenship, whereas Cleon apparently used it to articulate a view of leadership.

My reading of Pericles' funeral oration suggests that through the striking erastes metaphor, the speech proposes that the ideal Athenian citizen is not a servant of the city but an active, energetic participant in the construction of its greatness. The metaphor urges citizens willingly and affectionately to offer their city fine and extraordinary gifts in the form of public service and patiently to tend to the city's developing needs. It further urges them actively to guide the city in the exercise of its own powers and to help frame its conception of its best interests and aspirations. The metaphor also suggests that democratic citizenship demands that obviously unequal parties—the city and each individual citizen—struggle to forge a relationship of mutuality and reciprocity. Such an achievement would be beautiful, praiseworthy, honorable. Pericles' metaphor indicates that an ideal of reciprocity between city and citizens animated Athenian democratic politics. Of course, we need look no further than the rest of Thucydides' own narrative to find the Athenians failing to live up to this conception of democratic citizenship under the stresses of war. Nevertheless, these are aspects of the patriotic self-image that the Athenians created and clung to in their efforts to persevere in their experiment in democracy,[84] and to which Pericles (and Thucydides) gave superior expression at a moment of political crisis.

[83] Plato, too, exploits the "lover of the demos" metaphor for all its possible corrupt implications. An orator's love of the demos can be a vulgar sort of love, his critique of rhetoric suggests, a love aimed not at bettering the "target" but rather at manipulating him into serving the leader's own personal pleasure and benefit (see *Alcibiades I* 132a).

[84] I disagree with Loraux's argument in *The Invention of Athens* insofar as she maintains that the funeral oration does not represent any original democratic thinking, only aristocratic glosses on Athenian democratic life.

Chapter Four

CITIZEN AS *THEATĒS* (THEATER-GOER): PERFORMING UNITY, RECIPROCITY, AND STRONG-MINDEDNESS AT THE CITY DIONYSIA

EVERY YEAR in early spring, the Athenians staged an elaborate, days-long festival in honor of the god Dionysus. The City Dionysia was a magnificent, enormous, politically significant undertaking and was recognized as such in its own day.[1] Its celebration included processions, choral competitions, sacrifice, feasting, revelry, and dramatic competitions (for which the works of Aeschylus, Sophocles, Euripides, and Aristophanes were produced). Thousands of citizens of all ranks participated. As this was an open event held during sailing season, many foreign visitors attended as well.[2] Modern scholars estimate that the Theater of Dionysus in Athens held between 14,000 and 17,000 persons—about two and one-half times as many as the Pnyx, the site of Assembly meetings.

For citizens, participating in this event was not a private or leisure activity but a vigorous civic practice closely identified with the exercise of democratic citizenship.[3] For example, the act of being in the audience at

---

[1] Pericles brags in the funeral oration that Athens celebrates plenty of festivals throughout the year (Thucydides 2.38). Other sources confirm that Athens sustained an unusually large number of festivals ("Old Oligarch," *Constitution of the Athenians* 3.2; Aristophanes *Clouds* 300ff.) and were thus sometimes regarded as "more pious than other people" (Pausanias 1.17.1, 24.3). Large festivals, and especially the City Dionysia, formed part of the "sociocultural structure" of democracy at Athens (Josiah Ober and Barry Strauss, "Drama, Political Rhetoric and the Discourse of Athenian Democracy," in *Nothing to Do with Dionysos: Athenian Drama in Its Social Context*, ed. John J. Winkler and Froma Zeitlin [Princeton: Princeton University Press, 1990], p. 237). Aristotle explains, for example, that by converting the private rites of prominent families into a smaller number of public, and publicly funded, festival celebrations, the democratic reforms of Cleisthenes brought the poor into leading elements of worship (*Politics* 1319b20–30).

[2] The City Dionysia was the high point of the Athenian festival calendar and probably a major panhellenic event as well. The size of the audience, as Simon Goldhill has observed, makes this festival "the largest single body of citizens gathered together not only in the Athenian calendar but also throughout the Greek world, except perhaps for the Olympic games (for which figures are not readily available), or certain major battles." See his "The Audience of Athenian Tragedy," in *The Cambridge Companion to Greek Tragedy*, ed. P. E. Easterling (New York: Cambridge University Press, 1997), p. 58.

[3] This point is now well established in the scholarly literature on Greek politics. It is stressed both by interpreters of tragedy and comedy who read drama in its social context and

plays, "of being a *theatēs* . . . [was] not just a thread in the city's social fabric, it . . . [was] a fundamental political act."[4] To attend the theater was to constitute a mass gathering designed to hear critical speech regarding political matters and to "play the role of judging *politēs* [citizen], the mainstay of democratic decision-making."[5] On this occasion Athenians also enacted an official perception of the excellence of their democratic polis. That is, festival rituals involved citizens in the display of developing elements of the Athenian civic self-image.[6] In particular, being theater-goers and festival spectators (*theatai*), I propose, engaged citizens in performing three substantive elements of the Athenian democratic self-image: the idea of a unified demos, the aspiration to reciprocity between city and citizens, and the conviction that the ordinary, nonelite citizen is

---

by historians of Greek politics who respect the centrality of cultural practices as well as governing institutions in the Athenian understanding of democracy. See, for example, Easterling, ed., *The Cambridge Companion to Greek Tragedy*, J. Peter Euben, *The Tragedy of Political Theory* (Princeton: Princeton University Press, 1990), and *Corrupting Youth* (Princeton: Princeton University Press, 1997); J. Peter Euben, ed., *Greek Tragedy and Political Theory* (Berkeley: University of California Press, 1986); Winkler and Zeitlin, eds., *Nothing to Do with Dionysos*, R. Osborne and S. Hornblower, eds., *Ritual, Finance, Politics: Athenian Democratic Accounts Presented to David Lewis* (Oxford: Clarendon, 1994); Alan Sommerstein, Stephen Halliwell, Jeffrey Henderson, and Bernhard Zimmerman, eds., *Tragedy, Comedy and the Polis*, papers from the Greek Drama Conference, Nottingham, U.K., 18–20 July 1990 (Bari: Levante Editori, 1993); Rush Rehm, *Greek Tragic Theater* (New York: Routledge, 1992); Christian Meier, *The Political Art of Greek Tragedy* (New York: Cambridge University Press, 1993); Simon Goldhill, *Reading Greek Tragedy* (New York: Cambridge University Press, 1986); Josiah Ober, *Mass and Elite in Democratic Athens* (Princeton: Princeton University Press, 1989); Jean-Pierre Vernant and Pierre Vidal-Naquet, *Myth and Tragedy in Ancient Greece* (New York: Zone, 1990); J. R. Green, *The Theatre in Ancient Greek Society* (New York: Routledge, 1994); Barbara Goff, ed., *History, Tragedy, Theory: Dialogues on Athenian Drama* (Austin: University of Texas Press, 1996).

[4] Simon Goldhill, "The Seductions of the Gaze: Socrates and His Girlfriends," in *Kosmos: Essays on Order, Conflict and Community in Classical Athens*, ed. Paul Cartledge, Paul Millett, and Sitta von Reden (Cambridge: Cambridge University Press, 1999), pp. 105–24, at p. 106.

[5] Ibid.

[6] On the importance of this festival as a source for Athenian political ideology: W. Robert Connor, "City Dionysia and Athenian Democracy," *Classica et Mediaevalia* 40 (1989): 7–32; John J. Winkler, "The *Ephebes*' Song: *Tragoidia* and *Polis*," *Representations* 11 (1985): 25–62; and Simon Goldhill, "The Great Dionysia and Civic Ideology," *Journal of Hellenic Studies* 107 (1987): 58–70. Connor suggests that the City Dionysia functioned as a sort of "freedom festival." Winkler proposes that the seating arrangements in the theater formed a "map of the body politic" and that in attending the citizens performed a visual image of the administrative structure of the democratic polis. Goldhill proposes that the set of rituals carried out in the theater immediately prior to the dramatic productions engaged the citizens in enacting democracy's claim to provide them with a route to preeminent glory and power. In this chapter I extend in political theoretical directions the findings of these (and other) classicists.

intellectually capable. This chapter explores precisely how certain patterns of behavior and arrangements of icons that make up the celebration manage to convey these meanings.[7]

THE EVENT

The City Dionysia began in the evening with the staging of a reenactment of the advent of the god Dionysus into Athens.[8] Sometime before the festival, the cult statue of Dionysus was placed in a small temple outside the city. The Athenians gathered at this temple, offered sacrifices at its altar, sang hymns, and, by torchlight procession, escorted the cult statue back to the Theater of Dionysus in Athens.

On the first day of the festival, the poets made formal announcements regarding the plays to come. Each of the three poets participating in the dramatic competitions in turn mounted a platform located in the agora and described the subjects of the trilogy of plays he had prepared for performance. The following day was full. It began at daybreak with the staging of another larger and more inclusive procession.[9] We do not know the complete make-up of the procession, but we do know that it included not only Athenian men young and old, wealthy and poor, but also high-born

[7] Of all the festivals on the Athenian calendar, I focus on the City Dionysia for three reasons. First, the state of the evidence and scholarly literature permits detailed study of the symbolic dimension of this event. Second, the City Dionysia was one of the most salient opportunities the Athenians had to make their abstract status as members of a specifically *democratic* polis into a tangible, observable reality in their daily lives. Third, on this occasion the Athenians—playwrights and audience members—were invited to be reflective regarding such questions as "Who are we?" "In what does our unity consist?" and, "What is distinct about our city?" The answers enacted in the ritual activity implicitly characterize democratic citizenship in certain ways. On the Pananthenaia and democratic ideology: Jenifer Neils, ed., *Goddess and Polis: The Panathenaic Festival in Classical Athens* (Princeton: Princeton University Press, 1992; Jenifer Neils, "The Panathenaia and Kleisthenic Ideology," in *The Archaeology of Athens and Attica under the Democracy*, ed. W.D.E. Coulson, Olga Paglia, T. Leslie Shear, Alan H. Shapiro, and Frank L. Frost, Oxbow Monograph 37 (Oxford: Oxbow, 1994), pp. 151–60; Victoria Wohl, "*Eusebeias heneka kai philotimias:* Hegemony and Democracy at the Panathenaia," *Classica et mediaevalia* 47 (1996): 25–88; and Lisa Maurizio, "The Panathenaic Procession: Athens' Participatory Democracy on Display?" in *Democracy, Empire and the Arts in Fifth-Century Athens*, ed. Deborah Boedeker and Kurt A. Raaflaub (Cambridge, Mass.: Harvard University Press, 1998), pp. 297–318.

[8] The following description of the festival relies on the assessment of the evidence by A. W. Pickard-Cambridge, *The Dramatic Festivals of Athens*, revised by J. Gould and D. M. Lewis (Oxford: Oxford University Press, 1968), supplemented by various recent works identified here in the notes.

[9] For a "tentative reconstruction" of the *pompē*, see Christiane Sourvinou-Inwood, "Something to Do with Athens: Tragedy and Ritual," in Osborne and Simon, eds., *Ritual, Finance, Politics*, pp. 269–89.

Athenian girls, noncitizen residents of Athens (metics), and Athenian colonists. Each group was elaborately clad and carried particular offerings. We do not know the route the procession followed, but it is likely that it wound its way through the agora and perhaps ended up in the Theater of Dionysus at the base of the Acropolis. Throughout the procession, the participants and thousands of spectators would have had a clear view of the impressive monuments of the Acropolis, along with the civic buildings and numerous commemorative statues placed in the agora. Spectators and marchers were not solemn or reserved but lively, even raucous. Their demeanor should not suggest that the event was simply fun and games. This was a holy day. Normal time was suspended. No Assembly meetings or public business could be conducted. Even prisoners were released on bail so that they could be present. When the procession arrived at the altar, the animals were slaughtered. The fatty portions of the meat were reserved for the gods as burnt offerings (the thick smoke such tissue produced was thought to reach the gods); the remaining meat was distributed among the citizens. The Athenians referred to the evening as a *kōmos*—a great party filled with feasting, drinking, letting loose, and general revelry, including music and dancing in the streets. Sometime during the day of the grand procession, the Athenians conducted choral competitions,[10] with the city awarding prizes for the finest performances.

For the next three days (the third, fourth, and fifth days of the festival), the Athenians and foreign visitors spent nearly every daylight hour in the theater, eating and drinking as the performances were going on. With all the spectators gathered but before the performances began, the Athenians staged still more civic rituals. Indeed, they chose this moment to stage a series of exceptionally evocative rituals.[11] First, the priests purified the theater. Second, the ten generals (*stratēgoi*)—the very top military officers at Athens—came forward to pour libations. Third, a herald proclaimed the names of a small number of individual citizens who, it had been determined earlier, had done something exceptionally praiseworthy for the city during the past year. These individuals came forward to be crowned before the assembled crowd. The herald also proclaimed the names of the slaves who had been freed during the course of the previous year. Since the city kept no official record of slaves, such a public display of a change in status was probably the best insurance against any later challenge. Fourth, the

---

[10] On the choral competitions, see Robin Osborne, "Competitive Festivals and the Polis: A Context for Dramatic Festivals at Athens," in Sommerstein et al., eds., *Tragedy, Comedy and the Polis*, pp. 21–38.

[11] For discussion of these preperformance rituals in detail, see Goldhill, "Great Dionysia and Civic Ideology."

members of the Delian League brought the annual tribute due Athens into the orchestra of the theater for all to see.[12] Fifth, a herald announced that the city would recognize the young war orphans who had reached the age at which they were to begin their formal military training. These boys came forward, paraded in the orchestra of the theater clad in full armor, and retired to special seats down front.

The eagerly awaited dramatic performances could now begin. A large number of citizens attended. On each of the three days of theater, a single poet staged a trilogy of tragic plays and a light, short satyr play. Then came a single comedy by a different poet. By the end of the three days of dramatic performances, the audience would have experienced three tragic trilogies, three satyr plays, and three comedies. Each contest (choral, tragedy, comedy) was judged by a panel of ordinary citizens. This panel was selected by lot in an elaborate way designed to minimize corruption. The completion of the dramatic competition concluded the religious program of the festival.

Representing the Unity of the Democratic Polis

Both the idea of a group and the status of member are abstractions. They need to be represented before they can be celebrated. The ritual activity performed during the City Dionysia created a visual image of the city as a whole and engaged participants in experiencing their identity as members of it.[13] Celebrating the festivals together became a powerful source of common identity and solidarity. Xenophon reports that in a speech delivered in 403 (when Athens was suffering intense civil strife), a man pleaded for reconciliation by appealing to the citizens' sense of unity: "We have shared with you in the most holy religious services, in sacrifices and in splendid festivals."[14] The festival was a site where the class and status differences among the members of the polis were both highly visible and inscribed with meanings that helped diffuse the ever-present potential for civic un-

---

[12] This practice began when the Athenians moved the treasury from Delos to Athens, that is, when the Delian League first metamorphosed into the Athenian Empire. They exhibited the wealth in the form of a set of earthenware jars, each of which was packed with silver. Each jar held twenty-six kilograms of silver, the equivalent of one talent (6,000 drachmas).

[13] The City Dionysia was certainly not the only occasion to perform this function. Other festivals, Assembly meetings, military exercises and campaigns, as well as other practices gave the Athenians many opportunities to "see" the polis as a whole and experience their status as members. On the Panathenaia see note 7 above.

[14] *Hellenica* 2.4.20–21. The rituals also made the proceedings sacred, thereby helping to foster affective ties to the polis. See Barry Strauss, "Ritual, Social Drama and Politics in Classical Athens," *American Journal of Ancient History* 10 (1985): 74–75.

rest. The public treasury[15] paid the poets and actors and supplied the prize money as well, and the wealthiest citizens were required to undertake liturgies, sponsoring dramatic productions and choral performances and providing animals for sacrifice. Because the preparations for the festival employed many and the actual celebration engaged many more, the festival occasioned a considerable redistribution of wealth. The Old Oligarch even complains that the numerous Athenian festival events were really ways in which the poor soaked the rich:

> As for sacrifices and rituals, festivals and temples: knowing that it is not possible for every poor man to sacrifice and feast and establish sacred places and have a great and beautiful city to live in, the commoners have discovered how to manage these things. Thus the city sacrifices many victims under public auspices. And it's the populace that feasts and receives shares of the sacrificed animals.[16]

In addition, the festival enacted an acceptance on the part of the mass of citizens of the existence of inequalities of wealth accompanied by firm demotic control over the cultural norms prescribing the proper uses to which great wealth can be put, as well as over the appropriate routes to personal distinction.[17] For example, wealthy citizens financed the dramatic productions. After choosing which poets were to compete in a given year, the chief magistrate at Athens assigned each poet a sponsor (*chorēgos*). The law identified the minimum the sponsor had to spend in support of such things as stipends for the performers (actors, chorus members, musicians) and crew members during their time in reheasals and the construction of sets and costumes. Each elite citizen serving as choregos in any particular year sought to be singled out as the most magnificent benefactor of the city. The sponsors, and especially the winning sponsor, received high honor and public prestige that could translate into political clout. The losing choregoi would no doubt have been extremely disappointed, possibly even furious. They had not achieved as full a measure of honor and public prestige by means of their service as a choregos as they had probably hoped. The rituals thereby also made visible inequalities of status among members of the elite.

---

[15] These funds came from sources such as the publicly owned silver mines and tribute paid Athens by its "allies." Only wealthy citizens paid "taxes" in democratic Athens. These were levied in the form of mandatory sponsorship of a civic event (chorus) or other need (e.g., outfitting a trireme) and special wartime contributions of money (*eisphora*).

[16] "Old Oligarch," *Constitution of the Athenians* 2.10, translation by Charles M. Gray in *The Greek Polis*, ed. Arthur Adkins and Peter White (Chicago: University of Chicago Press, 1986), p. 52.

[17] Ober, *Mass and Elite*.

The rituals also marked the differences between the members of the demos (i.e., citizens) and noncitizen residents of Athens (i.e., female Athenians, metics, slaves), as well as between Athens and its "allies," legitimating them by making them appear sanctioned by the authority of the gods under whose auspices and in whose honor the Athenians staged this whole event. For example, the participation of female Athenians and metics in the festival was carefully prescribed and far more limited than that of the citizen men. Specially chosen young women of Athens were prominent in the procession. Metics also marched in the procession, clad in elaborate robes of deep purple that advertised their wealth. Citizens who marched, on the other hand, were free to wear whatever they liked. The procession thus acknowledged the presence in the polis of both women and metics and their own strivings for honor. But the festival activity also marked their exclusion from the demos, the governing body.[18]

The festival activity also represented Athenian relations to other poleis. For example, the Athenian colonists participated in the procession pulling carts containing giant phalluses. An erect phallus had on other occasions been used to symbolize military victory. The carts drawn by the colonists probably alluded to the military victory that was part of a process of colonization. In addition, the "allies' " presentation of tribute in the theater advertised not only Athens' wealth but also the city's dominant position in interpolis relations.

The ritual activity of the City Dionysia marked these differences between the various participants not only to articulate a social hierarchy (regarding the place of women, slaves, free citizens, metics, and foreigners) and publicize the political authority of the demos over elite production (the evaluation of plays, for example), but also to link these actors to the common enterprise of the Athenian polis. Some of the ritual activity expressed what those in the citizen group could be thought to share across the divide of social and status inequalities and in virtue of which they all claim membership in the Athenians demos. Differences have to be marked in order for the boundary around the "in-group" to be drawn and for the more porous boundaries separating groups inside the in-group to be (wishfully) defined as relatively insignificant.

The Athenians understood the civic import of the ritual activity of the City Dionysia. Significantly, "the official responsible for all the organization of the City Dionysia was not the basileus, the old religious official of the community, but the archon, the political leader," who, beginning in

---

[18] The exclusion of the metics from the demos was also marked by their lack of any right to share the meat meal that followed the sacrifice, segregation from the citizens in the theater, and absence of representation on the panel that judged the performances.

487, was selected by lot.[19] This archon selected the poets and actors to be part of the dramatic competitions and assigned specific actors to specific poets. He also selected the sponsors for the plays. In addition, the procession, feasting, organization, and financing of the choral and dramatic competitions, the seating arrangements in the theater, and the preperformance rituals all involved the Athenians in apprehending, sanctifying, and developing affective ties to the structure of the democratic constitution.

For example, ritual activity repeatedly displayed the Cleisthenic division of the citizens into ten administrative units called "tribes." The creation of these groupings reduced the influence of propertied families by creating basic units of political organization that mixed up citizens of different social status and regional attachment. Aristotle considers this reform a major step in the process of Athenian democratization.[20] This new structure is evident in the organization of the choral competition. Each of the ten tribes supplied one chorus (five supplied a chorus of men and five a chorus of boys). In addition, each of the ten tribes selected a poet and a flute player for its entry into the choral contest and assembled the individual chorus members from among its residents. Each tribe selected its own choregos for this competition. He had to assume the financial responsibility of training and costuming the chorus and flute players. The total of 500 participants in the choral competition reflected another aspect of the new Cleisthenic political order—it was the same as the total number of citizens who served on the Council (*boulē*), fifty from each tribe.[21]

The activity around the dramatic productions also advertised the organization of the city into tribes as well as other institutions of the new democratic order. Before the plays began, the ten generals, one from each tribe, poured libations, and ten citizen-judges, one from each tribe, were selected to evaluate the plays. The seating arrangements in the theater formed an image of the overall institutional structure of the Athenian democratic polis.[22] The amphitheater was probably divided into thirteen wedges.[23] Men currently serving on the Council, the archons, priests of

---

[19] H. W. Parke, *Festivals of the Athenians* (London: Thames and Hudson, 1977), p. 129.

[20] *Constitution of Athens* 21.

[21] Connor, "City Dionysia and Athenian Democracy," p. 22.

[22] Winkler, "The *Ephebes'* Song," p. 30.

[23] Goldhill cautions that reconstructions of the seating arrangements in the theater, while accepted by numerous scholars, are actually based on very little direct evidence. I take the way this reconstruction fits the general pattern of representing the tribal structure of the polis to be more reason to accept this view of the seating arrangements. See Goldhill, "Representing Democracy: Women at the Great Dionysia," in Osborne and Hornblower, eds., *Ritual, Finance and Politics*, pp. 347–70; and Goldhill, "The Audience of Athenian Tragedy," pp. 54–68.

gods and goddesses, foreign dignitaries, and individuals being specially
honored by the city (e.g., those who had received crowns and orphans
who had paraded) sat in the central wedge. The five wedges on either
side of the center were reserved for citizens of Athens, each wedge being
designated for affiliates of one of the ten tribes. Foreign visitors and metics
sat in the two outermost sections. The egalitarian seating of citizen men
inside each wedge reflected the equal citizenship of rich and poor, noble
and ordinary.[24] Some argue that if women did attend the performances,
they probably sat apart from the men, perhaps being seated in the uppermost sections of each wedge reserved for a particular tribe.[25] Yet with or
without female Athenians, the theater seating formed a "map of the body
politic."[26]

The physical setting of the theater easily recalled the legislative institution of Athenian democracy, the Assembly. The Theater of Dionysus and
the Pnyx were laid out similarly. The relation of the assemblymen to the
orator's platform in the Pnyx was parallel to that of the audience members
to the stage building that served as backdrop and actors' place in the theater. These two groups—the audience at the festival and the voting body—
were in many ways largely synonymous, and the plays before them often
draw on this identity.[27] Ober and Strauss show, moreover, that playwrights
and orators "each referred to the other's genre, by references to actions,
symbols, codes, vocabulary, paradigms and rituals." They continue, "Oratory drew on the audience's experience of theater; drama drew on the
audience's experience of political and legal speeches. By so doing, each
genre implicitly taught its audience that being an Athenian was a comprehensive experience, that there was no compartmentalized division be-

---

[24] Ober, *Mass and Elite*, p. 152. Winkler speculates that the spirit of egalitarianism may
be behind the attraction of the circular orchestra. "One of its features is that it gives an
equally good view of the dancing to all in the audience, right, left, and center. It also enables
the members of the audience to view one another. These are democratic principles." John J.
Winkler, "*Phallos Politikos*: Representing the Body Politic in Athens," *Differences* 2, no. 1
(1990): 29–43, at p. 39.

[25] On the question of women's attendance, see Anthony Podlecki, "Could Women Attend
the Theater in Ancient Athens?" *Ancient World* 21 (1990): 27–43; Jeffrey Henderson,
"Women and the Athenian Dramatic Festivals," *Transactions of the American Philological
Association* 121 (1991): 133–47; Goldhill, "Representing Democracy"; and idem, "The Audience of Athenian Tragedy." See also Jeffrey Henderson's brief response to Goldhill in
"Attic Old Comedy, Frank Speech and Democracy," in Boedeker and Raaflaub, eds., *Democracy, Empire and the Arts*, p. 409 n. 94.

[26] Winkler, "The *Ephebes'* Song," p. 32.

[27] Peter Arnott, *Public and Performance in the Greek Theater* (London: Routledge, 1989),
p. 14. See Ober, *Mass and Elite*, pp. 152–53, for more elaboration of the near-identity of
assemblymen and theatai.

tween esthetics and politics."[28] Thucydides' Cleon calls the Athenians "spectators (*theatai*) of speeches" (2.38.4).

The strong links between the work of the Assembly and that of the theater would have been reinforced by two additional practices. First, by the time of Ephialtes, money from the public treasury supported the purchase of theater tickets by citizens (the theoric fund). The payment of these sums recalled the stipends paid for Assembly attendance and jury service. Second, Athenian law specified that a special Assembly meeting be held in the theater on the day immediately following the conclusion of the festival. The law also specified the agenda for the meeting.[29] The continuity of the activity of the theater with that of the Assembly is also noted by Plato, who names theaters along with Assemblies, courts, and army camps as the "common meetings places of a multitude" (*Republic* 492b). Isocrates also acknowledges the continuity, complaining that there is no parrhesia (frank speaking) in Athens except in what he takes to be two problematic venues of public debate—the Assembly and the theater (*On the Peace* 14). The theater audience was continuous with the demos also in that a subset of members was selected by lot to sit in judgment of fellow citizens. The integrity of the judges in the theater and of jurors in the democratic courts was even subject to similar safeguards. Both panels were selected in a complex manner designed to minimize corruption.[30]

The organization of the ritual activity repeatedly suggested that whatever divided the citizen body (capacity to serve as a choregos, for example),

[28] Ober and Strauss, "Drama, Political Rhetoric and the Discourse of Athenian Democracy," p. 270.

[29] At this meeting the Assembly reviewed, indeed scrutinized, the conduct of the officials who had organized the whole event. Overseeing and planning the particular elements of the festival were not the province of a special elite but rather were the responsibility of magistrates selected by lot who were now to be held accountable. The Assembly could pass decrees praising (or admonishing) individual officials if it so chose. The Assembly also heard individuals who wished to complain about the misconduct of any nonofficial (that is, complaints about someone having violated the sanctity of the festival). The Assembly could review the grievances and record a view of their merits, but this was not a judicial proceeding. At most it was a prelude to litigation.

[30] Ober, *Mass and Elite*, p. 244. Just before the performance of the first play began, the archon came forward to select the judges of the competition. Sometime before the festival began, ten sealed jars containing the names of citizens who wished to serve as an official judge had been deposited on the Acropolis in the care of the appropriate officials. The jars were now brought into the theater and the archon drew one name from each jar at random. These ten individuals swore to give an impartial verdict. Immediately following the last performance the judges selected the winners. Each of the ten judges wrote his order of merit on a single tablet. The ten tablets were placed in a single jar. The archon then drew only five tablets from the jar and on these five lists the contest was decided. On the selection of jurors, see Aristotle *Constitution of Athens* 63–69.

certain common experiences united them, marking them as members of the citizen body. These experiences were being born a free citizen, being a member of the "nonpartisan" intermediary civic groups (deme, tribe), attending meetings of the Assembly, and serving as juror, Council member, or magistrate. The ritual activity interpreted for the Athenians the normative significance of particular political institutions that they had fashioned through material struggle.[31]

ENACTING DEMOCRATIC NORMS

Reciprocity between City and Citizen

The City Dionysia staged an unabashed display of Athenian wealth, military power, and artistic accomplishment. It was "an occasion for marking [not only] the structure of [but also] the magnificence of *democratic* Athens."[32] The ritual activity mingled display of Athens' identity as a democracy (its constitutional structure and its attachment to freedom) with its understanding of its own greatness (its power, prosperity, and vitality). In the performance of the City Dionysia, the Athenian celebrated the coincidence of these two achievements—democracy and greatness.[33]

The ritual activity of the City Dionysia enacts not only that citizens had certain experiences in common but also that specific norms ought to guide their practice of citizenship. The rituals suggest ways in which the Athenians ought to think about the demands of democratic citizenship. They enact relations of reciprocal, mutual exchange understood on the pattern of benefaction and gratitude, between individual citizens and the city.

The rituals of the City Dionysia form almost a catalogue of exemplary ways in which citizens could perform benefactions for the city and the city could express its gratitude. The exchange may appear unbalanced. Importantly, however, each of the unequal partners to the exchange incurs significant obligations to the other. As discussed in Chapter Three, the mutual-exchange model suggests that though unequal, the parties are not—and should not be—in a relation of dominance and subordination. It also implies that the deterioration of the relation into one of dominance and subordination is an ever-present danger against which citizens must guard.

---

[31] In concluding his essay on the Balinese cockfight, Clifford Geertz writes: "Societies, like lives, contain their own interpretation. One has only to learn how to gain access to them." I approach the ritual activity of the City Dionysia as containing an Athenian self-interpretation. Clifford Geertz, *The Interpretation of Cultures* (New York: Basic, 1973), p. 453.

[32] Winkler, "The *Ephebes'* Song," p. 30, my emphasis.

[33] Pericles in the funeral oration also links Athens' achievement of greatness to its democratic constitution and habits of life. See Thucydides 2.36.

Formally announcing the names of special benefactors of the city and ceremoniously bestowing a crown or garland on the honorees in the theater immediately before the performances began most obviously represents, in symbolic form, the benefaction/gratitude model of relations between citizen and city on display at this festival. Demosthenes noted explicitly that those witnessing the crowning applauded not only the generosity or intelligence of the individual being honored but also the city's exhibition of gratitude (*On the Crown* 120). This display of gratitude functioned in part to stimulate those assembled to do public service. But the ritual did not suggest that public service was one's duty. Rather, it downplayed the mandatory aspect of service, representing the performance of the liturgy as being voluntary in an important way.[34] The crowning ritual demonstrated that benefaction would not go unnoticed or be taken for granted. It showed that individual benefactors would be formally recognized by the whole city. We need only recall how fiercely competitive was the Athenian political environment to understand why the crowning ritual resonated so with the elite as well as with the masses. The city's display of gratitude and the honor that accrued to the individual benefactor exhibited the city's fulfillment of its part in the mutual exchange.

The preperformance rituals are filled with symbolic representations of benefaction eliciting the city's gratitude. For example, the strategoi—exemplary benefactors of the city by virtue of having distinguished themselves in battle and having served as military and political leaders—poured the libations and took special seats in the theater. The parade of war orphans in the orchestra also reminded those assembled that the city was responsive to the benefactions performed by their now-deceased fathers. The men had given the city their bodies and lives. The city, in turn, gave them an honorable public funeral and assumed their paternal responsibilities toward their surviving male children. The presentation of the boys in the theater recalled for the audience that the city had indeed sponsored the education and military outfitting of the orphaned boys. The proclamation read on this occasion confirms that the city's actions were uppermost in the celebrants' minds: it did not dwell on the deeds of the fathers, but ceremoniously identified what the city had done for the boys in gratitude

---

[34] The citizen's formal right to refuse being assigned a liturgy also helped represent this expenditure as voluntary. The assigned liturgist could challenge whether his wealth was great enough to obligate him to perform these services. This man could officially name another citizen either to perform the liturgy in his place or to agree to a complete exchange of property (*antidosis*). If the other citizen refused the offer, a court decided which one was required to perform the liturgy. The procedure required both parties publicly to reveal fully their private wealth. See Matthew Christ, "Liturgy Avoidance and *Antidosis* in Classical Athens," *Transactions of the American Philological Association* 120 (1990): 147–69.

to the fathers.[35] In the Theater of Dionysus, the city also marked its gratitude to Harmodius and Aristogeiton, legendary "tyrant-slayers" and
"founders of democracy." The Athenians celebrated these two men as exemplary benefactors of the city, honoring them in many ways, including
granting their descendants special seats in the theater in perpetuity.

The organization and production of the dramatic competitions also
modeled the way exemplary benefaction by individual citizens would be
matched by the city's expression of great gratitude. In this case, the poets
and choregoi were the benefactors; the honor, public acclaim, and prizes
bestowed on them constituted the city's display of gratitude. The practice
of awarding prizes not only to the winner but to the other competitors as
well should be understood in this connection. The city could have regarded this whole group of individuals as illustrious benefactors. Each
used personal skills and financial resources to develop an event of importance to the whole demos.

Choregoi were especially potent symbols of the benefaction/gratitude
model of relations between citizens and city because their public service
could be easily quantified. Many elected to spend more lavishly than the
law required[36]—the competition for the added honor of being singled out
from among other benefactors was fierce. The victors won not only special
recognition at that moment but also lasting fame. Winners were permitted
to erect a tripod celebrating the victory in a public place, and the names
of the victors were inscribed in the public record.

The rituals did not mask the existence of great inequalities of wealth
and status among the citizen body. Rather, they provided a setting in
which the democratic polis negotiated these inequalities. In the festival
context, wealth had a particular meaning. It was an opportunity to "perform the role of a democratic citizen" in a highly dramatic way.[37] The
festival was thus a site of contest in that the wealthy citizens could use this
opportunity to assert their status as one of the "better" or "notable" people, who deserve, in their view, some sort of special treatment from the
polis. The official ritual context contained this claim, however, offering a
bounded interpretation of the reach of the distinction one could earn on
this occasion.

---

[35] Aeschines *Against Cteisiphon*; Isocrates *On the Peace* 82.

[36] Though the festival represented the benefaction as between the individual and the
whole city, wealthy citizens commonly referred to their discharge of the responsibilities of a
choregos as an exchange between themselves and the demos. In forensic oratory (e.g., Lysias
Defense against a Charge of Taking Bribes) we find wealthy speakers citing their past munificence in an effort to gain the favor of the demos (i.e., to get a public decision—court case—
to go "their way").

[37] Simon Goldhill, "Power and Politics and the *Oresteia*," paper presented at the conference "Teaching the *Oresteia*," Northwestern University, Evanston, Illinois, 21 April 1996.

The festival placed many grand examples of benefaction before the polis and engaged the assembled celebrants in enacting the city's bestowal of great gratitude on the individual benefactors. In so doing, the rituals invited likening the performance of modest acts of participation (i.e., forming a theater audience, a jury, an assembly) to grand acts of munificence deserving of recognition, honor, and the gratitude of the whole city. Some of Pericles' comments in the funeral oration are helpful. The funeral oration focused on a grand act of benefaction—dying in battle. Pericles explicitly identified dying in battle as the most glorious contribution a man could offer, one that will be met by great gratitude on the part of the whole city (Thucydides 2.43).[38] But Pericles also asks how, save dying in battle, an ordinary citizen, one who does not possess either extraordinary talent or great wealth, could hope to be a benefactor of the city and garner the honor attached to such status. He proposes that democracy provides all citizens, regardless of social and economic status, with multiple avenues to political participation, that is, to an active part in determining the course of public policy (serving on the Assembly or Council), administering public decisions and organizing civic events (serving as a magistrate), or settling litigation (serving as a juror). In democracy, public service is not beyond the capacities of any citizen. Fitting these ordinary practices into a model of reciprocal benefaction, Pericles not only affirms that all citizens can serve, but further celebrates that their service will not pass unnoticed, will not remain unsung. Pericles' oration sings of them, albeit collectively. Pericles attributes the honor and glory the city has achieved to the pervasive democratic patterns of life that all citizens have a part in sustaining.

Other examples of Athenians assimilating common acts of political participation to grand acts of munificence like liturgy performance can be found in some of the language and iconography of service as a magistrate, Assembly member, or juror. Every magistrate (selected by lot) ordinarily wore a crown in the course of his duties.[39] A relief scupture depicting a bearded, seated Demos being crowned by Demokratia adorns the inscription recording the Law against Tyranny of 337/6.[40] The official language

---

[38] For discussion of dying in war as triggering an exchange, see Clifford Orwin, *The Humanity of Thucydides* (Princeton: Princeton University Press, 1994), pp. 22–23.

[39] Demosthenes *Against Aristogiton II* 5; Mogens Herman Hansen, *The Athenian Democracy in the Age of Demosthenes*, trans. J. A. Crook (Oxford: Blackwell, 1991), p. 229.

[40] The law dates to a year or so after the Athenians lost a critical battle in the struggle with Macedon and thus to a tense period during which the Athenians feared the imposition of a tyranny and subversive plots by individuals eager to curry favor with Philip. For the text, translation, brief commentary on the inscription as well as a plate of the relief, see B. D. Meritt, "Greek Inscriptions," *Hesperia* 21 (1952): 355–59. For discussion of the law, see Martin Ostwald, "The Athenian Legislation against Tyranny and Subversion," *Transactions of the American Philological Association* 86 (1955): 103–34.

employed to indicate a citizen who has not yet cast his vote parallels the term used to identify one who, though eligible, has not yet performed a liturgy. As Dover has pointed out, the cry of the jury-service-loving Philocleon in Aristophanes' *Wasps*—"What I yearn for . . . [is to hear] the herald say . . ., 'Who is unpolled? Let him stand up' " (*tis apsēphistos; anistasthō*, 753–54)—is probably not a poetic invention but a formal expression similar to that found in documentary inscriptions identifying "those who have not sponsored a chorus" (*achorēgētos*).[41]

Common Citizens as Intellectually Strong

The experience of theater-going involved Athenian citizens in enacting a substantive characteristic they wished to attribute to themselves as democratic citizens. In particular, they enacted the ordinary Athenian man's claim to be intellectually capable. Many ancient critics of democracy maintain that democracy is fundamentally incoherent and unstable because it relies on poorly educated, thoughtless, or at least intellectually vulnerable people to render political decisions, that is, to steer the ship of state.[42] These attacks amount to charging the mass of ordinary citizens with being weak-minded. The Athenian democrats were aware of this criticism. And they recognized the threat to the health of the democratic polis were these charges to ring true. Athenian public discourse is full of references to the Athenians' claim to be able to deliberate and thus, as Pericles is made to suggest, to be able to educate action (Thucydides 2.43). The celebration of speaking with parrhesia that we found in forensic and deliberative oratory functioned in a similar way. Orators characterized themselves as freely speaking with painful frankness, and their hearers as people capable of digesting difficult truths. The ritualized speech employed in oratory projected an image of the intellectual strength of the citizens. It was an image of strong-mindedness, not in the sense of pigheadedness but in the sense of possessing intellectual stamina, a capacity for reflection, an openness to criticism, and an ability to master new subjects and critically evaluate leaders. It was also an image of risky intellectual engagement with practical concerns, not one of contemplative detachment. This image was most boldly displayed in the ritual practice of attending the dramatic performances, that is, of being a theates. It was en-

---

[41] K. J. Dover, "The Language of Classical Attic Documentary Inscriptions," *Transactions of the American Philological Society* 112 (1981): 9–12. Translations from the *Wasps* are from *The Comedies of Aristophanes*, vol. 4, *Wasps*, edited with translation and notes by Alan H. Sommerstein (Warminster: Aris and Phillips, 1983), pp. 75, 204.

[42] For example: "Old Oligarch," *Constitution of the Athenians*; Megabyzus and Darius in Herodotus *Histories* 3.80–89; Cleon in Thucydides 3.37–38; the parable of the ship in Plato's *Republic* 488a–e.

acted by the behavior of the audience during the productions, especially the audience's boisterous involvement in the action of the plays and strong identification with the chorus.

The citizen audience did not sit politely and quietly in the theater. They did not simply listen passively,[43] then digest the poet's ideas and rethink their own commitments in private. Athenians shouted at the stage, wept, hissed, booed, stomped their feet, threw figs. They were not merely talkative, but noisily engaged with the performance. Robert Wallace shows that a systematic review of the sources indicates that the audience was itself a "performer" during the plays: it was, he stresses, "both vocal and even physically active during theater performances. . . . The public itself performed quite vigorously in the theater during both the fifth and fourth centuries, sometimes even interrupting the drama."[44]

The performances were challenging in many senses. The content of the plays was both intellectually demanding and emotionally unsettling. Tragedy portrayed the complete unraveling of social fabric, personal identity, political and moral norms. Comedy mocked daily practice, the democratic style of life and social norms, humiliating its named and unnamed targets with unrelentingly obscene and crude references. Both tragedy and comedy at times even subjected to rigorous scrutiny specific policy decisions made by the demos. To some extent, the poets adopt the role of the true frank speaker. Jeffrey Henderson has noticed this in regard to the comic poets. He observes that the comic poets "claim to be distinct from the politicians and litigators whom they routinely criticize, but at the same time they regard themselves as genuinely political voices: like other speakers [orators], they consistently claim to benefit the polis by giving it good, honest advice and by attacking those who would harm it, and like other speakers they express concern about the potential risks of their outspoken-

---

[43] Cf. the representation of the effect of poetic performance on listeners in Homer. The common effect is one of magic, of rendering the listeners speechless, passive, helpless (e.g., the Sirens). Homer also portrays heroic words as being heard in silence, even as eliciting an initial response of silence on the part of hearers (e.g., *Odyssey* 8.234, 11.333, 20.320). (My thanks to Ahuvia Kahane for these references.) The conduct of the audience at the dramatic performances in the democratic city thus appears explicitly to oppose an earlier understanding of the relation between poetic performance and audience, as well as between edifying words and hearers.

[44] Robert Wallace, "Poet, Public and 'Theatocracy': Audience Performance in Classical Athens," in *Poet, Public, and Performance in Ancient Greece*, ed. Robert Wallace and Lowell Edmunds (Baltimore: The Johns Hopkins University Press, 1997), pp. 97–111 at p. 106. Wallace collects the evidence for the various forms of "audience performance" at the dramatic festivals. Also see Christina Dedousi, "Greek Drama and Its Spectators: Conventions and Relationships," in *Stage Directions, Essays in Ancient Drama in Honour of E. W. Handley*, ed. Alan Griffiths (London: Institute of Classical Studies [University of London], 1995), pp. 123–32.

ness."[45] In taking on this role, I want to stress, the poets also cast the members of the theater audience in the demanding role of hearers of parrhesia. Performing this role, as we saw in Chapter Two, required a significant measure of intellectual strength.[46]

The theatai were rowdy not merely because they thereby had the most possible fun at a recreational event or because the poets were skillful in manipulating their passions, but also because displaying their emotional and intellectual involvement in the theatrical production expressed democratic ideals appropriate to the occasion and because the festive environment encouraged unrestrained displays of such involvement. Citizen-spectators' rowdy behavior dramatized immediately that citizens are strong-minded and that reflection provoked by the plays would have practical import, that is, would issue in a perspective, a view, and ultimately, in actions. Perhaps the reflection provoked at this time exacerbated divisions among the citizenry or polis members more broadly. Or such intellectual work might occasion a moment of true political insight. But in either case, boisterous behavior enacted the audience's claim to have strong minds capable of directing action. The practice of judging the productions and awarding prizes—that is, of issuing a decision—not only fits with the competitive ethos of the society but also stresses the Athenian patriotic claim that, for them, action issues from mental work. By being theatai and meeting the challenge of the plays, especially in passing judgment on their merits, Athenian citizens enacted a claim to be intellectually capable folk.

This is precisely how Plato reads the Athenians' noisy behavior in the theater. In the *Laws*, the Stranger proposes that the "unmusical shouts" and "clappings" (700c) of the many during Dionysiac celebrations are the public expression of their self-understanding as knowers of the difference between good and bad music and consequent claim to act with authority in evaluating the performances. This intellectual confidence travels into other spheres of life, the Stranger continues, creating a veritable "theatocracy" (*theatrokratia*), by which he means the prevalence of the opinion that "everyone is wise in everything" (*hē pantōn eis panta sophias doxa,*

---

[45] Henderson, "Attic Old Comedy," p. 260.

[46] Accordingly, Aristophanes praises the intelligence of his audience. See *Wasps* 65, 1013–14; *Knights* 233; *Clouds* 521, 575; *Frogs* 677, 1109–18. Comedy claims to challenge each audience member to take up the role of hearers of parrhesia in earnest by confronting the audience with representations of a pitifully gullible demos, of self-serving, manipulative leaders, and hero(in)es who realizes the promise of parrhesia. On the comic stage, the least among the Athenians (e.g., the poor, the old, women) rise to speak, assume risk, criticize the powerful (orators, political leaders), and influence action. See Henderson, "Attic Old Comedy," p. 268: "By frankly criticizing the powerful, the comic hero(ine) did what isegoria and parrhesia ideally allowed but could not fully provide for."

Laws 701a). Of course, Plato is highly critical of the role of theater-going in Athenian public life. What I want to stress is that he considers the noisy, rowdy behavior in the theater to signal not simply bad manners, but the masses' claim to a measure of intellectual capability.

Recent scholarship on ancient theatrical performance emphasizes that the poets, too, considered the audience to be involved in displaying their intellectual self-confidence during the productions. Rehm stresses that the poets assumed the active participation of the audience in their productions and anticipated significant audience responses as they fashioned their texts.[47] To appreciate how this is possible, we must first note that as the performances took place in full daylight, the actors could see the audience, the audience could see the actors, and the members of the audience could see one another.[48] Playwrights were not aiming to create a "seamless dramatic illusion."[49] Rather, the audience could be "an active partner, free to comment, to be commented upon, to assist, or to intervene" in the theatrical production.[50] Of course, this was one of the strategies the playwrights used to provoke reflection. They counted on certain responses and worked them to stimulate self-awareness and criticism in their audience. But the unruly behavior of the citizen audience also made it clear that the members of the audience, delighted in and wished to advertise their part in the serious mental business of dramatic performance.[51]

The "strong identification"[52] of the mass of citizen spectators with the chorus also occasioned the citizens' enactment of a claim to intellectual capability. The chorus took up a highly demanding task, the performance of which implicitly confirmed the intellectual capacities of audience members because a large number of citizen spectators would have, at some time in their lives, themselves been in a dramatic chorus. Each year, a substantial number of citizens was selected—we do not know how—to participate as the chorus in the Dionysian festival. Citizens always formed the chorus not only for the choral competitions but also for tragedy and comedy.

[47] Rehm, *Greek Tragic Theater*, pp. 20–30.

[48] Arnott, *Public and Performance*, p. 11.

[49] Rehm, *Greek Tragic Theater*, p. 45.

[50] Arnott, *Public and Performance*, p. 11.

[51] Since the idea of a "participating" rather than a passive audience may have already been present in the practice of epic poetry (see Richard Martin, *The Language of Heroes* [Ithaca: Cornell University Press, 1989], p. 232), it is possible that the democratic city found elaboration of the role of the audience in newly developing forms of oral performance created for a contest (tragedy and comedy) both easy and effective for fashioning emergent democratic norms.

[52] Oddone Longo, "The Theater of the Polis," in Winkler and Zeitlin, eds., *Nothing to Do with Dionysos*, pp. 12–19. Also see P. Easterling, "Form and Performance," in Easterling, ed., *The Cambridge Companion to Greek Tragedy*, pp. 151–77.

These citizens were ordinary citizen volunteers, not professional orators or actors. A dithyrambic chorus traditionally had fifty members, a tragic chorus consisted of twelve or fifteen, and a chorus in comedy might have had as many as twenty-four members. As there were five groups of boys and five of men competing in dithyramb, and a different chorus for each tragic trilogy and for each comic poet, about 600 Athenian males received choral training as part of the preparation for a single Dionysia.[53] Rehearsals probably took up the better part of a year as these men trained hard for the performances.[54] Choral training was the largest part of the production process. It was the major expense and required the most time-consuming rehearsals.[55]

The Athenians explicitly identified choral training as part of men's education. Aristophanes indicates that good politicians are educated through physical training in the palestra and music and choruses (*Frogs* 729). Plato treats as uncontroversial the suggestion that "the uneducated man will in our view be the one untrained in choral performances and the educated ought to be set down as the one sufficiently trained in choral performances" (*Laws* 654a). To the extent that these citizens performed this central role in each production well, they advertised their own capacities. When the herald proclaimed, "Bring on your chorus," to mark the start of the performances, we can presume that utterance meant more than, "Let the performance begin." It meant something like, "Show us (citizens) your (poet) skill at teaching." It might even have suggested something like, "Bring on your lesson," where "lesson" referred not only to the substantive themes and point of the play but also to the embodiment of the poet/director's lesson—the well-trained chorus.[56]

That the Athenians regarded the poets as teachers of adults is not news.[57] The technical term for dramatic poets chosen to produce plays was *didaskaloi*, from the verb *didaskō* ("to instruct"). The occasion of the City Dionysia highlighted the playwrights' roles both as teachers of the chorus

---

[53] Choral competitions as well as dramatic performances were part of other festivals as well. The total number of Athenians who would receive choral training in any given year was therefore significant. See Glenn Morrow, *Plato's Cretan City* (Princeton: Princeton University Press, 1960), pp. 311–12.

[54] Arnott, *Public and Performance*, p. 23. We should bear in mind that dramatic performers, much like athletes, were engaged in a dangerous competition for honor and thus were probably highly motivated to perform well. See also Bruce Heiden, "Emotion, Acting and the Athenian Ethos," in Sommerstein et al., eds., *Tragedy, Comedy and the Polis*, p. 150.

[55] Rehm, *Greek Tragic Theater*, p. 25.

[56] There may also be a strong identification between political leaders (orators) and principal actors. Demosthenes and Aeschines both had close ties to the theater. See Ober, *Mass and Elite*, pp. 154–55.

[57] See, for example, Aristophanes *Frogs* 1054–55.

and as educators of the polis in general. As Rehm has stressed, "The Greek phrase for directing a play was *didaskein choron*, 'to teach a chorus.' The list of victors in the dramatic competitions was called the *didaskaliai*, indicating that the prizes were given for directing and not for writing." Rehm captures the extraordinary learning experience citizens enjoyed when they served as tragic-chorus members:

> [The poet/director] work[ed] with a group of players to bring together music, movement, and a highly literate and demanding text. A good deal of learning took place via oral repetition, since it cannot be assumed that the performers could read. . . . The choral melodies were taught by ear . . . the patterns of dance must have been worked out "on their feet." . . . The same twelve performers . . . played the chorus in all four plays—three tragedies and a satyr-play—composed by a given tragedian. To get a sense of what this meant in practice, consider Aeschylus' production of the *Oresteia* in 458 b.c. The same group of performers appeared as a chorus of Argive Elders in *Agamemnon*, a group of captured slave-women in *Chorephori*, the terrifying spirits of vengeance called the Furies in *Eumenides*, and a band of (presumably) randy satyrs in the last satyr-play, *Proteus*. Not only were the masks, costumes, and personae different, but the style of movement, the music, the level and quality of emotion, and countless other factors shifted from play to play. Since there was only one performance, the chorus were compelled to master a wide range of material without the benefit of preview audiences.[58]

Of course, "No one disputes the experience of play-going at the Dionysia was supposed to be broadly educational, a school for citizenship in the Athenian democracy."[59] I am proposing that the spectators experienced the chorus not only as a medium through which the poet's words reached, unsettled, and thereby educated them, but also as a living symbol of the capacity of the poet/director to instruct his fellows and of the citizens themselves to think and learn in concert with others.

By attending and participating in the dramatic performances, and by considering such activities as much a part of Athenian political life as serving on a jury or fighting in battle, the Athenians acted out an idealized image of citizenship that highlighted the citizens' intellectual agility and strong-mindedness. The ritual practice of theater-going implied that Athenians do not crumble in the face of criticism, nor do they collapse when confronted by painful and probing questions. This account of the

[58] Rehm, *Greek Tragic Theater*, p. 26.

[59] Paul Cartledge, "The Greek Religious Festivals," in *Greek Religion and Society*, ed. P. E. Easterling and J. V. Muir (Cambridge: Cambridge University Press, 1985), pp. 126–27. See also Goldhill, "The Audience of Athenian Tragedy," pp. 66–67.

symbolic import of some of the rituals of the Festival of Dionysus can illuminate Pericles' boast in the funeral oration that Athenians are lovers "of wisdom without softness."[60] His own explanation, one that stresses the links between thought and action, makes a little more sense in juxtaposition with the rituals' symbolism. Pericles continues, "In our enterprises we present the singular spectacle of daring and deliberation, each carried to its highest point, and both united in the same persons, although with the rest of mankind decision is the fruit of ignorance, hesitation of reflection" (Thucydides 2.40.3). In each venue, he emphasizes, both thought and action are united: knowledge produces not hesitation and softness (*malakias*) but daring (*tolma*).

It is plausible that the practice of theater-going helped citizens develop "the mental infrastructure"[61] that facilitated the conduct of the mental work they had to perform in the Assembly and courts. First, it afforded citizens an opportunity to become comfortable with and sophisticated about the interpretation of fictionalized material. In the theater, citizens performed the mental task of divorcing the man from the argument, the actor from the mask. This is important because it enabled citizens to gain some critical distance from the actual elite status of a politician and accept him in the role of an advisor to the people.[62] Most often stressed is the possibility that the theater nourished a citizen's "capacity to act with foresight and judge with insight" by exposing him to depictions of the frightening possibilities that inhere in the complexities of everyday life.[63] I would add that the physically demanding aspect of theater attendance was significant. The audience at a City Dionysia attended five performances on a single day (tragic trilogy, satyr play, and a comedy) in the open air and sun—and did this three days in a row. Perhaps by bringing people to the limits of physical comfort and of mental concentration, the theater-going experience unsettled normal ways of thinking. This physical experience helped the audience gain the remove necessary for the mental venture of imagining the unimaginable.

This view of the relationship between the dramatic performances and democratic citizenship suggests that we see the safety of an extremely patriotic setting (the festival) as permitting the theatai to become engrossed in plays with painful content, as allowing them to achieve the remove necessary for critical thinking, and ultimately as encouraging a more critically self-aware embrace of democratic structures. This is, in

---

[60] *Philosophoumen aneu malakias* at 2.40.1. Translation from P. J. Rhodes, *Thucydides Book 2, Edited Greek Text, Translation and Commentary* (Warmister: Aris and Philips, 1988).

[61] Meier, *Political Art*, p. 4.

[62] Ober, *Mass and Elite*, pp. 152–55.

[63] J. Peter Euben, "Introduction," in idem, ed., *Greek Tragedy and Political Theory*, p. 23.

part, the case.[64] But this is not the whole story. If my reading of the symbolic import of the Athenian behavior in the theater is right, then the Athenians enact in the theater a model of a deeply engaged citizen/deliberator, not one of a citizen distinguished by the measure of intellectual detachment he can achieve. Theater rituals do not suggest that the Athenians understood themselves to be moving between arenas, honing skills in one (theater) that were especially useful in another (Assembly). Rather, it suggests that they understood the "mental venture of politics"[65] to be seamless, inclusive; that thought and action take place in all these venues. The activity of citizens in the theater honed intellectual skills and enacted a celebration of citizens' capacities for reflection, but it did so in intimate partnership with an enactment of the connectedness of precisely this work to practical concerns. Theater rituals reined in the part intellectual detachment might play in the practice of Athenian democratic citizenship, especially in deliberative arenas.

Reciprocity and strong-mindedness are not often thought to be central norms of Athenian democratic politics. This is to the detriment of our understanding of Athenian civic ideology. A glorification of almost selfless devotion to the "state" is as wrong-headed an interpretation of the Athenian image of proper relations between democratic citizens and the city as is the view that the Athenians embraced radical individualism.[66] Similarly wrong is the presumption that the Athenian democracy embraced the notion of the rule of men who were intellectually unremarkable, let alone "unschooled." Rather, the ritual activity insistently involved both city and citizens enacting their strivings to sustain relations of mutual benefaction, to form a unified whole, and to recognize that ordinary citizens have capable minds.

[64] Charles Segal crisply elaborates the point: "The tragic performance itself exists in a kind of contradiction. . . . As part of the civic ritual of Athens, the performances in the theater of Dionysus affirm the social order at a state-sponsored occasion in a public and holy place. Tragedy also endorses that order through its lofty poetic language, traditional and dignified, through the elaborateness of the state-financed costumes and the discipline of the dancers, and through the choral odes, which often celebrate the city or the moral and heroic values of the city or comment upon the action from the point of view of ordinary citizens. Yet the narrative material of the myths that tragedy dramatizes shockingly violates this order with the most feared and abominated pollutions: matricide, incest, patricide, fratricide, madness. The actual *content* of these works denies what their ritual *context* affirms." *Dionysiac Poetics and Euripides' Bacchae* (Princeton: Princeton University Press, 1982), p. 14. Emphasis in original.

[65] Meier, *Political Art*, p. 43.

[66] Clifford Orwin also challenges this assumption. Commenting on the Periclean funeral oration, he writes: "Pericles sketches a society in which the fullest development of the citizen is compatible with the greatest devotion to the city. . . . Athens sacrifices neither citizen to city nor vice versa." *Humanity*, p. 16, also see pp. 22–23.

The rituals of the City Dionysia were hardly anomalous in stressing these ideals. The preceding chapters have also shown that these were key elements of the Athenian democratic imaginary. I have examined these features of the Athenian self-understanding and political life not only to deepen our understanding of Athenian democratic life, but also to set up a new context within which to read Plato's political thought. It is to this project that I turn in the chapters that follow.

PART TWO

Plato's Democratic
Entanglements

Chapter Five

UNSETTLING THE ORTHODOXY

Familiarity with the features of the Athenian political imaginary detailed in the preceding chapters makes it possible to recognize the textured nature of the relationship of Plato's thought, especially his depiction of philosophic labor, to the Athenian democratic tradition. Plato's writings unquestionably urge readers to adopt a highly skeptical attitude toward democracy. They counsel us to look beyond the powerful allure of democracy, that is, to be constantly on guard lest we become attached to democracy in a manner reminiscent of a pitifully infatuated lover's attachment to a beloved. But they also contain hesitations, caveats, and reconsiderations regarding the reach and conclusiveness of the critique of democracy as well as outright appropriations for philosophy of elements of Athenian democratic discourse.

PHILOSOPHER AS TYRANT-SLAYER

Plato disputes the popular characterization of the philosopher as at best politically useless, and at worst a corrupting influence on the young[1] in part by grafting the outline of the story of the tyrant-slayers Harmodius and Aristogeiton onto his presentation of the philosopher's activities, especially in the *Republic*. Plato submits that the philosopher is the most vigilant and effective subduer of menacing tyrants (in the soul and the city), a liberator from civic ills and founder of a just regime, a model civic benefactor, and one whose erotic attachments (to philosophy and truth) prove the salvation of the city. While these features of his thought are well-known, the stunning parallel with the imagined excellence of Harmodius and Aristogeiton enshrined in Athenian myth is not. Recognizing that Plato connects his philosophical and political project with democratic antityrantism does not, of course, entail judging him to be a democrat. It does, however, direct us to confusingly interrelated parts of his thought. Indeed, tracking the parallel between the tyrant-slayers and the philosopher further, we see that it structures Plato's understanding of the problem of democracy. The parallel extends to the portrait of the development of tyranny from democracy in *Republic* Books 8 and 9. Plato's depiction of democracy as exquisitely vulnerable to collapse into tyranny does not

---

[1] Most famously in Aristophanes' *Clouds*.

explain the dynamics of Athenian history, nor does it address the variety of changes that have occurred in actual regimes. Aristotle complains about this feature of *Republic* 8, pointing out that the history of Greek cities shows that regimes change form in all directions and for reasons more diverse that Plato has Socrates speak of in *Republic* 8 (*Politics* 1316a1–b30).[2] But it does address head-on a key element of the Athenian imaginary. It engages Athenian preoccupations with the threat of tyranny and especially the conceit driving the Athenians' veneration of Harmodius and Aristogeiton. The popular myth celebrates Harmodius and Aristogeiton as having made Athens *isonomos*, that is, a place of political equality and responsible ruling—most of all, a place of resilience in the face of aspirants to tyranny. Plato locates the excellence of philosophic rule in *its* organic attachment to the exercise of power in a responsible, nonabusive manner. Plato's moral and political philosophy also envisions a form of tyranny that democracy cannot equip citizens to repel. Somewhat paradoxically, Plato represents taking up philosophy and empowering it politically as the embodiment of one's traditional duty as a democratic citizen to be a "tyrant-hater and killer rather than admirer and emulator."[3] The parallel works in another way as well. The popular myth also idealizes a reciprocal relationship between citizens and city. While Thucydides is at pains to undermine the imagined coincidence of a self's public and private interests, Plato appropriates the ideal. He reduces the conflict between an individual's civic duty and personal concerns by identifying both with properly caring for one's soul. Plato represents the project of philosophy as at once both continuous and discontinuous with that of Athenian democracy at the level of the imaginary.

These links to the Athenian myth of the tyrannicide are too general to establish that Athenian democratic discourse had a substantial impact on Plato's thought.[4] In the chapters to follow, I recover and explore in detail

---

[2] It does resonate with the Sicilian experience of tyranny; see the discussion of Finley below.

[3] Kurt A. Raaflaub, "Stick and Glue: The Function of Tyranny in Fifth-Century Athenian Democracy," in *Popular Tyranny*, ed. Kathryn Morgan (in preparation).

[4] Plato explicitly mentions the tyrannicide myth in only two places in the entire corpus. Pausanias appeals to the traditional version in his eulogy of Eros in the *Symposium* (182c), and Socrates delivers a fanciful retelling of it at *Hipparchus* (229b-d). The part of the *Hipparchus* in Plato's examination of the contours of the Athenian ideal of coincidence of private and public concerns is the subject of my current research. I argue that Plato addresses the import of the myth in both the Athenian imaginary and Thucydides' *History*, and that Friedlander is correct to see this work as a very early Platonic dialogue. On the *Hipparchus*, see the translation by Steven Forde and interpretative essay by Allan Bloom in *The Roots of Political Philosophy: Ten Forgotten Socratic Dialogues*, ed. Thomas Pangle (Ithaca: Cornell University Press, 1987); Paul Friedlander, *Plato 2*, trans. from the German by Hans

Plato's explicit and sustained appropriation for philosophy of three peculiarly democratic strategies of civic discourse: *parrhēsia* (frank speaking), *epitaphios logos* (encomiastic public funeral oratory), and being a *theatēs* (theater-goer). In this chapter, I take up questions that are preliminary to that enterprise. I examine the aspects of Plato and his work that are often taken to support the orthodox reading of the philosopher as a notorious antidemocrat, including his elite personal background, his dismay over the fate of Socrates, his disdain for the common man, his recommendation in the *Republic* of a positive political doctrine marked by autocratic institutions, his actual founding of an exclusive institution at Athens (the Academy), and the experimental tenor of his personal involvement in Syracusan politics. None stand scrutiny.

THE MATTER OF BIAS

I will not reduce Plato's words to an expression of the biases of his family or class.[5] Biographical information can certainly help us interpret a text. But as far as we know, democratic leaders of the fifth and early fourth centuries were also from affluent or highly placed families.[6] In addition, Plato's work radically challenges the foundations of his culture, including key beliefs associated with his class.

Regarding an assumed "oligarchic bias," we need only note that Plato's writings are indeed unambivalently opposed to granting special political standing to a few on the basis of their exceptional wealth; that is, they oppose oligarchy.[7] This is sometimes obscured by a mistaken way of reading the discussion of regimes in *Republic* Book 8. If one approaches this passage as a story of the decline of regimes rather than as a typology of regimes, oligarchy appears "closer to" the ideal city and, by implication, "better" than democracy. As it is proximate to tyranny, democracy appears "farthest removed from" the ideal city and therefore the "worst" regime. But, as Saxonhouse has recently stressed, a word for "decline" does not appear in the Book 8 passage. We instead hear of "changes" (*metaballei,*

Meyerhoff (New York: Bollingen Foundation, 1964), pp. 119–28; and the astute remarks of C. W. Fornara, "The 'Tradition' about the Murder of Hipparchus," *Historia* 17 (1968): 419 (note 71).

[5] Ellen M. Wood and Neal Wood come dangerously close to such a position in their *Class Ideology and Ancient Political Theory* (New York: Oxford University Press, 1978). They view Plato's "teaching" as a "product of an aristocratic mentality" (p. 126).

[6] Cleisthenes and Pericles were from elite families, and Demosthenes and Cleon were affluent.

[7] This point needs stressing because although specialists continue to drive the point home, the characterization has yet to take hold more broadly.

545d), "movement" (*kinēthēnai*, 545d), and "mistaken" (*hēmartēmenas*, 544a) regimes.[8] The language employed by Socrates at the opening of Book 5 supports the accuracy of Saxonhouse's observation. At this point, Socrates brings his description of the ideal city to a tentative close and attempts to move on to consider "the others," that is, other regimes (*tas allas*, 449a). Socrates calls his city in speech "good" and "right" (*agathēn* and *orthēn*, 449a1) and the others "bad and mistaken" (*kakas . . . kai hēm-artēmenas*, 449a). Socrates continues, trying to order the investigation to come. "There are four forms of badness" (*en tettarsi ponērias eidesin ousas*, 449a), he states bluntly, suggesting further that he speak of them simply "in the order that each appeared to me to pass from one to another" (*hekastai ex allēlon metabainein*, 449b). He says nothing about the order of their relative merit. Socrates' partners in discourse do not let him proceed, of course, demanding that he explain his earlier passing remarks about the "community of wives" practiced by the guardians. Socrates does not return to the matter of the "other" regimes until Book 8.

The portrait of the oligarchic city in *Republic* Book 8 is not one that stresses its proximity to the ideal but, more accurately, one that highlights "misery and division."[9] The portrait of democracy, coming after that of oligarchy, emphasizes its pleasures and attractions. Saxonhouse elaborates on her important observation thus:

> The move to democracy is not a "decline." It is a blessing, with the extremes of poverty and the evils associated with oligarchy left behind and the divisions between rich and poor surmounted. To achieve this, though, there must be the violent overthrow of the oligarchic regime. . . . After the violence of the transition to democracy, we arrive at a regime of softness and gentleness, no longer plagued by faction and without compulsion.[10]

Socrates describes democracy, at least initially, as making possible a life that is colorful, beautiful, attractive, easy, gentle. Due to the freedom it encourages, democracy is also exquisitely vulnerable to some problematic tendencies. Nevertheless, judging from the account of the quality of life enjoyed by citizens, democracy is a marked improvement over oligarchy.[11] Even though in democracy the many are undisciplined and without standards (making it exceedingly difficult for them to sort through the myriad opportunities before them and therefore making them unable consistently

---

[8] Arlene Saxonhouse, "Democracy, Equality, and *Eidē*: A Radical View from Book 8 of Plato's *Republic*," *American Political Science Review* 92, no. 2 (June 1998): 273–83, at p. 274.

[9] Ibid., p. 278.

[10] Ibid.

[11] Plato never defends the rich against the poor, the wealthy class against the needy class.

to pursue virtue), the situation in oligarchy is worse. In oligarchy, a few systematically and with great conceit pursue wealth. In oligarchy a powerful elite enshrines the wrong standard and reduces the remaining mass of people to beggars.

Plato does, of course, advocate a form of "aristocracy" (rule of the "best men") in the *Republic*. But he does not conflate oligarchy and aristocracy. Rather, he is constantly at pains to delineate the proper criteria for setting some small set of men apart from the rest, that is, for marking them as "best men" and entrusting them with political power. He mercilessly robs of any claim to be a significant factor not only simple citizenship status (democracy's criterion) and wealth (oligarchy's criterion), but also nobility of birth, family status, and physical beauty (traditional aristocracy's criteria).[12] He constantly insists that only the capacity to attain knowledge is relevant. This capacity is, moreover, rigorously trained, checked, and tested in all potential philosophers (and thus rulers) until their fiftieth year (*Republic* 540a–b). Only then are philosophers required to use their knowledge of the Good, each in turn, as "a pattern for ordering city, private men, and themselves for the rest of their lives" (540b). I am not trying to escape some of the elitist implications of Plato's view. Rather,

---

[12] For an opposing view, see Jennifer Tolbert Roberts, *Athens on Trial: The Antidemocratic Tradition in Western Thought* (Princeton: Princeton University Press, 1994), pp. 84–86. She suggests that Plato "was distinctively a Greek aristocrat who shared numerous traditional convictions with the bulk of his class" (p. 85). But the convictions she identifies with the elite were hardly theirs alone. She names a "blithe acceptance of slavery; an inability to see a political structure larger than the polis; a preoccupation with physical beauty . . .; a strong belief in heredity; and a disdain for manual labor" (ibid.). To some extent, each of these was shared by the mass of Athenians. For example, even men of modest income owned household slaves, and the demos as a political body collectively owned slaves and strenuously resisted granting citizenship to manumitted former slaves when presented with such a proposal. Further, what larger political structures did the democrats embrace, or even dare to imagine (besides empire, which was embraced by the elite as well)? In addition, consider Plato's panhellenic sympathies in his discussion of the ideal city's treatment of other Greeks in times of war (*Republic* 470e–471c). And were any Greeks not preoccupied with physical beauty? Consider Pericles urging the Athenians to gaze upon the city as if its lover, as discussed in Chapter Three. This surely suggests that an appeal to alluring beauty resonated with the demos. Furthermore, the Athenians of all classes shared a strong belief in the principle of heredity, though aristocrats extended it to domains of life that the democrats opposed. For example, citizenship was a birthright; there was no usual naturalization process that even lifelong residents like metics could initiate. Moreover, regarding Plato's provisions for the reproduction of the three groups in his ideal city of the *Republic*, his reliance on eugenics and specific mention of the possibility of "social mobility" highlights that the criteria for membership in the guardian group is intellectual capability, not birth. He treats heredity as an expedient, not as a foolproof method for identifying bright children and a sure source of rights. Disdain for manual labor is an aristocratic conviction both in the sense of being held by this group and in the sense of serving their material interests. Plato's expression of it is tempered, however, by his regular interest in craft analogies.

it is essential to identify his view's distance from the contemporary ideology of oligarchy as well as aristocracy and democracy.[13] Plato thoroughly divests the contemporary notions of "best men" of any of its usual content.

One might object that after the discussion of the tyrannical soul in Book 9, Glaucon does indeed rank the various regimes of soul according to their possession of happiness, and that he does so in response to Socrates' explicit request for him to do so (580b). This passage cannot bear the necessary interpretative weight. Socrates' response to Glaucon's ordering ignores the positions two, three, and four (timocratic, oligarchic, and democratic). He is talking only of Glaucon's good sense in identifying the just soul as happiest and the tyrannical one as most wretched. Socrates does not endorse the entire ranking. Plato here leaves room for his readers to consider the relative attractions of the other regimes. Armed with these models, readers are now better equipped to evaluate their own societies and others with which they might have some lived experience.

DISMAY OVER THE FATE OF SOCRATES

Plato was of course profoundly troubled by the injustice of the condemnation and execution of Socrates.[14] But there are several reasons to hesitate before taking his account of the unsurprising character of this turn of events (*Gorgias* 521d) to mean that he proposed a necessary and complete opposition between philosophy and democracy. First, entering politics at Athens was a risky endeavor for anyone, not just a philosopher. Plato has Socrates stress this in the *Gorgias*. To be a true political player is, he argues in this text, actively to care for the well-being of the Athenians, something he claims he does in a fashion superior to that of the most celebrated rival pairs of political leaders of the Athenians—Pericles and Cimon, Themistocles and Miltiades. Unlike Socrates, Plato suggests, these leaders did not attempt to modify citizens' passions but only to make them even wilder or more effective in their pursuit of their desires. Nevertheless, every one

---

[13] For the conventional ideology of oligarchy, see "Old Oligarch", *Constitution of the Athenians*.

[14] The relation of the historical Socrates to Athenian democracy has received considerable attention in recent years. See Introduction, note 23 above, for references. I am persuaded that Socrates' own moral views, to judge from the evidence of Plato's texts, were in significant but not all ways democratic, that his relation to the democracy was highly complex, and that his views may have been easily misinterpreted during the difficult times following the end of the Peloponnesian War. See W. Robert Connor, "The Other 399: Religion and the Trial of Socrates," in *Georgica: Greek Studies in Honor of George Cawkwell, Bulletin*, suppl. 58 (London: Institute of Classical Studies, 1991), pp. 49–56.

of them was punished by the Athenians. Socrates recalls: "At the end of Pericles' life, they [the Athenians] convicted him of theft, and nearly condemned him to death" (516a). He continues:

> Didn't [the Athenians] ostracize [Cimon] so that they wouldn't hear his voice for ten years? And didn't they do the same to Themistocles, and punish him with exile as well? And Miltiades of Marathon—didn't they vote to throw him into the pit, and but for the *prutanis* wouldn't they have thrown him in? (516d–e)

Socrates adds: "And perhaps they'll seize on you [Callicles], if you're not careful, and on my companion Alcibiades" (519b). Plato does not have Socrates stress that only good men are likely to perish if they enter political life, or that as a philosopher Socrates is at greater risk of being the target of some action than anyone else. Rather, he emphasizes that there is a haphazard quality to life in the democratic city. There is no way of predicting how the demos will treat anyone.

A key passage is Socrates' response in the *Gorgias* to Callicles' suggestion that Socrates seems strangely confident that none of the things that happened to these celebrated leaders will happen to him. Socrates says: "I am really senseless, Callicles, if I don't think that anything might happen to anyone in this city" (*anoētos ara eimi, ō Kallikleis, hōs alēthōs, ei mē oiomai en tēide tēi polei hontinoun an hoti tuxoi, touto pathein*, 521c.). What follows is Socrates' account of why it is that, should it come to pass that he is brought before a court, he considers it likely that he will be misjudged and draw the most severe punishment, death. There is no necessity that the philosopher will be the target of some political attack. Indeed, the Athenians tolerated Socrates for decades, as it did the Academy of Plato.[15] What Socrates stresses is that should the philosopher be summoned to give an account of his life to the demos, grave misunderstandings are likely.

In *Letter 7*,[16] Plato reiterates that chance (*tuchē*) and misunderstandings played central roles in the attack on and death of Socrates. Writing about

---

[15] For discussion of an Assembly decree forbidding philosophers from setting up a school at Athens years after Plato's death in the year 307 and its annulment in the courts the following year, see P. A. Brunt, "Plato's Academy and Politics," in his *Studies in Greek History and Thought* (New York: Oxford University Press, 1993), pp. 314–34 at Appendix A.

[16] The authenticity of *Letter 7* and *Letter 8* is generally accepted, though debate goes on. The following views are representative: Glenn Morrow, *Studies in the Platonic Epistles*, with a translation and notes, *Illinois Studies in Language and Literature* 18, nos. 3–4 (Urbana: University of Illinois, 1935); J. Harward, *The Platonic Epistles*, trans. with intro. and notes (New York: Arno, 1976); Ludwig Edelstein, *Plato's Seventh Letter*, *Philosophia Antiqua* 14 (Leiden: E. J. Brill, 1966). Most recently: Robert Brumbaugh argues that methodological and stylistic aspects of the text of *Letter 7* "come close to certainty in establishing the *Letter*'s authenticity" ("Digression and Dialectic: The *7th Letter* and Plato's Literary Form," in *Pla-*

the closing years of the Peloponnesian War, and in particular the period in which Socrates was tried and condemned, he says:

> Now many deplorable things occurred during those troubled days, and it is not surprising that under cover of the revolution too many old enmities were avenged; but in general those who returned from exile acted with great restraint. By some chance (*kata de tina tuchēn*), however, certain powerful persons brought to court this same friend Socrates [who had refused to arrest Leon on orders of the Thirty], preferring against him a most shameless accusation, and one which he, of all men, least deserved" (*pantōn hēkista Sōkratei prosēkousan*, 325b–c).[17]

The inclusion of "by some chance" focuses attention on the haphazard quality of politics of the period, as does the dramatic juxtaposition of "many deplorable things" and "acted with great restraint." In addition, the description of Socrates as a man who "least deserved" his fate echoes Thucydides' language praising Nicias as a man who, "of all the Hellenes in my time, least deserved his fate" (*hēkista dē axios ōn tōn ge ep' emou Ellēnōn es touto dustuchias*, 7.86.5). What could be accomplished by inviting a comparison of the fate of Socrates with the Thucydidean account of the fate of Nicias, an Athenian general and rival of Cleon and Alcibiades who perished horribly in Sicily? In addition to depicting Nicias as opposed to aggressive imperialism,[18] Thucydides presents him suffering "the most extreme peripety of fortune,"[19] despite his own efforts to be cautious and prepared. Plato's language alludes to this feature of the Thucydidean understanding of Nicias as a reminder that Socrates' fate was similarly a result, at least in part, of happenstance. Plato here treats Socrates' death as evidence for the disorderliness of democratic politics—not for its essential nastiness.

A passage in the *Statesman* raises more questions about the impact the death of Socrates had on Plato's view of the necessary nature of democracy. Here the fate of the historical Socrates did not prevent Plato from having the Eleatic Stranger explicitly argue in Socrates' company that of all the likely-to-exist, flesh-and-blood regimes, democracy is best because it is least capable of perpetrating great evil (303a–d). This passage warrants

---

tonic Writings/Platonic Readings, ed. Charles Griswold [New York: Routledge, 1988], p. 91) and Brunt considers the depiction of Plato's politics and concerns in *Letter 7* to be accurate ("Plato's Academy and Politics"). See also Josiah Ober, *Political Dissent in Democratic Athens* (Princeton: Princeton University Press, 1998), pp. 162–65.

[17] The *Menexenus* voices the same judgment (244a).

[18] Nicias was concerned to preserve empire and Socrates opposed such a goal totally, so I do not want to make too much of this link.

[19] Walter Schmid, *On Manly Courage: A Study of Plato's* Laches (Carbondale: Southeastern Illinois Press, 1992), p. 7.

careful analysis. The interlocutors in the *Statesman* are discussing the relative merits of imperfect, actually existing regimes. The Eleatic Stranger expresses reasons for a qualified acceptance of democracy for political life. The passage's modest praise of democracy attributes the attraction of this form to its being the weakest and least dangerous of known regimes—that is, to the likelihood that it affords the best protection against tyranny. A democratic regime, the Stranger points out, is least capable of perpetrating great evil, even if it is also least capable of achieving greatness. The rule of the many, he says, "is weak in all respects . . . because under it offices are distributed in small portions among many people" (*Statesman* 303a). This argument contrasts with the argument in *Republic* that democracy precisely does not provide adequate protection from the dangers of self-serving leaders and mob action, that is, that democracy breeds tyranny. But the passage is also striking for the way it directly engages the Athenian civic self-image.

According to the patriotic view, democracy does not promise perfect, errorless rule. Rather, it promises that ordinary life will be less oppressive and more pleasant here than in other known regimes. We found these themes in Pericles' funeral oration as well as in Otanes' praise of democracy in Herodotus' "Debate on the Constitutions." These themes also form the grounds on which the *Statesman* passage delivers its qualified praise of democracy.

This passage has much in common with Otanes' argument in Herodotus. Both turn on a suspicion of power. In Herodotus' account, Otanes proposes that because power will tempt even the most virtuous man, it is prudent to rely on the wide distribution of power, and not on the strength of a man's character—that is, on his virtue—to insure that power is exercised responsibly. Similarly, it is dangerous, he says, to recognize formally any claim to superior competence, because such a claim will foster hubris and therefore invite arbitrary, ill-considered, and self-interested ruling. Popular government ensures moderate rule, he suggests, because by relying on the lot and rotation it recognizes no special claims when it invests someone with power, and it counteracts the dangerous effects of even this power by holding all officers to account, and conducting deliberations in the open. The thrust of Otanes' argument is that a wide distribution of power best protects against its abuse. The *Statesman* passage delivers a noticeably similar account, proposing that in the absence of a man of perfect wisdom and virtue in whose hands power could be trusted (301c5–d3), and assuming that the regimes lack good written law codes (good from a scientific, philosophic point of view), life will be least difficult (302b5) in a democratic regime. In a contest with monarchy and oligarchy, democracy should, for these reasons, win the support of thoughtful and reasonable people.

But although the *Statesman* passage expresses a certain measure of agreement with the Athenian understanding of the attraction of democracy, it also delivers fierce criticism of that understanding. The Athenians prided themselves on their lawfulness. They praised their constitution for its grounding in the rule of law and in the reasonableness of individual citizens. Yet the praise of democracy in the *Statesman* asserts that democracy is only the best of the imperfect regimes likely to exist; it defines these regimes as *lawless* or, more accurately, as poorly ordered, that is, as possessing badly designed legal codes. Praising democracy as the least dangerous regime does not entail celebrating the laws that characterize existing democracies, most importantly Athens. Quite the contrary. Democracy's attractions, as described, derive from a prior recognition of the poor quality of its legal codes as a whole.[20]

The passage thus does not function to present a doctrine about democracy at odds with those expressed in other places; rather, it raises questions about the adequacy of the laws that characterize democratic societies. It asks the reader to scrutinize those laws. I propose that we read the tensions regarding democracy in the *Statesman* passage as representing Plato's appreciation of the difficulty of passing a final, single judgment on so complex a phenomenon as democratic government and ways of life. Instead of presenting a settled view, this dialogue works to unsettle the reader in a particular way. The straightforward criticisms of democracy would be likely to upset anyone comfortable with an existing democratic state of affairs. The explicit expressions of acceptance shake the confidence of a dedicated opponent of democracy. The dialogue disturbs the reader in both ways simultaneously. Thus the *Statesman* passage exemplifies the complexity of the treatment of democracy in Plato's texts.

DISDAIN FOR THE COMMON MAN

Plato's dialogues are consistently and unequivocally opposed to the institution of majority rule. Unlike Aristotle, Plato has little confidence that a widely held opinion is likely to have more merit than a minority view, or even a view held by one alone.[21] He holds fast to the notion that there is a body of knowledge and a set of technical skills the possession of

---

[20] Glenn Morrow demonstrates that in the *Laws*, Plato draws on specific Athenian democratic laws in his development of the legal code for a hypothetical new city. Certain laws of democratic Athens have merit, especially when balanced by laws of a different cast. Plato crafts a "mixed constitution" for his hypothetical Cretan city. *Plato's Cretan City: An Historical Interpretation of Plato's* Laws (Princeton: Princeton University Press, 1990).

[21] *Politics* 1281a11. See Jeremy Waldron, "The Wisdom of the Multitude: Some Reflections on Book 3, Chapter 11 of Aristotle's *Politics*," *Political Theory* 23, no. 4 (1995): 563–84.

which enables an individual to think intelligently, indeed correctly, about political matters, and that good politics is about empowering this knowledge. Moreover, and this time like Aristotle, he expects physical and other forms of economically driven labor to retard the development of one's reason and, thus, one's intellectual sophistication and capacity to exercise political power responsibly. He expects such a person to be too thoroughly enmeshed in private concerns to be able to adopt the perspective of the whole (whole self or whole city). Nevertheless, Plato's thought is not entirely dismissive of the intellect of the common man. To bring this feature of his thought to the fore, we must distinguish between Plato's unequivocal opposition to majority rule as a strategy for achieving responsible ruling and his putative disdain for the intelligence of the common man.

Three parables in the *Republic* seem to suggest that Plato had no confidence at all in the mental capacities of ordinary men. The parable of the ship (488a–e) depicts the captain/demos as slow-witted and vulnerable to the shrewd, self-interested leading crewmen/politicians eager for control over the resources of the ship/polis. It portrays the captain/demos and crew/politicians as unable to recognize the man truly capable of intelligent leadership, the navigator/philosopher, seeing him only as a stargazer. Socrates also likens the mass of citizens to a wild beast that can be calmed only by tending to its appetite (493b–c). Perhaps most damning, however, Socrates argues that the "biggest [i.e., worst] sophist" is not any individual of that description but the many when they sit down together "in assemblies, courts, theaters, army camps, or any other common meeting of a multitude" (492a–c). These parables do point to a weakness of democratic regimes—its reliance on majority rule, which Plato construes as a form of rule by force. But to take the parables as dismissive of ordinary men in general is to fail to attend to two complexities.

First, such an interpretation is "profoundly inconsistent with the Socrates of other dialogues, a Socrates who is committed to the possibilities of educating the individual, to talking to all who will listen, be they citizens or foreigners, old or young, male or female (e.g., *Apology* 23b)."[22] Socrates does indeed display this disposition in the *Republic* as well. At 518c–d Socrates interprets the allegory of the cave as indicating that education is not like putting sight into blind eyes. Rather, he says, the story (*logos*) indicates that "this power [to know] is in the soul of each" (*tautēn tēn enousan hekastou dunamin en tēi psuchēi*) and education is a matter of

---

[22] Arlene Saxonhouse, *Athenian Democracy: Ancient Theorists and Modern Mythmakers* (Notre Dame, Ind.: University of Notre Dame Press, 1996), p. 89. She notes the unreflective way in which the parables are often cited as proof of Plato's disdain for the mental capacities of ordinary people.

directing and training the instrument with which each (*hekastos*) learns.[23]
Second, it is to fail to see that Socrates does not introduce these parables
simply to criticize ordinary men for their essential stupidity but rather to
explain why the mass of men tend to hold a negative opinion of philosophy. The parables attribute the opinion of the masses regarding philosophy to two things: the vulnerability of philosophy to slander and the
practice of reasoning in groups.

The parable of the ship stresses the vulnerability of philosophy to misunderstanding and, as a result, to a reputation for being politically useless.
When one does not understand the art of navigation, a man who spends
his time gazing up at the stars seems a useless passenger. The parable also
suggests a predicament that all the people on the boat share. How is a
navigator to demonstrate the importance of his skill, short of being given
the opportunity to practice it? The abstract nature of his knowledge makes
it difficult for him to convey to the captain and crew that he indeed knows
something relevant. For them even to fathom the value of the navigator,
they have to either learn navigation or experience a ship guided splendidly
under a navigator's direction. The parable does not portray the captain
and crew members as just plain stupid (though the crew is depicted as
malicious). It links the bad reputation of philosophy to something other
than the poor-quality minds of the many. It links it to their inexperience
and ignorance of justice. The parable casts the people, at least in part, as
victims of circumstances, not just as hopelessly dumb.[24]

The parables as well as other passages that register explicit criticisms of
democracy also do not denigrate the capabilities of people individually.
Rather, Socrates attacks the practice of addressing large groups on the
grounds that it is inhospitable to the process of education. In such settings,
it is easiest for men to be swayed by appeals to their unreflective appetites,
rather than by any careful effort to move them toward a critical understanding of their own best interest (*Republic* 493c–e). In the *Gorgias* Socrates states: "I know how to produce just one witness to whatever I say—
the man I am having a discussion with, whoever he may be. . . . I know
how to put the question to a vote to one man, but I don't even have a
dialogue with the many" (474a5–10). In addition, Socrates consistently
blames leaders trained by sophists, and not necessarily the people themselves, for the difficulties created and endured as the result of poor collective decisions. "The blame for the many's being harshly disposed toward
philosophy is," Socrates says, "on those men from outside who don't be-

---

[23] Cf. Allan Bloom, *The Republic of Plato, Translated with Notes and an Interpretive Essay* (New York: Basic, 1968), p. 465 n. 3.

[24] For a different reading of the ship parable, see Harvey Yunis, *Taming Democracy: Models of Political Rhetoric in Classical Athens* (Ithaca: Cornell University Press, 1996), p. 163.

long and have burst in like drunken revelers, abusing one another and indulging a taste for quarreling" (*Republic* 500b). The account of the metamorphosis of democracy into tyranny in *Republic* Book 8 also blames leaders for the troubles endured by the citizenry. Here Socrates argues that a democratic city ordinarily divides into three parts, which he identifies as the fierce political leaders, the wealthy, and the people. He portrays both the wealthy and the people as victims of the self-aggrandizing "leaders" (564d–565e), who misuse power to steal from both. In the *Crito* Socrates offers that while "the many" are capable of no great good, neither are they capable of great evil (44d–e). Plato's writings portray the majority of men as basically decent individuals who, when gathered in groups, become more inclined to follow their appetites due to the influence of rhetoricians, sophists, politicians, and poets. This view certainly attacks the wisdom of democratic political structures (large assemblies and majority rule), but it does not quite so severely question the mental capabilities of ordinary human beings. It points to the fragility of their mental capacities, rather than to their essential stupidity. This focus should be telling, for it is a limitation that, in Plato's portrayal, even those blessed with philosophic natures share with their less intellectually ambitious fellows. After all, Plato spends a great deal of time explaining why it is that even the most promising young minds can become corrupted. He even claims that it is such people who are likely responsible for the perpetration of great civic evils (*Republic* 491e–492a).

Turning to the *Laws*, we find a similar complaint about a crowd's capability to act intelligently (758b). But, in the imagined city of the *Laws*, where the political culture of the society protects citizens from "bad" influences, Plato is perfectly comfortable with unphilosophical ordinary men and women individually being entrusted with considerable—though not total—political power. In the city of the *Laws*, such people serve as magistrates of a dazzling variety and vote on the selection of important office-holders. As voting would not have been considered a democratic practice in Plato's time but rather a privilege granted to those considered worthy or especially able, extending the vote to ordinary people suggests a confidence in their capabilities, at least under certain circumstances.

THE "DOCTRINE" OF THE *REPUBLIC*

Another factor often taken to confirm the view that Plato's dialogues argue for a wholesale rejection of democracy is the profoundly autocratic character of the positive proposals recommended in the *Republic*. To question this view, we need not approach the images of highly centralized power, human breeding, and censorship, for example, with intellectual receptivity. Plato's favorable presentation of these ideas must be unaware of their future ominous form. Indeed, the *Republic* actually displays deep and abiding suspicion of absolute power.[25]

Plato's direct discussion of the philosopher-ruler was possibly even informed by his city's grappling with a raging issue of his time: how best to reduce or remove the threat of the abuse of power,[26] most dramatically symbolized by the threat of tyranny. Constitutional alterations in the direction of oligarchy—adopted by the Athenian demos in a frantic attempt to avert the installation of a foreign tyrant at the end of the Peloponnesian War—had proved disastrous. The Athenians suffered enormously under the rule of an ever more brutal and exclusive oligarchy, which came to be known as the rule of the "Thirty Tyrants." Abroad, Syracuse, a prosperous city that not long before had helped defeat the Athenian naval forces, had since become subject to the absolute rule of Dionysius I. Moses Finley describes the rise of Dionysius to power in terms that recall Plato's account of the rise of a tyrant in *Republic* Book 8. Finley tells us that Dionysius came to power "by demagogic appeals to the poorer classes" during a time of crisis.[27] The result was that "whatever spark of popular participation still existed in Sicilian politics at the end of the fifth century was snuffed out under Dionysius I. Henceforth, Sicilians were to be subjects rather than citizens; and all further political action took the form of destructive dynastic struggles, conspiracies and civil wars."[28] The *Republic* and the rest of Plato's dialogues explore the question of justice against this background of practical, immediate concern and with the Athenian conceit about being heirs to Harmodius and Aristogeiton in mind.

Plato argues that the emergence of democracy accompanied the identification of the appropriate aims of politics, but not the development of institutions that could deliver on this promise. Democratic institutions, he stresses in the *Republic*, will not meet or solve the problem of corruption and the attendant threat of tyranny. They cannot deliver the fine goal of responsible ruling, as Otanes has claimed in Herodotus' "Debate on the Constitutions." At first glance, Plato's strategy of meeting the challenge of

[25] Wolin noted this. He writes: "The argument for entrusting the philosopher with absolute power did not originate in a naive attitude towards the temptations of power, much less in the secret craving for *étatisme*. It came, instead, from two entirely blameless aims, the good of the whole and the avoidance of tyranny." Sheldon Wolin, *Politics and Vision* (Boston: Little, Brown, 1960), p. 55.

[26] Socrates explicitly criticizes democracy for allowing various forms of abuse of power to flourish despite its claim to insulate politics from the forces of corruption. As Derrida noted, in *Republic* Book 8 (555e), Plato argues that a "drawback of democracy lies in the role that capital is often allowed to play in it.""Plato's Pharmacy," in *Dissemination*, trans. Barbara Johnson (Chicago: University of Chicago Press, 1981), p. 82.

[27] M. I. Finley, *A History of Sicily* (London: Chatto and Windus, 1968), p. 75. Compare *Republic* 565a–566d.

[28] Finley, *A History of Sicily*, pp. 86–87.

corruption appears to rely heavily on the inner strength and good sense—that is, the "character"—of the individuals invested with the power to eradicate corruption. In this way, the city of the *Republic* does not seem to exhibit any interest in specifically democratic strategies of securing responsible rule. Rather, it appears more in tune with the manner in which proponents of oligarchy and monarchy "solve" the problem of corruption and threat of tyranny: they claim that the empowered elite are "the best men." And Plato at times describes the well-governed city as the true aristocracy, or the place where the "really rich rule, rich not in gold but in those riches required by the happy man, rich in a good and prudent life" (521a). Plato's adoption of the language of "best men" (even if it is emptied of all conventional, recognizable content) makes it easy to spot its nondemocratic aspect. But like the *Statesman* passage discussed above, the *Republic* also embraces a democratic insight into the problem of corruption. Socrates in the *Republic* relies in large measure on the design of social and political structures to minimize, ideally to eradicate, corruption.

Like the Athenians, Plato experiments with using institutional structures to prevent the persons entrusted with great power from abusing it. Athenian democracy tries parceling out political power in small portions (majority rule) and imposing multiple mechanisms of accountability on those who exercise small and large amounts of power (e.g., *dokimasia*, *euthunai*, *graphē paranomōn*, threat of dishonor, *atimia*, ostracisim, fines, secret ballot, assigning jury assignments and administrative duties by lot and rotation). Plato explores the possibility that different structures would more reliably generate responsible ruling. He focuses not on accountability or wide dispersal of power, but on the radical separation of the spheres of economic/private life and political life. Those who participate in commerce, consumption, and private family life will not have access to political power, and those who exercise political power will have no access to commerce, consumption, and private attachments. The radical separation of these spheres of life, articulated in the division of labor between the gold, silver, and bronze groups in city, addresses the material and psychic sources of corruption. In this city, bribery and nepotism should not be perennial problems. The guardians have gold in their souls and therefore no need of it in their pockets. They have an extended "family" and no need for special personal attachments. They have an understanding of the good of the whole and find their own contentment in its pursuit.

Plato's ideal regime would succeed not only at battling corruption but also at reducing the sources of civic conflict. Plato holds that in this regime, the bronze group will not yearn for political power any more than the guardians will yearn for affluence and personal lives (e.g., 466b–c). Why not? He seems to assume that the structure of the life of the guardians as well as the rigors of their education gives the laboring group reason to be confident that those charged with ruling will not be corrupt.[29] The laboring group will not, in Plato's view, desire involvement in politics chiefly because its participation is no longer tied to the achievement of responsible ruling (as it was in the view of Otanes in the Herodotean "Debate on the Constitutions"). But, he also implies, another reason they will not intensely desire political involvement, is that the life of ruling is not an apparently pleasant one. Those in the laboring group will believe that it is they, and not the guardians, who live the more pleasant lives. That is, they will have money and luxuries, a more unrestrained erotic life, and the personal pleasures and honors of households and families. The myth of the metals provides ideological justification for the laboring group's inclination to accept its position in the social hierarchy and exclusion from politics by suggesting that the members of this group are naturally less capable of practicing politically relevant forms of intellectual endeavor (they have bronze in the soul). But the structure of the regime also provides hefty material incentives for unphilosophical people to remain content not to share in ruling.

In the ideal city, not only are the nonrulers conceived of as lacking a desire to rule, so are the rulers. Socrates structures the ideal city so as to allow only those "who are not lovers of ruling (*mē erastas tou archein*) to go to it." Otherwise, he continues, "rival lovers will fight" (*hoi anterastai machountai*), and factionalism, indeed all sorts of civic ills, will surely ensue (521b). Only if we "discover a life better than ruling for those who are going to rule" (521a) might a well-governed city be possible.[30] The crispest expression of Plato's deep concern about the ruler's relations to his own passions comes in the stress on the reluctance of the philosopher to assume power. The philosopher must be compelled to return to the cave—to give up the pleasures of pure thought and take up the practical challenge of ruling for a set period of time. The compulsion is not, of course, physical, but rather moral. It tests the philosopher's rational self-mastery of his own (sometimes peculiar) appetites as well as his moral resolve. Everything Plato has written up to this point leads us to appreciate the tremendous allure of a life spent in an intellectual embrace of the

[29] Richard Kraut makes this point: "Although Plato is . . . in favor of giving extraordinary powers to rulers who themselves have a philosophical understanding of the human good, he is not unconcerned about the possibility that such power might be misused or arouse resentment. It is partly for this reason that private wealth and the family are abolished in the ruling class: These powerful sources of political corruption and favoritism must be eliminated in order to give reasonable assurances to those who are ruled that they will not be exploited by those who are more powerful." "Introduction," in *The Cambridge Companion to Plato*, ed. Richard Kraut (Cambridge: Cambridge University Press, 1992), p. 12.

[30] Also 520d: "That city in which those who are going to rule are least eager to rule is necessarily governed in the way that is best and freest from faction."

Forms to the exclusion of all else. And yet Socrates makes it clear that the philosopher is self-controlled even in the face of such exquisite desire. At 520d–e, he asks Glaucon if it is conceivable that the philosophers will be unwilling to serve, preferring instead to spend all their time pursuing the pleasures of contemplation. Glaucon emphatically says, "Impossible!"— for these are just men, and it is a just injunction. Paradoxically, assuming power is the supreme test of the philosopher's justice, self-control, and incorruptibility. By serving politically, the philosopher performs a most stunning enactment of his or her fitness for ruling.

Plato invites us to consider the guardians and, in particular, the philosopher-ruler as alternative "model benefactors." Just as the demos required the wealthy in Athens to spend large portions of their fortunes in ways that benefited the whole polis (sponsor a chorus or play, outfit a trireme, provide animals for public sacrifice), justice compels the philosopher to use his or her intellectual "riches" in a way that benefits the whole. In both cases, the city as a whole tolerates inequality but still determines the appropriate use to which greater resources can be put. In democratic Athens, there was inequality of wealth and social status; in the ideal city, it is inequality of intellectual achievement and political status. In Athens, the demos actually had authority over the assignment of liturgies. In the ideal city of the *Republic*, the interest of the whole, but not the actual judgment of the many, guides the determination of the purposes to which great intellectual achievement may be put. Plato has transformed that most useless pursuit, philosophy, into the most honorable and memorable form of public benefaction. He even fits the lives of philosophers into the conventional pattern of mutual exchange. The reluctant rulers give the city a "rest from evils" and receive this benefit along with everyone else.

Does the philosopher receive any other special benefits? Plato suggests the answer is yes. The special education philosophers receive in order to prepare them for this political task (that is, the ways in which their talents are nourished) is a benefit, because without it they would not have progressed to experience Truth and the finest form of life possible (an intellectual one, albeit one punctuated by the unpleasant work of ruling "each in his turn," 540b). Plato also provides for the ideal city to enact its gratitude to the guardians and philosophers. Guardians "must be given honors, both while living and when dead, and must be allotted the greatest prizes in burial and in other memorials" (414a).[31] Upon the death of philosophers who have served as rulers, he provides that "the city makes public memorials and sacrifices to them as to spirits, if the Pythia is in accord; if

---

[31] Socrates stresses similar points in his depiction of how the city will respond to a guardian's death in battle (469a–b). Cf. *Laws* 697a, where the Athenian insists that they must consider how the city is to dispense honors.

not, as to happy and divine men" (540b). Note that the memorial is not to supremely altruistic, self-sacrificing individuals, but to people who, in performing great benefactions, procured for themselves happiness and closeness to the gods.

Plato surely does not design structures and practices that democrats, ancient or modern, would embrace. Nevertheless, Plato's depiction of an ideal city draws on a democratic insight in seeking a route to responsible ruling in the design of the city's constitutional structure and cultural patterns of life.

To appreciate additional layers of complexity in the *Republic*'s proposal for autocratic rule, it is necessary to keep in the front of one's mind that Socrates presents the idea of a marriage between philosophy and political power in response to Glaucon's worry about the "realizability" of the imagined polis. At 471d–e, Glaucon insists that even if he grants that the imagined city is good, it remains necessary to show that it is also possible, that it could come into being. First, Socrates briefly, but sternly, reminds Glaucon that the theoretical project should not be evaluated on the basis of realizability (472b3). He stresses that he, together with his interlocutors, is "making a pattern in speech of a good city" (*paradeigma epoioumen logōi agathēs poleōs*, 472e). As a pattern (*paradeigma*), it aims to capture conceptual relationships. Socrates continues: "Is what we say less good [at portraying these things] on account of our not being able to prove that it is possible to found a city the same as the one in speech?" (472e). Socrates extracts from his friend an admission that "it is the nature of acting to attain to less truth than speaking" (473a1–3) and that as a result it would not be reasonable for him to compel Socrates to "present it [the city] as coming into being in every way in deed as we described it in speech" (473a).[32] He insists that it is unreasonable to expect that "what we produced in words is in all respects reproduced by experience."[33] Socrates emphasizes that Glaucon should, like him, be content to use the city in speech to direct attention to what it is about the way cities behave today that keeps them "from being governed in this [ideal] way and with what smallest change . . . a city would come to this manner of regime" (473b).

The course of this exchange is significant. Socrates translates Glaucon's question about realizability from a policy-implementation issue into a theoretical question. Socrates uses Glaucon's concern with practicality to

---

[32] Adam notes that Plato acknowledges here that he is contradicting a common view: "Most men would of course admit that a perfect scheme must usually be modified if it is to be put in force. But they would not allow that lexis has more truth than praxis; for the truth of a theory—they would say—is best tested by experience." James Adam, *The Republic of Plato*, Greek text edited with critical notes, commentary, and appendices, 2 vols., 2d ed. (New York: Cambridge University Press, 1965), p. 328.

[33] Translation modified following ibid., p. 329.

move him to exercise his theoretical imagination—to conjure up a world in which the issue of implementation would not be a problem. This involves asking Glaucon to doubt the givenness (naturalness) of the existing political culture he knows. Socrates acknowledges that the ideal city will appear horribly unrealizable at the moment. He wants Glaucon to accompany him as he labors to portray under what circumstances this city in speech might indeed appear fathomable and workable to a wide audience, even to the populace at large. Socrates is daring to say, and attempting to engage Glaucon in apprehending, that to bring theory and practice closer together, it is the world that must change. A good political theory requires no emendation on account of practicality issues. The full import of the philosopher-ruler passage can now come to the fore.

Socrates takes it upon himself to capture in a few words the way in which the world would have to be different such that the structure of the ideal city could appear attractive. That is, he wishes to identify what "smallest change" would logically entail (at least) a majority of the myriad ways in which the world would have to be different for us to imagine citizens greeting Socrates' proposals with interest and enthusiasm, rather than with bemused curiosity and, ultimately, contempt. The formulaic encapsulation he offers is that "unless political power and philosophy coincide in the same place [and the] numerous natures who at present pursue either to the exclusion of the other are forcibly debarred . . . there is no rest from ills for cities . . . nor I think for humankind, nor will the regime we have now described in speech ever come forth from nature, insofar as possible and see the light of the sun" (473d–e).[34] I suggest that the passage proposes that once people have a taste of what sound philosophic rule (that is, a rest from evils) is like, they will find the structure of the ideal city compelling.[35] To put it another way, Plato is here concerned with representing under what circumstances public opinion would favor—or at least treat respectfully—the numerous proposals that make up the city of speech as detailed by Socrates. The passage may even suggest that since forward-looking understanding of the promise of philosophic rule is beyond the grasp, beyond even the imagination, of all but a tiny few who live in Athenian democracy, public opinion will never favor this constitutional arrange-

---

[34] Translation modified following Adam, *The Republic of Plato*, p. 329.

[35] We find a catalogue of the evils that would no longer inflict men at *Republic* 464c–465d. They include: being drawn apart by claims to ownership, ubiquitous lawsuits and complaints, factionalism, the escalation of small quarrels into big problems, assaults on parents and the elderly, flattery, want and grief over the difficulty of raising children without sufficient means, going into debt, ignoble deeds occasioned by desperate need of money. When those men charged with political power do not suffer these evils, Plato assumes, there will no doubt be a dramatic improvement in the quality of legislation and justice that governs the lives of all members of the society.

ment until the public actually has an experience of the political empowerment of philosophic knowledge. This is why he calls the whole
formulation "very paradoxical" (*polu para doxan*, 473e): it is very much
at odds with prevailing views of common sense. But it is precisely the
contingency of what passes for "common sense" that Socrates wants to
stress.[36] The philosopher-ruler passage suggests that only the experience
of the best variant of "happiness" could dislodge the current prejudices
and possibly render the constitutional structure of the *Republic* irresistible
from a commonsense point of view. Oddly, the philosopher-ruler passage
may be the most practical, grounded moment in the entire text. Here
Plato is addressing how the felt interests of people are formed and re-
formed as well as acknowledging how thoroughly impractical his vision
must appear at a given historical juncture. He is also far from minimizing
the enormity of the change he has dared to envision.

Glaucon playfully addresses how far from common sense Socrates' view
is by suggesting that many will be moved to consider it a glorious and
wonderful deed to "do you in on the spot." Defend yourself in speech
and get away, he urges Socrates, reminding him that the alternative is that
he will "really pay the penalty in scorn" (474a). This obvious allusion to
the fate of the historical Socrates effectively keeps the question of the force
of popular beliefs in the front of the reader's mind. Glaucon then point-
edly says at 474b, "Try to show the disbelievers (*apistousin*) that it is as
you say." Note that he does not say, "Show the ignorant that you are
right." Rather, his words direct Socrates to address the formation of people's confidence or trust (*pistis*) in an idea, not in their grasp of its truth.
And so Socrates takes up the issue of explaining not only what philosophy
is but also why it is routinely slandered.

The other places in the *Republic* where Socrates discusses the question
of realizability support this reading. At 541a–b, Socrates proposes that it
is hard for this ideal constitution to come about, but it is not impossible.
He repeats his earlier point that only the coincidence of political power
and philosophy could occasion the birth of such a regime. Then he turns
to consider precisely how one might accomplish its establishment. He asks
what might be the "quick and easy way" (541a) to set it up. His answer
is the infamous proposal for philosophers to begin with a population of
children—that is, to send all the citizens over ten years old into the country and keep only the children in the city and have philosophers raise them.
What does this proposal mean? Does it suggest that Socrates recognizes
that he must quite extensively dupe folks into believing in his plan and
that only impressionable young children could be so brainwashed? I do

---

[36] Compare the discussion of opinions regarding common meals at *Laws* 780c.

not think that is quite right. Socrates is interested not in simply duping folks but in the fair issue of how easy or difficult it is to craft customs, norms, and practices that reach into both public and private life and that will tend to support the smooth functioning of the new institutions, and thereby the true happiness of the population. The drastic character of the proposal highlights the importance of cultural norms and customs to the project of collective living. The passage proposes that "the quickest and easiest way" to establish the new regime would be to avoid having to undo old prejudices (having to move others to "despise the current honors," 540d) and get straight to the business of setting new mythologies, norms, and idealizations in motion. To insist that Plato's attention to this dimension of political life amounts to an embrace of brainwashing is to adopt something akin to Rousseau's view that all cultural norms and local practices are nasty forms of indoctrination inimical to the development of an authentic personality. Instead, I suggest we see in this passage an indication that Plato acknowledged that all governing regimes can be supported or unsettled by cultural formations. He is deeply involved here with the question of how it is that a person or people can imagine themselves out of a dominant discourse.

If starting with children is the "quick and easy way" for the constitution of the ideal city to be established, we should assume the implied lengthy, more difficult way to accomplish the same goal to be the way practiced by Socrates. His constant questioning of the merits of conventional ways of thinking about justice, happiness, and virtue is the slow, painful way to unsettle antiphilosophical prejudices, that is, to turn people toward an understanding of the political relevance of philosophy. Perhaps we could even imagine that Socrates' individual critical conversations amount to efforts to coax the mind of an adult into an open condition that resembles the mind of a child (into *aporia*).

Interpreting the proposal for the rule of the philosopher-king in the *Republic* as tantamount to a wholesale rejection of everything Athenian democracy stood for in Plato's time not only misses the peculiar links to democratic ideas I track in this book, but also presupposes that the Platonic dialogues, and especially the *Republic*, express the author's settled, substantive political doctrine.[37] Yet nowhere in the dialogues does Plato speak in his own voice. He does not address the reader or participate in the conversations and speeches depicted. Doctrines and programmatic statements are developed throughout the different works. But nowhere does Plato, the author, give the reader an unequivocal, explicit endorse-

---

[37] See Diskin Clay, "Reading the *Republic*," in Griswold, ed., *Platonic Writings/Platonic Readings*, p. 269.

ment of any particular view as his own. To find the author's intended doctrine in the dialogues, one would have to assume that it is presented through a mouthpiece (presumably Socrates) or that it can be discerned by following clues left by the author as to his "real" or "deepest" teaching hidden in the letter of the text. The first method typically pays too little attention to the dramatic structure of the dialogues; the second focuses on it. Both, however, assume that the project of the dialogues is to communicate the author's settled beliefs, and that the reader's project is to illuminate his doctrine.[38] I find both views problematic. Neither adequately confronts the interpretative challenge of "Platonic anonymity"[39] or "Plato's silence."[40] A reading must be based, as most recent scholarship on the question of Platonic writing insists,[41] on some understanding of why it was not only politically important but also philosophically necessary to write dialogues, that is, to keep his own voice completely absent from the entire corpus. The considerable literature on the issue of why Plato wrote dialogues and to what end he "never lifts the veil of anonymity"[42] has for too long been ignored by many commentators on Plato's political thought.[43]

Plato addresses the practice of attributing doctrines to him in *Letter 7*. Here Plato writes that the fact that the tyrant Dionysius composed a book in which he sets out firm political views is good reason to doubt that the tyrant understands the nature of philosophic practice. In the key passage, Plato writes:

[38] See Kraut, "Introduction," for discussion of the trends in the scholarship.

[39] Ludwig Edelstein, "Platonic Anonymity," *American Journal of Philology* 83 (1962): 1–22.

[40] L. A. Kosman, "Silence and Imitation in the Platonic Dialogues," in *Methods of Interpreting Plato*, ed. J. C. Klagge and Nicholas Smith (Oxford: Clarendon, 1992), pp. 73–92.

[41] Griswold, ed., *Platonic Writing/Platonic Readings*; Klagge and Smith, *Methods of Interpreting Plato*; Gerald Press, *Plato's Dialogues: New Studies and Interpretations* (New York: Rowman and Littlefield, 1993).

[42] Edelstein, "Platonic Anonymity," p. 16. There is an excellent bibliography on the scholarship on this issue in Griswold, ed., *Platonic Writings/Platonic Readings*.

[43] Vlastos' work, the influence of which has been substantial, falls in this category. See Diskin Clay's review of Vlastos' *Platonic Studies* in *Arion*, n.s. 2, no. 1 (1975): 116–32, esp. 127–31; and, for more elaboration, Clay, "Reading the *Republic*". See also David L. Roochnik, "Terence Irwin's Reading of Plato," with Irwin's reply in Griswold, ed., *Platonic Writings/Platonic Readings*, pp. 183–93. Two recent studies of Plato's political philosophy show little interest in the interpretative challenge posed by "Platonic Anonymity." See C.D.C. Reeve, *Philosopher-Kings: The Argument of Plato's Republic* (Princeton: Princeton University Press, 1988); and George Klosko, *The Development of Plato's Political Theory* (New York: Methuen, 1986). In contrast, see Kraut, "Introduction." Kraut notes that this aspect of Plato's thought commands much attention today. His own view is that Plato used the dialogic form to remind readers that "oral exchange is the essential tool of philosophy" and to warn readers against the "misuse of books" (p. 27).

I hear he [Dionysius] wrote a book on the matters we talked about, putting it forward as his own teaching, not what he had learned from me. Whether this is true I do not know. . . . So much at least I can affirm with confidence about any who have written or propose to write on these questions, pretending to a knowledge of the problems with which I am concerned, whether they claim to have learned anything at all about the subject. There is no writing of mine about these matters, nor will there ever be one (*oukoun emon ge peri autōn esti sungramma oude mēpote genētai*). For this knowledge is not something that can be put into words like other sciences (*rhēton gar oudamōs estin hōs alla mathēmata*); but after long-continued intercourse between teacher and pupil, in joint pursuit of the subject, suddenly, like light flashing forth when a fire is kindled, it is born in the soul and straightaway nourishes itself. And this too I know: if these matters are to be expounded at all in books or lectures, they would best come from me. Certainly I am harmed not least of all if they are misrepresented. (341b–d)

Plato's comments suggest that any philosophic insight he himself might have gained as a result of his intense, sustained, patient, difficult, and disciplined investigations is not something that he has put into words. There is no "writing of mine" on these matters, he says, because the intellectual process of grasping an insight is "like light flashing forth when a fire is kindled." When he continues, "It is born in the soul and straightaway nourishes itself," he probably means that the insight stays there, in the soul, and cannot travel to the written page. In this significant digression from discussion of his relations with Dionysius and Dion in *Letter 7*, Plato reiterates compactly, and in dramatic language, a theory of knowledge that, he indicates, he has tried to expound in other places.[44] This account of knowledge proceeds in stages: the name, the definition, the image, the knowledge, and last, the object itself, which is grasped suddenly like an insight, not as the result of a linear demonstration. Along the way, Plato's *Letter 7* offers indications of what part in this process written dialogues can play and, accordingly, suggests a way of reading the dialogues.

The digression on knowledge in *Letter 7* stresses that true knowledge cannot usually be represented in words.[45] But an eagerness to undertake and sustain difficult, lengthy, and multiple encounters with the variety of

---

[44] For discussion of this dimension of *Letter 7* and its relation to other texts, see Hans Georg Gadamer, *Dialogue and Dialectic: Eight Hermeneutical Studies on Plato*, trans. P. C. Smith (New Haven: Yale University Press, 1980); and Kenneth Sayre, "Plato's Dialogues in Light of the *Seventh Letter*," in Griswold, ed., *Platonic Writings/Platonic Readings*, pp. 93–109. There is a substantial literature on Plato's explicit discussion of the problem of writing in the *Phaedrus*. See especially Derrida's "Plato's Pharmacy."

[45] Most scholars treat this as a problem peculiar to writing, but Sayre ("Plato's Dialogues in Light of the *Seventh Letter*") has argued that Plato treats it as a problem that besets oral communication just as severely.

names, definitions, images, and accounts concerning any subject can nurture the gestation of a moment at which an insight might be had and grasped. Plato continues:

> The truth and error about any part of being must be learned together, through long and earnest labor. . . . Only when all of these things—names, definitions, and visual and other perceptions—have been rubbed against one another and tested, pupil and teacher asking and answering questions in good will and without envy—only then, when reason and knowledge are at the very extremity of human effort, can they illuminate the nature of any object. (344b)

His own dialogic texts, this suggests, can be seen as accounts of such rubbing and testing. They are resources for readers' vicarious conversations.[46] Plato's dialogues

> give us a strong sense of what it would be like to listen to a dialectical debate or even to participate in it; they perhaps give us a stronger sense of what is involved in such a debate than we could have acquired by actually attending an ordinary dialectical discussion. For they represent paradigmatic debates between model characters in characteristic settings in a most vivid and realistic way. To this end they display an impressive mastery of a wide array of literary techniques.[47]

The vicarious experiences of dialogue pull readers in different directions at different moments, managing to disorient them, to move them toward clarity, and to unsettle them again.[48] The dialogues do not present settled views for the reader to accept or reject.[49] The details of the dialogues pro-

---

[46] Compare Charles Kahn: Plato created "a set of rigorous discussions on virtue and education without any definite conclusions, designed to perplex and provoke his readers and thus to produce in them the kind of intellectual stimulation he had himself received from Socrates. . . . The extraordinarily lifelike characterization of the participants gives the reader the illusion of overhearing an actual conversation." *Plato and the Socratic Dialogue: The Philosophical Use of a Literary Form* (New York: Cambridge University Press, 1996), p. 57.

[47] Michael Frede, "Plato's Argument and the Dialogue Form," in Klagge and Smith, eds., *Methods of Interpreting Plato*, p. 201. For an extensive discussion of the relationship between Plato's literary artistry and philosophical concerns (one that is unsympathetic to the idea that the dialogues contain expressions of Platonic doctrine), see Kahn, *Plato and the Socratic Dialogue*, passim.

[48] See J. Peter Euben, *The Tragedy of Political Theory* (Princeton: Princeton University Press, 1990), for a sustained investigation of how the dialogues work upon the reader in this way. I also find helpful the idea that the reader constructs a "second dialogue" in her own mind during the reading process, suggested by Alan Bowen, "On Interpreting Plato," in Griswold, ed., *Platonic Writings/Platonic Readings*, pp. 49–65, following E. N. Tigerstedt, *Interpreting Plato* (Uppsala: Almquist and Wiksell, 1977).

[49] Charles Kahn refers to this erroneous supposition as the "fallacy of transparency," *Plato and the Socratic Dialogue*, pp. 41–42. See also Martha Nussbaum, *Fragility of Goodness* (New York: Cambridge University Press, 1986), p. 127.

voke, irritate, inspire, and confuse. Of course, the dialogues prompt thinking along certain lines. They are not "neutral." Plato presents particular
views because he believes, at least tentatively, that they have merit.[50] But
having merit should not be confused with being "endorsed" by Plato. The
dialogues do not positively offer something we can unproblematically call
Plato's own settled, substantive doctrine.

Above all else, the dialogues provide the experience of enlivening, difficult, sustained mutual philosophic questioning. But they also elicit substantive questions, one of which this book investigates. For ancient readers, the question was: "What is the moral significance of democracy?" For
us the questions are: "How did the Athenian democrats and Plato conceive of the moral significance of democracy as they knew it?" and "Of
what theoretical and historical interest is that?" Following up the complexities resident in these questions, I propose a further question: "What
kind of engagement with democratic ideals and cultural practices do the
dialogues sustain?" Only in the context of the civic symbols and arguments of the period can we conceive of Plato's reader in a historically
responsible and intellectually robust way, or ask how Plato's texts register
a debt to a tradition that they subject to rigorous criticism.[51]

THE WORK OF THE ACADEMY

Plato's founding of the Academy and his involvement in the politics of
Syracuse are also usually taken to support two problematic assumptions.[52]
The first is that Plato had a settled political "doctrine" that is unequivocally hostile to democracy. The second is that the Academy was a training
ground for statecraft, particularly for the training of would-be philosopher-kings or the advisors to, or advocates of, such a political leadership.
But what we know of the Academy, as well as of Plato's involvement in
the affairs of Sicily, does not support these assumptions. The dialogues,
including the *Republic*, do not amount to a clever presentation of a political doctrine that it was Plato's personal aim to realize in practice through
the Academy or through his own personal involvement in Sicily.

---

[50] Kraut, "Introduction," p. 29.

[51] Compare Hayden White's suggestion of a semiological study of classic texts. His aim,
as he says, is to "unpack the rich symbolic content of [the] work . . . [and] return it to its
status as an immanent product of the culture in which it arose." *The Content of the Form:
Narrative Discourse and Historical Interpretation* (Baltimore: The Johns Hopkins University
Press, 1987), p. 213.

[52] See Brunt, "Plato's Academy and Politics," p. 282, for a review of influential scholarship
that worked with these assumptions. He offers a complementary argument "that the conception they represent is largely mistaken" (pp. 282–84, at p. 282).

Founded at Athens by Plato in the year 387 B.C., the Academy sustained a far more open intellectual environment than is commonly supposed.[53] First, though membership was a matter of formal affiliation, it was not restricted in principle to the elite strata of society. Second, the training did not amount to the indoctrination of "pupils" in an ideology.

Modest living and simplicity were hallmarks of the style of life maintained at the Academy. Plato's own wealth, supplemented by gifts, was sufficient to finance the collection of books, maintenance of the building, and the hosting of symposia.[54] The Academy charged no fees during Plato's lifetime, suggesting that the school was not socially exclusive. Moreover, Plato's published works were at least somewhat available to readers outside the Academy.[55] Consider two well-attested cases.[56] First, Axiothea, a woman who later took part in the school disguised as a man, came to the Academy after reading a book of the *Republic*. Second, Nerinthos, a Corinthian farmer, came to study at the Academy after being impressed by his reading of the *Gorgias*. In spite of the absence of fees, however, only the financially secure or independently wealthy could probably afford to attend regularly. The young men seeking to educate themselves for leadership at Athens (or elsewhere) who came to the Academy were probably typically from the upper classes. The Academy may have been exclusive in a different sense, one that may have distinguished it from other would-be educators who set up shop in Athens. By making membership a matter of formal affiliation unconnected to the payment

---

[53] On the Academy's open intellectual environment, see Harold Cherniss, *The Riddle of the Early Academy* (Berkeley: University of California Press, 1945); Debra Nails, *Agora, Academy and the Conduct of Philosophy* (Boston: Klower Academic Publishers, 1995); Brunt, "Plato's Academy and Politics." On the Academy, also see John Patrick Lynch, *Aristotle's School: A Study of a Greek Educational Institution* (Berkeley: University of California Press, 1972); C. B. Armstrong, "Plato's Academy," *Proceedings of the Leeds Philosophical and Literary Society* 7 (1953): 89–196; Anton-Herman Chroust, "Plato's Academy: The First Organized School of Political Science in Antiquity," *Review of Politics* 29 (1967): 25–40; H. I. Marrou, *A History of Education in Antiquity*, trans. George Lamb (Madison: University of Wisconsin Press, 1982 [1945]); and Eduard Zeller, *Plato and the Older Academy*, trans. Sarah Frances Alleyne and Alfred Goodwin (New York: Russell and Russell, 1962 [1888]). I am discussing here the character of the Academy during Plato's lifetime. Its operation changed after his death, introducing, for example, fees and the formalization of courses of study. Full review of the ancient sources regarding the activities of the Academy is beyond the scope of this study. I focus here on demonstrating that the scholarship on the Academy forcefully challenges the soundness of these two assumptions.

[54] Armstrong, "Plato's Academy."

[55] Perhaps several other dialogues, notably the *Gorgias*, were used as advertisements for the philosophical mission of the Academy. See Nails, *Agora*, p. 217

[56] Sources are, for Axiothea, Themistius *Orations* 23.295c–d; for Nerinthos, Aristotle frag. 64. For brief discussion of these two cases, see Nails, *Agora*; and Lynch, *Aristotle's School*, pp. 57–58.

of fees, Plato could conceivably have been reserving the right to refuse "membership" to those "whom he discovered to be incapable of, or insincere about, the rigorous study of philosophy."[57]

Plato's Academy did not impose upon students a program of study modeled on the education of the guardians as outlined in the *Republic*. The evidence is consistent only with the view that the Academy was organized loosely as a "community of advanced members and of younger students; it was not simply a group in which one person was the expert and the rest a following in search of their leader's services or doctrines."[58] Cherniss' assessment is similar: Plato did not "teach" his associates a doctrine "and did not even resolve their disagreement about the meaning of what he had written on the subject by laying down an authoritative interpretation."[59] Rather, there was debate and disagreement at the Academy, even—perhaps especially—over the interpretation of Plato's written works. "All the evidence points unmistakably to the same conclusion: the Academy was not a school in which an orthodox metaphysical doctrine was taught, or an association the members of which were expected to subscribe to the theory of ideas."[60] In sum, the Academy under Plato's leadership was not a sectarian community.[61] Instead, the manner in which individuals conducted their investigations as members of the Academy supports the conclusion that in setting up this school, "Plato held to the Socratic belief in *sunousia* [conversation] as the basis of higher education,"[62] that is, he not only insisted on discussion as a method but also carefully cultivated an open intellectual environment.[63]

---

[57] Nails also wisely cautions against the use of the terminology of "initiate" to describe members of the Academy (*Agora*, pp. 213–14).

[58] Lynch, *Aristotle's School*, p. 55; Armstrong, "Plato's Academy," p. 93.

[59] Cherniss, *Riddle of the Early Academy*, p. 78. The dialogue form rigorously avoids suggesting that the key point in any investigation is what an authoritative figure thinks. This is one reason why, in addition to avoiding his own voice, Plato employs a variety of interlocutors; this may also be why Socrates is increasingly absent or only marginally present in the later dialogues. Readers, the dialogic form strongly implies, must not be led to substitute the authority of a great man for their own reasoned judgment. Only the authority of truth should prevail.

[60] Ibid., p. 81.

[61] Armstrong also argues that Plato's leadership was not dogmatic but largely "suggestive and advisory." He maintains that the great value of the Academy to the students, apart from providing the opportunity to hear the great thinkers of the period who gathered there, "was not so much that it gave them systematic knowledge, as that it taught them a fresh mental approach to problems, trained them in character by association with good men, and brought them into a new intellectual and social atmosphere" ("Plato's Academy," pp. 93–94).

[62] Lynch, *Aristotle's School*, p. 63.

[63] Kraut is therefore correct to suggest that for Plato, "written works can serve a purpose, but only so long as they are accompanied by philosophical dialogue" ("Introduction," p. 21). It is possible, moreover, that dialogues were used in the Academy to teach the method-

Cherniss' characterization of the Academy focuses on the conduct of metaphysical investigations and has thus been largely overlooked when scholars consider the character of the Academy's political training.[64] One common view is that insofar as Plato's Academy was concerned with educating men for public affairs, it was concerned with producing potential philosopher-kings, or at least with producing individuals committed to the establishment of such an institution, as well of other institutions described in the *Republic*.[65] Chroust, for example, bluntly states: "There is little doubt that the Platonic Academy was intended to realize [the] training program [articulated in the *Republic*]."[66] Plato, in Chroust's view, "harbored a relentless hatred for [the] restored democracy . . . [and] wished to establish a 'training center' for people who would one day overthrow that despised regime."[67] Even those who do not read the *Republic* as Plato's blueprint for an institution of learning nevertheless sometimes assume that the *Republic* represents a fixed political program that Plato aimed to realize in practice through the Academy.[68] Armstrong, for example, suggests that in the Academy, Plato sought "converts" as "instru-

---

ology of philosophical investigation (Nails, *Agora*, pp. 215–30). Gadamer's observations may support this view. He urges that the question of how to proceed is always at issue in the dialogues. He writes: "In Plato the discussion is about dialectic, whether in the *Phaedo*, *Republic*, *Phaedrus*, *Sophist*, *Parmenides*, or the *Seventh Letter*. It always has to do with resisting the sophistic tricks of obfuscation in the use of arguments, and to hold fast to the idea of what is really meant by dialogue." Hans Georg Gadamer, "A Reply to Nicholas P. White," in Griswold, ed., *Platonic Writings/Platonic Readings*, p. 266.

[64] Summing up his main point, Cherniss writes, "The metaphysical theories of the director were not in any way 'official' and the formal instruction in the Academy was restricted to mathematics." This view enables him to make sense of Plato's choice of Speusippus over Aristotle as his successor as director. See *Riddle of the Early Academy*, p. 82.

[65] For discussion of a related view, in particular that the *Republic* was intended to be "implemented," if not in total then in part, through reform efforts, see George Klosko, "Implementing the Ideal State," *Journal of Politics* 43 (1981): 365–89. He does not discuss the Academy.

[66] Chroust, "Plato's Academy," p. 26.

[67] Ibid., pp. 27–28.

[68] Gadamer's comments on the program of study at the Academy require review. He suggests that the *Republic* is not a serious political utopia but a clever presentation of the education of the ideal philosopher-king. In his view, the model developed in the *Republic* actually details the structure of activities that Plato sought to sustain at the Academy. He sums up his view in this way: the *Republic* is "a brilliant literary utopia in which a counterfeit civic order is made to represent (indirectly and with pointed allusions) the course of instruction in the academy, the propaedeutic training for the doctrine of ideas" (*Dialogue and Dialectic*, p. 97 n. 10). If we modified Gadamer's point in the following way, it would have some force: remove both the suggestion that the *Republic* details the regimen at the Academy and the notion that the Academy was a training ground for would-be philosopher-kings, and focus on how the *Republic* represents (through argument, characterization, and dramatic context) the stages and processes of serious dialogue and progressive argumentation (that is, effective philosophical inquiry). Gadamer comes close to modifying his argument in precisely this

ments of reform" to promote his political views.[69] But, as Brunt puts it, "There is no ancient authority for this modern notion."[70]

Ancient sources link Plato's Academy to the practical political activities of several individuals.[71] Scholars sometimes take these links as evidence for the indoctrination model of political training at the Academy. These personal links do not warrant characterizing the way the Academy conducted political training as departing from the open way it conducted general philosophical training. For example, the ancient sources suggest those who were "associated with" Plato's Academy included not only notorious tyrants, but also prominent Athenian statesmen such as Phocion, Demosthenes, Lycurgus, and Hyperides. Each of these Athenian statesmen participated in democratic politics: Phocion as an elected military general and orator, Lycurgus as an orator and elected financial magistrate, Hyperides as an orator, and Demosthenes as a particularly powerful orator. Although these individuals often opposed the specifics of Athenian military policy toward Macedon, none is reported to have challenged the fundamental legitimacy of democracy. None tried to change the regime at Athens. Indeed, these leaders all contrived to preserve the regime even during the rise of Macedon.[72]

Plutarch indicates that Plato sent Phormio to Elis in response to that city's request for assistance in revising their laws. Phormio is reported to have counseled the city to "curtail the powers of an oppressive oligarchy

---

way when he reviews a passage in *Letter 7* where Plato considers "the means by which an insight may be reached" (p. 96).

[69] Armstrong, "Plato's Academy," p. 102.

[70] Brunt, "Plato's Academy and Politics," p. 288.

[71] Links between Plato and specific individuals, in addition to the well-known figures named in the Platonic dialogues and Dion, Aristotle, and Speusippus, appear in the following ancient sources. Phocion: Plutarch *Life of Phocion* 4. Hyperides and Lycurgus: Diogenes 3.46. Demosthenes: Plutarch *Life of Demosthenes* 5. For a thorough analysis of the named individuals linked to the Academy in one source or another, see Brunt, "Plato's Academy and Politics"; also see Zeller, *Plato and the Older Academy,* p. 30 n. 64, for a collection and brief review of the reliability of the ancient sources asserting links between Plato and political actors. Saunders usefully divides the ancient evidence for the political activity of Academy members into two categories. The primary sources are the dialogues of Plato, chiefly the *Laws.* The secondary sources (ones that report on the activities of Academy members) are the Platonic *Epistles;* the list of pupils in Diogenes Laertius' *Life of Plato* (3.46–47); Athenaeus 508d, 506e–f; Plutarch's *Lives,* chiefly that of Dion; scattered remarks in the *Moralia;* and the list of politically active Academics in Plutarch *Against Colotes* 1126d. See Trevor Saunders, "The RAND Corporation of Antiquity? Plato's Academy and Greek Politics," in *Studies in Honor of T.B.L. Webster,* vol. 1, ed. J. H. Betts, J. T. Hooker, and J. R. Green (Bristol: Bristol Classical Press, 1986).

[72] On Demosthenes' vision as "Plato-tinged," see Yunis, *Taming Democracy,* pp. 237–77, at pp. 236–37. Democracy continued to exist at Athens even after Athens' defeat by Philip's forces at Chaeronea in 338 B.C. Democracy ended only when Athens lost its independence and had to submit to Antipater, regent of Macedonia, in 322 B.C.

and introduce a more 'democratic constitution.' "[73] Other sources also suggest that the Academy was approached on numerous occasions for help with revising a city's laws, drawing up new laws for a new colony, or some other practical assistance.[74] Yet the ancient accounts of Plato's involvement with or supposed influence upon particular statesmen are extremely difficult, if not impossible, to assess. Plato's admirers (for example, Plutarch) link him with celebrated statesmen as regularly as his detractors (for example, Athenaeus) link him with notorious assassins and tyrants. Accordingly, we cannot always, if ever, really tell when these authors are being selective or when they are being more imaginative. The variety of practical activities with which ancient authors link "associates of" Plato is more telling than any single association. It indicates that the Academy was not so thoroughly and unquestionably associated with any particular political program that any suggested link would appear ludicrous to an ancient reader.

Moreover, we must not accept uncritically the notion that someone who is said to have frequented the Academy during some portion of his life can be identified as a serious "pupil" of Plato. Although a variety of men interested in being "educated" (possibly for public careers) may have come to the Academy, as Brunt urges, these should be "sharply distinguished from those who immersed themselves in Plato's dialectic and metaphysics." The rest, Brunt offers, "would have been alienated by the seeming irrelevance of the disciplines to which they were asked to attend, and have fallen away unless they had acquired a zest for the mastery of abstract studies."[75] Moreover, we must take care to consider the evidence for Plato's attitude toward the practical political efforts of those with whom he did have a strong association. For example, Letter 7 and Plutarch's Life of Dion indicate that Plato had a high opinion of Dion's mind and general moral outlook and engaged in dialectic with him, but they do not indicate that Dion acted on Plato's "instructions," or even initially "in conformity with his principles."[76] These sources in no way suggest that Dion sought out training with Plato in an effort to prepare to take up the project of trying out the idea of the philosopher-ruler in practice of that Plato had urged Dion to consider such a plan.

The political training offered by the Academy during Plato's lifetime probably focused on developing knowledge of the complexity of the problems and dilemmas likely to be faced in politics and some useful techniques

---

[73] Chroust, "Plato's Academy," p. 36.

[74] See Morrow, Plato's Cretan City, for discussion of the political activities of the Academy; and Zeller, Plato and the Older Academy, p. 30 n. 64, for a collection of the ancient evidence.

[75] Brunt, "Plato's Academy and Politics," pp. 285, 287.

[76] I have borrowed some phrasing from Brunt, ibid., p. 288. Plato's relations with Dion are discussed below.

of analysis. Most likely, to the extent that the Academy sought to train potential leaders, it developed individuals' capacities to think theoretically about moral and practical problems of politics, to be highly self-reflective about their choices and their costs—not to apply stock (uniformly anti-democratic) solutions to specific empirical problems.[77] The most compelling evidence for this view is the character of the *Laws*, the work to which Plato devoted the closing years of his life, when the Academy enjoyed a reputation for training political advisors.[78] The setting of the dialogue places the interlocutors in the "historically familiar situation" of legislating for a new city. This hypothetical city is being established under the sponsorship of Cnossos and other Cretan cities and under the guidance of an Athenian. Morrow shows that in crafting the legislation appropriate for this colony, the Athenian Stranger draws on both philosophical principles and "accurate and extensive" knowledge of the details of the law codes and normative practices of many Greek poleis, including Athens and Sparta. Morrow proposes that this dialogue probably was intended to provide a "norm for the other members of the Academy."[79] As such, it "encouraged them to gain a wide knowledge of the history and characters of actual states"[80] and training in dialectic. For example, the procedures adopted by the advisors in the *Laws* (the Stranger and his companions) include devoting considerable time to discovering all sorts of information about the city in question. They seek out details about its physical location and natural resources as well as the temper and character of its populace. Their practice implies that the Academy would counsel advisors that they need to do research—sociological and otherwise.[81] The account of the cultural practices to be sustained by the city of the *Laws* also includes a proposal to send a highly regarded citizen abroad for a period of up to ten years to observe other cities. This individual is imagined to return bearing descriptive accounts of other ways of doing and thinking that the noctur-

---

[77] Morrow proposes something similar in his study of the *Laws*. He writes, "Perhaps the chief purpose [of the Academy] in [Plato's] eyes, was the training of statesmen, or legislative advisors, imbued with the insights of philosophy"(*Plato's Cretan City,* p. 5). I would be more cautious about suggesting that the chief aim of the Academy was the training of "legislative advisors" rather than the development of an environment conducive to learning dialectics.

[78] Though there is a general belief among scholars that the Academy enjoyed this reputation, the evidence is far from conclusive. See Saunders ("The RAND Corporation of Antiquity?") for an assessment of the foundation for this general belief.

[79] Morrow, *Plato's Cretan City,* pp. 4–6. He also suggests that Plato's interest in providing the "norm" explains "why Plato should have devoted the closing years of his life to the composition of such a painstaking piece of hypothetical legislation as the *Laws.* . . . It may . . . have been intended as a kind of model for use by other members of the Academy" (p. 9).

[80] Ibid., p. 5.

[81] This point is stressed in Saunders, "The RAND Corporation of Antiquity?"

nal council must engage seriously.[82] The *Laws* suggests that political training at the Academy involved developing students' abilities to think theoretically about real, practical challenges, not to acquire a commitment to
the imposition of specific, antidemocratic institutions in all cases. The
Laws does not propose, for example, that new methods of educating people were to be "handed down on a take-it-or-leave-it basis, nor imposed
in a new state in a brutal and uncompromising manner: [they were to be]
tentative, adaptable, and flexible, fine-tuned to the citizens' beliefs and
habits."[83]

Insofar as the *Laws* may have provided a guide of some sort for members
of the Academy who were called upon to give practical advice regarding
the construction or reform of constitutions, it suggests that members must
do empirical political research—that is, be sensitive investigators into a
city's circumstances, practices, and myths—as well as be steadfast in one's
love of virtue and commitment to philosophy.[84] The advisors of the *Laws*
display the knowledge gleaned from careful study of the details of democratic practice. They exhibit no inclination to condemn wholesale this
form of government. For instance, the Athenian Stranger explains to his
two Dorian interlocutors that there are two "mothers of regimes" (*eisi
politeiōn hoion mēteres duo tines*, 693d) from which all the rest derive—
monarchy and democracy. In order for a legislator to achieve "freedom
and friendship, together with prudence," the Stranger insists, the polity
must partake of both forms of government (693e). He characterizes the
city of the *Laws* as a temperate combination of monarchy and democracy, a
mixed form of constitution that avoids the excesses to which each "mother
form" alone is prone.

After Plato's death in 347 B.C. (twenty-five years before Macedonia
gained control of Athens), the Academy became more regularly linked
with advising monarchies and tyrannies. The most celebrated of these ties,
of course, is Aristotle's association with Alexander. Other individuals were
associated with more violent actions (both tyrannicides and attempts to
install absolute rulers). Events of the late fourth century, with the rise of

---

[82] The practice of the research-*theoroi* is the subject of extended discussion in Chapter
Eight.

[83] Saunders, "The RAND Corporation of Antiquity?" p. 208.

[84] On this point I disagree with Brunt's characterization of Plato's theoretical outlook as
"indifferent to the data of historical experience" ("The Model City of Plato's *Laws*," in his
Studies in Greek History and Thought, pp. 275–76). Brunt is right to state that Plato is not
primarily interested in historical explanation and that he does not observe the actual behavior of states and individuals in order to confirm the accuracy of his theory. And he is right to
stress that the political training was largely in abstract thinking ("Plato's Academy and Politics," p. 332). But, as this book demonstrates, there are other ways in which a theorist can be
profoundly interested in historical data and "abstract thinking" can be informed by practical
experiences.

monarchic Macedonia and the spectacular military conquests of Philip and Alexander, had much to do with this development. Before the end of the fourth century, the independent city-state was a thing of the past. The functioning of institutions of democratic politics in such a state became a matter of historical interest.

Personal Involvement in Syracusan Politics

Scrutiny of the account of Plato's personal involvement in the politics of Syracuse in *Letter 7* and *Letter 8* also reveals that this aspect of his biography fails to support the view that Plato had a positive political doctrine that he aimed to realize in practice, or that he was personally unequivocally hostile to democracy. *Letter 7* is our only good source for Plato's involvement in the politics of Sicily. Other accounts of the events either ignore Plato altogether or clearly rely on this letter for evidence.[85] Before turning to these issues, let me recall some of the historical context.

Syracuse had sustained a moderate democracy during the second half of the fifth century. But during the fourth century, it underwent political upheavals. Several years after Syracuse defeated the Athenian naval forces at the end of the Peloponnesian War, a Carthagian invasion created an "anarchic situation."[86] In this setting, Dionysius I was able to seize a tyranny at Syracuse. Plato visited Syracuse three times during the period of the tyranny of Dionysius I and his son, Dionysius II. From sources other than *Letter 7*, we know that soon after Plato's final visit to Syracuse, Dion, a young relative of the tyrant whose intellect Plato admired and who had spent time at the Academy, led a military effort to depose Dionysius II. Companions of Dion's from the Academy as well as other Syracusan exiles made up his force. He accomplished a stunning victory over the considerably larger forces of Dionysius II and was welcomed in Syracuse. The Syracusan Assembly was convened, and Dion was given special powers to overhaul politics. Yet he soon got caught up in intense civil conflict and rivalry with a popular Syracusan advocate of a "radical" democratic regime that pledged to redistribute land. Dion handled this conflict poorly. Twice he magnanimously declined to use his power legally to reprimand or even

---

[85] For discussion of the reliability of these additional sources, see Brunt, "Plato's Academy and Politics," pp. 314–32. The sparseness of additional biographical information on Plato dating from the classical period indicates that, as Moses Finley has suggested, "the Greeks of [Plato's] day had a rare indifference to the private lives of their poets and philosophers." "Plato and Practical Politics," in his *Aspects of Antiquity* (New York: Viking, 1968), p. 77. The same could not be said of their interest in the lives of their political leaders, however. Diogenes Laertius (second century A.D.) did, of course, compose a "Life of Plato" in Greek (Book 3 of his *Lives*).

[86] Finley, *A History of Sicily*, p. 75.

exile his opponent for various offenses. Later, however, he apparently contrived to have this rival assassinated. Soon after this assassination, Dion was himself murdered by a trusted companion, Callippus.

Letter 7 is addressed to Dion's grieving friends, who had apparently written to Plato for advice. But Plato's letter offers little practical advice beyond urging Dion's friends to follow the general principles to which Plato and Dion had been devoted. The general tone of *Letter 7* indicates that it was written with a wider audience in mind and intended as a semipublic document. Finley suggests that "Plato and his Academy must have had a bad press for their connection with the whole sordid mess in Sicily, in which several men associated with them in the public mind were implicated." He proposes that Plato perceived that an *apologia* was called for, and for this purpose composed and distributed the letter.[87] The letter suggests that Plato believed his own motives in going to Sicily had been terribly misunderstood and that he was eager to correct this misunderstanding. For example, the letter claims to offer an account of "the bold purpose I [Plato] had in setting forth from home." It insists that it was "not what some persons had ascribed to be" (328c). Morrow writes:

> [Plato] realized that the central purpose of his political and moral teaching, and the ideals that guided him and Dion in Syracuse, were in serious danger of being completely misunderstood by his friends as well as his enemies; and the importance of the issue involved called forth from him an effort that resulted in one of the most impressive of all his written compositions.[88]

We learn from *Letter 7* that Plato's first trip to Syracuse (around the year 387) was a personal visit to meet with Pythagorean philosophers. It explains that while in Sicily, Plato met Dion, a twenty-year-old relative of the tyrant Dionysius I. He instructed the youth and found him an extraordinary student. Plato states that Dion had a quick and agile mind, a keenness and ardor that he had never seen matched in another student (*Letter 7* 327b). In the short time they spent together, Dion developed a strong determination to live a "life of virtue." The letter does not say that he wanted to live a "life of philosophy."

Plato's second trip to Sicily took place twenty years later. *Letter 7* explains that, upon the death of the notoriously brutal and oppressive tyrant Dionysius I (in 367), Dion hoped that the new youthful ruler, Dionysius II, could, with Plato's help, be moved to "desire the noblest and best life." Dion reportedly urged Plato that through his and Plato's combined efforts, the younger Dionysius could be moved to establish "throughout

---

[87] Finley, "Plato and Practical Politics," p. 80; also Brunt, "Plato's Academy and Politics," pp. 322–23.

[88] Morrow, *Studies in the Platonic Epistles*, p. 56.

the land a true and happy life without the massacres and deaths and the other evils" (327d). He could perhaps be influenced to abandon the brutal ways and excessive living that had characterized his father's rule, thereby immediately improving the lot of Syracusans and setting the stage for peaceful change in the direction of constitutional government. Dion succeeded, moreover, in persuading Dionysius II officially to invite Plato to his court. The letter reports that Plato agonized over whether to make the trip. He had reason to be confident of Dion's character but not that of the young tyrant. In the end, he hesitantly decided to journey to Sicily.

The whole effort ended in disaster. Plato was strict in his instructions to the young tyrant, insisting that he begin training his mind and passions by studying geometry. But Dionysius II was impatient and, as Syracuse was rife with civil conflict, came to suspect that Dion was plotting with Plato to undermine his rule. The tyrant acted on this fear by forcing Dion into exile. He detained Plato for some weeks after his expulsion of Dion, *Letter 7* reports, because Dionysius II was jealous of the esteem in which Plato had held Dion and repeatedly tried, to no avail, to gain Plato's backing for himself.[89] Dion spent about ten years in exile. For some of that time he lived in Athens and kept company with Plato, now his friend as well as his teacher, and with other Academy members.

Plato's third and last trip to Sicily took place about ten years later (in 357), in response to an urgent summons by Dionysius II. The tyrant claimed to have had a change of heart and professed a new, sincere interest in being instructed. The letter does not say whether Plato believed the tyrant, although the fact that Dionysius II did not also recall Dion to Syracuse at the same time might well have made him suspicious. Plato likely knew Dion was preparing an assault on Syracuse from exile, and acted in the interest of trying to reconcile Dionysius II and Dion so as to prevent a bloody civil war in Sicily: "I, an Athenian citizens, a friend of Dion and his ally, came to the tyrant in order to bring about friendship, not war, between them" (333d). Plato found, however, that Dionysius II had not had a change of heart after all. Soon after the philosopher's arrival, the tyrant seized Dion's property. At this point, Plato tried to leave but was detained for months while the tyrant attempted to bribe him to support the expulsion of Dion. Failing in this enterprise, Dionysius II finally allowed Plato to leave. Soon after, Dion mounted a successful attack from exile on the tyrant. Dion later perished, as we noted above, in the civil strife that followed.

Letter 7's account of Plato's activities in Sicily never suggests that his aim was to conduct a political "experiment," that is, that he had gone

---

[89] For a detailed account of Plato's personal involvement with Dion and Dionysius II, see Morrow, *Studies in the Platonic Epistles*, pp. 137–67.

there in order to try to establish something akin to the ideal state of the *Republic*.[90] As Finley writes of *Letter 7* (and *Letter 8*, to which we will turn below), "Nothing in either letter . . . warrants the view that Plato proposed to convert Dionysius II into a philosopher-king and thus realize on the earth the ideal state of the *Republic*."[91] Plato shows no sign in this letter of having a high opinion of Dionysius II's intellect or of expecting great outcomes from the continued concentration of supreme power in a single individual. Rather, as Morrow emphasizes, "the most emphatic and forceful portion of Plato's advice in *Letter 7*, the part which he must have put in italics (if the anachronism may be permitted) in the manuscript sent to the friend of Dion, is his condemnation of unlimited power: [quoting Plato] 'Do not enslave Sicily, nor any other city, to human despots, but let the laws be sovereign' " (334c).[92] The practical political concerns behind Plato's work in Syracuse were, according to the letter, simply those of someone eager to find a way to end tyrannical oppression and factional struggle in a peaceful manner. These goals did not require the implementation of the putative plan of the *Republic*.[93] The letter also explicitly stresses that Dion's plea for Plato to journey to Sicily the second time was an intensely personal trial for Plato. The chief factor in his decision to go to Sicily was fear of self-reproach (328c5–6). He feared betraying both Dion and philosophy:

> Above all I was ashamed lest I appear to myself as a pure theorist (*pantapasi logos monon*), unwilling to touch any practical task—and I saw that I was in danger of betraying Dion's hospitality and friendship at a time of no little real danger to him. (328c–d)

> In so going I discharged obligation to Zeus Xenios and cleared myself of reproach from philosophy, which would have been dishonored if I had incurred disgrace through softness or cowardice. (329b)

---

[90] In his Editor's Prologue to Klagge and Smith, eds., *Methods of Interpreting Plato*, Klagge mistakenly treats as uncontroversial the idea that Plato went to Sicily "to carry out the programme of the *Republic*" (p. 5).

[91] Finley, "Plato and Practical Politics," p. 80. See also Morrow: "To accuse Plato of trying to make of Dionysius a philosopher-king after the model of the philosopher-guardians in the *Republic* is to misconceive Plato's program at Syracuse"; *Studies in the Platonic Epistles*, pp. 55–56.

[92] Morrow, *Studies in the Platonic Epistles*, p. 148.

[93] Brunt stresses that the assumption that Plato sought to implement the plan of the *Republic* in Sicily is ludicrous in part because, although the letter reports the reflections of Plato on his choices and enterprises, it does not present Plato as "reflecting that he had long been preparing pupils for the kind of task" he was invited to undertake. Furthermore, none of the conditions the *Republic* identifies as necessary for philosophic rule to develop were in place—for example, prevailing luxury had not been curbed, and no class of guardians existed in Sicily. "Plato's Academy and Politics," p. 326.

The importance of the issue of Plato's loyalty to Dion in accounting for his activity in Syracuse should not be underestimated. Plato's significant attachment to Dion combined with Dion's pleading to involve Plato personally in the affairs of Syracuse. If it is also correct, as some evidence suggests, that Plato's relationship with Dion had developed into one of erotic friendship, the personal pull would have been strong indeed.[94]

Letter 7 involves a familiar Socratic issue—the sort of life an individual will choose. The stakes were unusually high in this case because the young man questioning what sort of life to choose, Dionysius II, had just assumed supreme power in a city that had for years been menacing the other city-states of Sicily and had become notorious throughout Hellas as the site of a vicious tyranny.[95] Plato's success at moving Syracusan politics in the direction of peaceful change to constitutional rule would have brought great benefits not only to the city of Syracuse, but to all of Hellas, as well as to the person and family of his friend, Dion. Plato's efforts to facilitate this change likely took the form of conveying to the ruler "a certain view of the world, certain standards of moral and political conduct, which we may broadly describe as 'Academic', with the aim of seeing those standards applied in day-to-day life."[96] His efforts were likely aimed at the moral education of the ruler.

The stakes were high for Plato personally as well. Responding to Dion's request would involve a long journey, a long stay abroad,[97] and possibly a risk to his own life. The challenge facing Plato as he weighed Dion's plea was not, "Is this a chance to realize the plan for an ideal city as outlined in the *Republic*?" but rather, "Should I take on in actuality a challenge not unlike the one depicted in the *Republic*—to convince a young man with

---

[94] The evidence for an erotic attachment between the two consists of a few lines of elegiac verse lamenting Dion's death attributed to Plato's hand by the second-century A.D. writer Diogenes Laertius (3.30). Nussbaum has argued that the lines are highly erotic. She states: "The last line reads, literally, 'O Dion, you who drove my *thumos* [heart/spirit] mad (*ekmēnas*) with *erōs*' " *Fragility of Goodness*, p. 230, with full translation at p. 200. Brunt cautions that if the author is Plato, he must be "recollecting passion he had felt for Dion at their first meeting; it would have been bizarre if *eros* persisted in long years of separation until 353 when Plato was at least 75 and Dion about 57" ("Plato's Academy and Politics," p. 329 n. 94). See also C. M. Bowra, "Plato's Epigram on Dion's Death," *American Journal of Philology* 59 (1938): 394–404. Nussbaum also reads the *Phaedrus*, a dialogue largely about erotically charged friendship, to suggest that many complexities in the text can be understood if we imagine Socrates and Phaedrus to "stand for" Plato and Dion (*Fragility of Goodness*, pp. 229–30).

[95] "The picture that Plato draws in the ninth book of the *Republic* of the tyrannical man was copied in all probability from the living reality which the character and career of Dionysius presented to the Greek world." Morrow, *Studies in the Platonic Epistles*, p. 50.

[96] Saunders, "The RAND Corporation of Antiquity?" p. 209.

[97] Saunders emphasizes that the evidence suggests that "the Academy must always have been prepared to have its advisors spend a considerable period on the job" (ibid., p. 203).

the opportunity to wield unlimited power, in the *Republic* a man in possession of Gyges' ring, to choose instead a life of virtue, self-regulation, and
restraint?" Dion's plea had brought Glaucon's challenge to life. As *Letter
7* tells it, Plato had been asked to carry out a concrete task, that is, to use
philosophy and his intellectual skills to try to turn the mind of a young
man "towards goodness and justice" (328d), not to make him into a philosopher-king. *Letter 7* repeatedly states that as he thought about the task
he might have before him, Plato wondered whether he was man enough
to dare to do this, whether he was a coward, and whether, by implication,
philosophy truly is as useless as most men believe. Plato portrays himself
in *Letter 7* as concerned with the practice of a sort of "philosophic statesman," as described by Stephen Salkever: "The work of the philosophical
statesman is not to design institutions, laws, or policies, but to persuade
citizens of the primacy of the question of the good life or of human *arete*,
over the questions of power, security, and honor."[98] As the letter tells it, a
chance to "implement" the "policies" advocated in the *Republic*—or even
those of the *Laws*—did not figure into Plato's deliberations. Rather,
Dion's plea opened up a chance to raise questions, especially the question
of the good life, in a way that might influence for the better the character
of a regime.[99]

The text of *Letter 8* was presumably written after Dion's grieving friends
once again pressed Plato for advice. It opens by acknowledging the gravity
of the situation in which the Syracusans find themselves. Factional fighting
is raging, tearing the city apart. Each faction's desire for total victory over
its rival drives its leader to commit great evils (353c–d). As a result of
this "endless round there is danger that both the tyrannical party and the
democratic party will be completely destroyed" (353e). This is not an
abstract danger. Syracuse is in imminent danger of falling prey to the imperial designs of other cities. "The whole of Sicily will have practically lost
the Greek language and will have come under the empire and dominion
of the Phoenicians or the Opici," *Letter 8* warns (354e).

Neither *Letter 7* nor *Letter 8* lends support to the view that Plato entered
Syracusan politics in an effort to "realize" the plan of the *Republic*. Both
display Plato's concern to distance himself from a mistaken interpretation
of his interest in Syracusan affairs. *Letter 8* goes further still. It also implies
that philosophic practice is in some ways positively dependent on elements
of the Athenian democratic culture.

---

[98] Stephen Salkever, "Socrates' Aspasian Oration: The Play of Philosophy and Politics in
Plato's *Menexenus*," *American Political Science Review* 87, no. 1 (1993): 133–46, at p. 135.

[99] In line with this interpretation, I reject Nussbaum's suggestion that Dion and Plato
attempted "to spend their lives together and to govern a philosophical city" (*Fragility of
Goodness*, p. 229). Appreciating the closeness of their personal relationship does not entail
this interpretation of their concrete political aims.

When Plato uses his own voice in *Letter 8*, he stresses that he is writing in the spirit of "all frankness" (*pasa parrhēsia*, 354a3). To speak with parrhesia, as we have seen, is to risk saying what one knows will be unpopular but what one nevertheless is convinced is best. We shall see in Chapter 6 that Plato links this value with the practice of philosophy. Such speech partakes of Athenian democratic ideals. Plato's general advice, which counsels the factions not to seek total destruction of their rivals but to reconcile, would surely have been unpopular. Addressing the antidemocratic faction, *Letter 8* states, "I advise the tyrant to shun his name and the reality it stands for, and to change his government to a kingship if he can" (354a–b). It continues,

> Now this is the point of my present recommendation to you all: let those who are aiming at tyrannical power shun and flee from what senseless and insatiate men call happiness; let them try to change into the form of kings and subject themselves to kingly laws, thus acquiring the highest honors from their willing subjects and from the laws. (354c)

Addressing the democratic faction, the letter also warns, "Likewise I advise those who cherish the ways of freedom and shun the yoke of slavery as something evil, to beware lest by an excessive and ill-timed thirst for freedom they fall into the affliction of their ancestors, the excessive anarchy they experienced as a result of their unmeasured passion for liberty" (354d). The advice to each side presented in Plato's own voice would probably not have been popular with either one. The advice to the democrats may appear more troubling to us. Plato here displays his belief that the establishment of democratic institutions will be unable to deliver moderate, responsible ruling. But we should not neglect to appreciate that the general advice to both sides mobilizes an attitude characteristic of the democratic view and preeminent in the Athenian civic self-image—a strong suspicion of power.

When Plato does move to consider specific, concrete reforms, he casts them as promoting responsible ruling. But Plato does not deliver this advice in his own voice. Rather, he impersonates the ghost of Dion. He crafts an imaginary speech by Dion to the Sicilians. This literary device enables Plato to address his audience as compatriots and as persons with whom he has some personal ties, rather than from the standpoint of a meddling outsider (no matter how respected). This is especially important as Plato, like Thucydides, recognized that domestic factions engaged in serious strife often became emboldened and hardened in their hatreds when expecting help from a friendly foreign power. Plato's impersonation of Dion is an effort to avoid playing the role of such a foreigner.

Dion's speech (from the grave) begins, not surprisingly, by exhorting the Syracusans to care for their souls above riches. It then suggests institutional reforms, recommending in particular that the leaders of the three rival factions become joint kings, "three in number" (356b). The speech clarifies "kingly rule" (*archē basilikē*) by describing it as "responsible" (*hupeuthunos* at *Letter 8* 355e), attaching to it a principle usually claimed and celebrated by advocates of a democratic organization of power (for example, Otanes in Herodotus' "Debate on the Constitutions"). This is the only appearance of the term *hupeuthunos* in the Platonic corpus.[100] It refers to the accountability of office-holders for their administration. *Hoi hupeuthunai* at Athens were, for example, magistrates who had to submit their accounts to public auditors (*logistai*) at stated intervals. The word recalls specific, recognizable practices of democracy pioneered by the Athenians and drawn on by Plato in creating the city of the *Laws*.[101] At the only moment at which a Platonic text (albeit through the ghost of Dion) explicitly delivers suggestions for specific institutional reforms in an actual, historical city, it recommends that personal authority be checked by a recognizably democratic practice closely associated with the Athenian constitution.

Dion's ghost's advice to his friends continues with more suggestions regarding the restrictions that need to be placed on personal authority. His further advice is not of a specifically democratic cast, but neither does it favor investing absolute power in an individual. Dion's ghost suggests that the kings be in control of the temples and have other, related responsibilities. The power to make war and peace, however, should rest not in the hands of the kings, but in those of a body of thirty-five "guardians of the laws ruling in conjunction with the assembly and the council (*dēmos* and *boulē*)" (356d).[102] The ghost of Dion explicitly states that the kings are to be subject to the laws. He recommends various courts of law, with judges selected from among outgoing magistrates. He states that kings should never be involved with a case that might involve executing, deporting, or imprisoning a citizen. The kings are to be "like priests," that is, they should remain untainted by any association with bloodshed, imprisonment, or exile. This likening of the kings to priests suggests that the kings perform symbolic, unifying functions rather than exercise considerable political power. The duties of these kings sound more like those of the archon-basileus (king-archon) in democratic Athens than of a philosopher-king of the *Republic*.

[100] This is noted by Leonard Brandwood, *A Word Index to Plato* (Leeds: W. S. Maney and Sons, 1975), p. 917.

[101] On the relation between the proposals of the *Laws* and Athenian practices of scrutiny and audit, see Morrow, *Plato's Cretan City*, pp. 215–29.

[102] Finley's brief reference to this passage is misleading, as it suggests that the advice amounted to a proposal for a "collective tyranny" ("Plato and Practical Politics," pp. 78–79).

Plato's advice, delivered in his own voice and in Dion's, seems to have made no visible difference at Syracuse. Civil war engulfed the city for several years, coinciding with the last of Plato's life. Plato died before the Sicilians' appeal to Corinth[103] for help initiated a series of events that ended with the successful efforts of Timoleon to secure Sicily's freedom from tyrants, restore democracy, fight off foreign enemies, and bring peace to the island.

Plato's involvement in Syracusan politics should be viewed in the context of Plato's personal obligations to Dion as well as in the context of the kind of political activity undertaken at the Academy. It was decidedly not linked to a concern to implement the plan of the *Republic*.[104]

Although Plato's dialogues are unquestionably and radically critical of elements of Athenian democracy, it is not accurate to claim further that they attack democracy unrelentingly. Rather, as we have seen, the explicit treatment of democracy in Plato's writings is marked by qualifications, hesitations, ambiguities, and even a measure of ambivalence. These moments in the texts are not anomalous. I reject the idea that these moments fail to represent "the real Plato," the Plato who crafted an other-worldly standpoint from which to condemn politics in general and democracy most vehemently. Rather, they bespeak a deep engagement with the ways of Athenian democracy in Plato's writings. In the chapters that follow, I examine the contours of Plato's entanglement with three aspects of the political culture of his native city: frank speaking, encomiastic public oratory, and theater-going. I do not challenge that the critique of democratic governing institutions is a major theme in Plato's writing. I do raise questions about whether he is unambiguously opposed to democratic culture.[105] The next three chapters recover Plato's reliance on the imagery and language of specific democratic cultural practices. In particular, I track how the ethos and culture of democratic Athens subtly inform his presentation of the work of philosophy.

[103] Corinth had some ties to Sicily. Corinth's colonies developed into the independent city-states of Sicily.

[104] Klosko is correct to argue that Plato's "involvement in Syracuse should be seen in the light of the Academy's tradition of political activity rather than as an attempt to fulfill the exalted hopes of the *Republic*" (*The Development of Plato's Political Theory*, p. 186). But Klosko is wrong to insist that the *Republic* was designed as a model for reform, only to be put aside (as a model, not as philosophy) as Plato grew older and less optimistic.

[105] *Contra* viewing the driving aim of Plato's works as "the suppression of democratic culture" (Peter Steinberger, "Who Is Cephalus?" *Political Theory* 24, no. 2 [1996]: 172–99, at p. 186).

Chapter Six

PHILOSOPHER AS *PARRHĒSIASTĒS*
(FRANK SPEAKER)

Plato folds a subtle affirmation of the celebrated democratic ideal of free and frank speech (*parrhesia*) into his dialogues—indeed, into arguments repudiating democratic politics. He defends the specifically democratic conceptualization of parrhesia and appropriates it for philosophy. Moreover, he does not simply use the term ornamentally while substantially altering its content. Rather, he appropriates it to depict the difficult relationship between philosophic and democratic practice.

In this chapter, I examine precisely how Plato draws upon the ideal of parrhesia as the Athenians understood it in his representation of the practice of philosophy, as well as in his account of the fundamental failure of democratic politics actually to sustain parrhesia. I find that for Plato, philosophy best fulfills the demands of the ethos of parrhesia. Paradoxically, then, for him a strong commitment to the democratic ideal of parrhesia leads one to question the adequacy of a democratic organization of political authority.

Plato recognizes that democracy claimed parrhesia as a defining feature of its politics. In Book 8 of the *Republic*, Socrates describes democracy as "a city full of freedom (*eleutheria*) and frank speech(*parrhēsia*)," (557b).[1] He also links parrhesia and philosophy in works from every period of his life. Three times in the *Laches*, Plato relies upon the notion of parrhesia to describe some of the psychological preconditions for conducting philosophic inquiry (178a, 179c, 189a). In the *Gorgias* on six different occasions, Plato relies on parrhesia to explain the psychological disposition needed of one who is to participate in a serious search for the truth as distinct from a competition for rhetorical victory (487a, 487b, 487d, 491e, 492d, 521a). At several key moments in the *Republic*, features of the practice of parrhesia are implicated in Socrates' efforts to construct a "city in speech." In the *Laws*, too, Plato links a commitment to the ideal of parrhesia to the progress of a serious intellectual inquiry into political matters. Moreover, in *Letter 8*, Plato even speaks of his own advice con-

---

[1] Parrhesia was a "watchword" of democracy, as Adam notes in reference to *Republic* 557b. James Adam, *The Republic of Plato*, Greek text edited with critical notes, commentary, and appendices, 2 vols., 2d ed. (New York: Cambridge University Press, 1965).

cerning the affairs of Syracuse in the aftermath of Dion's death as being offered "in all frankness" (354a).[2] There are discernable and significant patterns in Plato's treatment of parrhesia.[3]

The *Laches*: Recognizing *Parrhēsia*

On one reading, the *Laches* is a "failed" dialogue, inconclusive. It poses the question, "What is courage?" without providing a satisfactory answer. But the dialogue as a whole does positively argue a relevant and significant point.

The dialogue opens at the home of Lysimachus, who boldly admits that he and his friend Melesius are both undistinguished sons of very distinguished fathers (Aristides "the Just" and Thucydides the general, respectively). He says that he and his friend are unhappily ignorant of the best way to educate their sons for greatness. Lysimachus then announces that he has invited Nicias (the statesman and general) and Laches (the general), two distinguished Athenians and parents, to his home in order to seek their advice. Laches and Nicias agree that this is indeed a good idea, but Laches proposes that they also include Socrates among those whose advice they will consider. Socrates happens to be present and has thought much about the question now being raised. Nicias agrees.

Socrates does participate in the inquiry, and it is on his prodding that the question, "Should the boys watch a display of martial arts?" metamorphoses into, "What is courage?" In the course of the argument, although the participants reach no agreement on the "What is" question, the dialogue ends with the interlocutors agreeing on the practical matter of what kind of instruction the boys should receive. Laches, Nicias, and Lysimachus explicitly agree that they would choose to place their children in the care of Socrates. But Socrates resists.[4] He suggests that since none of the assembled company has demonstrated any positive knowledge, there is no basis on which to prefer any one of them as a guide. He proposes instead

---

[2] On the authenticity of the letters, see Chapter 5, note 16 above.

[3] Plato does, on occasion, make use of other common meanings of parrhesia—for example, the outspokenness of Alcibiades in the *Symposium* (222c1–2), the speech of intoxicated persons in the *Laws* (649b2–3, 671b3–4) and *Phaedrus* (240e5–6), and candid speech among friends in the *Charmides* (156a8). In this chapter I have restricted my investigation to Plato's consistent use of the term to raise the issue of the relation between an aspect of democratic life and philosophy.

[4] Foucault mistakenly reports that Socrates accepts the role. Michel Foucault, "Discourse on Truth: A Study of *Parrhēsia*," transcript of lectures given in English at the University of California, Berkeley, 1983, transcribed by Joseph Pearson, Department of Philosophy, Northwestern University, p. 57.

that they should all join together in a collective search for the best possible teacher—for themselves as well as for the boys. "What I do not advise is that we remain as we are," Socrates states. He then reiterates the collective project he has in mind: "Let us join together in looking after both our own interests and those of the boys." Lysimachus, the one who had originally raised the issue and begun the search, agrees for the company: "I like what you say, Socrates," he states (201a–b). He then asks Socrates to return to his house the very next day to start making plans. Socrates agrees, bringing the dialogue to a close.

The *Laches* thus culminates by affirming the practical usefulness of Socratic philosophy.[5] Along the way, it articulates some necessary preconditions for one to participate in such philosophic activity. The dialogue illuminates what "joining together" to conduct a philosophic investigation entails. This dimension of its project makes prominent use of the ideal of parrhesia. Plato uses the term "parrhesia" three times in the *Laches* (178a, 179c, 189a). As the *Laches* is a very short text, this is proportionately more frequent than in any other dialogue. The first two mentions appear in Lysimachus' effort to describe his own eagerness to seek help in determining how to educate his son. The third appears in Laches' description of his eagerness to converse with Socrates.

Lysimachus uses "parrhesia" at the very opening of the dialogue to describe the kind of speech he expects of Nicias and Laches, whose advice he is seeking, as well as to describe his own disposition as a hearer:

> [Melesius and I] think it especially right to be frank (*parrhēsiazesthai*) with you. Now there are some people who make fun of such frankness, and if anyone asks their advice, they don't say what they think, but they make a shot at what the other man would like to hear and say something different from their own opinion. But you we considered capable not only of forming a judgment but also, having formed one, of saying exactly what you think (*gnontas haplōs an eipein ha dokei humin*), and this is why we have taken you into our confidence about what we are going to communicate to you. (178a–b)

The text stresses the importance of this opening by having Lysimachus reiterate the same point later in the same speech. "We shall be frank with you (*parrhēsiasometha pros humas*), exactly as I said in the beginning" (179c2).

Lysimachus' appeals to the ethic of parrhesia are revealing. He invokes the ideal to explain in detail his embarrassing situation vis-à-vis his children. While he can speak of his father's great deeds, he can relate no great

---

[5] For a different interpretation of the *Laches* and extensive discussion of the text's historical setting, see Walter T. Schmid, *On Manly Courage: A Study of Plato's* Laches (Carbondale: Southern Illinois University Press, 1992).

deeds of his own to his son. He appeals to parrhesia in order to utter this fact publicly because he is ashamed that it is true. Yet he realizes that he must dare to expose the truth about himself if he is to learn. He appeals to the ethic of parrhesia in order to be able to admit his own shortcomings and his own ignorance of how best to give his son an excellent education. He also appeals to the ethic of parrhesia to seek the help of experts, or at least two men who, because of their own accomplishments, he has reason to believe may be expert on this matter. Lysimachus makes clear what he expects of his counselors, Nicias and Laches: their considered judgments, boldly stated.[6]

Right from the start, the dialogue subtly suggests that the ethic of parrhesia has important implications for philosophy. Plato represents an individual's (Lysimachus') commitment to parrhesia as expressing his courage in admitting his own ignorance on how best to educate his son. An admission of ignorance is the first step in the direction of philosophy. Lysimachus' commitment to parrhesia also accounts for his eagerness to seek the counsel of experts in this moral matter, and thus potentially to take another step in the direction of philosophy. At this early stage in the dialogue, Lysimachus does not intend to undertake a philosophic investigation. Rather, he wants a parrhesiastic encounter more akin to good and frank political deliberation. He solicits advice in the form of speeches to which he will listen. But, the course of the dialogue shows, persons with a true commitment to parrhesia might gently and successfully be turned toward a philosophical approach, and if not toward the practice of philosophy, then at least toward a recognition of its value.

The other appearance of the term "parrhesia" in this dialogue emphasizes the same point, but farther along in the turning toward philosophy. It appears in a speech by Laches, and it explicitly refers to Socrates. Laches finds Socrates a person "privileged to speak fair words and to indulge in every kind of parrhesia" (188e–189a). At this point in the dialogue, Nicias and Laches have given their speeches of advice, and they disagree. The company then turns to discuss how best to proceed. Their language now embraces the terminology of political deliberation. The participants speak of having taken counsel and of needing a tie-breaking vote. Yet the company has already moved away from a deliberative setting: the listeners, Lysimachus and Melesius, are not cast as voters. Rather, the listeners ex-

---

[6] The difficulty of speaking frankly even about matters regarding which one is considered "expert" is made almost palpable in the presence of Nicias. At the time of the dramatic setting of the *Laches*, Nicias is at the height of his political influence at Athens. But not ten years later he is, according to Thucydides' account and as Plato's readers would have known full well, incapable of speaking boldly of his opposition to the Sicilian campaign (6.9–15). He even speaks deceitfully in a failed effort to halt the campaign (6.20–23). Instead, his words inadvertently further arouse the Athenians' passions for the enterprise (6.24.2).

press a wish to defer to the judgment of the advisors (Nicias and Laches)
but find themselves in a bind because the advisors disagree. They turn to
another expert in an effort to break the tie, and so they ask Socrates for
his view. But Socrates refuses to cooperate. He suggests that he is not a
competent expert in the matter at hand and that it is "by knowledge that
one ought to make decisions, . . . and not by majority rule" (184e), even
a majority of apparent experts.

Socrates' remark has some intensely antidemocratic content. He takes
the reliance on majority rule to embody a willingness to give up the pursuit
of knowledge. But the remark is also oddly democratic in spirit. Socrates
is reminding the company that the truth of an utterance and the sincerity
of a speaker matter, not the social standing of the speaker. Socrates is appealing to the ethos of parrhesia. His target is the practice of deferring to
the judgment of a reputed expert rather than thinking critically for oneself. He stresses that what a simple majority of the respected and accomplished men here assembled (Nicias, Laches, and Socrates) thinks is no
more authoritative than what any other simple majority thinks. Implicitly,
the comment jabs not only at democracy but at the oligarchic rule of the
400 (the government of "the best men"), and possibly also at the so-called
mixed constitution of the 5,000, with its focus on those of hoplite status—
two short-lived Athenian experiments with rule by the majority of a few
conventionally successful (and presumably expert) men.

Socrates argues for a different method of investigating how to educate
one's son. He proposes that instead of giving speeches, the participants
try to define the expert they seek by adopting a rigorous practice of question-and-answer. Socrates wants Lysimachus to question Nicias and Laches. Lysimachus proposes that Socrates do the questioning and asks his
guests/advisors if they will comply. Faced with this possibility, Nicias and
Laches offer back-to-back commentaries on what they know of Socrates'
method and character. They reflect on what kind of experience they may
be agreeing to suffer, using their knowledge of Socrates as a guide.

Nicias states that he knows Socrates' words. He knows he will be inter-
rogated aggressively and that his whole manner of life will come under
scrutiny. He knows that his listening role will not be thoroughly passive
but, on the contrary, quite demanding. After presenting a striking account
of the nature of talking with Socrates, Nicias agrees to submit to his questioning (187e–188c). Laches, on the other hand, knows only something
of Socrates' deeds. He recalls that he and Socrates served together in battle
during the Peloponnesian War[7] and that Socrates there showed himself to

---

[7] The Athenians were defeated by the Boeotians under Pagonas at Delium in the fall of
424, the eighth year of the war. Alcibiades refers to the conduct of Socrates in the retreat at
Symposium 220eff. See also *Apology* 28e. For an account of the battle, see Thucydides 4.91–

be a man of great valor and honor. It is on the basis of his knowledge of Socrates' deeds that Laches judges him to be worthy of speaking with parrhesia. Laches then notes that should Socrates actually possess the ability to speak frankly, an ability that Nicias implicitly stressed in his account of the Socratic method, he (Laches) would be eager to submit to being examined by Socrates. Laches says he is confident that Socrates maintains a "harmonious" relation between his deeds and words. He calls such a man "musical" and indicates that he himself often appears to be a "discussion lover" because of the enthusiastic way in which he welcomes what is said by a man such as Socrates (188d–e). But, Laches also states, when he finds himself suffering through the speeches of men of bad character addressing fine subjects like virtue and wisdom, it "distresses me [Laches]" (188e). Laches reiterates this point at the end of his brief speech:

> I present myself as someone for you to teach and to refute in whatever manner you please, and, on the other hand, you are welcome to any knowledge I have myself. . . . This has been my opinion of your character since that day on which we shared a common danger and you gave me a sample of your valor. . . . So say whatever you like (*leg' oun ho ti soi philon*). (189b9–10)

When the members of the company resume their investigation, they adopt the question-and-answer method. And although they do not end up agreeing on a definition of courage, they do come to agree on the value of the method. Plato represents Laches' serious interest in parrhesia as the key to his own willingness to consider, and ability actually to see, the value of Socrates' philosophic approach.

Foucault has suggested that the descriptions of Socrates uttered by Nicias and Laches indicate that they viewed Socrates as a *parrhēsiatēs*. He proposes that Nicias' explanation of what talking to Socrates is like amounts to a "portrayal of Socrates as a *parrhēsiastēs* . . . from the perspective of the one who is 'tested,' "[8] and that Laches' recollection of Socrates' deeds amounts to an account of the "visible criteria, the personal qualities, which entitle Socrates to assume the role of touchstone (*basanos*) of other people's lives." I think this is right. Plato portrays Nicias and Laches relying on their own understandings of parrhesia to convey what it might mean to engage Socrates. The two men turn to the ethos of speaking with parrhesia to claim some understanding both of what prerequisites one must bring to a serious philosophic investigation and of what such activity

---

96. Also see R. S. Sprague, *The* Laches *and the* Charmides, trans. with an introduction and notes (New York: Bobbs-Merrill, 1973), p. 17.

[8] Foucault, "Discourse on Truth," p. 60. Foucault stresses that Nicias casts him in such a role despite the clear difference between Socratic parrhesia and democratic parrhesia in the Assembly: Socratic parrhesia requires a face-to-face relationship.

will be like. In so depicting Nicias and Laches, moreover, Plato relies on the ethic of parrhesia to convey another feature of philosophic practice: the need for willing, active audience cooperation.

A passage from Book 8 of the *Laws* also shows Plato's concern to tie not only intellectual disposition but also personal qualities as evidenced by deeds to one's capacity to practice parrhesia. Book 8 opens with the Athenian Stranger taking up the complex matter of how to legislate for the organization of the festivals and sacrifices that will occupy citizens much of their time. The Athenian quickly moves to the matter of who should be permitted to compose and sing the poems of praise and blame that will decorate the festivities and constitute their educational value. He concludes that those chosen should not simply be men of a certain age who display a certain talent but, most importantly, should be men "who are artists of noble deeds" (829d). To these men (selected by the guardians of the laws) will be given "the prize of being the only ones who may exercise parrhesia in musical competitions" (829d). They may compose freely and expect their compositions to be sung unedited. Parrhesia here may appear to have a certain implication of guardedness and self-censorship. But that is the point. For Plato, to exercise parrhesia is not simply to say whatever pops into one's head, but to say what one thinks best. It involves discrimination and moral seriousness.

Laches' concern for the character and virtue of a speaker (harmony in his soul) has roots in the Athenian understanding of the ideal of parrhesia. For one to be able to get away with publicly speaking intense criticism, one had to make a case for one's own worth, integrity, and virtue. Orators, as we saw in Chapter Two, cited their deeds to bolster the claim to personal integrity—but often the deed named was the simple act of daring to speak, given how risky it was to rise before the Assembly. An orator might also cite words spoken on other occasions or material benefactions (e.g., liturgies) performed in the past. The kind of concern for character we find in Laches' admiration for a "musical life" brings a new twist to the Athenian concern for the integrity of the speaker. The "harmonious fitting together of one's words and deeds" at least resembles, if not positively constitutes, a very aim of Socratic examination.[9] Socrates seeks to convince people to accept the striving for such a harmonious condition of the soul as the most important thing in one's life.

In the *Laches*, Plato may be distinguishing philosophic parrhesia from political parrhesia. Whereas philosophic parrhesia aims to produce a har-

---

[9] See Hans Georg Gadamer, *Dialogue and Dialectic: Eight Hermeneutical Studies on Plato*, trans. P. C. Smith (New Haven: Yale University Press, 1980), pp. 1–2. Also note that in the *Gorgias*, Gorgias is portrayed as incapable of participating in a philosophic investigation, a state Socrates sums up as "not harmonic." Socrates, on the other hand, says that he will speak freely and will not choose to be "discordant." See *Gorgias* 457e and 481d.

monious form of life (*bios*), political parrhesia aims to produce political criticism. Other texts too show that Socratic parrhesia is different from political parrhesia. They also indicate that Plato appropriates the ideal of parrhesia for philosophy. But Plato does not simply appropriate the ideal for philosophy, empty it of its contemporary political associations, and give it entirely new meaning.[10] Rather, Plato subtly manipulates its patriotic, political associations to illuminate the relation of this democratic practice to philosophy, as well as to engage his readers in thinking about how far a devotion to this democratic ideal will lead one, gently, to interest in philosophy. In Plato's usage, parrhesia is an intellectually and morally significant ideal.

THE *GORGIAS*: EMBRACING *PARRHESIA*

The *Gorgias* is central to interpreting the evaluation of democracy in Plato's texts. Apart from some short passages in the *Laws*, nowhere else in the dialogues does Plato directly address the institutions and achievements of his native city.[11] Here speakers comment specifically on Pericles, Themistocles, Cimon, and Miltiades, as well as on oratory and the courts. Nor is the criticism as abstract as in the *Republic*. The *Gorgias* attacks the whole way of life at Athens that "measures its 'power' by the number of ships in its harbours and of dollars in its treasury, its 'well-being' by the standard of living of its citizens."[12] The *Gorgias* may also be a deeply personal work. More than an affirmation of the *Apology*, the *Gorgias* is in some sense "Plato's Apology."[13] As Dodds has suggested, "Behind it stands Plato's decision to forgo the political career towards which both family tradition and his own inclinations had urged him, and instead to open a school of philosophy."[14] Every page of the *Gorgias* calls its reader to a new way of living and to the possibility of statesmanship enriched by a capacity to think theoretically about political affairs. Socrates brings the dialogue to a close by commenting to Callicles that once we have begun to practice this new way of life together, "then finally . . . we'll undertake political business. . . . We'll deliberate about whatever we think fit [and] we'll be better at deliberating than we are now. . . . So let us . . . follow this account [of justice and virtue] and call others to follow it" (527d).

Given an agenda arguing against the moral integrity of democratic institutions, it is striking that this dialogue makes dramatic use of the Athenian

[10] On this point I disagree with Foucault, "Discourse on Truth," pp. 63–64.

[11] E. R. Dodds, *Gorgias: A Revised Greek Text with Introduction and Notes* (New York: Oxford University Press, 1959), p. 32.

[12] See ibid., p. 33.

[13] See ibid., p. 31 (note 1), for discussion of this phrase.

[14] Ibid., p. 31.

democratic ideal of parrhesia in its representation of the practice of philosophic examination. The term "parrhesia" appears six times in the *Gorgias* (487a3, 487b1, 487d5, 491e7–8, 492d2, 521a6). In each instance, it refers to the disposition needed for one to participate in a serious search for truth as distinct from a competition for rhetorical victory. This use of the term signals a subtle acknowledgment of certain morally compelling features of democratic life, even though this point does not fit neatly with the dialogue's overall systematic criticism of democracy. Plato's use of parrhesia represents the practice of philosophy, exemplified by Socrates' life, as in some sense organic to Athenian aspirations.

This dialogue is not narrated by one of the participants or recollected by an individual, but enacted. The action depicted in the *Gorgias* takes place a short time after a public demonstration of rhetorical skill by the celebrated rhetor Gorgias.[15] The crowd has moved inside, and Gorgias has agreed to take questions. Socrates prompts Chaerophon to ask, "What is rhetoric?" Polus, Gorgias' pupil, offers to respond, but Socrates asks Gorgias to submit to questioning himself, and Gorgias agrees. After a little while Polus does take over, and then Callicles. The setting amounts, therefore, to a question period in the presence of at least part of the large audience that had assembled to hear Gorgias.[16] The action of the dialogue— the spectacle witnessed by the assembled crowd and envisioned by the reader—is Socrates' encounters with a succession of interlocutors. The *Gorgias* displays the kind of question-and-answer method of investigation that, for Socrates, in some ways constitutes philosophy.

The display is supplemented at various points by explicit accounts of the features of this method. Early in the dialogue, Socrates explicitly raises the issue of the relation between the general climate of free speech in Athens and the practice of philosophy. When Polus moves to take over for Gorgias (461b), Socrates asks him to refrain from making long speeches. Polus responds: "What? Won't I be at liberty to say as much as I want to?" (*ouk exestai moi legein hoposa an boulōmai*, 461d9). Socrates adds, "Indeed it would be hard on you . . . if you came to Athens, where there is the most liberty to speak in Greece (*hou tēs Hellados pleistē estin exousia tou legein*), and then you were the only one here denied it" (461e1–3). He goes on to suggest that if Polus cares about the discussion at hand, he will seek to "examine and be examined" and not make speeches. The passage

---

[15] On the historical Gorgias, see ibid., pp. 6–10. Dodds argues that Gorgias was not and is not represented as either a sophist or an original philosophic thinker, as some modern scholars have suggested. Rather, he was more simply a celebrated rhetor, one who was clever at speaking (*deinos legein*), that is, able to alter the appearance of things with words.

[16] Ibid., p. 118.

indicates that the general climate of free speech characteristic of a demo-cratic polis raises the possibility of doing philosophy, though it by no means guarantees its practice. Polus does not, after all, prove capable of carrying out such an examination.[17]

The most important passage of the *Gorgias* for understanding Plato's interest in parrhesia depicts Socrates' excitement about the apparent frank-ness exhibited by Callicles. After listening to Callicles' defense of natural strength as the proper standard for justice, Socrates exclaims that a fruitful dialogue is possible with Callicles and that he is fortunate to have stum-bled across this marvelous man. Certainly the substance of Callicles' argu-ments is far more challenging than what had been said by either Gorgias or Polus. But Socrates does not stress Callicles' extreme position. In fact, he indicates that Callicles is not an extremist but only an honest, frank exposer of the logic of a commonly held view. Socrates stresses Callicles' parrhesia. Callicles, in contrast to Polus and Gorgias, appears to possess all three necessary prerequisites for a serious investigation into how we ought to live—knowledge, goodwill, and parrhesia (487a)—whereas Gor-gias and Polus possess only knowledge and goodwill. The significance Soc-rates attaches to Callicles' parrhesia appears most vividly in the well-known passage in which Socrates calls him a "touchstone." Socrates remarks:

> If you agree with me about anything in the discussion, then this will have been adequately tested by me and you, and it will no longer need to be brought to another touchstone. For you would never have conceded it either from lack of wisdom or from excess of shame, nor would you concede it to deceive me; for you are a friend to me, as you say yourself. In reality, then, agreement between you and me will finally possess the goal of truth. (487e)

Callicles' embrace of parrhesia creates the possibility of truth because, since Callicles' frankness is without shame (487b1, d5), or, as it is put later at 492d2, he frankly says "what others think but aren't willing to say," he may be able to articulate a consistent view. Callicles' parrhesia helps him avoid getting caught in the contradictions embedded in conventional moral attitudes, where both Polus and Gorgias were tripped up. Socrates eschews these attitudes to listen only to "my beloved philosophy" (481d), while Callicles promises to listen only to his own mind. Unlike Polus and Gorgias, moreover, Callicles regularly appeals to "nature." His frankness plays a key role in this Socratic dialogue because it enables him to criticize conventional, traditional expectations and boldly state what the logic of an argument reveals (491e7–8).

---

[17] See especially the way he responds to Socrates' objection to his discussion of the tyrant Archelaus at 471d–472d.

In addition to linking parrhesia and the practice of philosophic examination, Plato has Socrates assert, and then exploit, the association of these two to confront Callicles' attack on the moral and political usefulness of philosophic inquiry. Callicles allows that boys may profitably engage in philosophy but asserts that it is a soft, wasteful, even ridiculous activity for adults. He insists that an adult practicing philosophy "is bound to end up being unmanly" (*anandrōi*, 485d4). Socrates' response revolves around valorizing the intellectual and moral courage associated with an embrace of speaking with parrhesia. In so doing, he makes Callicles finally appear unmanly himself for failing to practice parrhesia. Callicles is tripped up precisely on the issue of how far he will honor the principle of parrhesia. Socrates shows him that to be consistent, that is, to be a manly, shameless practitioner of parrhesia, he must not recoil from acknowledging that his view of the happy life as one that allows for the most satisfaction of pleasures would lead to the conclusion that the life of a *kinaidos* (*ho tōn kinaidōn bios*, 494e)—an adult man who takes pleasure in the passive role in anal penetration—is happy. But this figure is reviled in Greek culture as thoroughly unmanly,[18] and Callicles cannot bring himself to praise such a life. Callicles will not continue to speak with parrhesia about the subject at hand because his own manliness is now at stake. He might not bend to conventional attitudes about justice, but he will to those governing masculinity.

Plato continues to stress Callicles' failure to live up to the ideal of parrhesia in the closing pages of the text. He has Socrates ask whether he, Socrates, should struggle as would a doctor to make the Athenians better or whether he should serve them and seek to gratify them. Socrates recalls for Callicles his earlier embrace of parrhesia: "Since you began by speaking frankly to me, it's only just that you should go on saying what you think" (521a). But Callicles counsels Socrates to serve the demos—not, we are led to believe, because he thinks it is what is best or right, but because he considers the risk in doing otherwise too great. "If you don't . . .," Callicles begins—but Socrates jumps in: "Don't tell me what you've often told me, that anyone who wants to will kill me." Callicles is, of course, urging Socrates to be a flatterer. Having given up parrhesia, Callicles is reduced to advocating precisely the kind of risk-averse conventional attitude he had earlier derided.

Socrates' characterization of true statesmanship in the *Gorgias* has much in common with the political role of speaking with parrhesia glorified in the Athenian civic self-image. Doing philosophy is represented in the *Gorgias*: as steadfastly opposed to flattery; as personally daring, dangerous, and courageous for the speaker; as performing an unpleasant but ulti-

---

[18] For discussion of the *kinaidos*, see Chapter 3, note 60 above.

mately beneficial service for the polis by subjecting beliefs to rigorous criticism; and—most deeply—as committed to the exposure of truth. Plato appropriates the role of speaking with parrhesia for philosophy (and Socrates) in his effort to articulate the political and moral work philosophy can do.

THE *REPUBLIC*: PRACTICING *PARRHESIA*

The *Republic*'s treatment of parrhesia in Book 8 is more complex than that in either the *Laches* or the *Gorgias*. This part of the *Republic* delivers some of the strongest criticisms of democracy to be found in the Platonic corpus. But here, too, there are subtle indications that the democratic virtue of parrhesia interested Plato. The idealized role of speaking with parrhesia provided a framework for the expression of unconventional and challenging views in Athenian political debate. As in the *Laches* and the *Gorgias*, Plato in the *Republic* explores the relation between this role and philosophic practice.

The general context of the key passage from the *Republic* (557bff.) is Socrates' account of a typology and transformation of regimes and souls—in particular, the account of the metamorphosis of democratic life into tyranny. At the start of this passage, Socrates asks, "Isn't the city full of freedom and parrhesia?" Adeimantus replies, "That is what is said, certainly." Yet what follows describes a democratic polis completely lacking in the practice of critical parrhesia, understood as the frank expression of considered judgment. Democracy is portrayed as a regime in which citizens practice no discrimination; they treat all views and desires as equally deserving of attention and pursuit. In addition, Socrates directly criticizes freedom and, to a lesser extent, equality, but does not criticize the ideal of parrhesia at any point in his argument.

The absence of any explicit attack on parrhesia in this part of the text is striking, though we should be careful not to make too much of the observation of an absence. Freedom of speech was a highly celebrated, and highly controversial,[19] feature of democracy. Moreover, a well-known attack on democratic parrhesia would fit in quite well with a line of reasoning pursued here. Parrhesia on the comic stage, for example, was attacked as nothing more than baseless, abusive speech, speech uninformed by any thoughtful point but uttered simply for the pleasure of the hearers or for the fun of raising a ruckus. Parrhesia in the Assembly was criticized by Isocrates (who defends it in other places) as reckless speech, hardly tied to any commitment to the exposure of truth and practice of intelligent criti-

---

[19] See the attack on free speech (both isegoria and parrhesia) in "Old Oligarch," *Constitution of the Athenians* 1.6–9.

cism, or to the project of discerning good from bad choices.[20] Such views of parrhesia could have formed part of Socrates' case against the lack of discrimination that he takes to be characteristic of democracy. But Plato does not have Socrates develop such an attack on democratic parrhesia, here or elsewhere. Instead, he continues, even in this mature work, to represent the Athenian conception of parrhesia as valuable for substantive reasons. Parrhesia as an ideal remains in the dialogues a practice linked in important ways to the project and practice of philosophy. In addition, Socrates used this term to enlist Athenian attachments to the ideal in order to reduce his interlocutors' suspicions of philosophy. I plot these two connections by looking in turn at several sections of the *Republic*: the picture drawn of democratic life; the account of the metamorphosis of oligarchic man into democratic man; the description of the fully democratic man; the discussion of the transformation of a democratic regime into a tyranny; and the depiction of Socrates' introduction of the idea of women guardians and of the philosopher-ruler.

The opening of Plato's discussion of democracy in Book 8 (557b4–558c6) suggests ways in which certain features of democratic life support philosophic endeavor. These do not directly engage the issue of parrhesia, as do the later parts of Book 8, but they do raise the general issue of the complexity of the relation between philosophy and democracy in Plato's work.

The beginning of the passage appears to register appreciation of the human and material diversity sustained by a democratic culture, as well as recognize the possibilities for leading an independent private life that democratic government creates. Democracy, as we have seen, is said to be a place where one can "live as one likes" (557b).[21] As a consequence, Socrates declares, the regime will produce a variety of sorts of people. He then likens the city to a many-colored robe that delights all who see it, and to a shop that carries an extraordinary variety of goods. What's more, here individuals are not compelled either to rule or to be ruled, to make war or to keep peace. The citizens are gentle toward convicts, shun pettiness in their personal relations, and expect no special training of those who choose to take up political leadership or action.

The first of the features of democratic life taken to be supportive of philosophic activity is the lack of compulsion. Should a "transcendent nature,"[22] that is, a philosophic nature, appear in a democracy, its owner

---

[20] *On the Peace* 14. See also Euripides *Orestes* 905, where "parrhesia" is used to suggest "ignorant outspokenness."

[21] See also Aristotle *Politics* 1310a31 and 1317b11.

[22] Socrates calls a philosophic nature "transcendent" (*huperbeblēmenēn phusin*, 558b) when instead of growing from the rigorous training outlined in the *Republic*, such an individual appears to spring from the midst of a badly structured city.

could choose a private life of philosophy. Plato allows that such natures might emerge in a democracy, moreover, for in addition to providing the example of Socrates' life, he has Socrates actually remark that "*all* sorts of human being come to be" in a democracy (557c1). The "all" I take to include philosophers. We know that Socrates took full advantage of the opportunity to refrain from the active part in politics available to citizens of a democracy in order to live a (long) life of philosophy. Plato, too, chose not to participate actively in politics (*Letter 7* 324c–326a). This is appropriate behavior for a philosophic soul in a corrupt polis, according to *Republic* Book 6 (496a–e).

Socrates comments further that the extraordinary human variety present in democratic Athens makes it a convenient place in which to take up consideration of the specifically political question of regime choice. "Because . . . it contains *all* species of regimes, the man who wishes to organize a city, as we were just doing," Socrates says, "must go to a city under a democracy" (557d4–9). This comment raises two problems of interpretation. First, what could it mean for a specifically democratic city to "contain" or "have" (*echein*) all species of regimes? Second, why is this significant for the conduct of a philosophic inquiry?

On the first question, could it mean that a democratic politeia incorporates institutions of various sorts so that it can observe them? This seems unlikely, because the city would not "contain" or "have" all sorts of institutions. Could it mean that since the city is open to foreigners and its own citizens may travel, knowledge of other regimes is possible to obtain? Could it be a reference to the historical development of a democratic city? Based on Adeimantus' response to Socrates, I favor a different answer. A democracy sustains the kind of openness that allows all regimes to be tried out *in speech*. Adeimantus notes that in a democracy, one seeking the best regime "wouldn't be at a loss for patterns (*paradeigmata*) at least" (557e). The *Republic* itself exemplifies how democracy can "contain" or "have" even the perfect regime—its citizens can create it in thought and discussion and publicize it. This is, moreover, the only sense in which the perfect regime, and therefore truly all regimes, could possibly exist in a democracy. At 472d10–e1, Socrates calls the project of Book 5 the making of a "pattern in speech of a good city" (*paradeigma epoioumen logōi agathēs poleōs*). The ideal city is one *paradeigma*.[23]

Why is this variety necessary for the conduct of a philosophic inquiry? Arlene Saxonhouse suggests that the openness and lack of discrimination characteristic of democratic life are also necessary preconditions for the

---

[23] Compare Plato's suggestion that democracy contains a multiplicity of *paradeigmata* to Pericles' suggestion in the funeral oration that Athens is a *paradeigma* for all Greece (Thucydides 2.37.1). Also see Adam, *The Republic of Plato*, p. 235. Also compare *Laws* 811d–e.

start of a philosophic inquiry.[24] Saxonhouse observes that the discussion of democracy in the *Republic* emphasizes "not . . . the autonomy and the self-expression of the many, not . . . the will of the people—but . . . the acceptance of the principle of openness and thus a resistance to discrimination, whether it be between the ugly and the beautiful, the male and the female, the wise and the foolish." She then argues that "philosophy requires . . . that openness, that initial refusal to discriminate."[25] Saxonhouse relies on a reading of the dramatic structure of the dialogue to develop the point. I would add that we also find the indebtedness of political philosophy to a democratic cultural climate in Socrates' explicit remark about the need for an inquiry like his own to take place in a city under a democracy (557d4–9).

In Book 8 Socrates also describes democracy as a regime of "choice." There is no settled, single, determined way of life sanctioned or promoted by this regime, the passage emphasizes. The authority of tradition is not strong. Instead, individuals are confronted with many decisions and options and rely only on their individual judgment for guidance. At several points Socrates stresses this point by repeating that in a democracy there is "license" (*exousia*, 557b5, b8, d4). This translation of *exousia* is standard but a little misleading. The Greek does not imply deviation from a norm but rather the absence of an overarching norm and the practice of individuals generating their own personal standards, or rejecting any standards whatsoever. Where there is exousia, there is no settled course that applies to all. Every individual is thought to be in possession of the power and authority to determine his or her own way. "There is neither order nor necessity in his [democratic man's] life," as Socrates puts it (561d5–6: *oute tis taksis oute anangkē epestin autou tōi biōi*).

Democratic life therefore raises the questions for citizens, "How am I to decide?" and "How should I lead my life?" These questions require, Socrates insists, the most careful consideration. Socrates' strong criticism of democracy follows from his contention that most people in democracy generally do not give these matters the attention they deserve and that democracy itself makes this possible. People instead usually make decisions on the basis of what is momentarily pleasant and delightful, unencumbered by any conception of the relative worth of the various human pleasures and desires. They therefore lay themselves open to extreme dangers. Their choices are no more thoughtful than if they were determined by lot (561b4).

---

[24] Arlene Saxonhouse, "Plato and the Problematical Gentleness of Democracy," in *Athenian Democracy* (Notre Dame, Ind.: University of Notre Dame Press, 1996).

[25] Ibid., p. 112.

Democracy is a regime of self-conscious creation. When Socrates states that one must come to a democracy if one wishes to build or organize a regime—that is, to take up a project like that of the *Republic* (557d)—Plato is acknowledging that the very project is indebted to a democratic insight: styles of life and of regimes are not given but made; they should be understood as the products of self-conscious human creation.[26] It is possible here, as perhaps nowhere else, consciously to order one's own life, to build a regime in one's self. And it is not only possible but also greatly needed here. The Myth of Er at the close of the *Republic* reiterates the value of philosophic insight for one born into a condition of choice.

These remarks of Socrates raise the attentive reader's interest in the relation between philosophy[27] and democracy. They suggest not only the possibility but perhaps also the necessity of practicing philosophy in a democratic setting. They implicitly admit that among actual regimes, democratic life sustains the cultural environment most conducive to philosophy. Democracy does not sustain a cultural environment conducive to the political empowerment of philosophy. The many factors that converge to prevent such an empowerment are the subject of Book 6, as well as arguably the entire Platonic corpus.

It is in this context that we should understand a potentially troubling passage from the *Republic*. At 497a Socrates suggests that "no regime at all"—and this would have to include democracy—is "suitable for philosophy." He continues, "Not one city today is in a condition worthy of the philosophic nature." The point at this moment in the dialogue is that no actual regime is persuaded of the political usefulness of philosophic knowledge. Socrates is not contradicting the suggestion that, among actual regimes, democracy sustains a cultural environment that is most conducive to the development of moral and political philosophy. Rather, he is suggesting that no available regime permits the full flowering of a philosophic nature because none requires the philosopher to rule. The dialogue suggests that the members of the "suitable" polis, though they need not be philosophic, must understand the political role philosophy is to play if that society is to be able to sustain itself for more than one generation of a philosophic ruler.[28]

[26] See Cornelius Castoriadis, "The Greek Polis and the Creation of Democracy," *Graduate Faculty Journal* 9, no. 2 (1983): 79–115.

[27] By philosophy I mean here moral and political philosophy. The same connections do not obtain if we consider natural philosophy. On the emergence of political philosophy—and political theory—as distinct from natural philosophy, see Sheldon Wolin, "The Invention of Political Philosophy," in his *Politics and Vision* (Boston: Little, Brown, 1960), pp. 28–34.

[28] See Adam, *The Republic of Plato*, p. 33.

The striking comment about how a man wishing to set up a city ought to go to a democracy is immediately preceded by a comment that gently warns of democracy's capacity to lure people away from the search for critical truth. The passage indicates Plato's appreciation of the diversity characteristic of a democratic culture, but also signals that such material diversity can be distracting.

> It [democracy] is probably the fairest of the regimes (*kallistē haute tōn politeiōn*). . . . Just like a many-colored cloak decorated in all hues, this regime, decorated with all dispositions, would also look the fairest (*kallistē an phainoito*) and many perhaps . . ., like boys and women looking at many-colored things, would judge this to be the fairest regime (*kallistēn an polloi krineian*)." (557c)

This passage combines a vivid, memorable image of the diversity characteristic of democratic life with an elegant summary of the harshest criticism of democracy voiced in all the dialogues of Plato. It suggests the seductive powers of democracy and the manner in which democracy dulls people's powers of discrimination—two of the features of democracy that Plato presents as precipitating a transformation into tyranny. The passage does not celebrate diversity but acts principally as a warning: the variety characteristic of democracy is charming and delightful to the point of reducing the judgment of many to something akin to that of children and women.[29] The use of *polloi* for "many" subtly suggests that "the many"— the (male) citizenry—are debased by democracy in this way.

The passage also suggests precisely how democracy manages to charm its members. The language conjures up an image of the *peplos*, an elaborately embroidered robe specially made for the cult statue of Athena in the Parthenon. Every four years, women chosen by the polis wove a new peplos that was presented to the cult statue on a grand and solemn ritual occasion, the Panathenaic Procession. The bearers of the new robe led the great procession from the agora up to the Acropolis. It was an unusually inclusive event, as citizens, metics, children, and women all figured in the procession, and there were crowds of spectators. This occasion, unique to Athens, was so closely associated with the city's assertion of its greatness that it became the subject of the Parthenon frieze. In alluding to the procession, the passage suggests that the spectacles orchestrated by democra-

---

[29] I therefore think that Adam is only partially correct when he proposes that the many-colored robe "is symbolical of kaleidoscopic diversity and changefulness" (*The Republic of Plato*, p. 235). He also suggests that the soul of the democratic man appears to contain a sort of "kaleidoscopic succession of polities" (ibid.), and that democratic man is a "chameleon of human society" (ibid., p. 240).

cies (Athenian democracy is the real subject), especially religious festivals, exemplify the way the regime charms its members. This fits with what Plato argues later in the *Laws*. The Athenian Stranger comments,

> A fear came over me as I reflected on the problem of how someone will manage a city like this . . . where sacrifices, festivals, and choruses are the preoccupations of everyone throughout their whole lives. How, in this city, will they ever avoid the desires that frequently cast many down into the depths, the desires that reason, striving to become law, orders them to avoid? (835d–e)

The juxtaposition of these two comments at the very outset of the *Republic*'s discussion of democracy in Book 8—one on the "many-colored robe" and the other advising the man wishing to organize a city to come to a democracy (557c and 557d)—functions to remind the reader of the impossibility of rendering an unequivocal final verdict on democracy.[30] The democratic regime has a highly complex mixture of attractions and dangers.

The *Republic*'s account of the emergence of democratic man from oligarchic man (559dff.) continues to draw the reader to consider the relation between philosophy and democracy. It does so by raising the issue of parrhesia. In this passage the transformation of oligarchic man into democratic man is attributed to a curious dynamic between true and false speech.

Oligarchic man becomes democratic man when a young man experiences growth in the variety and quantity of his desires. The oligarchic norms imposed by his father, which once regulated his desires and their satisfaction, lose their hold, liberating all desires and declaring them equally deserving of satisfaction. The completion of the change is signaled by the young man's attachment to the ideals of freedom and equality. These ideals celebrate the defeat not only of oligarchic standards of discerning good and bad desires, but of any and all standards of discernment. Democratic individuals live "in accord with a certain equality of pleasures . . . fostering all on the basis of equality," and they consider this life "sweet and free." Such a life is much admired chiefly for the variety the individual can experience (561e).

But Socrates does not attribute the change from oligarchic to democratic man simply to the onslaught of desires and the rejection of oligarchic

---

[30] While Adam notes that Plato "was fully alive to the wonderful variety and colour of Athenian life," he is not exactly right to continue, "but even on this ground democracy did not appear to him worthy of praise" (*The Republic of Plato*, p. 234). The *Republic* here does not produce explicit praise; it does, however, register an understanding of the peculiar brilliance of the regime.

standards. He also attributes it to the young man's soul being "empty of true speeches" (560b9)[31] at the crucial moment when he was confused and suffering inner turmoil. These speeches, "the best watchmen and guardians in the thought of men whom the gods love" (560b9–10), were absent from his mind. Instead, while his mental conflict raged, he was supremely vulnerable to the influence of "false and boasting speeches" (*pseudeis dē kai alazones logoi*, 560c2). These false, boasting speeches closed his mind to any help he may have received in gaining new direction. They "close the gates of the kingly wall within him" (560c3–4) to any help that might have been forthcoming from strengths residing within him, or from older men. Those boasting speeches purge order "from the soul of the man whom they [the pleasures] are seizing . . . they [boasting speeches] proceed to return insolence, anarchy, wastefulness, and shamelessness from exile, in a blaze of light, crowned and accompanied by a numerous chorus" (560d9–e4). This imagery may refer to Alcibiades' return to Athens and the procession to Eleusis that he orchestrated. Once we make this identification, then among the "older men" whose help the boastful democratic man (Alcibiades) resists, we would certainly include Socrates.

At this point it is necessary to consider to what "false and boasting speeches" is supposed to refer and the relation of these speeches to the idea of parrhesia. We can immediately rule out the kind of false speech (lies, myths) that the *Republic* promoted both for the education of children (376eff.) and in the presentation of the "noble lie," also called the "myth of the metals" (414bff.). The false speeches at work in ushering in a disorderly soul have no use, medicinal or noble. They are destructive and tend to incite the passions. Uttering such false speeches is distinctly unlike speaking with parrhesia. Far from counseling critical evaluation and scrutiny of all known alternatives or expressing one's considered judgment, such speeches imply disregard for standards.

I suspect that the phrase "false and boasting speeches" refers to the (false and boasting) words of politicians and perhaps poets. Such an interpretation would fit the critique of these forms of speech that runs throughout the *Republic* (and plays a major role in the *Apology*). It would also fit with an explicit connection made later in this larger passage. Book 6 had reminded us that slanderous speech against philosophy is one of the reasons a city fails to recognize the political value of philosophy, and therefore continues to suffer. The usual slander is that philosophy is a useless, if not vicious, activity. This slander (*diabolē*) is perpetrated, moreover, by those who themselves seek to exercise power (rhetors, poets),

---

[31] "Speeches" is awkward here, but I have opted for it because it is necessary to convey the sense of *logoi*, which suggests not just words but accounts and arguments.

though they lack the knowledge necessary to do so in a way beneficial to the polis.[32]

Now, in this passage, democratic political leaders are represented as catering to the growing desires of the people rather than attempting to direct or educate them. This sort of speech on the part of the politicians figures centrally in the account of the demise of democracy and the emergence of tyranny (564eff.). In discussing the tyrant's rule at the end of Book 8, Socrates explicitly recalls the earlier decision to banish the poets from the ideal city. The poets, he says, "extol tyranny as a condition 'equal to that of a god' " (568b4–5), and "gathering crowds, and hiring fine, big and persuasive voices, they draw the regimes toward tyrannies and democracies" (568c2–4). The role of false speeches in the emergence of democratic man and the striking remark about the soul of the young man being "empty of true speeches" raise serious doubts about the ability of political leaders and the poets—the very citizens democracy counts on to speak with parrhesia and provide "true speeches"—to perform the task of educating action.

How are we to understand the references to "true speeches"? Socrates gives no explicit indication of exactly what they are or from where such speech is to come. We can infer from the work such speeches are capable of doing—establishing some inner order and averting the eventual danger of suffering a tyranny—that "true speeches" guide a critical review of the alternatives facing an individual. In the description of the fully democratic man, Socrates states that the democratic soul "doesn't admit true speech or let it pass into the guardhouse" (561b9–10), that is, into his mind. Such a soul rejects any interest in discerning good from bad desires or recognizing the need to indulge some and control others. He displays no interest in establishing some conscious order. Instead, the democratic man holds that "all [pleasures] are alike and must be honored on an equal basis" (561c3–4). "True speech" must therefore be speech that evaluates critically the merit of acting on any of many and various felt desires.[33] In this way it is like the practice of both critical parrhesia and philosophy. Plato implicitly chooses the general, abstract term "true speeches" to make it possible to observe what is common to both practices—the commitment to truth and the concern to discern good from bad options for action.

---

[32] See the image of the ship at *Republic* 488a–e.

[33] True speech may also be speech that illuminates the value of philosophy, that is, that argues for its political usefulness. This is the implication of Socrates' references in Book 6 to his own speeches aimed to counter the slander of philosophy (489d and 499a). The failure to give an adequate hearing to such speeches is given as part of the reason why reasonably fine natures often do not turn toward philosophy but are lured away by the glorious possibilities associated with other pursuits (and therefore why one willing to pursue philosophy is so very rare), as well as why the city does not insist that true philosophers rule (499b8–10).

Another account of how democracy generates a need for "true speech" appears later in Book 8. Here Socrates allows that democratic man can attain a certain kind of equilibrium. The difficulty is that this equilibrium is due purely to uncontrollable factors such as luck and aging (561a8–10). Socrates argues that "if he [democratic man] has good luck and his frenzy does not go beyond bounds—and if, also, as a result of getting somewhat older and the great disturbances having passed by, he readmits [moderation and order] and does not give himself wholly over to the invaders, then he lives his life in accord with a certain equality of pleasures" (561a8–10). To whichever pleasures happen to come along, he submits himself, "as though [the pleasure] were chosen by lot" (561a–b). Such a man will do gymnastics at one moment, drink at another, and engage in politics at a third (561c–d). Socrates concludes this part of the passage by suggesting that such is the life of an *isonomikos anēr*, a man attached to the law of equality. The term "isonomikos" instantly recalls the celebrated democratic principle of isonomia (political equality), which was, in the democratic mind, strongly associated with the kind of order, balance, and lawfulness thought to characterize the life of a democratic citizen. The text here admits that a commitment to equality can do the valuable, indeed essential, work of keeping one's desires in check and providing order. But it is distinctly unreliable. It requires considerable help from forces beyond human control—chance and nature. Such dependence is acutely problematic. Only one way emerges of adequately addressing the need for order: some exposure to true speech, that is, the active intervention of the intellect.

The issue of parrhesia surfaces in another curious way in the account of a democratic regime's slide into tyranny (562a7ff.). Socrates begins this passage by emphasizing the extreme attachment to freedom characteristic of democracy. He makes greediness for freedom the chief cause of the slide (562b–c). But greediness for freedom is not itself the agent of the disastrous change; the citizens do not all become tyrannical and anarchic. Rather, the climate of greediness provides the condition under which the people will swiftly fall victim to the vicious designs of a few or of one.

The argument begins by describing how the greediness affects daily life. Socrates mentions first the corruption of politics. Liberating the insatiable desires of many makes it possible for a "bad wine-bearer" to become a leader (*prostatēs*), in which case the city gets drunker (562c9–d2). Freedom spreads to everything, including private relations and the behavior of beasts, causing anarchy. No distinctions can be maintained. Citizens, metics, and foreigners will become indistinguishable (562d–563a). Slaves will be no less free than their owners, and freedom will erupt in the relations among men and women (563b). Socrates' description of the excesses of freedom is interrupted at this point by an odd but telling comment by Adeimantus. "Won't we," Adeimantus interjects, "with Aeschylus 'say whatever just came to our lips?' "Socrates responds, "Certainly, I will do just that" (563c1–2).[34] He then goes on to utter the daring (because offensive) remark that even beasts are freer in a democratic city. They move about the city virtually unrestrained, "bumping into whomever they happen to meet on the road" (563c). Both the uninhibited character of the speech Socrates and Adeimantus are practicing and Socrates' affirmation of his intention to continue to speak in this manner remind the reader of the issue of parrhesia. That the image they conjure up is also funny may suggest some allusion to the parrhesia of the comic poets. This brief exchange between Adeimantus and Socrates brings to the fore, if only for a moment, the possibility that Socrates and his interlocutors are practicing parrhesia. They are speaking out. They are saying what they think, following the argument where it leads, exposing truth. In the midst of the anarchy that is democracy, their own practice of parrhesia names the problem and suggests a course of treatment. The juxtaposition does more than hint at a relation between parrhesia and the practice of philosophy.

The concluding remark of this passage is even more telling. Socrates finishes by saying that the radically democratic city in which beasts behave as they wish—the one about to generate a tyranny—is a city "full of freedom" (*mesta eleutherias gignetai*, 563d1). This comment repeats the exact phrase that Socrates had earlier used to introduce democracy, but with one glaring change. Rather than being a city full of freedom and parrhesia (*kai eleutherias hē polis mestē kai parrhēsias gignetai*, 557b4–5), the city is now described as full of freedom only. This omission is deliberate. It implicitly denies the orthodox claim that Athens is a place full of parrhesia because it proposes that parrhesia is not truly practiced by the citizens (chiefly politicians and poets) on whom the Athenians rely for it. As long as the city rejects philosophy, it is a city full of freedom untempered by the critical power of parrhesia. It is for this reason a city in great danger. On this interpretation, Plato defends the ideal of parrhesia rather than attacking it. He suggests that the very regime that professes to honor parrhesia actu-

---

[34] *Oukoun kat' Aischulon . . . "eroumen hoti nun ēlth' epi stoma"*; and *panu ge . . . kai egōge houtō legō*. The implication here is that a serious, critical thought will be expressed, not that a passing fancy will receive the same treatment as a serious conviction. Adam discusses the possibility that this passage links up with Aristotle's *Nichomachean Ethics* 1111a9ff. (*The Republic of Plato*, p. 248). If so, the passage could further imply speaking in a manner that reveals some important truth. It would also fit with Socrates' profession of ignorance even at the moment he utters elements of a positive doctrine. Aristotle, discussing the possibility that a man can be ignorant of what he is doing, cites people who inadvertently reveal a secret and plead, "It slipped out of their mouths . . . as Aeschylus said of the mysteries" (translation from the *Ethics* is from R. McKeon, ed., *The Basic Works of Aristotle* (New York: Random House, 1941). Note that these religious rites were supposed to remain secret; revealing their details was punishable in severe ways.

ally lacks it. Democracy, it seems, has generated a need for a practice it cannot in fact provide.

Parrhesia also plays a role in the *Republic*'s account of how a tyrannical regime evolves. Socrates maintains that tyranny has its origins in the development of conflict among the various members of the city due to the greed of some. He begins by observing that people will not assemble to conduct business without receiving some compensation. The leaders of the people, in order to promote themselves, aim to satisfy the appetite of the people by contriving to take from the wealthy. The wealthy defend their interests, believing the people to be deceived by slanderers. They become committed oligarchs out of the experience, however, and enter into political rivalries with the leaders of the people, or plot to overturn the government. The people, eager to defeat the oligarchs and egged on by their leaders, move to protect the democracy and satisfy their greed by fostering a strong leader. A tyrant, Socrates proposes, then "grows naturally, he sprouts from a root of leadership" (565d1–2). A leader's chief resource in the democratic context, we must remember, is his speech. Leaders are those who successfully persuade the Assembly time after time, gaining for themselves a position of authority with the people. Speech is the primary instrument by which a tyrant initially promotes himself. The emerging tyrant is an example of a deceitful speaker manipulating the felt desires of the people to gain personally.

Socrates' subsequent account of the emergence of the full tyrant offers a scenario in which the false speech of the politician plays a central role. A leader brings an unjust charge against a wealthy man, seeking to seize his wealth to satisfy the greed of his followers. The leader in effect murders the man and starts rumors about the cancellation of debts and redistribution of land (more false speech). This action incites the wealthy to seek to slay this emerging tyrant, or to turn the people away from him by means of their own strong, even slanderous, speech. If they fail, however, the leader is likely to become a tyrant, as he has already tasted blood. He tricks the people (more false speech) into allowing him to form a private bodyguard and is then firmly installed.

Where is the celebrated practice of parrhesia in this story? Parrhesia, truthful political criticism, was supposed to be the Athenians' front line of defense against the potential for abusing the power of speech and the threat to the integrity of the democratic political order. The patriotic self-image celebrated parrhesia for its capacity to perform precisely this role. Yet parrhesia is absent from this account. In Plato's tale of the fall of democracy, the people simply ride along; they do not name abuses or criticize the prosecution of policy. Instead, either they are drunk with booty, or their minds are closed through the influence of false speech. Once the tyrant is well-established, it is made clear that the powers of true persuasion and critical speech are no match for the use of physical force and violence in ways unaccountable to the people. The fate of those who desperately turn to parrhesia at this point reveals the cost of its neglect at an earlier time.[35] A citizen suspected by the tyrant of having "free thoughts" (*eleuthera phronēmata*, 567a5–6)[36] or of being discontented with the tyrant's rule will simply be killed (sent to fight in a drummed-up war). Even a person from the tyrant's inner circle who attempts to address the tyrant frankly in an effort to resist the perpetration of horrors will simply be killed.[37]

This account of the slide into tyranny would not have struck the average Athenian democrat as odd. Quite the contrary. Fear and suspicion of political leaders was common. The Athenians worried about deceitful oratory and the virtue of their advisors, that is, the strength of their advisors' commitment to the priority of the public interest over the promise of private benefit. The Athenians considered their city to have reliable mechanisms in place to check these threats (among these would be a commitment to parrhesia). If in fact those mechanisms were reliable, Plato's text would be wrong in pressing the absence of true parrhesia and the extreme vulnerability of a democratic polity and a democratic citizen.[38] Nevertheless, the language works implicitly to reduce Athenian democrats' suspicions of philosophy by suggesting that philosophy has a political use in fulfilling the role of advising the polis in a spirit of parrhesia.

At two crucial moments in the argument of *Republic* Book 5, Plato's depiction of Socrates' disposition highlights the fact that he is speaking especially boldly, that he is daring to venture where the argument leads, that he is daring to say what he truly thinks. These passages are Socrates' introduction of the possibility of women guardians (450cff.) and the idea of the philosopher-king (473cff.). Although the term "parrhesia" does not appear in these passages, other constructions emphasize that the progress of the philosophic investigation requires a willingness to speak frankly. The characteristics attributed to Socrates at these moments echo some of the characteristics patriotically associated with one who dares to speak with parrhesia.

[35] The link between the failure to practice parrhesia and the development of severe problems recalls Demosthenes' warning that democracy is in danger when citizens fail to practice parrhesia (*On Organization* 15).

[36] The use of the phrase "free thoughts" is noteworthy for its recognition of the intellectual freedom presupposed by the ethic of parrhesia.

[37] Socrates' description of the death of this individual at 567b may be a reference to the fate of Theramenes during the period of the Thirty Tyrants. See Aristotle's defense of him in *Constitution of the Athens* 28.5, 32.2, 33.2, 34.3, 36.1–37.1.

[38] Perhaps an example of the unreliability of these mechanisms is Thucydides' account of citizens who opposed the Sicilian expedition being frightened into silence after the majority became enthused with the enterprise during the speech of Alcibiades (6.24.4).

The introduction of the idea of women guardians is replete with references to the many great risks run when one speaks uncommon or radically critical things. Socrates identifies the specific risks he is about to assume: the proposal will seem impossible, and his credibility will be doubted (450c); he will prove to be mistaken and cause harm to his fellows, albeit involuntarily (450e–451a); and he will be laughed at (451a). Socrates' articulation of these risks reminds the reader of the practice of speaking with parrhesia. The list recalls Assembly oratory in which the speaker appeals to the ethic of parrhesia and highlights the great risks he is undertaking in order to emphasize his personal integrity. The characteristically Socratic worry about being mistaken also recalls the politician who appeals to parrhesia to indicate that he is offering his understanding of the truth in all seriousness, but not as an absolute certainty. The worry about eliciting laughter also strongly evokes the ethic of parrhesia. It was on the comic stage that the limits of Athenian toleration of parrhesia were pushed most aggressively. The interlocutors' assurance to Socrates that he should assume the risks because "your audience won't be without judgment, or distrustful, or ill-willed" (450d) also evokes the practice of parrhesia, suggesting the characteristics one expects of the hearers in a parrhesiastic encounter. Glaucon's final exhortation to "be bold and speak" (*tharrēsas lege*, 451b5) reiterates the ethic of parrhesia just before Socrates introduces his radical idea.

The introduction of the idea of the philosopher-king also subtly manipulates the ethic of parrhesia to encourage the reader to consider seriously the radical proposal about to be uttered. Socrates begins by noting that he and his interlocutors must identify "what is badly done in cities today" and demonstrate "with what smallest change . . . a city would come to this [ideal] manner of regime" (473b). He then states briefly and forcefully that the small change he has in mind will probably drown him in a wave of laughter and ill repute, but that nevertheless, "it shall be said" (*eirēsetai d'oun*, 473c7). He then addresses his readers and interlocutors in the imperative: "Consider what I am going to say" (*skopei de ho mellō legein*, 473c8–9). The risks he has identified include not only being laughed at but also something more akin to the risks undertaken by orators: losing one's standing with the public. The "small change" that can illuminate the transformation of the city is, of course, the marriage of philosophic knowledge and political power. When Socrates reiterates the need for this "small change" later in Book 6, he again emphasizes that he is speaking in the spirit of parrhesia. He refers to the argument he made as "fair and free speech (*logōn . . . kalōn te kai eleutherōn*) of the sort that strain[s] with every nerve" and recalls that when he first made the proposal, he "was frightened; but, all the same, compelled by the truth [to continue]" (499a).

The *Laws*: Practicing *Parrhēsia*

The terminology of parrhesia figures prominently in three passages in the *Laws*. In all these instances we find Plato turning to the idea and language of parrhesia to represent the practice of critical intellectual work. The first two concern the activity of interlocutors in the dialogue. The third appears in the Athenian Stranger's depiction of intellectual labor practiced by a member of the ideal city.

In Book 7 of the *Laws*, the Athenian Stranger turns to the question of how the women of this second-best city ought to live: are they to receive the same training as men, or are they to follow a distinct regimen? In taking up this question, the Athenian Stranger criticizes the way women live in Sparta. At this point the Spartan interlocutor, Megillus, turns to the Cretan interlocutor, Kleinias, and asks, "What are we going to do? . . . Are we going to let the stranger run down Sparta in front of us this way?" Kleinias' reply is significant. He states simply, "Yes. Parrhesia has been granted him and we have to let him go until we've gone through the laws in a way that is entirely sufficient" (806c8–d2). Here an explicit appeal to the group's commitment to the ideal of parrhesia affirms two things crucial to the progress of the investigation: the expression of criticism, and the interlocutors' willingness to see the argument through to the end. The idea of speaking with parrhesia comes up again only a few paragraphs along, this time from the Athenian Stranger. The issue now is what kind of poetry it is proper for the laws to permit citizens to encounter. After the Athenian Stranger has identified some of the known (historical) options before the lawmaker, but before he conducts any critical analysis, he pauses to remind his interlocutors of their commitment to the ideal of parrhesia. "Now isn't it the case that you're urging on me to speak with parrhesia in order that I might show . . . which part of what they say is fine and which is not?" (811a5–7).[39] Kleinias responds, "What else but that?" Again, a commitment to parrhesia is represented as crucial to the company's ability together to sustain the investigation.

At *Laws* 835c4 (Book 8), we find a dramatic appropriation of the ideal of parrhesia for philosophy. The Athenian Stranger here admits that the regulation of the sacrifices and festivals that the city is to celebrate is a particularly difficult task. Though some small changes may make little difference, there are other matters of grave importance "about which it is difficult to be persuasive, and which are in fact the task of the god, if it were somehow possible to get orders . . . from him." The Athenian continues:

---

[39] Translation slightly modified.

As things stand now, what is required, in all probability, is some daring human being, who by giving unusual honor to parrhesia (*hos parrhēsian diepherontōs timōn*) will say what in his opinion is best for the city and the citizens. Speaking before an audience of corrupt souls, he will order what is fitting and becoming to the whole political regime; opposing the greatest desires, and having no human ally, all alone he will follow reason alone. (835c)

What is the force of "honoring parrhesia," of boldly stating criticism rooted in one's opinion of what is best? This passage goes on to suggest the special quality of the lone man's opinion. It is rooted in "reason alone" and "has no human ally." Plato here straightforwardly appropriates the democratic ideal of parrhesia for the practice of philosophy. "Honoring parrhesia" here amounts to uttering truthful opinions grounded in knowledge of "what is fitting and becoming" to the conduct of public affairs, specifically the scope or application of the laws. Such knowledge has a strong kinship to the knowledge that Socrates fosters, philosophic knowledge. In the Athenian Stranger's vision, philosophic parrhesia is practiced not in a one-on-one examination but in the delivery of truthful criticism to a large audience. This is more like the democratic parrhesia praised by Demosthenes, but this speaker's criticisms do not seem destined to be scrutinized by the people or subjected to a vote. This speaker has special standing and authority. Plato's invocation of the ideal of parrhesia here helps him to articulate a role he sees as required in this imagined city.

Plato implicates parrhesia, a cherished ideal of democratic politics, in the very practice of philosophy. He portrays the ideal of parrhesia as substantively attractive and rhetorically useful. He manipulates appeals to the ethic of parrhesia to draw the Athenian reader into the investigation at hand and to articulate the demands such an investigation places upon its practitioners. The patterned treatment of this democratic ideal in the texts reveals Plato reflecting on philosophy's complex relation to democracy.

Chapter Seven

REMEMBERING PERICLES: THE POLITICAL AND THEORETICAL IMPORT OF PLATO'S *MENEXENUS*

THE *MENEXENUS* is a far more interesting dialogue than is usually supposed.[1] In this dialogue, Plato has Socrates recite a funeral oration purportedly composed by Aspasia not only to advance his well-known critique of rhetoric but also to engage the Thucydidean construction of Pericles'

[1] The *Menexenus* has received little sustained attention, in large part due to the difficulty of fitting Socrates' recitation of a funeral oration into a traditional view of Plato's political concerns. Scholars a generation ago even treated the text as spurious, despite the compelling evidence for its genuineness—Aristotle twice cites it (*Rhetoric* 1367b8, 1415b3). Accepting it as authentic, scholars today focus on explaining why Plato uses this genre of oratory. On how the *Menexenus* advances a critique of rhetoric, see E. F. Bloedrow, "Aspasia and the Mystery of the Menexenus," *Wiener Studien* 9 (1975): 32–48; Robert Clavaud, *Le Ménexène de Platon et la rhétorique de son temps* (Paris: Belles Lettres, 1980); L. J. Coventry, "Philosophy and Rhetoric in the Menexenus," *Journal of Hellenic Studies* 109 (1989): 1–15; E. R. Dodds, *Gorgias: A Revised Greek Text with Introduction and Notes* (New York: Oxford University Press, 1959), pp. 23–24; M. M. Henderson, "Plato's *Menexenus* and the Distortions of History," *Acta Classica* (Cape Town) 18 (1975): 25–46; Charles Kahn, "Plato's Funeral Oration: The Motive of the *Menexenus*," *Classical Philology* 58 (1963): 220–34; Nicole Loraux, *The Invention of Athens: The Funeral Oration in the Classical City* (Cambridge, Mass.: Harvard University Press, 1986); Donald J. Maletz, *Plato's* Menexenos *and the Funeral Oration of Pericles* (Ann Arbor, Mich.: University Microfilms International, 1975); Andrea Nightingale, *Genres in Dialogue: Plato and the Construct of Philosophy* (New York: Cambridge University Press, 1995), pp. 106–7; Stephen Salkever, "Socrates' Aspasian Oration: The Play of Philosophy and Politics in Plato's *Menexenus*," *American Political Science Review* 87 (1993): 133–46; Arlene W. Saxonhouse, *Fear of Diversity: Political Science in Ancient Greek Thought* (Chicago: University of Chicago Press, 1992), pp. 111–22; J. A. Shawyer, *The Menexenus of Plato*, edited with an introduction and notes (Oxford: Clarendon, 1903). For discussion of the text as a "poorly executed spoof" of funeral oratory, see Paul Shorey, *What Plato Said* (Berkeley: University of California Press, 1933), pp. 137–41; and A. E. Taylor, *Plato: The Man and His Work* (London: Methuen, 1949). For discussion of how the *Menexenus* might address specific policies pursued by the Athenians, see Pamela Huby, "The *Menexenus* Reconsidered," *Phronesis* 2, no. 2 (1957): 104–14; Kahn, "Plato's Funeral Oration"; and Maletz, *Plato's Menexenos*. For discussion of the *Menexenus* as an "ironic indictment of Athens," see Bruce Rosenstock, "Socrates as Revenant: A Reading of the *Menexenus*," *Phoenix* 48 (1994): 331–47. For an overview of the issues in earlier scholarship, see Shawyer, *The Menexenus* (1903). For a review of the issues in the more recent scholarship, see R. E. Allen, "Plato's *Menexenus*, Translation and Commentary," in *The Dialogues of Plato*, vol. 1 (New Haven: Yale University Press, 1985), pp. 319–43.

significance for Athens and for us. Plato here considers the enduring meaning of the life of Pericles. At stake is "an act of memory."[2] In particular, in the *Menexenus* Plato attacks his contemporaries' veneration of Pericles, rejects the model of democratic citizenship based on erotic relations attributed to Pericles in Thucydides' *History of the Peloponnesian War* in favor of one based on family relations, and considers the theoretical import of a key strategy of Athenian democratic discourse at which Pericles reportedly excelled—the *epitaphios logos* (eulogy spoken at the public funeral for war dead).[3] The *Menexenus* also shows how much Plato's thought is indebted to practices of Athenian democracy even as it delivers a critique of Athenian politics. For instance, we find in the *Menexenus* Plato appropriating for philosophy at least part of the intellectual mission that the Athenians associated with the practice of the funeral oration.

PLATO'S OPPOSITION TO THE VENERATION OF PERICLES

We must first recall Thucydides' explicit judgment of Pericles before tracing the conversation with this view sustained in the *Menexenus*. Though the progress of Thucydides' narrative of the war suggests that the historian's final judgment on Pericles is not entirely glowing, when he pauses at the end of Pericles' third speech (2.65) to comment on the leader in his own voice, he delivers strong praise.[4] Thucydides notes that Pericles did not live much longer and asks the reader to imagine the enormity of this loss for the Athenians. Hindsight reveals that Pericles had been the most thoughtful leader of the Athenians. The policies he advocated seem, in retrospect, to have been truly in the best interest of the city. At this moment Thucydides even comes close to lamenting the Athenians' inability to stay on the course Pericles had recommended. Had Pericles lived, Thucydides suggests, Athens might have won the war. He also specifies the

---

[2] Jacques Derrida, *Politics of Friendship*, trans. George Collins (New York: Verso, 1997), p. 95. He is explicitly commenting on Plato's *Menexenus*.

[3] Only Salkever also considers whether in the *Menexenus* Plato investigates the possibilities raised by democratic life and politics. In "Socrates' Aspasian Oration," he suggests that the *Menexenus* explores the possibility that philosophy can utilize rhetorical techniques and ritual occasions in an effort to communicate with the demos. The content of that communication is not to be found in advocating specific substantive ideas, but in insisting on placing certain questions on the agenda of public debate (e.g., the kind of language appropriate to political speech). I find this argument insightful and plausible. But it does not explore how much of a debt Plato's texts owe to the tradition they criticize. Salkever considers how far philosophy can deign to take the form of ordinary politics without corrupting itself or its message.

[4] Thucydides does not consistently confirm the positive evaluation voiced at 2.65 but rather subjects it to considerable scrutiny as the narrative proceeds. See S. Sara Monoson and Michael Loriaux, "The Illusion of Power and the Disruption of Moral Norms: Thucydides' Critique of Periclean Policy," *American Political Science Review* 92, no. 2 (1998): 285–97.

personal and intellectual qualities that made Pericles outstanding. Pericles not only could see what was best, he also could control the demos, that is, he could "lead them [the multitude] instead of being led by them" (2.65.8). As a result, under his leadership democracy was, in Thucydides' judgment, "in words" (*logōi*) a democracy but "in action" (*ergōi*) the "rule of the first man" (*hupo tou prōtou andros archē*, 2.65.9), and the Athenians averted the difficulties usually associated with democratic politics. Thucydides praises Pericles as a model statesman, a leader who appears to have kept democratic politics from deteriorating into factional disputes and the pursuit of personal ambition. All the leaders who came after him, Thucydides states, sought only to gratify themselves and their hearers, and politics took a turn for the worse.

It is not hard to imagine this explicit evaluation of Pericles gaining some popularity in the post–Peloponnesian War years, despite the historian's subtle efforts to raise questions about the truth of this preliminary assessment.[5] This view vindicates imperial aspirations (which were far from dead) and lays the blame for Athens' suffering in the latter years of the war on a set of "bad" advisors. This view also affirms that the war could have turned out differently, that there was nothing inevitable about Athens' defeat. Venerating Pericles had other attractions as well. His memory was not mired in continuing factional disputes, and he was a champion of democratic institutions. He could be a fitting symbol for a *restored* democracy struggling to reestablish some civic solidarity across social and economic divisions that had recently erupted in civil war. Though Pericles was a "leader of the people" (*prostatēs tou dēmou*), he was also held in good repute by the elite at Athens.[6] Venerating Pericles in the postwar period could be a strategy for asserting the continuity of the democracy of the years following the rule of the Thirty Tyrants with the vibrant democracy of the prewar period, linking the restored democracy with the imperial glory, commercial success, artistic vitality, excellent reputation, and civil peace that distinguished the earlier time.

From Plato's point of view, the stakes involved in the struggle to attach symbolic meaning to the memory of Pericles must have been great. Plato's writings aim to unsettle their readers' confidence in the adequacy of the

[5] Writing two generations after Thucydides, Aristotle offers an assessment of Pericles that he treats as uncontroversial and that indicates that the evaluation voiced at Thucydides 2.65 had indeed gained some currency. Aristotle writes: "As long as Pericles was the leader of the people, the state (*politeia*) was still in fairly good condition, but after his death everything became much worse" (*Constitution of Athens* 28.1). Harvey Yunis observes that the "Thucydidean exaltation of Pericles had begun to dominate popular understanding" by the mid-fourth century (*Taming Democracy: Models of Political Rhetoric in Classical Athens* [Ithaca: Cornell University Press, 1996], p. 143, with note 13, for useful points of comparison in orators).

[6] Aristotle *Constitution of Athens* 28.1.

moral and political outlook that a veneration of Pericles seems designed to solidify. They question whether the (soul-ignoring) understanding of human flourishing that Periclean Athens represents is really attractive. But whereas many dialogues aim to induce *aporia* (intellectual discomfort, uncertainty), the *Menexenus* begins with a mild version of it. The dramatic setting of the *Menexenus* indicates that this work assumes that the matter of whom the Athenians should admire—that is, what is praiseworthy and, by implication, blameworthy behavior—is an open question. At the start of the dialogue, Menexenus tells Socrates that he has just come from the agora, having gone there to see whom would be chosen to deliver the eulogy at the upcoming public funeral rites. But, he reports, no choice was made today.[7] The action of this dialogue continues under the assumption that the question, "Whom should we choose?" remains open.

---

[7] Menexenus playfully mentions that perhaps tomorrow they will choose Archinus or Dion. Of course, neither was a real possibility, and he knows it. Archinus was too brutal and Dion was not an Athenian. So why does Plato have Menexenus ironically mention these names? I speculate it is to develop Menexenus' characterization, specifically to indicate he is a capable interlocutor.

By having Menexenus mention Archinus, Plato lets us know that Menexenus will see the irony in Socrates' outrageous account of Athenian history in the oration he is about to recite. In particular, it suggests that he can see through its account of one key episode—the period of the restoration of democracy after the defeat of the Thirty. In Socrates'/Aspasia's telling, the returning exiled democrats and the former partisans of oligarchy were so fabulously gentle toward one another that men everywhere now look to Athens as a model of how to conduct civil war (243e–244b). As Fine suggests, the restraint showed by the people, and in particular by the returning exiles (partisans of democracy), during this period was extraordinary given the violence of the oligarchic domination. (See John V. A. Fine, *The Ancient Greeks: A Critical History* [Cambridge, Mass.: Harvard University Press 1983], p. 523.) The Athenians had reason to be proud of the reconciliation they had achieved. But, as Aristotle stresses (*Constitution of Athens* 40), only the harsh measures advocated by Archinus enabled the Athenians to live up to the terms of the amnesty—not each party's readiness and friendliness toward each other, as suggested at *Menexenus* 243e (*asmenōs kai oikeōs*). Archinus attacked the leading democrat's proposal to enfranchise noncitizen men (metics, slaves) who had fought for the restoration; contrived illegally to terminate earlier than expected the period in which elite citizens were permitted to migrate, thus forcing some to stay against their will; and recommended using brutal measures (including the death penalty) to enforce the immunity from prosecution for those citizens who wished to stay but who had been members or supporters of the Thirty. (On Archinus, see Fine, *The Ancient Greeks*, pp. 523–55.)

By having Menexenus suggest that the Athenians might choose Dion, a foreigner whose intellect Plato admired, Plato indicates that this interlocutor understands that the spatial boundaries of a particular polis cannot contain the question at hand. The issue in question in this dialogue is not simply who among our local citizens should get this honor, but, broadly speaking, what is the nature of admirable conduct, and to what form of excellence should we aspire? Dion was a member of the Syracusan royal family who was personally linked to Plato and who led a force of exiles to depose a brutal tyrant. He proved an incompetent ruler and was assassinated by an associate. For Plato's account of his intellectual and personal

Plato articulates the political stakes in properly assessing Pericles most clearly in the *Gorgias*. Here Plato criticizes the tendency of his contemporaries to venerate the memory of Pericles by setting up a rivalry between Pericles and Socrates for the title "most *politikos* citizen."[8] He attacks Pericles, along with Cimon, Themistocles, and Miltiades, for feasting the Athenians, that is, for "supplying them with what they had an appetite for" rather than making "the citizens better" (517b).[9] The appetite he has in mind is for empire and material riches. Several times the text identifies the delicacies distributed at the feast: "docks, shipyards, and walls," structures necessary for and symbolic of empire. Plato portrays Pericles as stuffing the demos with tasty, but ultimately unhealthy, treats. He does not stand up to the demos; he does not articulate painful truths. Rather, he cleverly panders to them. The *Gorgias* argues that all these highly regarded leaders—and Pericles is singled out for special disdain—did not make the citizens better, only "wilder" (516d2). This is familiar territory: here we see Plato's critique of democratic politics for its reliance on rhetoric that breeds only panderers rather than leaders, that is, men who cater to the city's desires rather than seek to modify them in significant ways.[10] Yet the specific way in which the *Menexenus* furthers the argument of the *Gorgias* is not familiar at all.

Precisely how does the *Menexenus* take on Thucydides' evaluation of Pericles?[11] The allusions in the *Menexenus* to Thucydides, to Pericles, and

---

relationship with Dion, see his letters addressed to Dion's grieving friends after his murder (*Letter 7* and *Letter 8*), with discussion above in Chapter 5.

[8] Especially *Gorgias* 515c–519c, but also 455d–e, 472b, and 503c. *Politikos* refers to a man who is "political" in the sense of being "polis-minded."

[9] Socrates challenges Pericles' reputation for greatness by way of questioning whether he ever "improved" an associate, including his sons, fellow citizens, foreigners, even slaves in the *Protagoras* 319e3–320a; and *Alcibiades I* 118d–e, 119a.

[10] Plato names Pericles as an exemplary orator in several dialogues: *Symposium* 215e5; *Phaedrus* 269a6, 269e1, 270a3; *Gorgias* 472b2, 503c2; and *Theages* 126a9. The allusions to Pericles in the *Menexenus* thus also link this text to the general Platonic critique of rhetoric. On these links, see Yunis, *Taming Democracy*, pp. 136–39.

[11] Allen ("Plato's *Menexenus*"), Kahn ("Plato's Funeral Oration"), and Maletz (*Plato's Menexenos*) see Thucydides as the target of Plato's criticism in the *Menexenus* but miss the target's more specific mark—the construction of Pericles' significance. Similarly, two commentators have observed that in this text, "Plato himself forces the comparison between his own funeral oration and Pericles' " (Rosenstock, "Socrates as Revenant," p. 333; Saxonhouse, *Fear of Diversity*, pp. 117ff.), but both assume that Plato's aim is to engage the substantive arguments put forward by Pericles. While this is a part of the project of the *Menexenus*, it is only a part. The *Menexenus* includes direct and sustained allusions not just to the historical figure Pericles and his policy but specifically to Thucydides' assessment of his lasting symbolic import. Yunis sees the Periclean funeral oration of Thucydides as Plato's "ostensible target" (*Taming Democracy*, p. 139) in the *Menexenus*, but only on his way to a discussion of the *Gorgias*. Yunis does not consider the *Menexenus* in detail.

specifically to Thucydides' construction of Pericles' significance are not hidden, nor are they few. The allusions to Thucydides begin with Plato's adoption of some language that his contemporaries would probably have recognized as peculiar to Thucydides' writings.[12] Socrates is made to use the term "Peloponnesians" (236d)—language only Thucydides uses to refer to the people of this geographical region. Other authors, as well as all of Plato's other dialogues, consistently use terms such as "Spartans" or "Lacedaimonians."[13] Other allusions quickly focus on Thucydides' construction of Pericles. Menexenus goads Socrates by asking him if he could put together a funeral speech on short notice were he to be elected orator. Socrates says in response that he could do as well as Pericles because they share a teacher (235e). My teacher, he continues, "has made many other people good orators, one of whom surpasses all the Greeks, Pericles son of Xanthippus" (235e). Menexenus immediately recognizes the teacher as Aspasia, Pericles' mistress. Socrates attributes authorship of the speech he recites in this text to Aspasia: it was "pieced together" out of the "left-overs" from the one she had written for Pericles some time ago (236b), an obvious reference to Pericles' funeral oration. Another strong allusion to Thucydides appears in this brief, dense passage. Socrates suggests that praising Athenians among Athenians is not a very difficult task and that even someone "less well instructed" than himself—for example, one who was trained in rhetoric by Antiphon—could do it (236a). This is a swipe at Thucydides' assessment of Athenian leaders, as he had identified Antiphon as a highly capable thinker and speaker (8.68.1–2).

Textual parallels between the speech Socrates recites and the Periclean oration as found in Thucydides' text also provide a link with the Thucydidean Pericles. These parallels include the use of the *logos/ergon* antithesis at the start and a direct quote from the ending of Pericles' oration at the close of the Aspasian speech.[14] In addition, by presenting the exhortation to the survivors that closes Socrates' speech as a report of the actual words once spoken by now dead soldiers, Plato alludes to Thucydides' insertion of speeches into his narrative. Thucydides uses literary artistry to prompt his reader to treat his reconstructed speeches in the same way that Socrates asks his listeners to treat his impersonation of the dead: as if they were "the very voices of the men themselves" (246c). Moreover, Plato's inclusion of a passage in which Socrates reflects on the method used to compose this portion of his speech sustains a powerful allusion to Thucydides' account

---

[12] Maletz, *Plato's Menexenos*, p. 38.

[13] Plato ordinarily uses the term "Lacedaimonians" to denote the people of the Peloponnese. See Leonard Brandwood, *A Word Index to Plato* (Leeds: W. S. Maney and Sons, 1976), on the pattern of Plato's word use.

[14] See Kahn, "Plato's Funeral Oration," pp. 222–23; and Rosenstock, "Socrates as Revenant," pp. 333–34.

of his method. Plato has Socrates say, "I shall tell you what I heard from these men, and what things they would be glad now to say to you if they had the power, as indicated by what they said then" (246c). This recalls Thucydides' comment at 1.22.1:

> With reference to the speeches . . ., some I heard myself, others I got from various quarters; it was in all cases difficult to carry them word for word in one's memory, so my habit has been to make the speakers say what was in my opinion demanded of them by the various occasions, of course adhering as closely as possible to the general sense of what they really said.

Socrates' funeral speech also suggests—and questions—Thucydides' explicit judgment of Periclean leadership. For example, when Socrates moves to describe the constitution that nourished the men of Athens, he uses language that echoes Thucydides' contention that Pericles ruled at Athens as "first man" and that the resulting political order was a democracy in name only (2.65.9). Let me cite the *Menexenus* passage in full.

> The same constitution existed then as now, aristocracy, and under this we dwell as citizens now. . . . One man calls it democracy, another what he pleases. But in truth it is Government by the Best, with the approval of the multitude. . . . While the multitude has control over most things in the city, they give authority and rule to those they *believe* are the best, and no one is excluded by reason of physical weakness nor poverty nor ignorance of his fathers nor, as in other cities, esteemed by reasons of their opposites. There is but one standard: he who *seems* to be wise or good is to rule and govern. (238c–d, emphasis added)

The Socratic/Aspasian oration continues: "The cause of our constitution is equality of birth. . . . We defer to each other in nothing except the *appearance* of virtue and wisdom" (238e–239a, emphasis added).

Socrates' hesitation about the proper name of the regime he lauds in this fictive eulogy of a fictive city may have theoretical import. Derrida proposes that it points to the gap between the name and the concept of a thing, signaling that it is precisely in this space—the gap—that Plato's thought operates. He then reads Plato's hesitant effort to affix, however loosely, the name "democracy" to the imagined Athens of the funeral oration as an effort to stress an abstract aspect of an idealized regime: "The required approbation of . . . the greatest number."[15] My proposal that the phrasing engages Thucydides' evaluation of Periclean leadership supports his reading. Referring to Periclean Athens as a democracy "in name" and yet also (in concept) the "rule of the first man," Thucydides stresses that Pericles enjoyed the approval of the many. Thucydides had reasoned that

---

[15] Derrida, *Politics of Friendship*, p. 101.

democratic institutions prevailed at Athens, but that by the force of his oratory and the intelligence of his vision Pericles was able to lead. In the case of Pericles, he maintains, the people deferred to one who was wise and good—or at least was the closest thing to wise and good that any had encountered. By contrast, the prevalence of the language of appearances (*doxa*) in the *Menexenus* passage cited above questions that judgment: On what basis did and does Pericles enjoy the appearance of virtue and wisdom? Should he really have been so respected, and should he continue today to be lauded above all others? Was he really wise and good? The *Menexenus* does not answer these questions, but it does stress their importance. In particular, the *Menexenus* questions the core of Thucydides' case for the exceptional excellence of Pericles voiced at 2.65. Plato's text engages the subtle critique of the Athenian tendency unreflectively to embrace the example of Pericles that Thucydides himself advances in the rest of his narrative and challenges a crucial assumption upon which rests the view that the memory of Pericles should serve as a symbol of Athenian aspirations in the postwar years: the belief that Pericles bears no responsibility for the painful course of events that led up to the Athenian defeat, that is, for the course of the war after his death. How does it do this? The *Menexenus* advances this issue through the account of Athenian history that forms the next part of the funeral oration recited by Socrates.

Two things stand out about this account of Athenian history. First, the text contains a blatant anachronism. Socrates recounts events that happened long after his death. This anachronism serves to link Pericles to the course of the war after his death. Socrates even speaks of Pericles at one point as if he were still alive (235e),[16] yet Pericles had died some thirty years earlier. Second, the irony in this account is quite thick. The tale focuses on the autochthonous birth of the city and the Persian Wars, skips over the amassing of empire, then presents a highly satirical account of the events from the Peloponnesian War down to the Corinthian War. The account perpetrates some extraordinary falsifications of history. It contends, for example, that Athens stood with Sparta against Persia during the Corinthian War, when in fact Athens stood with Persia against Sparta. While we must expect any funeral oration in the Athenian tradition to portray Athenian history selectively, indeed generously, the account Socrates recites is striking for the number and enormity of its falsifications. In part, the ironic features of the oration critique rhetoric in general and funeral oratory in particular. They ridicule these forms of public speech for their reliance on manipulations of fact and outright untruths in order to inflate the citizens' patriotic pride.

---

[16] See Allen, *The Dialogues of Plato*, 1: 319.

The *Menexenus* unmasks the funeral speech. Thucydides' own text, however, had already unmasked the bravado and self-deception in the Periclean funeral speech. Thucydides' telling of the war's history reveals that Athens in actuality did not so closely resemble the image constructed by Pericles in his oration—an image of perfect unity, tolerance, prudence, and intelligence. The sanitized account of the Peloponnesian War in the *Menexenus* and its gross distortions of the Corinthian War stand in stark contrast to Thucydides' own account of the Peloponnesian War, both in its details and in its methodology. The erroneous history in the *Menexenus* suggests, in my view, that to describe recent Athenian history in a manner analogous to the way Pericles described democracy at Athens in his famous speech is to disregard, paper over, indeed wish away, real vulnerabilities and real causes of adversity. To venerate Pericles is to praise someone who would act in such an irresponsible way.

So far I have argued that the *Menexenus* unsettles the glowing evaluation of Pericles voiced at one point in Thucydides' writings (2.65) and disturbs the Athenian practice of taking Pericles to exemplify the kind of virtue to which citizens should aspire. The *Menexenus* does not itself make the case that Pericles indulged Athenians' appetites for advantage and made the citizens "wilder" instead of "better" (as does the *Gorgias*). Nor does it directly make the case that Pericles' "best vision" produced the horrible course of the war after his death. But the *Menexenus* does hint at these conclusions, conclusions that, I have argued elsewhere, Thucydides himself also considered.[17] Its attack on the veneration of Pericles perhaps also links the *Menexenus* to another driving aim of both the *Gorgias* and the *Republic*, that is, undermining the apparent attraction of tyrannical power. We must remember that Thucydides depicts Pericles in his third speech explicitly referring to Athens' possession of empire as being a "tyranny" (2.63.2) and recommending that the Athenians hold onto it.

PLATO'S REJECTION OF PERICLES' MODEL OF DEMOCRATIC CITIZENSHIP

The *Menexenus* engages the specific content of the Periclean vision of citizenship implicit in Thucydides' report of Pericles' funeral oration. In particular, the *Menexenus* opposes Pericles' use of the citizen-as-lover (*erastēs*) metaphor in his celebrated comment: "Gaze, day after day, upon the power of the city and become her [the city's] lovers (*erastai*)" (2.43.1). Pericles' erastes metaphor proposed that individuals understand the demands of Athenian citizenship to involve reciprocal relations of mutual exchange between themselves and the city. The *Menexenus*, I argue, also

---

[17] Monoson and Loriaux, "The Illusion of Power."

favors a reciprocal model of citizenship but proposes that family obligations, not conventional erotic attachments, best capture the dynamics of the exchange.

The *Menexenus* does not explicitly argue against the appropriateness of the erastes metaphor proposed by Pericles. Rather, the dramatic structure of the *Menexenus* suggests that a rejection of this metaphor frames the entire discussion that constitutes this text. The most important evidence for this is the role of Menexenus, the young man after whom Plato titles the text, as significant interlocutor in the *Lysis*.

The *Lysis* provides, as one commentator observes, "two contrasting pictures of love and friendship."[18] Socrates first encounters Hippothales, an adult man in love with a young boy, Lysis. The men assembled tease Hippothales for behaving in a ridiculous fashion in his attempt to win the boy's affection. For example, he sings excessively flattering poetry about the boy and his family. Socrates comments that this is not the right way to behave toward a beloved. A lover should not try to win a beloved like a trophy. The company then asks Socrates to explain what the right way to express love would be. Socrates offers only to give an example, not to provide an explanation. He then leads the men inside the nearby wrestling school to contrive to engage Lysis in a conversation intended to exemplify the proper approach. Plato portrays Hippothales as so thoroughly infatuated with the boy that he cannot face him in this setting but must hide, hearing the exemplary conversation only by eavesdropping.[19]

As Socrates begins to speak with Lysis, it becomes clear that his discussion will not be flattering but rather educative in tone and purpose. It also does not treat the boy as a passive receptacle of the wisdom imparted by a teacher or mentor. He is not a vessel to be filled. Socrates engages him in a philosophic inquiry, asking him to explain the nature of friendship (*philia*), since he appears to know all about it judging from the exceptional relationship he has with another boy his age, Menexenus. The conversation requires that the boy himself (and later Menexenus, when he, too, enters the conversation) be an active, energetic inquirer rather than a passive listener. In fact, the example of how one ought to treat a beloved youth that Socrates develops approximates the equal, reciprocal friendship between the two boys—Menexenus and Lysis. It suggests that both parties, Socrates and his young interlocutor, must be active lovers of the inquiry at hand, and that sexual involvement is an impediment to that end.

---

[18] Donald Watt, "Plato's *Lysis*, Translation and Introduction," in *Plato: Early Socratic Dialogues*, ed. Trevor Saunders (New York: Penguin, 1987), p. 131.

[19] We can read this as suggesting that the kind of eros he experiences is an obstacle to membership in a philosophic community.

This model contrasts sharply with the lover/beloved paradigm ordinarily associated with erotic attachments and exemplified by Hippothales' attitude toward Lysis. Conventional in its educational tone, the *Lysis* is highly unconventional in its proposal of an active/active model. This active/active model is explicitly affirmed toward the end of the *Lysis*, when the interlocutors agree that "the genuine and not the pretended lover must be loved by his boy" (222a–b). This strong active response model was a radical view of erotic relationships during Plato's lifetime. The norms governing conventional relations between lovers and beloveds, as we saw in Chapter Three, detailed precisely how men and boys should act so as to protect the boy from behaving in a servile and therefore dishonorable fashion. Plato's stance deprives these carefully defined codes of conduct of their moral significance. Rather than accept the conventions normally associated with negotiations of relations between loving men and beloved boys, Socrates suggests in the *Lysis*—and later argues strenuously in the *Symposium* and *Phaedrus*—that the distinction between lover and beloved ought to be erased altogether. True eros seeks not an honorable way to the physical possession of a beautiful object (sexual gratification), but rather each lover's possession of the Good. The erotic desire one feels for another can arouse one to this pursuit and, importantly, such conduct (philosophy)—unlike pederastic sexual contact—is something both parties can pursue actively and simultaneously. For Plato, it is in philosophical community, not sexual union, that erotic passion is most fully experienced. In a dialogic partnership, there is "mutual erotic inspiration,"[20] rather than a carefully orchestrated barter relationship (wisdom for sexual favors). In the *Lysis*, Plato has Socrates argue for a radical new understanding of erotic experience that he links to philosophic activity.

Plato sustains this critique of conventional erotic relations throughout the dialogues. The active/active paradigm of relations consistently applies to the philosophical community, that is, to the erotic attachments among the members of the Socratic circle. Plato also stresses the centrality of an active posture to an understanding of true eroticism in his account of the philosopher's relation to the objects of his desire—Truth, the Forms, knowledge. He even borrows the language of the active partner in the conventional love relation to describe the philosopher's disposition. At *Republic* 501d, Socrates says philosophers are "lovers (*erastai*) of being and truth." He can do this without maligning the objects of desire (that is, likening them to a passive beloved) because in Plato's theory of eros, there are no passive parties. His view champions the active role and, di-

---

[20] David Halperin, "Plato and Erotic Reciprocity," *Classical Antiquity* 5 (1986): 60–80, at p. 70.

vorcing erotic expression from sexual conduct, makes it possible to eradicate the passive role altogether.[21]

The *Menexenus* alludes to the critique of the conventional understanding of eros developed in the *Lysis*. Menexenus' role as lone interlocutor in the dialogue that bears his name implies a reason for rejecting the Periclean erastes metaphor. Pericles' metaphor reinforces the conventional notion of eroticism and love relations because it relies precisely on normal negotiations of the active and passive roles in a pederastic love relationship to illuminate the demands of democratic citizenship.

The *Menexenus* also alludes to the erotic themes in the *Lysis* in the account of Menexenus' conversation with Socrates. This conversation sustains a playful parody of the language of gratitude (*charis*) and gratification (*charizomai*) that typically expressed the performance of sexual acts in the context of an honorable pederastic relationship. For example, when Socrates hesitates a little before reciting the speech, Menexenus urges him on: "Deliver it, and you will greatly oblige me" (*panu moi chariei*, 236c6). Socrates responds that perhaps you, Menexenus, will laugh at me, at which point Menexenus urges him on again. This is followed by a striking comment by Socrates that is clearly sexually suggestive (but not exactly arousing). He says, "I must surely oblige (*dei charizesthai*). Even if you told me to take off my clothes and dance for you, I could scarcely refuse (*charisaimēn an*), especially since the two of us are alone" (236c10–d3). This comment parodies the kind of humiliating action an infatuated lover (like Hippothales from the *Lysis*) might perform. Menexenus, whom we know from the *Lysis* to be quite bright, and who was said to have been present at Socrates' death (*Phaedo* 59b), then "passively" listens to the funeral speech. At the end, when the two resume their conversation, the vocabulary of gratitude again is quite apparent. Socrates asks, "Aren't you grateful to her [Aspasia] for her speech?" (*charin echeis tou logou autēi*, 249d10–11). Menexenus confirms that sentiment emphatically: "Oh, to be sure, Socrates—that is, grateful to her (*charin echō toutou*, 249d12) or whoever it was who recited it to you. And of course, I'm grateful to the man who recited it to me (*charin echē tēi eiponti*, 249e2)." The dialogue surrounding the recitation of the speech thus parodies the conventional model of appropriate behavior between an active adult lover, who gives, and his passive beloved boy, who expresses gratitude.[22]

---

[21] How far Plato imagines an individual philosopher's erotic passion for an idea might be reciprocated is unclear. There is an enormous body of literature on Plato's theory of eros. See Halperin's "Plato and Erotic Reciprocity" for useful notes reviewing the scholarship.

[22] The opening passage of the *Protagoras* and the introduction of Callicles in the *Gorgias* also parody the dynamics of gratification in the conventional love relation. The *Protagoras* opens with an unnamed friend teasing Socrates about his relation with the alluring young Alcibiades and prying, "How is he treating you?" "Just fine," Socrates says, judging from

The figure of Aspasia is another indication of Plato's interest in the critique of Pericles' erotic model of citizenship. Before exploring this point, we must of course recall that Socrates' attribution of his funeral speech to Aspasia links the text to Pericles and to the critique of rhetoric (the art Aspasia is reputed to have taught many Athenians, including Socrates and Pericles[23]). In addition, this attribution recalls the "chronological fantasies"[24] that mark this text. Keeping in mind the dramatic date of the dialogue, now we have Aspasia and Socrates conversing together long

---

the way Alcibiades spoke up for Socrates during a discussion with Protagoras. But then Socrates reports that oddly, he nearly forgot Alcibiades' presence altogether during his conversation with Protagoras—something the infatuated lover of the *Lysis* could not possibly have accomplished. The friend becomes excited and asks Socrates to tell him about the conversation. Socrates says he will count it a "favor" (owe *charis*, 310a5) to him for listening, and the friend says, "And vice versa if you'd tell us." Socrates responds, "That would make it a double favor" (*diplē an eiē hē charis*, 310a8). Mutual gratitude, of course, was not possible on the conventional model. Most important to notice, expression of intensely felt erotic passion and mockery of orthodox erotic practices frame the lively portrayal of the initiation of philosophic activity in the *Protagoras*.

In the *Gorgias* (481c–e), Socrates suggests that Callicles behaves like the ridiculous infatuated lover of the *Lysis* toward both of his two beloveds, the boy Demos and the Athenian demos. Callicles is unable to oppose their whims and rushes around in an effort to win their affections. Socrates says that he may also look ridiculous when he responds to the demands of one of his own beloveds, philosophy. Interestingly, though he names Alcibiades as his other beloved, there is no explicit mention of Socrates' famed ability to contradict him. Rather, there is at most the implication that love for philosophy gives Socrates the strength to oppose Alcibiades when necessary. To change Callicles' behavior, Socrates indicates, it would be necessary to stop his beloveds (Demos and demos) from saying what they do. Similarly, to change Socrates' behavior, it would be necessary to make his beloved, philosophy, say something different (to make a philosophical argument). The advantage of having philosophy as a beloved, we can speculate, is that she is not fickle. She "says always the same." Insofar as philosophy might reciprocate Socrates' eros, perhaps it is in providing this measure of stability and calm to its practitioner, enabling him to sustain a responsible erotic relation (intellectual and nonsexual) with a human beloved.

[23] Plutarch *Life of Pericles* 34.3–6.

[24] Pierre Vidal-Naquet, "Plato, History and Historians," in his *Politics Ancient and Modern*, trans. Janet Lloyd (Cambridge: Polity, 1995), p. 26. Vidal-Naquet suggests that Plato presents a confused historical timeline in the *Menexenus* deliberately as part of his effort as a philosopher to "break out of the chronological framework which was that of the city." He notes that the *Gorgias* blurs timelines as well (pp. 26–27). Also on the *Gorgias* as "cut free from chronological specificity," see Josiah Ober, *Political Dissent in Democratic Athens: Intellectual Critics of Popular Rule* (Princeton: Princeton University Press, 1998), pp. 191–92. Ober suggests that in the *Gorgias*, the "net effect is to foreclose the possibility of challenging Socrates' positions [regarding the condition of post-Periclean Athens] on the basis of close historical arguments" (p. 192). For discussion of the political import of representations of time in Greek thought, see Pierre Lévêque and Pierre Vidal-Naquet, *Cleisthenes the Athenian: An Essay on the Representation of Space and Time in Greek Political Thought from the End of the Sixth Century to the Death of Plato*, trans. David Ames Curtis (Atlantic Highlands, N.J.: Humanities Press, 1996).

after both were dead, about events that happened long after their deaths. Moreover, the gender of Aspasia may signal Plato's delivery of a challenge to conventional Greek understandings of eros.[25] In the context of the implicit commentary on Thucydides that runs through his text, suggesting that a woman drafted a funeral oration may also be a way of questioning Thucydides' efforts to fix the boundaries of the political by excluding from an account of the city's political history its religious practices, the lives of women, and the presence of philosophy and philosophers, for example.[26] But, if I am right in stressing that the memory of Pericles is the driving force of the dialogue, then Plato's striking use of this character should be putting in play some aspect of the conspicuous erotic relations that marked the legendary relationship between these two historical figures.[27]

Aspasia was perhaps the most famous woman in fifth-century Athens.[28] She was not Athenian-born but a foreigner, and she had a reputation for considerable intellectual capability (and for being a teacher of rhetoric).

[25] This interpretation would read Aspasia's significance on the model of Halperin's reading of the significance of Diotima in the Symposium ("Why Is Diotima a Woman?" in his *One Hundred Years of Homosexuality and Other Essays on Greek Love* [New York: Routledge, 1990]). Halperin seems to invite such a parallel but does not pursue it (pp. 122–24). Salkever ("Socrates' Aspasian Oration," p. 25 n. 48) says that the parallel of Aspasia with Diotima as interpreted by Halperin is compelling, but does not specify further what that parallel might signify. Other commentators interpret Aspasia's gender by classifying it as one more sign of the ironic nature of the speech. Saxonhouse (*Fear of Diversity*, pp. 113–22) considers it more fully, arguing that the female figure gives voice to the view of the mother, and thus emphasizes the speech's interest in the contrast between the unity of the public sphere and the unity of family. She also notes that Aspasia's speech focuses on the issue of origins and offers an unusual view of autochthony. See Wendy Brown ("Supposing Truth Were a Woman . . .: Plato's Subversion of Masculine Discourse," *Political Theory* 16 [1988]: 594–616) for another perspective on Plato's use of the female gender to signal a subversion of traditional Athenian attitudes on a variety of subjects. Brown does not mention the *Menexenus* or Aspasia's part in it at all.

[26] On the presence or absence of philosophers in Greek historical texts, see Vidal-Naquet, "Plato, History and Historians."

[27] Halperin (*One Hundred Years of Homosexuality*) observes that Plato's portrait of Aspasia exhibits "less interest in her than in her relations with Pericles" (p. 122). But while he sees that the figure of Aspasia in the work of other Socratic writers accompanies the treatment of erotic themes (pp. 123–24), he concludes that in Plato's *Menexenus*, she does not signal attention to erotic themes but only to what Halperin takes to be "the topic of that dialogue," that is, political rhetoric. He asserts that she "fits comfortably" into that dialogue because she "had a reputation for making her lovers into successful politicians [i.e., orators]" (p. 124). Halperin's acceptance of the usual, limited view of what is at stake in the *Menexenus* (the view that I challenge here) prevents him from seeing the way the figure of Aspasia works in that Platonic text.

[28] Sarah Pomeroy notes this (*Goddesses, Whores, Wives and Slaves: Women in Classical Antiquity* [New York: Schocken, 1975], p. 89). The brief summary of what we know of her life that follows is drawn from *The Oxford Classical Dictionary*, ed. N.G.L. Hammond and H. H. Scullard (Oxford: Clarendon, 1970), pp. 131–32.

The erotic relationship between Pericles and Aspasia appears to have been one of citizen and courtesan (*hetaira*), that is, she was a prostitute with whom Pericles developed a long-term erotic attachment. She lived with him after he divorced his legal wife. Their son, excluded from Athenian citizenship by Pericles' own law of 451/50, was legitimated by decree after his two sons by his former (legal) wife both perished in the plague. But this son also died before the close of the Peloponnesian War, having been one of the unfortunate generals at Arginousae. After Pericles' death, Aspasia lived with another man and, if we are to believe Plutarch's account, set up an establishment that educated young women to be courtesans.

Aspasia's standing as a famous *hetaira* was valuable for Plato. A hetaira was "at the highest end of the scale of commercially available sexual partners" in ancient Athens.[29] But, as Leslie Kurke argues, what distinguished the hetaira from the *pornē* (common streetwalker) was not simply the status and education of the woman, or even the length of time of the pair's sexual involvement, but the kind of exchange that the parties imagined to be taking place between them. Quite routinely, the male party to this commercial exchange wishfully viewed it as a form of gift exchange, that is, as if it were a *charis* relation. As Kurke points out, one ancient source even makes this explicit: "The fourth-century comic poet Anaxilas observed [that] the *hetaira* gratified her patron *pros charin*, 'as a favor.' "[30] Reviewing the iconographic evidence in which a hetaira's relation to the male symposiast is highly idealized, Kurke concludes that the inequality of their relation is "completely mystified as one of mutually comfortable and willing companionship."[31] Turning back to the case of Aspasia and Pericles, we can observe that the mystification of their exchange was so thorough that it was nearly assimilated to legal marriage and nearly modeled an exceptional case of male/female erotic relations: sexual, emotional, and intellectual partners and confidants.

Through the figure of Aspasia, Plato focuses the reader's attention on the precise target of his concern in the *Menexenus*: the enduring significance of the Thucydidean construction of Pericles as symbol. The presence of Aspasia importantly calls attention to the central image of Thucydides' rendering of Pericles' funeral oration, that is, to his urging of citizens to conceive of themselves as "lovers (*erastai*) of the city" (2.43.1). In Aspasia's dramatic presence, precisely what erotic relationship Pericles intends citizens to consult for some help in thinking through the demands of democratic citizenship becomes unclear. Are they to imagine

---

[29] Halperin, *One Hundred Years of Homosexuality*, p. 111.

[30] Leslie Kurke, "Inventing the *Hetaira*: Sex, Politics, and Discursive Conflict in Archaic Greece," *Classical Antiquity* 16, no. 1 (April 1997): 112.

[31] Ibid., p. 115.

themselves lovers of the city on the model of lovers of male citizen youths (*eromenoi*) or on the model of lovers of female courtesans (*hetairai*)? What kind of relationship of exchange is being invoked and lauded? Can a model of erotic exchange really signal the kind of reciprocity that ought to obtain between city and citizens?[32] The presence of Aspasia renders Pericles' metaphor unstable and therefore problematic, prying open space for Socrates to propose instead a familial-relations metaphor for understanding citizenship.

Plato rejects the erastes metaphor in the *Menexenus*, implying that Pericles is wrong to suggest, as he did in his funeral oration (2.43.1), that Athenians should turn to their understanding of norms regarding erotic attachments for some guidance in thinking about the relations between city and citizen. The metaphor Plato offers in its place further clarifies his substantive objections to the Periclean model of citizenship. The *Menexenus* proposes that relations among citizens as well as between citizens and city be understood on the pattern of (idealized) relations among family members. The text invokes qualities associated with the exemplary execution of the roles of parent (both mother and father) and son to create an ideal image of relations between the city and citizens. Socrates does not, however, dramatically announce this metaphor, as Pericles had done when he introduced the erastes metaphor. Rather, Socrates' speech develops the family-relations metaphor in the general language and set of images employed throughout the Socratic/Aspasian oration. For example, in its account of Athenian history, the speech identifies the land (*chōra*) and constitution (*politeia*) as nurturers of citizens on the model of parents, and especially on the model of the fertile and creative mother.[33] The speech also makes considerable use of the image of Athenian autochthony, a myth that symbolically asserts that all Athenian men possess a common ancestry.[34] (Other extant orations, with the exception of Pericles', appeal to this myth, but the *Menexenus* dwells on it.) Most intriguingly, this oration employs a striking literary device in the exhortation and consoling remarks that traditionally close this genre of public oratory. Socrates impersonates the dead soldiers (246c), thus enabling him to address the

---

[32] Pericles' relations with Aspasia were mocked in comedy, and perhaps Plato is counting on that background. For example, Aristophanes casts Aspasia as a whore and a madam whose behavior incited Pericles to start the Peloponnesian War (*Acharnians* 520–30).

[33] Saxonhouse, *Fear of Diversity*, pp. 113–22.

[34] For discussion of Plato's deployment of the myth of autochthony, see Derrida, *Politics of Friendship*, pp. 94–95; Nicole Loraux, *The Children of Athena: Athenian Ideas about Citizenship and the Division between the Sexes*, trans. Caroline Levine (Princeton: Princeton University Press, 1993); and Arlene Saxonhouse, "Myths and the Origin of Cities: Reflections on the Autochthony Theme in Euripides' *Ion*," in *Greek Tragedy and Political Theory*, ed. J. Peter Euben (Berkeley: University of California Press, 1986), pp. 252–73.

gathered survivors, the assembled citizens, as family (e.g., as "sons" [*o paides*] at 246d1).[35]

The family-relations metaphor of the *Menexenus* suggests that the bonds among citizens as well as between citizens and city are rooted in material necessity and nature. Pericles' view urges, in contrast, that the bonds between citizens and the city be understood as self-consciously and voluntarily pursued by both parties. The erastes metaphor implies that citizens must be thought of as freely choosing to enter into a relation with a city after having been attracted by its charms and virtues, opportunities and strengths. This free choice further implies that citizens have a direct, unmediated relation to the city. The citizens' equality with one another is understood as rooted in the recognition of the ability of each independently (indeed, autonomously) to sustain some significant relation with the city. In this way, Pericles' speech both praises equality and manages to assert that democracy at Athens amounted to the rule of the whole untroubled by intense civil strife. All, albeit in possession of different wealth, skills, or special talents, can perform benefactions for the city and in this way contribute to its excellence. Men of significant means can assume a liturgy (produce a play or outfit a trireme). Men of modest means can attend the Assembly, serve as jurors, and fight in battle. As we saw in Chapter Four, Pericles' funeral oration equates elaborate acts of munificence with modest acts of participation.

The family-relations model implicitly developed throughout the *Menexenus* offers a different view of how a city sustains unity among its citizens, how individuals become attached to a particular, concrete city, and how individuals can care for their native city's well-being. This is clearest in the way Socrates' funeral speech works with the myth of autochthony.

---

[35] Rosenstock ("Socrates as Revenant") goes so far as to argue that Plato uses literary devices to depict the resuscitation of a dead Socrates in order to portray Socrates addressing not only the Menexenus of the *Lysis* but a different Menexenus as well. "This other Menexenus is one of Socrates' sons." He offers Diogenes Laertius 2.26 as evidence for the name of one of the historical Socrates' biological sons. This son, "too young to have been taught by Socrates during his lifetime, [is] now, as he is coming of age, very much in need of his father's counsel" (p. 339). What would heeding his father's counsel entail? Rosenstock explains that a true heir of Socrates would be able to interpret the funeral oration delivered by Socrates in the following way: "The idealization of Athens, which on the surface seems mere flattery, now becomes, when it is read as the words of the executed Socrates to his son, both a condemnation of the city and an appeal to the reader to live in accordance with the ideals of virtue that guided Socrates' life" (p. 341). I object to Rosenstock's unreflective use of the term "condemnation" here. Socrates' relation to his city—even when awaiting execution, as detailed in the *Crito*—is far more textured. The most recent efforts to detail the links between Socratic practice and the democratic city are J. Peter Euben, *Corrupting Youth* (Princeton: Princeton University Press, 1997); and Gerald Mara, *Socrates' Discursive Democracy* (Albany: State University of New York Press, 1997).

As was often the case in this genre, an account of this myth begins the recitation of an idealized account of Athenian history. In the version recited here, the myth holds that the first Athenians did not descend from foreign migrants to Attica, but were borne and nursed by the very earth herself. Athenian ancestors, therefore, are identified as the original inhabitants of the land of Attica, and, most importantly, all Athenians are given a common ancestry. The ideological importance of this myth is easy to recognize. The exaltation of ancestors and focus on the nobility of birth were traditional aristocratic modes of asserting the special claims of certain individuals. The variety and inequality of family groups were, moreover, major sources of disunity in the polis. The myth of autochthony appropriates for the whole community and for every citizen an argument for special excellence based on origins and ties to land. It turns an argument that had been used to defend exclusive privileges into a justification for inclusiveness.

We can observe this transformation in the speech Socrates recites in the *Menexenus*. This speech first ties the achievement of political equality and unity to the recognition of common ancestry. For example, Socrates begins eulogizing the dead soldiers by praising the nobility of their birth. He does not distinguish each individual on this basis but traces the nobility of the undifferentiated mass of fallen soldiers to their common autochthonous origins. He focuses on praising "their mother herself" (237c), by which he means the earth. In so doing, he casts the citizens as brothers and his eulogy as one of "fraternal" democracy.[36] The earth, he continues, provided the original generation with a rich land that yields extraordinary nourishment in the form of opportunities for agriculture (particularly wheat, barley, and olives). The earth is also the original giver of paideia in the form of the guidance of the gods, and through them, *technai* (the arts). Only when these individuals have received sufficient nurturing from the earth are they, in this tale, able to establish a *politeia* (constitution). Socrates then explicitly ties the ability of the Athenians to sustain democratic institutions to the seriousness with which they regard their common origins.

> The cause of our constitution is equality of birth (*isou genesis*). Other cities are compounded of varied and unequal conditions of men, therefore their constitutions are also unequal in their diversity—they are tyrannies and oligarchies. And therefore they live acknowledging one another either as slaves or as masters. But we and those who belong to us do not think it fit to be either slave or master to each other: our equal birth according to nature (*he isogonia hēmas hē kata phusin*) compels us to seek equal rights according to the law (*isonomian . . . kata nomon*). (238e–239a)

---

[36] Derrida, *Politics of Friendship*, p. 93.

The myth of autochthony thus locates the source of unity in the polis in its ability to reduce, rather than incorporate, differences among citizens.

The *Menexenus* also uses a family-relations metaphor for citizenship in the exhortation to the living that closes the oration (246a–249c). While in other places the *Menexenus* reviles the practice of funeral oratory as cheap flattery, here it appears to make sincere use of this form of discourse and this public occasion. Using the rhetorical trope of *prosōpeia*, speaking in the voice of the dead (and in this instance, specifically in the voice of recent casualties of war), Socrates brings about the change of tone that characterizes this section.[37] From this point on in the speech, we find considerably less stinging satire, more straightforward and apparently heartfelt argument, and the direct expression of Socratic moral ideals. For example, this section draws on understanding of the responsibilities of a parent—and of surviving adults toward war orphans—to promote a view of the demands of citizenship very much like that in the *Apology*. It suggests that these responsibilities are analogous to the ones Socrates assumed by accepting a gadfly role. Socrates begins this section announcing, "It is necessary that all remembering these men should exhort their children, as in war, not to desert the station (*taxin*) of [your] forefathers, nor retreat and give way through vice" (246b–c). Socrates had earlier (*Apology* 28d7) explained his own determination to persevere in this role of exhorting and challenging in the face of danger (to be *politikos*) on the analogy of steadfastly remaining at one's station during the ordeals of war. Socrates suggests that both roles (being a good son and being a gadfly) are ways of striving to be truly politikos.[38]

The words attributed to the dead draw on the family-relations metaphor to develop a case for the Socratic view of political obligation and citizenship as defended in the *Apology*. The exhortation to the family members (children and parents, 246d–248c) does not portray the natural unit (family or polis) as rightfully demanding an allegiance that endures the loss of a particular member. It does not exalt the survival of the group and call upon the living to be willing to make similar (or appropriate) sacrifices when necessary. Rather, it stresses the importance of each remaining citizen's continuing struggle individually to live virtuously in the face of personal loss. The speech urges survivors not to mourn excessively but to honor the memory of loved ones by living well. The otherworldly voices explain that parents "bearing the misfortune with a heavy heart" dishonor

[37] Compare Plato's use of the rhetorical technique of prosopeia in *Letter 8*. Plato impersonates Dion's voice from the grave to address Dion's grieving and confused friends, especially as they attempt to be "heirs" to Dion's projects. Also compare Socrates' impersonation of the Laws in the *Crito*.

[38] See Rosenstock, "Socrates as Revenant," pp. 344–47, for another view of the relationship between the *Menexenus* and the *Apology*.

the dead by "behaving badly *toward themselves*." Parents who "bear it lightly and moderately . . . thereby live lives more beautiful, more upright, and more pleasing to us" (248c). The speech admonishes children not to be deterred in their own struggle for virtue (*aretē*, 247a) by the extraordinary reputation of their fathers. Rather, they are to strive to surpass their fathers in virtue. The speech suggests virtue is meant in a broad sense and not simply as a stand-in for valor. Even though the genre of the speech requires the extensive use of military vocabulary and reference to the future military exploits of survivors, the Socratic/Aspasian speech manages to suggest that the dead should inspire the survivors not only to great acts of valor on the battlefield, but also to living well. The language at times seems a mix of famous lines from the *Apology* and the *Republic*. "We believe," the dead propose, "that *life is not worth living* for a man who brings shame to *what is his own*" (246d). The otherworldly voices continue: "Practice [your own] with virtue, knowing that without this, all pursuits and possessions are shameful and bad. . . . All knowledge, when separated from justice and the other virtues, appears as unscrupulous, not as wisdom" (247a). The dead then urge that in surpassing their fathers in virtue, surviving sons can come to be accepted by their fathers "as friends" (*philoi para philous hēmas aphixesthe*, 247c1). This reference to *philoi* reveals that Plato has in mind a way for a young orphan to achieve equality with his father now that the usual democratic route, joining him in the ranks of full citizens, is no longer a possibility. This funeral oration's exhortation to children and parents collapses responsibilities to others and to the city into responsibilities to one's self.

The Socratic/Aspasian speech also quotes the proverb, "Nothing in excess" (247e), and urges survivors to practice self-reliance. The speech explains that depending on oneself is the best route to happiness. It counsels citizens to be temperate as well as courageous and wise (*houtos estin ho sōphrōn kai houtos ho andreios kai phronimos*, 248a). Depending on others to augment one's powers is risky, as their fortunes may rise or fall. This insertion is a haunting response to a lesson we could draw from Thucydides' narrative as a whole. So much of Thucydides' story of the war shows how an escalation of violence springs from individuals and factions, indeed whole cities, that hang their hopes on the expectation of help from others (the approaching Spartans or Athenians). The Melians have such false hopes. The entire story of the Corcyrean collapse into civil war begins by recounting how both factions became increasing bold (and cruel toward rivals) as each came to expect reinforcements from either Sparta or Athens. The Athenian navy at Syracuse was also emboldened by the expectation of reinforcements. Counseling the citizens to resist such imaginings, the funeral speech in the *Menexenus* suggests a way to avoid pursuing the same disastrous course of action that the Athenians (and others) had, as Thucydides reports, already suffered through once.

The reciprocal character of ideal city/citizen relations appears most clearly in the *Menexenus* in the last lines attributed to the dead soldiers. Citizens who have died to protect the well-being of their nurturing "parents"—the land and constitution (freedom)—now matter-of-factly declare that they expect, indeed are entitled to, something quite specific in return: "We bid the city care for our parents and our sons, fittingly educating the one, worthily tending the other" (248d). The terms of the exchange are treated as noncontroversial. The dead do not even amplify the point, but say only: "We know that this will be sufficiently cared for without our bidding" (248d). With this comment, Socrates' impersonation of the dead ends, and he begins once again to speak in his own (Aspasia's) voice. But while the dead do not dwell on this matter, Socrates' Aspasian continuation of the speech leaves none of the implications of this comment unexposed. Rather, the concluding remarks of the oration are devoted to explicating those last lines.

The city reciprocates its fallen heroes' actions through the workings of law, Socrates emphasizes.[39] These laws, however, do not cast the city unrelentingly in the role of surrogate parent. Rather, the city returns the citizens' actions (deaths) by performing multiple familial roles. The city must "stand to the fallen in the apportionment of son and heir, and to their sons as a father, and to their parents as guardian, allowing all aid to all at all times" (249c). At this point, the speech emphasizes the practical things that the city is required by law to do. For example, the city must assume the job of educating the sons of the fallen; in particular, the city must sponsor these boys' military training and outfitting. Toward the fallen themselves, however, the city must act as dutiful son and attend to the burial and proper eulogy. The city also fulfills the role of upstanding male adult by assuming the responsibility of caring for the elderly parents of the fallen. This section repeatedly emphasizes the lavish ways in which the city fulfills each of these roles. The city nurtures the orphan boys earnestly, Socrates reports, so that "their orphanhood [should] be as little before their minds as possible" (249a4–5). When they reach manhood, the city sends them out "arrayed in full armor" (249a7). If they should die in battle, not only will the city perform "for all in common the customary

[39] Pericles' model had assumed that reciprocity is accomplished through the performance of serial benefactions. Though some of these are mandated by law, even these retain the appearance of being voluntary. For example, a citizen who is called upon to perform a liturgy (e.g., sponsor a chorus) because he is deemed wealthy enough to owe this service to the polis can refuse by initiating a legal procedure known as antidosis. Socrates focuses, in contrast, on definite, uncontestable responsibilities outlined in law, those which citizens and city must perform.

[funeral] rites" (249b6), but it will add the conduct of "gymnastic contests and horse races and all sorts of music" (249b7–8) to the ceremony. The *Menexenus* thus suggests that Athenian norms of family obligations can best guide one in understanding how to maintain honorable, reciprocal relations between the city and citizens.

PLATO'S THEORETICAL INTEREST IN FUNERAL ORATORY

Though Plato is consistently suspicious of the ability of oratory to teach, or even to sustain an inquiry, the *Menexenus* demonstrates Plato has a theoretical interest in the project of funeral oratory.[40] The primary function of the official funeral speech was to give public expression to an orthodox conception of the potential excellence of the democratic polis. Its performance articulated civic and personal virtues to which the Athenians could aspire and that they could imagine themselves to exhibit. It was an occasion on which Athens "invented" and "reinvented" itself in narrative form,[41] a collective effort to define a specifically Athenian conception of a "good city" and display its achievement. The practice of funeral oratory of this sort was, moreover, an innovation unique to democratic Athens. Nicole Loraux succinctly states the case for treating the *Menexenus* as critical to the interpretation of Plato's rootedness in the Athenian democratic tradition: "If [Plato] has chosen the funeral oration as his target, it is because in the *epitaphioi* [funeral orations] the city recognizes itself as it wishes to be. . . . The *Menexenus*, then, is a minor dialogue only for those who fail to see in the funeral oration its character as civic discourse."[42]

Plato's writings explicitly engage the concerns of funeral oratory. For example, two of the most outstanding features of the ideal city of the *Republic*—perfect unity of the whole citizenry and complete absence of civic troubles—echo the central patriotic claims of the orthodox portrayal of Athens in the Periclean funeral speech as well as other extant epitaphioi (those of Lysias, Demosthenes, Hyperides). In the Periclean oration, for instance, the rule of the whole demos and the avoidance of civil conflict form the central organizing principles of much of the speech. In addition

---

[40] Though I am in agreement with much of Andrea Nightingale's account of Plato's thoroughgoing critique of the erotic encomium in the *Lysis* and the *Symposium* (*Genres in Dialogue*, pp. 93–132), my argument departs from hers in proposing that Plato explores in the *Menexenus* not only the problems but also the possibilities that inhere in another variant of encomiastic discourse, the *epitaphios logos*. Nightingale does not examine the *Menexenus* in detail but characterizes Plato's treatment of the *epitaphios* in this text as part of his "opposition to eulogy," which she sees as "part and parcel of his attempt to both define and legitimize philosophy" (p. 106).

[41] Loraux, *The Invention of Athens*.

[42] Ibid., p. 312.

to these substantive similarities, the structure of the *Republic* parallels the structure of all the extant epitaphioi. Each one sets out to construct a "city in speech" for public display. The epitaphioi and the *Republic* offer images that self-consciously aim not to describe Athenian life accurately but to illuminate the political and personal virtues to which people should aspire, that is, to illuminate the possibilities for the city. Loraux has noticed this, writing, for example, that "in its essence and in its history, the Platonic city irresistibly suggests the city of the epitaphioi. Characterized like it by unity, the polis of the philosopher, like that of the orators, knows none of the mistakes and difficulties of earlier humanity."[43] Loraux here asserts a link between the discourse of a serious funeral oration and that of the *Republic*. Both ideally invent a polis that is imagined successfully to avert corrosive civil conflict and achieve extraordinary happiness and honor.

On the occasion of the funeral speech, the Athenians assembled were implored to perform the mental act of imagining themselves members of a fictional, idealized city and to take their cues regarding how they ought to behave in the messy real world from the crisply defined responsibilities they bear as members of this symbolic community. Plato's understanding of the practice of philosophy is very much like that of the practitioners (both speakers and hearers) of funeral oratory. Consider the discussion of the philosopher's project of founding a regime "within oneself" at *Republic* 591e–592b (end of Book 9). The philosopher is someone who can think his way out of his historical situation, that is, someone who, through the force of his intellect, can choose membership in a fine, imagined community—the ideal city. This membership illuminates for him the requirements of justice. It guides his decisions regarding the conduct of his own life in the messy material world. This ideal city does not, of course, "exist anywhere on earth." Rather, Socrates stresses, "In heaven . . . [is laid] a pattern (*paradeigma*) for the man who wants to see and found a city within himself on the basis of what he sees. It doesn't make any difference whether it is or will be somewhere. For he would mind the things of this city alone, and of no other" (*Republic* 592b). The philosopher's willful embrace of membership in this imagined city does not undermine his affective attachments to the city of his physical birth. Like imagining oneself into the ideal city of funeral oratory, the philosopher's embrace of a heavenly pattern functions to inform ordinary conduct, guiding it, infusing it with meaning and purpose beyond the mundane. Membership in this imagined community is an act of intellect and choice. Both Plato's writings and funeral oratory are designed to strengthen their readers'/hearers' resolve to persevere in the pursuit of (what each takes to be) virtue, undeterred by mournful features of ordinary life. For Pericles, these features

---

[43] Ibid., p. 301.

are mortality and loss. For Plato, they are the powerful allure of pleasures, the misleading appearances of things.

The *Timaeus* and the *Critias* also allude to the discourse of a funeral oration. In the *Timaeus*, for example, Socrates asks if someone can give an account of what the ideal city might look like "in motion . . . engaged in some struggle or conflict" (19b–c). The company urges Critias to do so because he knows of an old tale of a great Athenian war that he once heard from his grandfather, who is purported to have heard it from Solon. Critias agrees that this story can provide a useful model of the kind of action the ideal city would take. He then tells the myth of the conflict between ancient Athens and great island city of Atlantis. The description of the Platonic city in history thus takes the form of a eulogy of Athenian ancestors, which displays many parallels to the concerns of a funeral oration. Loraux writes, for example: "[When Plato] 'brings to life' the city of the *Republic* and compares it with other states with a view to testing its paideia, his eulogy of it is evidence of a complex relation with the funeral oration [as a practice] and with the [image of the] polis of the epitaphioi."[44] Plato draws upon the funeral oration understood as a strategy of civic discourse to elaborate the possibilities associated with the city of the *Republic*.

Aristotle's understanding of epideictic oratory suggests another way in which Plato's work is indebted to this Athenian practice. Funeral oratory is a species of epideictic oratory. Such speech, Aristotle explains in the *Rhetoric*, is not concerned to persuade a jury (as is forensic oratory) or advance a policy alternative (as is deliberative oratory) but to deliver praise or blame. Its "end" is the artful display of the honorable and disgraceful (1358b3–5) in the interest of arousing aspirations. The Periclean funeral oration glorifies the orthodox Athenian conception of excellence. It assumes the audience knows what is truly praiseworthy and blameworthy. In contrast, Plato's funeral oration interrogates the patriotic view. Nevertheless, Plato does not abandon the end of epideictic oratory nor the specific civic goals of funeral oratory.[45] Rather, he appropriates this project for philosophy. The entire corpus of dialogues contains the full articulation of an alternative view of what is truly praiseworthy as well as repeated attempts to induce readers to take up philosophy and to aspire to a certain kind of virtue.

Aristotle's curious suggestion that epideictic is suited to written composition (*Rhetoric* 1414a6) indicates the link between orthodox epideictic and Plato's work I am proposing. Aristotle advises practitioners of epideictic not to compose a linear narrative of facts but to present the evidence

---

[44] Ibid., p. 296.

[45] On this point I depart from the arguments of Yunis (*Taming Democracy*) and Nightingale (*Genres in Dialogue*).

(actions that illustrate the honorable) in a "disjointed" fashion: "From some facts a man may be shown to be courageous, from others wise or just" (1416b1–2).[46] This strategy of presentation not only works clearly to display the honorable but, Aristotle notes, also happens to render it suitable for reading. This strategy of composition recommended by Aristotle recalls the structure of the Platonic corpus, that is, the contained substantive focus of each dialogue's presentation of Socrates in action (e.g., what is courage, what is justice, etc.). The dialogues offer not only a display (*epideiksis*) of the honorable, but also an account (*logos*) of it. The point I wish to stress is that Plato appropriates for philosophy at least part of the intellectual mission that the Athenians associated with the most celebrated—and uniquely democratic—form of epideictic, that is, funeral oratory.

I have argued that the *Menexenus* develops two concerns that propel Plato's political writings. First, it sustains a critical commentary on the Thucydidean myth of Pericles, showing Plato to be deeply involved in the practical politics of his city. Second, it wrestles with the funeral oration as a species of public discourse, appropriating some of its features for philosophy. Viewed in this way, the *Menexenus* is not an odd, marginal piece of Platonic writing, as many scholars have argued. Rather, it is a key part of Plato's exploration of the relationship between aspects of Athenian democratic culture and the practice of philosophy. My investigation of Plato's attention to this relation continues in the next chapter with analysis of his use of a curious metaphor from the theater to depict philosophy and intellectual work generally.

[46] Translation from John Henry Freese, *Aristotle: The Art of Rhetoric* (Cambridge, Mass.: Harvard University Press [Loeb], 1982).

Chapter Eight

THEORY AND THEATRICALITY

A Puzzle

Plato's depictions of intellectual labor in his dialogues contain a puzzle. On the one hand, the dialogues voice some of the most aggressive attacks on the intellectual merit of theatrical enterprises in all of Western literature. Most famously, the *Republic* banishes poetry from the ideal city (607a–e). In the *Laws*, moreover, the Athenian Stranger decries the deterioration of democratic politics into a "wretched theatocracy" (*theatrokratia*, 701a1). On the other hand, Plato likens serious intellectual toil, including philosophic understanding, to being a theater-goer. Throughout his dialogues he sustains a delicate metaphor: "Intellectual labor is like the activity of being a *theatēs*," where *theatēs* refers to an audience member at the theater, during the dramatic competitions held on grand civic festival occasions. Plato builds this metaphor by making extensive and patterned use of a cluster of technical terms that the Athenians used to describe the experience of spectating in the theater. These terms, from which the English word "theory" derives, include *theōreō* ("to be a spectator," especially in the theater), *theōros* (the state ambassador sent to the oracles or games in other cities), *theōria* (the practice of sending theoroi to oracles and games abroad), *theōrēma* ("sight, spectacle"), *theaomai* ("to attend theater, gaze at, be a spectator"), *thea* and *theama* ("vision, sight, spectacle"), and *theatēs* ("theater-goer").[1] For example, in the *Republic*, Socrates speaks of philosophic understanding as the "*theōria* of all time and being" (*kai theōria pantos men chronou pasēs de ousias*, 486a7), and as "spectating what is" (*tēn tou ontos thean*, 525a1).

Commentators have not much noticed this puzzle. Focusing only on how this cluster of terms connotes a link between viewing and learning,[2]

[1] *A Greek-English Lexicon*, compiled by Henry George Liddell and Robert Scott, revised and augmented throughout by Sir Henry Stuart Jones, 9th ed., with supplement (Oxford: Oxford University Press, 1968). For discussion of the etymology of "theory," see Christopher Rocco, *Tragedy and Enlightenment: Athenian Political Thought and the Dilemmas of Modernity* (Berkeley: University of California Press, 1997), pp. 109–10 n. 10.

[2] This link predates Plato's usage. For example, "For the [Presocratic] Ionian physicists . . . the world itself becomes a spectacle, a vision of order understood through the systematic application of reason. For this process and its results the Presocratics use the word theorein, of which the root is *thea*, 'vision.' . . . These thinkers use the word *theōria* for observing the heavens." Charles Segal, "Spectator and Listener," in *The Greeks*, ed. Jean-Pierre Vernant (Chicago: University of Chicago Press, 1995), p. 192.

they stress that Plato suggests that philosophy is a better sort of vision, a training in "seeing" the Forms.[3] Plato does, of course, do this. Plato and others do use the terminology of theory to "signify mental activity, not the functioning of the eyes."[4] But Plato portrays philosophy as a form of "theorizing" for additional reasons as well. In particular, the studied deployment of this vocabulary signals an exploration of continuities between democratic politics and philosophic practice. The *thea-* cluster of terms, especially in the late fifth century and throughout the fourth, evoked not just a sensory experience of viewing and not just the mental activity of thinking. It also recalled the vigorous civic practice of being a theates whereby men experientially encountered their democratic citizenship.[5]

In this chapter, I show that Plato indeed sustains the metaphor that intellectual toil is like the activity of a theates throughout the dialogues. I examine the dramatic setting, the portrayal of the behavior of Socrates and other speakers, and the substantive arguments regarding the nature of intellectual work. I argue that the metaphor Plato employs asks one to consult one's own demotic experience as a theates for some help in imagining what the strange activity of philosophy is like as well as to understand its political import. In so doing, Plato does not necessarily render the practice of philosophy less odd, only more imaginable.

FOUR PATTERNS

Four patterns run through Plato's use of the theatrical imagery to represent serious learning, including philosophy. He relies on it to (1) indicate some kind of empirical observation, (2) mark critical steps in an argument developed by Socrates or an interlocutor in the course of a discrete text,

---

[3] Even scholars who are sensitive to the historical resonance of much of Plato's language treat the presence of this vocabulary strictly as an instance of the broader pattern of Plato's reliance on visual terminology to consider intellectual work. See Segal, "Spectator and Listener"; Michael Morgan, *Platonic Piety: Philosophy and Ritual in Fourth Century Athens* (Princeton: Princeton University Press, 1990), p. 124. On the practice of referring to vision in the representation of knowledge in various philosophical traditions, see David Levin, ed., *Sites of Vision: The Discursive Construction of Sight in the History of Philosophy* (Cambridge, Mass.: Massachusetts Institute of Technology Press, 1997).

[4] Rocco, *Tragedy and Enlightenment*, pp. 109–10 n. 10.

[5] The dialogues develop other metaphors for intellectual toil, notably a journey, erotic passion, or religious ecstasy. These share with the theates metaphor a stress on the active nature of the behavior as well as on the practitioner's engagement with, rather than excessive detachment from, the object. As my subject in this study is the use Plato makes of language and imagery that have clear democratic resonance, I do not pursue these at length. Note that Plato's use of the imagery and vocabulary of Greek religious practice (e.g., ecstatic rites, Eleusinian mysteries) has received sustained attention. See Morgan, *Platonic Piety.*

(3) describe the intellectual disposition characteristic of one who would take up philosophy, and (4) portray the somewhat mysterious experience of philosophic understanding. This last pattern is perhaps the most stunning deployment of the metaphor. Plato likens doing philosophy to becoming an exemplary *theates*. The paradox is that in Plato's view, the performance of an intellectual task conceived of as an important democratic civic practice, when done well (that is, philosophically), generates a devastating critique of democracy itself.

We can detect each of these four patterns in many texts, but only in the *Republic* are all present. There is, moreover, a highly instructive contrast between the use of this family of terms in the *Republic* and in the *Laws*, a contrast that illuminates the relationship between these two texts. Whereas the *Republic* dramatically highlights the third and fourth uses, the *Laws* stresses the first. In the *Republic*, the dominant image is of a *theates*, a theater-goer who is part of the polis staging the sight. In the *Laws*, the dominant image is of a *theōros*, one who travels to another city to be a *theates* of the sights staged there. Plato's use of this vocabulary may thus direct us to his sense of how the *Laws* is both continuous with and yet also a departure from the project sustained in the *Republic*. I focus in this chapter on examining the importance of these terms in each of these two major texts.

PRELIMINARY THOUGHTS ON THEORY AND THEATER-GOING

If Plato were to adopt a metaphor from the theater for philosophic work, we might expect him to suggest that serious intellectual work is a finer form of something akin to poetic production. And in fact, Plato does urge that philosophers replace the poets as creators of public *paideia* (education), and the dialogic form of writing that he creates, though not composed for theatrical performance, is deeply indebted to the tradition of dramatic writing.[6] But consistently throughout the corpus, and at times with great verve, Plato likens intellectual toil not to the composition or staging of a play, but rather to the theatrical experience of a play, that is, to the activity of being an audience member.[7]

How is practicing philosophy more like mobilizing the skills employed by a theater-goer than it is like using the skills of a poet? An obvious

---

[6] For discussion of the specifics of the debt Plato's genre of writing (dialogue) owes poetic production, see Martha Nussbaum, *The Fragility of Goodness* (New York: Cambridge University Press, 1986), pp. 122–35; and Andrea Wilson Nightingale, *Genres in Dialogue: Plato and the Construct of Philosophy* (New York: Cambridge University Press, 1995).

[7] I am not relying solely on the mere appearance of the *thea-* cluster of terms but also on Plato's deployment of them in connection with other thick references and strong allusions to the conduct of these civic practices.

answer is that the Athenian poet embraces his role as teacher, while the philosopher, as conceived of by Plato, claims always to be the student. But this begs the question. Precisely what skills do a theates and a poet utilize such that the activity of philosophy can be clarified by drawing an analogy to one (*theatēs*) and distancing it from the other (*didaskalos*)? To consider this question, let us look at Plato's insistence in *Republic* Book 10 that all mimetic poetry, despite its many attractions, be excluded from the ideal city.

In this passage, Plato does not simply reiterate his earlier point about the need to censor the works of poetry so as to eliminate morally undesirable elements from the education of the young. Here he objects to the practice of mimetic poetry *as a whole* (and that would include the entire works of Homer and the dramatists), likening it to the work of a painter: both craft images of images.[8] It is important to remember that poets were not simply authors of texts but also the directors of performances. Plato's critique is aimed not simply at rival writers but at rival practitioners of the training of men's minds. The poets could be thought to train the actors, chorus, and audience. To Plato, a poet in his capacity as author and director makes a compelling representation of an object in the world of becoming (596e). Plato objects to mimetic poetry because its skilled practitioners do not labor to distinguish the sensible from the intelligible. Rather, they aim to produce convincing imitations of lived experience or of the "look of things." Plato allows that the great tragedians are superior practitioners of the *technē* of mimetic poetry, that is, that they have in abundance the skill of composition and a command of poetic technique both directorial and choreographic. But mimetic poets, he stresses, have no understanding or knowledge of a thing, only the techne of how to represent the semblance of such understanding or knowledge. An individual would therefore be terribly wrong to think he can learn the art of, say, generalship from an intimate acquaintance with Homer, or political and moral responsibility from Sophocles and Euripides. But, Plato notes, that is exactly how most citizens approach such performances and texts. Plato further argues that practitioners of poetry must labor to appeal to the basest elements of

---

[8] James O. Urmson stresses that Plato considered all mimetic poetry here. He writes: "Plato is attacking mimetic poetry using as examples those poets whom he clearly believes to be the best" ("Plato and the Poets," in *Plato's Republic: Critical Essays*, ed. Richard Kraut [(Lanham, Mass.: Rowman and Littlefield, 1997], p. 230). I think Urmson is right to distinguish between the issues at play in Book 3 and those considered in Book 10. For critical discussion of the tendency to read Plato as banishing the arts more generally, see Alexander Nehamas, "Plato on Imitation and Poetry in *Republic* X," in his *Virtues of Authenticity: Essays on Plato and Socrates* (Princeton: Princeton University Press, 1999), pp. 251–78. For a comparison of Plato's critique of poetry with popular critiques of television today, see Nehamas, "Plato and the Mass Media," in *Virtues of Authenticity*, pp. 279–302.

their audiences' souls. Poets—as trainers of actors and choruses as well as authors of texts—must work to arouse in people vicarious experiences of extremes of emotion in order to sustain the convincing imitation. Success at this, Plato notes, is precisely what distinguishes a superior poet from the rest (605d), and presumably superior actors as well. Why Plato should be intent on resisting an analogy between the practice of philosophy and that of poetic production should now be clear. Though philosophers will replace poets as suppliers of civic stories and public paideia, their intellectual labors—despite their demonstrated facility with language and myth—cannot be understood on the model of poetic production.

But what about the experience of theater-going? What skills do people in this position exhibit? At first it seems Plato thinks that they exhibit none. He stresses the theater-goers' vulnerability to deception, intellectual corruption, and moral decay. But Plato indicates that these people are vulnerable not simply because they are stupid or weak-minded but because of the exceptional skill with which poets ply their trade. The poets' representations can be so compelling that one is misled into thinking that they offer insight into reality or truth. Dealing in appetites, they do not help individuals to practice critical self-reflection.[9] Nevertheless, in attending the theater, a person does enact a rudimentary distinction between "reality" and "appearance." He may get lost in the story and (from Plato's point of view) be led to misunderstand the nature of, for example, virtue, courage, and justice. But, even when experiencing exceptional poetry, he will ordinarily not make the mistake of believing that he was, for example, "actually witnessing a quarrel between Creon and Antigone, Oedipus questioning Teiresias, or Medea threatening vengeance."[10] The Athenians in the theater watched the masked actors and chorus, fully aware that the players were not the masks. Perhaps Plato found theatrical experience intellectually valuable in this elementary way.

Might Plato's use of the theates metaphor thus also signal his interest in the way experiencing tragedy develops valuable mental and moral sensitivities, even sharpens people's awareness that things are not always as they seem? Much recent scholarship on tragedy focuses precisely on showing how it subjects the established Athenian order to powerful criticism, exposing the violence, exclusions, and contradictions that inhere in Athenian political order's most treasured norms. This scholarship stresses that in portraying society on the verge of collapse, tragedy sensitizes citi-

---

[9] "Appetite's capacity for distortion and self-justification cannot, Plato thinks, be overestimated." Nussbaum, *Fragility of Goodness*, p. 155.

[10] Urmson, "Plato and the Poets," p. 227. Urmson believes that Plato was not seriously worried about this possibility (the halfwits). And that is my point. This measure of distinction was valuable to Plato.

zen spectators to the tentative, unstable, fragile nature of order as well as to its underside.[11] A recent reading of the *Oresteia*, for example, argues that the trilogy "both celebrates the triumph of a democratic civic discourse and exposes the legacy of violence, exclusion, and subordination directed at the 'feminine other' that accompanies that triumph."[12] Good theater draws spectators into experiencing that tension, and possibly into critical self-awareness and doubt. It is intellectually arousing as well as emotionally stirring. Regular theater attendance probably facilitated citizens' development of mental skills important for the practice of deliberation, for example, self-criticism, empathy, appreciation of the complexity of moral issues, recognition that things are not always as they seem, and an ability to enter the thoughts of another. Might Plato have appropriated the language of theater-going to suggest that philosophic toil offers a more "real" experience of coming to critical self-awareness than does hearing poetry—that is, that it offers an experience of critical self-awareness unclouded by experiences of intense emotions? Plato's insistence on likening the philosopher to a *theates* is part of his effort to stress that intellectual toil consists in navigating apparently compelling imagery and convincing fictions, not crafting them.

Plato's own distinction between writing philosophical dialogues and practicing philosophy supports this reading. Writing dialogues can be understood as a finer form of poetic writing. Dialogues set up a relationship with the reader that is in many ways like that between play and audience. For example, as Nussbaum observes, the reader "is invited to enter critically and actively into the give and take, much as a spectator of tragedy is invited to reflect (often along with the chorus) about the meaning of the events for his own system of values."[13] She adds, "What we find in . . . [the] dialogues, then, is theater; but theater purged and purified of theater's characteristic appeal to powerful emotion, a pure crystalline theater of the intellect."[14] But Plato's studied deployment of the *theates* metaphor reminds a reader that doing philosophy is not the same thing as writing dialogues. Doing philosophy is like what you, reader, are doing when you engage seriously with these texts, and indeed, when you think carefully

[11] See, for example, J. Peter Euben, ed., *Greek Tragedy and Political Theory* (Berkeley: University of California Press, 1986); J. Peter Euben, *The Tragedy of Political Theory: The Road Not Taken* (Princeton: Princeton University Press, 1990); Nussbaum, *Fragility of Goodness*; John J. Winkler and Froma Zeitlin, eds., *Nothing to Do with Dionysos: Athenian Drama in Its Social Context* (Princeton: Princeton University Press, 1990; Jean-Pierre Vernant and Pierre Vidal-Naquet, *Myth and Tragedy in Ancient Greece*, trans. Janet Lloyd (New York: Zone, 1980).

[12] Rocco, *Tragedy and Enlightenment*, p. 168.

[13] Nussbaum, *Fragility of Goodness*, p. 126.

[14] Ibid., p. 133.

about the complexities of your own life choices. Doing philosophy does not require or even utilize talents specific to good writing. The skills employed by the philosopher are more like those employed by the common theates. This emphasis directs attention to the kind of mental skill one employs when practicing philosophy and to the personal stakes that hang in the balance. For the poet, prizes, applause, and reputation were at stake. For the theates, the development of a strong and discerning mind—the capacity to make good life choices—was at stake.

PHILOSOPHER AS *THEATĒS* IN THE *REPUBLIC*

Plato introduces the image of the philosopher as an eager theates in the very first lines of the *Republic*. He portrays Socrates as having come to Peiraia in the first place to attend a festival (*katebēn chthes eis Peiraia . . . hama tēn heortēn boulomenos theasasthai*, 327a) and as willing to stay on for dinner and talk only because more spectacles will happen later in the evening. This is significant, as it is well known that the opening words of a Platonic dialogue allude to the central issues taken up in the text as a whole and that the *Republic* is exceptionally rich in such suggestive detail. The theatrical particulars of the setting—chiefly, the placement of the action at a festival occasion and at the home of Cephalus' son, Polemarchus—artfully signal more of the substance of the matters the company will take up. In particular, these details suggest that this philosophic conversation, like the Athenians on the occasion of the civic festivals, will confront two issues of great civic importance: "What is unity?" and, "What is worth engaging intellectually or, more economically, 'worth seeing'?"

Insofar as philosophic inquiry appropriates the festival occasion, the setting suggests that the practice of philosophy provides an alternative and better means by which an individual can develop a strong sense of being a member of a whole, that is, of a "we." In the opening passage of the *Republic*, Plato has Socrates use the singular forms of spectating terms to describe his trip down to the Peiraia as well as his reasons for making his trip (I went down . . . to pray to the Goddess . . . wanting to attend the festival: *katebēn, proseuxomenos, boulomenos theasasthai*, 327a1–3). Plato then has Socrates quickly switch to the plural to describe what he actually did there and how he left (after we had prayed and spectated, we went off toward the city: *proseuksamenoi, theōresantes, apēimen*, 327b1).[15] The "we" that gathers to talk with Socrates through the evening soon becomes even more inclusive than Socrates' initial "we," but they are all people who

---

[15] On a significant, subtle shift from the singular to the plural at *Gorgias* 500c–d, see Josiah Ober, *Political Dissent in Democratic Athens* (Princeton: Princeton University Press, 1998), pp. 206–7.

initially came for the celebration of the festival. The "we" comes to refer to Socrates, Glaucon, Adeimantus, Polemarchus, Niceratus, Thrasymachus, Cephalus, Lysias, Euthydemus, Charmantides, Cleitophon, and some unnamed others. This group represents some of the diversity that the Athenian polis struggled to hold together. It contains citizens, and metics of various backgrounds; young and old men; kinsmen (fathers and sons) and unrelated people; men of moderate and wild tempers; aggressive speakers, thoughtful interlocutors, and quiet people; devoted partisans of democracy and critics of democratic politics; sons of famous or wealthy fathers and anonymous folks. What common project can these diverse people share? How does the singular "I" come to be part of a "we"? How might these men form a unity?

Athenians relied on ritual action to accomplish this binding. Sacrifice, feasting, procession, and gatherings in theater and other viewing stands were key symbolic activities that nurtured the affective ties of discrete individuals to the idea of the demos or polis.[16] Setting the philosophic conversation at a festival and marking its role in Socrates' development of a sense of membership, Plato is noting that the political defense of philosophy is bound up with showing how it supports the civic project of unity, which, we learn, implies justice.

In light of the dialogue's interest in what constitutes a true unity, staging the action at the home of the metic Polemarchus was provocative.[17] His father, Cephalus, was a Syracusan whom Pericles is reported to have persuaded to reside in Athens.[18] He grew rich from his business as a shield manufacturer. His family thrived in the years of the Peloponnesian War but, after Athens' defeat in Sicily, suffered near ruin under the rule of

---

[16] The centrality of ritual action in forming a sense of membership in the ancient polis is well established in the scholarship. Morrow writes, for example, that festivals were civic in a "deep" sense "as powerful agencies in promoting unity of feeling among citizens and in fostering the sentiments of loyalty and devotion" to the city. Glenn Morrow, *Plato's Cretan City: An Historical Interpretation of the Laws* (Princeton: Princeton University Press, 1990 [1960]), p. 353.

[17] Setting the action at this particular festival may have been provocative as well. The festival represented at the opening of the *Republic* appears to be that of Bendis, a cult that celebrated ties between Athenian and Thracian peoples and that likely involved metics in its celebration. Socrates's reference to two processions (one by locals and one by Thracians) probably indicates that the celebration included a procession by native-born Athenian citizens from a particular deme and one by metics and/or visitors of Thracian origin. There is no strong consensus in the scholarship regarding the precise identity of the festival to which Plato alludes. Bendis is, however, the only suggestion that receives serious attention. The most recent treatment is Robert Parker, *Athenian Religion: A History* (New York: Oxford University Press, 1996), pp. 170–75.

[18] See Peter Steinberger, "Who Is Cephalus?" *Political Theory* 24, no. 2 (1996): 172–99, at pp. 172–73, for a comprehensive review of the surprisingly scant scholarly attention to the significance of Cephalus.

the Thirty. Their wealth was confiscated, and one son, Polemarchus, was executed. Another son, Lysias, was arrested but escaped to Megara. While in "exile," Lysias demonstrated such intense democratic sympathies that, upon his return in 403, the Assembly of the restored democracy voted to make him a citizen. But the Assembly revoked this offer less than a year later, an act that reiterated the importance the Athenians attached to nativity. Lysias remained at Athens and went on in the fourth century to become an accomplished speechwriter, composing many forensic works for delivery by others (metics could not address the courts themselves) as well as epideictic pieces (a funeral oration and Olympiac). The dramatic date of the *Republic* is the period of this family's prosperity in Athens. The actual date of composition is, of course, the first half of the fourth century, after the nightmare of the Thirty and the subsequent restoration of democracy. The action of the dialogue thus takes place at the home of one with a tenuous connection to the demos and in the "shadow" of the Athenians' experience of intense civil strife.[19]

This family's travails would have been well known to Plato's contemporaries. Its members were deeply involved with the democracy and yet remained always excluded from the governing life of the polis. They could at times be *suntheatai* (co-celebrants of theater and other festivities, as they are in the dialogue), though they could not be fellow *politai* (citizens). In the *Republic*, the common project they could share with citizens, the one that could bind them into a "we," is the search for knowledge, a search for which Cephalus and Polemarchus prove unfit, not ineligible. The setting thus alludes to the dialogue's rigorous consideration of the criteria for exclusion and inclusion in governing life and the relationship of such restrictions to the accomplishment of unity (justice).[20] The history of these men directs attention to the fact that the Athenians policed membership in the governing group quite strictly, something Socrates also proposes to do, though armed with new criteria.[21]

---

[19] For a different view of the significance of noting that the action of the *Republic* takes place "in the shadow of the Thirty," see Allan Bloom, *The Republic of Plato* (New York: Basic, 1968), p. 440 (n. 3). For another view of the import of the experience of the Thirty on the formation of Plato's dissident voice, see Ober, *Political Dissent*, pp. 162–65.

[20] A central reason for admitting women into the governing class in Book 5 is to direct attention to the radical nature of his consideration of the proper criteria for inclusion.

[21] Steinberger proposes that Cephalus represents "democratic man" and that his abrupt departure from the dialogue announces the "exile of the democratic spirit" from the conversation that is the *Republic* ("Who Is Cephalus?" p. 189). He asserts that Cephalus was a "patriarch of the democratic stronghold [Peiraia]," that he symbolizes the "democratic party," and that his sons were "leaders of the democratic party" (p. 185). But how could a metic be a patriarch of a deme? How could a metic be a leader of the "democratic party" (putting aside the imprecise and misleading use of the language of "party" to speak about the ancient world)? As David Whitehead stresses, "Even in demes where metics were numer-

In addition to the nature of unity, the dramatic opening passage of the *Republic* also raises the issue of what is "worth seeing/engaging," and thereby, as we will see, the issue of what significant intellectual labor is like. Asked in a cultural environment in which men prided themselves on being both producers and consumers of the greatest sights staged by any polis, as well as one in which men advertised their own claims to be capable and intelligent people by performing their role as theatai, this question must have resonated with Plato's contemporary readers. Plato indicates that the question, "What is worth spectating/theorizing?" frames the entire inquiry "reported" in the *Republic* in the following manner. Socrates and his companions acknowledge that the two processions Socrates traveled to Peiraia to see were "fine" (*kalē*, 327a4). Socrates is then urged to stay in Peiraia to witness more things "worth spectating" (*hēn axion*

---

ous and where they were made welcome . . . the lines of demarcation were plainly drawn. . . . In no sense was a metic a *member* of his deme of residence, or any other deme, and any who attempted to infiltrate a body of demesman did so at their peril." (David Whitehead, *The Demes of Attica, 508/7–ca. 250* [Princeton: Princeton University Press, 1986], pp. 84–85, emphasis in original. See also David Whitehead, *The Ideology of the Athenian Metic*[Cambridge: Cambridge Philological Society, 1977].) Steinberger neglects even to discuss the family's status as metics. He observes that Cephalus' family was "inextricably bound up with the culture of democracy" (p. 186) but misses the significance for Plato of this limitation of their link with Athens.

Placing the action at Cephalus' *oikos*, Plato brilliantly and with great economy also signals a number of other themes taken up in the dialogue as a whole. In relocating to Athens, Cephalus made a life choice that the dialogue subjects to vigorous criticism. He chose a life of money-making rather than citizenship (Julia Annas, *An Introduction to Plato's Republic* [New York: Oxford University Press, 1981], pp. 13–34). The family's losses may allude to how mistaken it is to link happiness and justice with the possession of wealth. It is not something fully within one's own power, unlike one's temperament (condition of soul), and so cannot guarantee happiness (C.D.C. Reeve, *Philosopher-Kings: The Argument of Plato's Republic* [Princeton: Princeton University Press, 1988], p. 5). It may also be that Cephalus represents the authority of the father and that his abrupt departure signals the theme of intergenerational conflict (Steinberger, "Who Is Cephalus?"), though this view does not account for why this particular father is featured. It may also be that Cephalus' age is symbolically potent. He is an elderly man. This may signal that distance from the lure of lusty passions is needed if one is to consider rationally the attractions of justice (Reeve, *Philosopher-Kings*, p. 5). Reeve suggests that Cephalus' age signals that he is "set in his ways" and an appropriate target for Socratic elenchus (pp. 6–8).

To these observations I would add that the fate of the historical Cephalus' two sons may recall the fate of Socrates. Polemarchus was unjustly executed by a political authority. Lysias' actions remind us of the option Socrates decidedly rejected. Lysias fled into "exile" and, though able to return, remained always a metic, never securing status *politēs*, though he certainly enjoyed a good career as a wordsmith. We can speculate that had Socrates fled, as Crito and others urged him to do, the most he could have hoped for would have been to live long enough to return at some later date when the political climate had improved. He may even have hoped to return to his gadfly activities. But he would always have remained *atimos*, in effect a metic in his native city.

theasasthai, 328a7)—specifically, the torch race on horseback and the subsequent all-night festival (*pannuchida*, 328a6). The performance of these sights will, Polemarchus adds, bring many young men together and provide an opportunity for talk (*dialexometha*, 328a9). In response to these points, Socrates' companion Glaucon says, "It seems we must stay" (328b2), and Socrates agrees. Of course, the conversation Socrates and his interlocutors take up that night is so lengthy that we readers must assume that they never do get to the festival, that is, to be theatai. Or do they? Plato's use of the theatrical vocabulary in the rest of the text—which I will track presently—suggests that in sticking with the philosophic discussion—performing and observing a dialogue—he and his interlocutors are not abandoning the worthy sights but, instead, are pursuing far finer ones.[22] Ironically, it is Cephalus who, in defecting from the conversation to attend a sacrifice, abandons the "sights worth spectating."[23]

Textual links between the language of the opening passage and that of the allegory of the cave also suggest that conducting a philosophical conversation is an alternative form of spectating/theorizing. Commentators have noted that the dramatic setting alludes to the cave analogy, but none appreciate the full extent of this allusion. The terms are here most sensibly translated into English by observational language. But this limitation must not obscure the range of allusions that Plato sets in motion. What appears as a visual experience is coded with multiple layers of civic significance. The two passages not only both refer to a "going down"

---

[22] I do not find compelling the suggestion that "all sight-seeing and even the dinner are completely forgotten in favor of the conversation about justice" (Leo Strauss, in *The City and Man* [Chicago: University of Chicago Press, 1964], p. 64). Though Strauss notes the prominence of references to spectating in the opening passage, he does not account for it. Instead, he seeks to minimize its theoretical interest. Strauss proposes that we view Socrates' interest in the sights in the first place as motivated by his effort to "cure" Glaucon of his political ambitions by turning him to philosophy. But first he has to get his attention, "gratify" him. Strauss suggests that we assume that Socrates "descended to the Piraeus for the sake of Glaucon and at the request of Glaucon" (p. 65). In my view, Socrates' "curiosity" about the festival is not a "mystery" explicable only by imagining the actions presumably taken by the parties "prior to the conversation" depicted in the *Republic* (p. 65). Socrates' initial interest in spectating is real, it is part of his interest in mining his own political culture for possibilities. It is part of Plato's investigation of the complexities that mark the relationship between philosophy and the Athenian democratic tradition. I am, however, in agreement with Strauss insofar as he stresses that the group's preoccupation with the conversation leads them to miss the torch race, and indeed, to show no interest in food, though they were gathered ostensibly for a meal. This turn in the action suggests that philosophical toil requires extraordinary control of one's sensory and bodily appetites.

[23] Nussbaum also suggests that the festival setting and figure of Cephalus raise "a question about value," that is, of "what is truly worthwhile, worth doing, and worth seeing, in a human life." But she does not discuss the role of the theatrical vocabulary in developing this theme. *Fragility of Goodness*, p. 137.

(*katabēn*, 327a1, and *katabateon*, 520c1), but to a going down *to do some active spectating*. In the cave analogy, the philosopher is represented as having to "go down" to join the others (in the cave) and to become habituated to "spectating" the dark things (*katabateon . . . ta skoteina theasasthai*, 520c1–3). In the opening line of the dialogue, Socrates is represented as having "gone down" to the Peiraia to be a spectator of a festival (*katebēn . . . tēn heortēn . . . theasasthai*, 327a1). In both passages, the ultimately inferior "sights" that a philosopher will abandon in favor of the objects of reason and intellection are represented by the imagery of darkness and firelight. Socrates is said to remain in Peiraia ostensibly to witness a torch race and nighttime festival (*tēn pannuchida theasometha*, 328a8), a situation that recalls the firelight that the cave-dwellers rely upon as well as the "darkness" to which the philosopher must become rehabituated when he returns to the cave (520c1–3, cited above).

Plato goes on in the *Republic* explicitly to develop a veritable list of alternative spectacles to which Socrates, his interlocutors, and readers of the dialogue turn their theoretical attention: "the city in speech" (369a5), "the feverish city" (372e9), "a beautiful soul" in harmony with a beautiful "form" (402d4), "all time and being" (486a7), "what is" (525a1, 582c8), "what is best in the things that are" (532c6), "democratic man" (545c2), the various dispositions and regimes delineated in Book 8 (545c6), "the city as a whole" (576e1), "the soul as a whole" (579e2), the immortal soul (611b), the pure soul (611c4), the soul maimed by evils (611d6), the things seen by Er during his time in the underworld (614d3). The sight of cleansed, disembodied souls choosing among the alternative, concrete lives spread before them, the image that closes the dialogue, is described in language that recalls Polemarchus' comment about the torch race at the very opening of the dialogue as a whole: it is a "sight worth seeing" (*tēn thean aksian einai idein*, 619e6, cf. 328a7).

The first pattern we can discern in Plato's reliance on this vocabulary to represent intellectual toil in the *Republic* is that it is repeatedly used to denote empirical observation of deeds that issues in some practical knowledge. It suggests not simple visual observation but rather a form of discerning, assessing. This usage is most dramatically present in Socrates' discussion of the education of the guardians, where it appears first in the description of how the adults judge the capabilities of the children, and then in that of the kinds of activity the children must take up in the course of their education. Socrates states that we "must observe" (*theateon*, 413d8) the children to determine which ones possess the mental and emotional qualities needed to endure training as guardians. A little later Socrates insists that training these children should include having them actually "spectate" adults in real combat situations. Children of guardians must be "spectators of war" (*theōrous polemou tous paidas poiein*, 467c2–7). Following up on this shocking suggestion, Socrates explains that the children should be led to the sight (*tēn thean*, 467e2), that is, to the battle, on horseback, so as to get the "fairest look" (*kallista theasontai*, 467e5, reiterated at 537a5) as well as to minimize the risk to their safety. The learning going on during the personal observation of exemplary deeds is more than training in "how to"; it is also a subtle nurturing of one's moral sensitivities. Watching real battles not only trains one in soldiering, it also exposes one to suffering.[24]

The second pattern evident in the *Republic*'s use of this family of terms is Plato's depiction of taking critical steps in the progress of the argument of the *Republic* as a whole. He represents these steps as "coming to apprehend something new," or adopting a new perspective. For example, in his early discussion with Glaucon about how they will be able to see sharply enough to recognize the attraction of justice and injustice (368c–d), Socrates famously suggests that they consider these things "writ large" (368d–369a). Socrates then asks, "If we should watch [spectate] a city come into being in speech (*gignomenēn polin theasaimetha logōi*), would we also see its justice coming into being, and its injustice?" (369a5–6). When Glaucon dismisses Socrates' first stab at fashioning a city in speech as "a city of pigs," Socrates retorts, "[Then] let's spectate a feverish city" (*phlegmainousan polin theōrēsōmen*, 372e9). Plato also evokes the experience of theater-going in his representation of taking steps in the argument. For example, Socrates describes Glaucon, the interlocutor who urges him not only to take risky steps in the argument (e.g., explicate the happiness of the guardians, the community of wives, and the practicality of the kallipolis), but to do so with fanfare rather than meekly, that is, to

---

[24] The link between learning as spectating and learning as developing moral sensitivities is present in other texts as well. In the *Laches*, interlocutors name witnessing real battles as valuable training for children and the spectacle of Socrates' behavior during the retreat from Delium as exemplary (179e3, 181a8). In the *Symposium*, Alcibiades also calls Socrates' behavior during this battle a fine spectacle (220a8). In the critique of rhetoric driving the *Gorgias*, Plato is mostly concerned to attack what typically pass for instructive or "worthy" sights. Regarding rhetoric, Socrates explicitly asks, What do its spectators gain? Pleasures? Gratification? Flattery? (502e1–503d3). Can spectacles give real benefits as well? The example he gives of a truly beneficial spectacle is revealing. He suggests that the sight in Hades of the nasty predicament of an "incurable" soul is a valuable spectacle (525c9) for other souls. It is frightening and instructive, pitiable and cautionary. It is wrenching. Returning to the *Republic*, we find there that Socrates relies on such terminology to describe Er's observation of souls choosing among possible lives at the close of the text (619e). Here it is the habitually just man who has no guidance from philosophy who, choosing too quickly, ends up beating his breast over his own thoughtlessness, for upon inspection, he sees that the life he has chosen will include an unwitting act of cannibalism involving his own children. All these instances link being an alert, involved, discriminating spectator with being an educated, thoughtful person equipped to make good life choices. They appropriate some usual associations with spectating to suggest the practical utility of being able to discern the worthiest sights, that is, of doing philosophy.

do so as a *suntheatēs* (523a7), a fellow audience member. When Socrates moves to consider the various forms of souls and regimes in Book 8, moreover, Glaucon observes that this is a "reasonable way for the spectating and judging (*hē te thea kai hē krisis*, 545c6) to take place." Combining a reference to *thea* with one to the practice of judging vividly recalls the dramatic competitions. At the close of the discussion of the merits of the various regimes and souls, Socrates asks Glaucon to turn now to decide which is happiest. Here again Plato does not just use a visual term but specifically alludes to the Athenian practice of theater-going. Glaucon explicitly likens his situation to that of the judges of dramatic competitions. What is your choice? Socrates asks; which is first, second, and so on regarding happiness? Glaucon says (580b–c) he will choose the regimes, like choruses,[25] in the order in which they came onstage (that is, kingship first and tyranny last).[26]

The new "spectacles" referred to in this cluster of usages in the *Republic* are often fictional images designed by the theoretical imagination. They are crafted by a human mind guided by philosophy. Even though we might thus want to compare philosophy with poetic production, Plato cautions us not to do so. Plato explicitly casts Socrates engaged in constructing "the city in speech" in the role of a theates, not that of a poet or composer.[27] This must be stressed if we are to understand the way Plato's use

---

[25] Bloom observes this allusion but does not see it as a part of a pattern, *The Republic of Plato*, p. 470 (n. 5).

[26] More examples of this pattern in the *Republic* include the following: (1) Socrates insists that those assembled persevere in their quest for some clarity regarding justice and injustice by turning their attention to what vice looks like: the many forms of vice are, Socrates offers, "sights worth seeing" (*aksia theas*, 445c2). Compare Thucydides' use of similar terms to describe the Athenian military forces assembled on the beach, ready to undertake the Sicilian campaign. Crowds came to see because it was a "sight worth seeing" (*kata thean hēken hōs epi' axiochreōn*, 6.31.1). (2) After the discussion of the nature of the philosopher, Socrates insists that the company can understand the slander of philosophy in actual cities by "spectating [a theoretical reconstruction of] the corruption of a philosophical nature" (*tēs phuseōs dei theasasthai tas phthoras*, 490e). (3) When the discussion moves to the happiness or misery of the tyrannical city and soul, Socrates insists that it is necessary for them to adopt a specific perspective, to become spectators of the whole (city or soul), if they are to recognize their respective happiness or wretchedness (*chrē holēn tēn polin . . . theasasthai*, 576e3; *an tis holēn psuchēn epistētai theasasthai*, 579e3).

The use of spectating terms to indicate taking steps in an argument is also present in the *Protagoras* (316a7, 352a6), the *Statesman* (260c6, 267e2, 281d9, 292d2, 299d7, 305b2), and the *Laws* (639d6, 676a6, 683a4, 686c1, 695c6, 702a, 720e7, 815b4, 816d8).

[27] One possible exception comes at 490c–d. Socrates is talking about the various virtues contained in the philosophic nature. He casts himself in the role of the chorus-master (the *didaskalos*, though he does not use the term) to suggest that he has presented a precise, coherent, and well-ordered conception of the relation between all the constitutive elements of the philosopher's nature. Socrates says: "If truth led the way, we wouldn't, I suppose, ever assert a chorus of evils could follow it. . . . Why then [in order to add moderation to this just and healthy constitution] must I force the rest of the philosophic nature's chorus into

of this vocabulary mobilizes Athenian ideals to say something about the practice of philosophy. It is well known that the Platonic texts set up philosophers and poets (and sophists as well) as rival "moral educators" (rival discerners of what is praiseworthy and blameworthy), as well as Socrates and Pericles as rival "benefactors" of the polis, that is, as rival claimants to the distinction "most *politikos* citizen." And it would be tempting to account for Plato's appropriation of theatrical metaphors entirely by linking it to his quarrel with the poets. This view would seem to fit with Plato's effort to argue that in a just city, philosophers would fill the role currently assumed by dramatists, or at least philosophers would censor materials produced by poets. But we must resist this temptation because it does not fit with the pattern of Plato's use of this terminology. When it comes to representing the ongoing activity of intellectual toil, including laboring to describe the ideal city, Plato consistently turns to images that liken robust intellectual work to audience performance.

The third pattern evident in Plato's use of the imagery of festival attendance and theater-going appears in his account of the disposition of the philosopher. Here the metaphor does some especially intricate work. Plato attaches the eager and excited attitude associated with the usual practice of festival attendance to intellectual toil. Philosophers are portrayed as insatiable consumers of spectacles. But, at the same time, Plato's usage draws a stark contrast between the desire to gratify one's appetite for sensory pleasures and the desire to locate the finest "sights" available. Plato uses the metaphor to stress that philosophers do indeed have pleasures and thrills in their lives at least commensurate with those typically experienced by Athenian citizens, but also to suggest that conventional sights will not elicit such a response from them. The dramatic setting conveys these thoughts. Socrates is portrayed as eager for the thrill of more spectacles, and then as preferring the spectacle produced by the philosophical conversation to the physical sight of the torch race. This portrait of the disposition of the philosopher is sustained throughout.

For example, Plato has the interlocutors explicitly compare philosophers and typical "lovers of sights" (*hoi philotheamones*, 475d–e) in an effort to explain what a philosopher is. Socrates indicates that the philosopher is

---

order all over again from the beginning? You surely remember that, appropriate to these, courage, magnificence, facility at learning, and memory went along with them." This passage is not at odds with my argument because its allusion to the chorus does not explain what Socrates is doing but rather reveals the character of the relations between the elements of the philosophic nature. It evokes the experience of being in a chorus that many in the audience could recall, not of being a chorus-master. It says to readers: "You know how intimate these parts are with one another and how carefully and precisely orchestrated their relations are." This passage thus actually supports my view that the text as a whole makes use of the imagery of spectating to depict the activity of philosophy.

"one who is willing to taste every kind of learning with gusto, and who approaches learning with delight, and is insatiable" (475c). Glaucon immediately adds that we will have to include some strange folks among the ranks of the philosophers. "Lovers of sights" in particular "enjoy learning" and clearly exhibit an insatiable appetite for what they take to be learning, though not for "discussion" (*logous*, 475d4). Instead, they "run around to every chorus at the Dionysia, missing none in the cities or the villages" (475d). What's important about the way this passage proceeds is that although Socrates and Glaucon agree that these lovers of sights are not philosophers, Socrates also explicitly allows that they are indeed "like philosophers" (*homoious men philosophois*, 475e2). Philosophers can be rightly understood, he explains, by thinking of them as "lovers of the sight [now understood as 'theoretical apprehension'] of truth" (*tous tēs alētheias . . . philotheamonas*, 475e4). Nonphilosophic lovers of sights delight both in sounds, colors, and shapes and in the way artists work with these resources. Philosophers, lovers of the "vision" of truth, on the other hand, delight not in the fair things but in "the fair itself" (*auto to kalon*, 476b10). The metaphor enables Plato to liken the philosopher's seemingly strange activities to those more ordinarily performed by citizens as they go about their lives. It is part of Plato's systematic effort to defend the philosopher and combat the effects of slanderous accusations of uselessness, incomprehensibility, impiety, oddity. The metaphor asks readers to interpret the philosopher's seemingly strange absorption in his efforts to locate and theoretically engage what he takes to be the finest of sights on the model of behavior not at all uncommon among the most devoted fans of the ordinary civic festivals.[28]

The fourth and last pattern to consider is the use of theatrical imagery in Plato's efforts to describe the character of philosophic understanding. In these cases, the "pure soul" conducts the action. The imagery represents the intellect's apprehension of an "intelligible object" as opposed to an experience of ordinary sensory (including visual) perception. This usage is perhaps most dramatically present in the cave analogy's depiction of the soul's journey upward (516a9, 516b6, 517b4, 517d6), though it also appears in the divided line (511c–d), the discussion of mathematics (525c2, 526e6), and the discussion of astronomy's difference from philosophy (529a1, 529b3).

After Socrates narrates the condition of the prisoners and what a release from their bonds would entail, he uses the theatrical terminology to de-

---

[28] Compare *Timaeus* 19b6, where Socrates likens his eagerness to hear an account of the ideal city (city in speech) engaged in a practical struggle (e.g., war) to his intense desire, upon seeing a beautiful creature at rest or represented in a painting, to observe (*theasasthai*) that creature engaged in some vigorous physical activity (e.g., a horse at full gallop).

scribe the predicament of someone who is capable of moving between these two realms, the sunlight and the cave. If someone were to be dragged from the cave into the light, he says, at first he would not be able to see the true things because his eyes would be unaccustomed to the sunlight. His first step toward gaining some understanding of his new situation would be his becoming a "theorist/spectator" of the things in heaven at night (516a9). After becoming accustomed to the daylight, he can become a theorist/spectator of the sun (516b4–7). Socrates also suggests that journeying up and out of the cave is coming to "theoretically behold the things above" (*thean tōn anō*, 517b4) and describes such activity as "divine theorizing" or, as translators usually render this passage, "divine contemplation" (*theiōn . . . theōriōn*, 517d6). Someone so skilled will, however, appear ridiculous when he joins those who dwell in darkness, especially when he is compelled "in courts or elsewhere to contest about the shadows of the just . . . and to dispute about the way these things are understood by men who have never seen justice itself" (517d). The philosopher's return to the cave requires a process of becoming habituated along with them to being "theatai of dark things" (*ta skoteina theasasthai*, 520c3).

Interestingly, Plato does not use the theatrical vocabulary to describe the prisoners viewing the shadows. They are watching a sequence of images, but they are not depicted as "spectating" or "theorizing." Rather, they only see. Plato turns to theatrical-performance vocabulary to describe the journey to the light and back again into the darkness, but now armed with philosophic understanding. The pattern of Plato's use respects the theatrical vocabulary's normal association with the process of learning—that is, of becoming knowledgeable, of conducting intellectual work—and its requisite involvement of a whole civic being. It respects the theatrical vocabulary's association with intense activity and not just the sensory experience of passively "seeing." Plato, of course, derides what tends to pass for learning in democratic Athens. But in presenting philosophy as a finer type of "audience performance"—a type that goes beyond sensory perception to distinguish between what is real and what is illusory—Plato suggests that philosophers ought to fill the civic role ordinarily associated with theatai at a dramatic competition.[29] That role is of intellectual work

[29] It is crucial to stress the active, possibly even creative (that is, not merely passive and observational), contributions of the audience to the theatrical experience to be able to see how they fit with Plato's depiction of philosophic labor. I use the term "audience performance" following both Robert Wallace ("Poet, Public and Theatocracy: Audience Performance in Classical Athens," in *Poet, Public and Performance in Ancient Greece*, ed. Robert Wallace and Lowell Edmunds [Baltimore: The Johns Hopkins University Press, 1997], pp. 97–111) and Susan Bennett (*Audience Performance: A Theory of Production and Reception* [New York: Routledge, 1990]). I mean to convey the active manner in which the Athenian

that is removed from the pressures of immediate policy and judicial decisions but is nonetheless politically relevant.

Not only the *Republic* but also the *Phaedo* (66e1, 99d–e, 109e–110a), the *Gorgias* (465d1, 523e4, 524e2), the *Symposium* (210c, 211d2, 211d7, 212a2), and the *Phaedrus* (247c1, 247c7, 247d4, 247e3, 249e5) rely on the imagery of audience performance to describe the activity of the soul engaged in rapturous philosophic understanding of some dimension of the human predicament. Perhaps the most memorable uses of this imagery include the *Republic*'s depiction of the apprehension of the Forms (486a7, 525a1), Diotima's depiction of apprehension of "beauty itself" in the *Symposium* (211d2, 212a2), and the *Phaedo*'s (111e3) depiction of the blessed's vision of the whole. In the *Phaedo* passage, Plato describes being blessed as being able to apprehend the earth from the perspective of the heavens, that is, "from above," and to notice that veins of colorful metals like gold adorn it.

Plato's appropriation of this theatrical imagery for philosophy in the *Republic* raises some questions regarding Plato's understanding of the relationship between philosophy and democracy. The strong association of theorizing and spectating with democratic civic practice did not, in Plato's view, undermine the metaphor's usefulness or compromise its soundness. Why not? The discussion of philosophy's relationship with astronomy in the *Republic* is useful in this connection.

Plato peppers his account of how studying astronomy can direct one toward "theoretical apprehension of being" (*ousian theasasthai*, 526e6) with language to which he strikingly returns in the description of the democratic regime in Book 8. Plato portrays both astronomers and philosophic inquirers as able to make use of lovely "decorations" (*poikilmata*) as "patterns" (*paradeigmata*) that may facilitate serious learning of a theoretical sort (529c–d, 557e). Plato uses the word Bloom translates as "decorations" four times in the brief passage about astronomy (529c) and repeats it five times soon after, in the description of the democratic regime (four times at 557c–d and once at 558c). The noun, *poikilia*, actually suggests more than the English word "decorations" conveys. It refers to something that is colorful, intricate, elaborate, lovely. The verb, *poikillō*, means "to work in colors, to embroider, embellish."[30] Plato's use of these terms in the astronomy passage suggests the extraordinary loveliness of

---

spectators experienced the theater. Wallace stresses the audiences' noisy, physical engagement with the performance to the point of being participants in the creation of the meaning of the event. As this view of the ancient theater-goer is not controversial and Wallace has already collected the relevant evidence in a convenient form, I do not review the ancient sources here. See Bennett, *Audience Performance*, for a theoretical treatment of the significance of an "emancipated" audience.

[30] Liddell and Scott, comps., *A Greek-English Lexicon*.

the objects studied by the astronomer—the stars and heavenly bodies. Plato also uses it to describe why democracy appears to be the fairest of the regimes (*kallistē autē tōn politeiōn einai*, 557c4). In this passage, which was also discussed above in a different context, Socrates says, "Just like a many-colored cloak (*himation poikilon*) embroidered in all colors (*pasin anthesi pepoikilmemon*, 557c5), this regime, embroidered (*pepoikilmenē*) with all dispositions, would also look the fairest. Many, like boys and women spectating such colorful things, would judge this the fairest regime (*hōsper hoi paides te kai hai gunaikes ta poikila theōmenoi kallistēn an polloi krineian*, 557c)."

This passage certainly highlights the apparent "loveliness" of democracy.[31] But is Plato endorsing or mocking the view that democracy appears the fairest regime because of its multiplicity? He is doing both. The conceit of the typical democrat is being mocked by the reference to women and children; at the same time, the philosopher's subtle insight regarding the intellectual resource its multiplicity provides is being endorsed.

Plato gently stresses the interest of democratic multiplicity to one with genuine philosophic abilities. Glaucon suggests that astronomy is useful for training toward philosophy, since plainly it "compels the soul to see the things above" (*dokei dēlon hoti hautē ge anangkazei psuchēn eis to anō horan*, 529a1–2). Socrates objects. "Looking upward" (*anō ... blepein*, 529b4) must mean "looking toward what is" (*peri to on*, 529b5), not just tilting your head back. "Even if a man were to learn something by tilting his head back and looking at decorations on a ceiling, you would probably believe he apprehends with his intellect, not his eyes" (*auton noēsei all' ouk ommasi theōrein*, 529b2–3). Socrates ridicules the suggestion that a physical orientation—rather than the orientation of one's intellect—can yield any knowledge. He does so, moreover, in a manner that responds to the characterization of himself in Aristophanes' *Clouds*.[32] "If a man, gaping up or squinting down, attempts to learn something of sensible things, I would deny that he ever learns—for there is no knowledge of such things—or that his soul looks up, rather than down, even if he learns while floating on his back on land or sea" (529b4–c1). Glaucon accepts the reproach gracefully and asks Socrates to explain in what way the study of astronomy might be helpful to the development of philosophic understanding. Here Socrates talks of the heavenly bodies and stars as if they were "decorations ... embroidered on a visible ceiling" (*poikilmata ... en horatōi pepoikiltai*, 529c7–8) and believed to be "the fairest and most

---

[31] For discussion of this passage's representation of democracy, especially its "variability," see Bruce Rosenstock, "Athena's Cloak: Plato's Critique of the Democratic City in the *Republic*," *Political Theory* 22, no. 3 (1994): 363–90.

[32] Bloom notes this allusion in *The Republic of Plato*, p. 466 (n. 17).

precise things" (*kallista* and *akribestata*, 529d1). His point regarding astronomical study is not complex. He simply refers to a view he had already developed in his discussion of geometry. Study of "decorations" (*poikilmata*, 529c7) can yield some knowledge only if one approaches them as "patterns" (*paradeigmata*, 529d7) for the sake of learning other things, that is, as carefully drawn diagrams (*diagrammasin*, 529e2–3).

I propose that Plato talks of "decorations" to direct the reader to some of his subtler thoughts about the relationship between philosophy and democracy. Democracy's loveliness is not simply deceptive, distracting, and generally problem-creating, though it is that.[33] It is also potentially a resource. Just like attention to the "decorations on the heavens" can yield some knowledge if one approaches them as "patterns" (*paradeigmata*, 529d7) for the sake of learning other things, the "decorative elements" of a democratic regime can be studied as patterns for the sake of learning finer things. Glaucon even says as much. Glaucon reasons that a man who desires to take up political philosophy "would not be at a loss for patterns" (*paradeigmata*, 557e1) in a democracy because democracy "contains" all species of rule (557d). Glaucon treats the lovely variety as a resource for philosophic conversation about justice, or, as Socrates puts it, for anyone trying to "organize a city [in speech] as we were just doing" (557d).[34]

Also meaningful in this connection is Plato's reference in the passage describing democracy's loveliness to the *peplos* (529c–d), the central symbol of the celebration of the Panathenaia, a grand civic festival on which occasion a richly embroidered cloak (*peplos*) was presented to the cult statue of Athena. This reference suggests a link between democracy's cultivation of loveliness and the celebration of the festivals. Accordingly, it suggests that training to be a "true" *theates* would constitute learning. Almost immediately after offering this possibility, however, Plato emphasizes that the ability to order these various paradigms, to discern their relative merits, is not something that democracy in fact cultivates. Socrates notes simply that democratic man "would choose the sort [of regime] that pleases him" (557d) and sums up his view thus: "[Democracy] is a sweet regime, without rulers and many-colored (*poikile*), dispensing a certain equality to equals and unequals alike" (558c). Democratic man is unlikely

---

[33] See Rosenstock, "Athena's Cloak," for discussion of how the *poikil-* language also develops the critique of democracy.

[34] The centrality of working with *paradeigmata* in Plato's view of serious intellectual endeavor is confirmed by the language at 540a–b. There Plato also describes the philosopher's work as ruler as an effort to use the "good itself" as a *paradeigma* to order (*kosmein*) a city, private men, and themselves for the rest of their lives. Also see *Laws* 811d–e, where the Athenian Stranger insists that "this discourse of ours" should be given to the guardians of the laws in the city they are crafting as a most useful tool for educating educators: nowhere could there be found a "better model" (*paradeigma* ... *beltion*, 811d).

to learn how to apprehend theoretically the patterns. This is a terrible circumstance, for only "if one *knows how* to be a theorist/spectator of the soul as a whole" (*ean tis holēn psuchēn epistētai theasasthai*, 579e3) will one be able to recognize the misery of the tyrant. Amidst the attention to the serious shortcomings of life in a democratic regime, these passages from the *Republic* nevertheless contain an acknowledgment of the real significance for philosophy of the apparent loveliness of democratic life.

THEORIST AS *THEŌROS* IN THE *LAWS*

Though the *Laws* incorporates many Athenian democratic innovations as well as traditions into the imaginary Cretan city and explicitly characterizes this second-best city as a mixture of democratic and aristocratic elements (756e), this text seems also to contain a sharp attack on radical democracy, and specifically on audience performance as the Athenians knew it. In the *Laws*, Plato blames developments in the theater for the dangerous excess of freedom in democratic society. The unnamed Athenian argues that the experience of being a theates, complete with its license to stomp feet and the like, nourishes an overconfidence in one's own judgment by assimilating the ability to assess what is pleasurable musical entertainment to the ability to evaluate the moral teachings expressed in a dramatic performance. It promotes, he argues, the belief that "everyone is wise in everything" (701b). People become fearless and, in the end, shameless—a civic condition he likens to a veritable "theatrokratia" (701a), by which he means rule of men possessed of the disposition of typical "spectators"—uninhibited, strong-minded, excessively confident, and noisy. Does this apparently wholesale attack on the behavior of auditors signal Plato's loss of confidence in the possibility of practicing a finer form of spectating, theorizing? Does the *Laws* give up on mining the familiar Athenian practices of audience performance for their philosophical possibilities, perhaps suggesting Plato is now in despair over the practical impossibility of uniting philosophy and political power, as one traditional reading of the relationship between the *Republic* and the *Laws* proposes?[35]

[35] Major works in political theory on the *Laws* are Morrow, *Plato's Cretan City*; Richard Stalley, *Introduction to Plato's Laws* (Oxford: Basil Blackwell, 1983); Leo Strauss, *The Argument and Action of the Laws* (Chicago: University of Chicago Press, 1975); Trevor Saunders, *Plato. The Laws. Translated with an Introduction* (New York: Penguin, 1970); Thomas Pangle, *The Laws of Plato* (New York: Basic, 1980); George Klosko, *The Development of Plato's Political Theory* (New York: Methuen, 1986); and P. A. Brunt, "The Model City of Plato's *Laws*," in his *Studies in Greek History and Thought* (Oxford: Clarendon, 1993), pp. 245–81. For discussion of the trends in scholarship on the *Laws* since 1960, see Charles Kahn's "Foreword" to the 1990 reissue of Morrow's *Plato's Cretan City*. For an accounting of the scholarship through 1975, see Trevor Saunders, *Bibliography on Plato's Laws, 1920–70, with Additional Citations through May 1975* (New York: Arno, 1976).

Some further probing of the theatrokratia passage combined with attention to the text's deployment of theatrical imagery in other places indicates that such conclusions are unwarranted. Instead, the pattern of Plato's use of this imagery in the *Laws* suggests quite the opposite. The passage decrying theatrokratia does not, for example, dismiss the experience of being a theates altogether, but laments the squandering of a resource, the metamorphosis of a possibility into a corrupting force. Plato explicitly uses this passage to stress that until the city and citizens accept the political import of genuine intellectual sophistication (capacity to discriminate), there will be, in language that echoes the *Republic*'s plea for recognition of the need to marry philosophical wisdom and political power, "no cessation of evils" (*mē lēxai pote kakōn*, 701c).[36] The condition he names "theatrokratia" at 701a is a terrible sign that a city is indeed quite far from such a recognition.[37]

Furthermore, in the rest of the *Laws*, Plato turns to the language of audience performance to represent behavior on the part of all the characters in this drama—the citizens of the imaginary Cretan city and all the participants in this dialogue. The crucial question for the present inquiry is, do these uses sustain the delicate metaphor, "intellectual labor is like the activity of a theates," that we have so far tracked in the *Republic* and noted in other texts? If so, do they also show signs of recording Plato's interest in the relationship between democratic life and the development of philosophic enterprises? The short answer to both questions is yes. To explain how so, I must first attend to some potentially misleading elements in the text.

Plato uses the theatrical language to represent the interlocutors' efforts to develop and follow the argument of the *Laws*, a pattern of use also evident in the *Republic*. However, unlike in the *Republic*, here it does not mark momentous moves but rather small steps. Moreover, the intellectual work of the Lawgiver and other high officials in the city of the *Laws* (assessing evidence, rendering judgment) is, on occasion, described in the language of audience performance (767e1, 862b5, 976d). But there is no apparently studied pattern of this use in the text as a whole. Also possibly misleading is the program of moral education of citizens detailed in the *Laws*. It relies heavily on censored sights and the well-regulated performance of spectating. The citizens of the imaginary Cretan city celebrate a full and varied regimen of festival activities. In fact, as Morrow has observed, the number of formal festivals with dramatic and musical contests,

---

[36] Cf. *Republic* 501e: *oute polei oute politais kakon paula estai.*

[37] Cf. *Laws* 659a–c, where the Athenian Stranger describes a corrupt theater as one where the judges show no independence but rather take their cues from the rowdy behavior of the audience, and where, as a result, the spectators "educate" the poets.

athletic games, and processions in this Cretan city will be considerably
"more than was usual in Greek cities."[38] But Plato does not characterize
the form of spectating performed on these occasions as independent intellectual toil. Rather, it is treated as a practice that facilitates the habituation
of ordinary citizens to a conception of virtue.[39] They do work not unlike
that of the preambles included in the written law code.[40] To find Plato
linking the cultural practice of theorizing/spectating with the practice of
philosophy we must look at the *Laws'* regulation of foreign travel, specifically its account of the intellectual work conducted by a citizen who goes
abroad to survey other cities and the civic import of his or her[41] mission,
and its account of the intellectual labors of the citizens who serve on the
"nocturnal council," an element of the city of the *Laws'* institutional
structure. Plato's treatment of these two matters displays a concentrated
and patterned use of the vocabulary of theorizing.

It is not surprising to find the comparison of intellectual toil and theorizing alive in this part of the text. The *Laws* does not invite its readers to
practice philosophy in the way that other dialogues in Plato's corpus do.
Here readers are presented with a law code as scripture, and interlocutors
are portrayed deferring to the authority of a lawgiver.[42] The *Laws* does not
depict interlocutors conducting an investigation, and the code presented
does not aim to kindle in citizens a passion for questioning. The only
account in this text of some variant of a serious contest of ideas takes
place among a small group of citizens in this imaginary city. The only
representation of investigations and examinations, and the only times
ideas here presented might rub up against alternative ways of thinking
and behaving, are when citizens travel abroad or consider the reports of
one who has traveled during a session of the nocturnal council.

---

[38] Morrow, *Plato's Cretan City*, p. 353, emphasis added.

[39] Such practices facilitate habituation first by exposing the citizen audience to legitimate
representations of the virtues to which they should aspire, thereby serving as "enchant-
ments" that, like the preambles to the laws, urge citizens to develop private aspirations
toward the public definition of praiseworthy behavior. Second, they effectively promote
solidarity among citizens. The proposal to include daily sacrifices should be read in this
connection. Third, they publicly *display* the ideals with which this city identifies itself.
(Plato's approach here is reminiscent of the interest in censorship in *Republic* Book 3.) All
of Plato's discussions of the conduct of these events in the imaginary Cretan city highlight
the way in which they involve citizens in enacting civic ideals. See Morrow, *Plato's Cretan
City*, for detailed study of how each proposal in the *Laws* draws upon practices of the historical Athens.

[40] On the preambles, see Andrea Nightingale, "Writing/Reading a Sacred Text: A Literary
Interpretation of Plato's *Laws*," *Classical Philology* 88, no. 4 (1993): 285–94, esp. p. 286.

[41] On female theoroi, see p. 233 below. On women in the city of the *Laws*, see David
Cohen, "The Legal Status and Political Role of Women in Plato's *Laws*," *Revue internatio-
nale des droits de l'antiquité* 34 (1987): 27–40.

[42] Nightingale, "Writing/Reading a Sacred Text," passim.

First, let us look at the Athenian Stranger's consideration of the imaginary Magnesia's regulation of citizens' foreign travel. Should foreign travel by citizens be allowed (950d)? The Athenian addresses this question at length. While he prohibits people under the age of forty from going abroad under any circumstances, and anyone at all from traveling for purely private reasons (950d–e), he explicitly allows, even elaborates upon, the usual practice of dispatching theoroi. A theoros was typically an envoy sent to a foreign city either for diplomatic reasons, to consult an oracle, or officially to represent the home city at a panhellenic festival (for example, at the Nemean or Olympic Games). The sending of such official missions was called *theōria*. The terms "theoros" and "theoria" could also denote a pilgrimage to a religious shrine. These terms stress the intellectual work conducted in visiting these places and reporting about them back home. The Athenian proposes that the city of the *Laws* dispatch not only these familiar theoroi, but also "other observation missions" (*theōrous allous*, 951a; *theoria*, 951c4) to travel for a longer period of time—up to ten years—for the twin purposes of surveying "the affairs of the other human beings [i.e., of various foreigners]" (*ta tōn allōn anthrōpōn pragmata theōrēsai*, 951a) and seeking out the conversation of "certain divine human beings" (*anthrōpoi theioi tines*, 951b). Plato portrays the work the new theoros conducts abroad as a searching empirical investigation of the practices (*nomoi*, *ēthē*, and *epitēdeumata*) of other cities as well as intense, possibly rational and philosophic, discussions with wise individuals whom, the Athenian readily admits, he may very well find even in badly ordered states (951b). The Athenian Stranger does not just permit such missions, but insists that they are a critically important public practice. He warns that without "this observation and search a city will never remain perfect; nor will it do so if they should carry out the observational missions badly" (*aneu gar tautēs tēs theōrias kai zētēseōs ou menei pote teleōs polis, oud'an kakōs autēn theōrōsin*, 951c). Nothing short of the maintenance of the health of the city through time pivots on the performance of a fine form of spectating by the special research-theoros. Why?

The research missions of the theoroi supply materials that sustain the living presence of philosophy in this city. We can get more of an idea of how this is so by comparing the qualifications the Stranger sets out for the traditional and the novel theoroi, and the depictions of how each is to be received by the city upon his return.

The traditional theoroi are described in a single sentence. They are to be over forty, and "the most numerous, beautiful, and best men possible" (*pempein de eis dunamin hoti pleistous hama kai kallistous te kai aristous*, 950e). The Athenian expects their behavior to advertise abroad the excellence of the city's moral fiber—these theoroi shall "give the city a good reputation in the sacred and peaceful gatherings . . . that is the counterpart to what is gained in war" (951a). He expects the return of these traditional theoroi from their "political trips" (950e) to reinforce younger citizens' confidence in and attachment to their city. They "will teach the young that the legal customs, pertaining to the regimes, of the others are in second place" (951a). This lesson is likely because the festival life of the imaginary city is so extensive and rich that foreign ways will seem wanting. Plato here seems to replicate the source of a similar conceit among the Athenians: the exceptional character of the city's festival events.

The labors of the traditional theoroi are not at all provocative. Not so with the novel research-theoroi.[43] Indeed, precisely because theirs can be provocative (and critical), the qualifications and return of the "other theoroi" receive extensive treatment.[44] The Stranger explains that such a theoros must be at least fifty, of good repute (especially in war—the common currency of honor in the Hellenic world), and a member of the board of auditors, and one must survive the careful scrutiny of the guardian of the laws (951c–d). The question of to whom the theoros must report immediately upon his return occasions a pause to describe in some detail the make-up of the so-called nocturnal council (951d–952d), a subject to which Plato returns at the close of the text (961a ff.). That is, the Athenian's efforts to describe who shall receive the information the theoros has collected, who shall be entrusted with the interpretation of this material, and precisely how this knowledge is to be put to the public use for which it was gathered, prompt the first account of this final element of this city's formal institutional structure.[45]

This council is to be made up of a "mixture of young and elderly men and shall be compelled to meet each day from dawn until the sun has risen" (951d). The older members are to include the ten eldest members of the guardians of the laws (chief magistrates), all those living who have served as a supervisor of education, and others judged meritorious. None

---

[43] Plato was not the first to rely on theoria to suggest going abroad to investigate/see the world. For example, in Herodotus' discussion of Solon at 1.30 we find *theōriēs heieken ekdemein*. But Plato's use of the term "theoroi" to denote a new class of official ambassadors is novel. See below for a discussion of Solon as theoros.

[44] Only Morrow (*Plato's Cretan City*) recognizes that this new institution is not a minor or marginal addition to the legal system and discusses it in any detail. Other commentators hardly even note its existence.

[45] On the logic of the late introduction of this element in the institutional structure of the *Laws*, see Morrow, *Plato's Cretan City*. On the imprecision of the common English translation of the Greek, *nukterinos sullogos*, as "nocturnal council" and the mistaken assumptions that flow from this habit, see V. Bradley Lewis, "The Nocturnal Council and Platonic Political Philosophy," *History of Political Thought* 19, no. 1 (1998): 1–20, at pp. 14–15. Lewis argues that the Greek strongly suggests informal, ad hoc meetings, not regular, institutionalized ones, and that a "more accurate, albeit homey, English translation would render *nukterinos sullogos* as something like 'nightly conference' or 'nightly meeting' " (p. 15).

of these individuals is to attend alone, but accompanied "by a young man between the ages of thirty and forty," of his own choosing (951e, also 961a–b). The members of the council are to hear accounts of the "legal customs among the rest of humanity" (952b) and to talk freely about them in comparison with those of their own city. They are possibly to consider how far this information raises questions about the adequacy of their own city's laws, or the need for a modification. But Plato here includes no mechanism by which this council can implement any changes that some or all of its individual members may deem necessary. Instead, he seems to assume that these citizens will always judge the laws of this city to be, all things considered, well ordered, and in need of no "innovation" (950a). And that may just be the point. The work of the research-theoros combined with that of the nocturnal council allows for the laws to be self-consciously and willingly *chosen* by a sample of honorable, capable, and somewhat philosophic citizens.

The scheme of awards and punishments meted out to theoroi engages citizens beyond the council members in enacting the choice-worthiness of their regime. Council members must identify whether going abroad has harmed, in no way altered, or improved the character of the individual theoros before he can rejoin society. If they decide that the theoros has returned corrupt, "he is not to associate with any young or elder man" (952c). If he abides by this rule, he may live "as a private man" (952d). But if he should be convicted in the popular court for being a "busybody in some way concerning the education and the laws," he is to die (952d). The theoros who has returned more or less the same should receive a little praise. The theoros who has returned significantly "better" (meaning more confident of the excellence of his own city's laws), however, should receive not only praise (952c) but possibly membership in the nocturnal council (961a) and certainly commemorative honors after death (952c). Both the popular court's conviction of the disgraced theoros and the recognition given to the honorable theoros involve citizens in representing the superior comparative value of their own laws.

The work of the council may also enact the idea that good arguments beyond the enchanting preambles stand behind the laws. Its work is chiefly exploratory and, at times, given the presence of sitting officials among its members, informally advisory. Its members are to consider the material collected by the theoros "seminar-style."[46] Plato stresses that what makes the council the "savior" (961d) and "safeguard" (960e) for the laws and this regime is that it performs the work of the "head" (961d), that is, of reason. The Stranger insists that the city needs to have some means of understanding its project (its "aim") so that it won't wander haphazardly

---

[46] Klosko, *The Development of Plato's Political Theory*, p. 218.

during times of stress (962d). The Stranger appeals to the imagery of the ship of state to focus on this point, stressing that the city needs some appreciation of the work of a ship's navigator as well as its crew so that it can prepare for and weather storms (961e). That appreciation is developed in the nocturnal council. Here members use the resources introduced by the research-theoros to provide themselves with a reasoned account of the excellence of their own laws. The institution of the theoros is designed to aid council members' efforts to get an accurate view (*akribestera skepsis thea*, 965c) by enriching their experience of "the many and dissimilar" (*tōn pollōn kai anomoiōn*, 965c), and thus their subsequent grasp of one unifying form. The council thus is, as the Stranger proposes, like an anchor for the entire city (961c).

Why Is Socrates Absent from the *Laws*?

In the *Laws*, Plato does not use the image of a theates, a spectator of local events, but turns instead to the image of the theoros, the foreign traveler-spectator, to represent serious, independent intellectual labor. Explaining why also helps elucidate why Socrates is not present in this dialogue, a knotty issue for commentators.

Most commentators explain Socrates' absence in the *Laws*—alone among the dialogues in the Platonic corpus—by noting that placing Socrates in Crete would have been historically awkward given that Socrates did not travel.[47] The speech of the Laws in the *Crito* includes the following account of Socrates' life choices:

> You have never left the city, even for a festival (*out' epi theōrian pōpot' ek tēs poleōs exēlthes*), nor for any other reason except military service, you have never gone to stay in any other city, as people do; you have had no desire to know another city or other laws; we and our city satisfied you. (52b)

But we know that at times Plato did not hesitate to violate historical accuracy for substantive ends.[48] In the *Menexenus*, Socrates is made to speak of events that happened after the dramatic date of the dialogue—indeed, after the death of the historical Socrates. We must seek a substantive reason for the absence of Socrates.

It has been suggested that his dramatic absence signals Plato's retreat from Socratic ideals. But the *Laws* is, as Morrow argues, fully concerned

---

[47] On Socrates in Crete as historically awkward, see R. B. Rutherford, *The Art of Plato* (Cambridge, Mass.: Harvard University Press, 1995), p. 275; and Strauss, *Argument and Action*, p. 1. Strauss quickly adds that this alone cannot account for Socrates' absence from the dialogue.

[48] Strauss notes this in *Argument and Action*, pp. 1–2.

with the key Socratic convictions that knowledge is virtue and that the political empowerment of genuine knowledge is the key to improving the lot of humankind. Strauss has suggested that perhaps the "emphatically political character of the *Laws* [i.e., its detailed, apparently practical policy proposals] would seem to explain why that work is the only Platonic dialogue in which Socrates does not participate, for Socrates was prevented by his *daimonion* from engaging in political activity."[49] But the Athenian Stranger is not himself engaging in any official political activity in this text. He is a visitor conversing with men whom he has met on the road about an abstract possibility. Nevertheless, Strauss' observation does direct us to the matter of the link between the absence of Socrates and the kind of intellectual activity portrayed here.

The *Laws* is a deep meditation on the possible political import of forms of intellectual labor in which the historical Socrates did not engage but in which Plato—judging not only from the text of the *Laws* but also from the elements of his biography that are known to us—certainly did. The absence of Socrates artfully records Plato's acknowledgment of the limitations of the life of Socrates as a model for understanding the full range of special knowledge that may be politically significant. Moreover, Socrates does not appear in the *Laws* because a different character was more suggestive of the concerns at hand. What we need to focus on is not the absence of Socrates, but the presence of the Athenian Stranger.

The unnamed Athenian is, as the letter of the text stresses, a "stranger" (624a, 625b, 625c, dramatically *o xene Athēnaie* at 626d and passim). The text itself provides valuable material for interpreting the significance of this figuration. During the discussion of the theoros and how the ideal city itself ought to receive visitors, we find a distinction between four "kinds of strangers" (952e). First, there are seasonal visitors on some private business. Second, there are theoroi of the traditional type—those who come to witness the sights (including festivals). These are described as tourists of sorts. Third, there are people on public business (treaties, trade). Fourth, there is the rare theoros who is a "counterpart" (*antistrophos*, 953c4) of our own research-theoroi. The Athenian offers that such a theoros would come to Magnesia either to view something of unsurpassed excellence resident here or to report on some such feature to another state. Such a person—and Plato explicitly notes that this theoros may be male or female (*xenous te kai xenas*, 953d9)—should be welcomed into the homes of the most virtuous. Plato crisply describes his or her intellectual labors. He or she is to "keep company with" one or two virtuous citizens, "teaching and learning" (*xunōn de toutōn tisi to men didaxas,*

---

[49] Ibid., p. 1.

to de mathōn apallattesthō, 953d). A theoros, he recognizes, may come from a less-than-ideal city.

It is plausible that the unnamed Athenian interlocutor models the stranger/theoros engaged in his empirical studies. Features of the dramatic setting support this identification. The Athenian Stranger is technically a theoros: he is traveling to visit the cave and Temple of Zeus, a religious shrine (625b). Further, he is an old man engaged in conversation with two other old men. This image of a private conversation among a stranger and two others, all over the age of fifty, recalls the account of how an ideal city ought to receive a theoros. Moreover, the noted (635a) absence of any young people in the present company indicates that the conversation does not parallel the discussion initiated by the theoros in the nocturnal council, but instead represents his prior labors. In the nocturnal council, as we have just seen, the information collected by a theoros is presented to a set of young people, albeit carefully selected ones, as well as to older men.

Plato's depictions of the labors of the Stranger in the whole text may supply an extended account of what the toil of a theoros is like. The Athenian Stranger is portrayed as eager to inquire as to the meaning and attraction of alien customs, and to report on Athenian ways. His initiation of a discussion of the purpose of Dorian ways—specifically common meals, gymnastic schools, and military exercises—opens the *Laws*. Moreover, Megillus' report that he once viewed (*etheasmēn*, 637b5) a whole city drunk at a Dionysia inspires, for the Stranger, not only a discussion of drunkenness but also an effort to consider whether an observer's opinion is of any consequence if not informed by some experience of (*etheasato*, 639d) the institution in question "correctly" conducted. That is, he moves to consider what makes an observation theoretically interesting. The Stranger represents his account of rightly ordered education in part to remedy his interlocutor's (and his reader's) inexperience of any such rightly ordered institutions in practice, and thus, it is implied, to improve his (and our) judgment. The Stranger's companions are urged to "learn from my [his] explanations" (*emou phrazontos*, 640a4).

The Athenian Stranger may also model another form of intellectual activity that Plato considered significant but in which the historical Socrates did not engage. The Stranger acts as an unofficial legislative advisor to Kleinias, the Cretan interlocutor who will soon be involved in crafting a constitution for a new colony. In being asked to help Kleinias, the Athenian Stranger may conduct some of the intellectual work of actual members of the Platonic Academy. The establishment of new colonies was in the fourth century still very much a part of Greek life, and Plato, as well as other members of his Academy, was approached to give advice to actual men in similar circumstances (as were other highly regarded intellectuals of the time). As Morrow notes, "The conversation [the Athenian] carries on with his companions is but an idealized version of the discussions that must have taken place on countless occasions among persons responsible for establishing a new colony."[50]

It remains for us to consider how Plato's use of the theatrical imagery in the *Laws* may record his interest in the relationship between philosophy and democracy. We must be cautious, because democratic cities were not the only ones to conduct such missions. We must ask in what way Athens specifically was connected with these theoretical missions, foreign travel, and the treatment of aliens. The exceptional and celebrated openness of Athenian democratic society—its tolerance, its openness to numerous foreigners, the mobility of its own citizens—is significant. Athens was, of course, a chief destination for the intellectually curious, for renowned intellectuals from the itinerant sophists to Aristotle, and for spectacle seekers from all over Hellas. The celebration of the City Dionysia, moreover, probably rivaled the four panhellenic festivals. Thus, not only is the Athenian politeia a spectacle usefully studied by travelers from other cities, but wise men of many backgrounds can often be found in this city. Despite his moral worries about "living as you like," Plato may have appreciated that Athens as a whole was apparently a superb resource for people interested in serious political research and intellectual stimulation of the sort that the novel theoros might undertake and the Lawgiver is assumed to have already undertaken.[51]

Another link between Athenian democracy and these theoretical missions (theoria) may be that the most celebrated theoros in Greek history was probably Solon, an Athenian statesman and poet closely associated

---

[50] Morrow, *Plato's Cretan City*, p. 4.

[51] Some may object, insisting that Plato is most interested in studying Spartan ways. Plato was indeed drawn to Spartan customs, but, as Stalley and Morrow have stressed, he always assesses them through the lens of Athenian society. Stalley writes: "Plato leaves us in no doubt as to his respect for the Dorian way of life, which was much admired by conservative elements throughout Greece, but at the same time he makes it clear that the Dorian tradition is fundamentally defective and needs to be reviewed in the light of Athenian wisdom. He thus distances himself from the orthodox conservatism of his day" (*Introduction to Plato's Laws*, p. 5). I would add that the dramatic setting offers further reason to find Stalley's suggestion compelling. The Athenian Stranger's two companions are both portrayed as having special "affection" for Athens. The Spartan Megillus reports that his family is *proxenos* of Athens (642b5), that is, officially charged to represent the interests of Athens in Spartan deliberative arenas. The Cretan Kleinias, moreover, reports that his ancestors had journeyed to Athens before the Persian Wars and had formed a bond of "guest-friendship" with citizens there (*exenōthēsan*, 642e). In response to these two figures' back-to-back declarations of affection for Athens, the unnamed Athenian replies, "It's likely, then, that you are ready to play your part as listeners" (*akouein*, 643a). Plato later depicts the two Dorians in large part being instructed by the unnamed Athenian. The Dorians are even explicitly referred to as students (*mathētai*, 770c). See Morrow, *Plato's Cretan City*, pp. 74–77.

in the Athenian imaginary with the city's democratic constitution (see Aristotle *Politics* 1273b34–1274a21 and *Constitution of Athens* 2.3, 5.1–12.5). Solon traveled abroad for ten years (chiefly in Egypt) following the institution of his reforms. In the *Histories,* Herodotus uses the language of theoria to describe his travels (1.29–30). Judging from his treatment in the dialogues, Plato admired Solon and the use to which he put his intellect.[52] In the *Timaeus* we can observe two parallels between Solon the traveler and the research-theoros of the *Laws.* The first comes in the course of Critias' recollection of the story of Atlantis (20e–25d), a tale Solon is said to have brought to Athens from Egypt. Critias' account of Solon's intellectual labors while in Egypt includes a report that Solon took up vigorous questioning of the Egyptian priests about ancient history (22a, 23d). The second parallel appears in the account of the use to which the interlocutors in the *Timaeus* put the story of Atlantis. They employ it as a resource for thinking further about the nature of the ideal city—the subject of their lengthy conversation only "yesterday" (26d–e, also 17c and 19b). *Timaeus* 17d–19a clearly identifies this ideal city discussed "yesterday" with the one detailed in the *Republic.* In the *Timaeus,* the Atlantis myth becomes a vehicle for imagining the ideal city of the *Republic* involved in a material struggle (20b) or a time of stress (e.g., in a war). This subject then leads to inquiries into issues like the origin of the universe and the order of the kosmos. Plato depicts the figures in the *Timaeus* relying on material originating from a theoros to raise the most searching and fundamental of investigations.

It is no longer easy to assert that "like all puritans, Plato hates the theater."[53] As we have noted, it is now widely recognized that the genre of writing Plato creates owes a positive debt to the Athenian tradition of dramatic writing. I propose further that through a studied deployment of theatrical metaphors for intellectual toil, Plato both acknowledges and explores philosophy's links to a specifically demotic (as opposed to elite) practice of Athenian democracy—theater-going. Thus, though the *Republic* and *Laws* both vigorously oppose the core principle of democracy, that is, the belief that the political arena ought not to recognize any claim to special knowledge, both texts also rely on variants of the practice of audience performance to portray the cultivation of "special knowledge." In

---

[52] See *Protagoras* 343a; *Symposium* 209d; *Republic* 599e; *Timaeus* 20e; and *Laws* 858e. For an assessment of Plato's treatment of Solon that stresses both the importance of the memory of Solon for the fourth-century Athenian democrats and the affinities between Solon's and Plato's political visions, see Morrow, *Plato's Cretan City,* pp. 76–86.

[53] Iris Murdoch, *The Fire and the Sun* (Oxford: Clarendon, 1977), p. 13.

the *Republic*, Plato relies on the imagery of the theater-goer (*theatēs*) to represent the education of the philosopher and its civic significance. In the *Laws*, he turns to the citizen-envoy dispatched abroad (*theōros*) to depict empirical research and its public import. In crafting a radical new account of how politically significant learning ought to be conceived, Plato found these concrete civic practices of Athenian democratic life in some ways illustrative. His vision of intellectual labor, though not democratic in outlook, remains nevertheless entangled with elements of Athenian democratic traditions.

Concluding Remarks

In these pages I have developed approaches to interpreting Athenian democracy and the complexities of Plato's political thought. Taking Athenian democracy to be a cluster of cultural practices and normative imagery as well as a set of governing institutions, I emphasized that ideas of antityrantism, reciprocal exchange, responsible ruling, frank speaking, unity, and strong-mindedness are central to the Athenian understanding of the demands of democratic citizenship. Placing Plato in the context of these contemporaneous understandings of democracy, I showed that although he contrasts the claims of democratic legitimacy and those of philosophical truth, he also explores how intimately linked are Athenian democratic politics and the practice of philosophy. In particular, I tracked Plato's embrace of the ethics of antityrantism, frank speaking, responsible rule, and reciprocity, and of parts of the intellectual missions of both funeral oratory and theater-going.

These continuities between Plato's political philosophy and the Athenian democratic tradition are subtle; Plato's recognition of this measure of union—his weaving of elements of what his contemporaries would regard as specifically democratic ideals and practices into his depiction of the activity of philosophy—is delicate. But these patterns of interest in democracy indeed coexist alongside the well-known criticisms of the democratic Assembly, popular juries, and the culture of freedom and equality. Plato remains politically and intellectually attached to democratic Athens even as he lays bare what he took to be its inadequacies.

Additional aspects of Plato's thought are ripe for interpretation using the approach I advocate here. For example, new dimensions of Plato's thought might emerge from a study of the cultural resonances of his use of the language and imagery of gender difference and family relations. There are, moreover, questions in democratic theory today that can engage the record of Athenian cultural practices and Plato's treatment of them. For instance, what improvement in our understanding of democratic deliberations today might come from attention to the Athenian practice of frank speaking? What questions about the demands of democratic citizenship today might rise from consideration of the centrality of reciprocity in the Athenian democratic imaginary? Throughout this study I have focused on identifying the intricacies of Plato's involvement with democracy as he knew it. Perhaps we can now bring Plato into conversations about democracy as we know it.

INDEX OF CITATIONS

INDEX

Academy, of Plato, 137–45; goals of, 139–42; and the *Laws*, 143–44; political influence of, 141–45, 146–53; and political research, 144; as source of law-givers, 141–42, 143–45; structure of, 138–40

accountability, and power, 127. *See also* responsibility

Adam, J., 130n, 154n, 167n, 169n, 170n, 171n, 175n

Alcibiades, 45–46, 47, 48, 172

Allen, D., 16n

Allen, R. E., 181n, 185n, 188n

anachronism: in the *Laws*, 232; in the *Menexenus*, 188–89

Andrewes, A., 23n, 43n, 46n, 47n

Annas, J., 215n

anonymity, Platonic. *See* voice, in Platonic dialogues

antityrantism: Athenian, 21, 29, 37; in Plato, 113–14. *See also* freedom; Harmodius and Aristogeiton; tyranny

Apology, of Plato, 27, 125, 161, 172; and the *Menexenus*, 199–200

aporia: in the *Menexenus*, 184; and philosophy, 133

Archinus, and the restoration of democracy, 184n

Arendt, H., 14n

aristocracy: distinguished from oligarchy in Plato, 117; Platonic attitudes toward, 127; in the *Republic*, 117, 127

Aristogeiton, motives of, 49–50. *See also* Harmodius and Aristogeiton

Aristotle: on epideictic oratory, 204–5; on Harmodius and Aristogeiton, 49–50; on Pericles, 183n

Armstrong, C. B., 138n, 139n, 141n

Arnott, P., 96n, 105n, 106n

Aspasia, in the *Menexenus*, 186, 193–96

Assembly: deception of, 59–60; decisions of, 15; *isēgoria* in, 56–57; *parrhēsia* in, 51, 56–63; as scrutinizer of drama, 97n; and the theater, 96–97

astronomy, and philosophy, 223–25

Athenian Stranger: as *theoros*, 233–35; and the work of Plato's Academy, 143–44, 234

Athens: beauty of, 72–74; as *erōmenos*, 74–87

audience performance, 103n, 222n, 223, 226–27. *See also* drama

autochthony, and citizenship, 196–99

Bambrough, R., 14n

Barker, E., 3n

Benardete, S., 33n

benefaction, toward Athens, 37, 39, 99–101; and class, 197; in oratory, 86; in the *Republic*'s ideal city, 129–30; Socrates' and Pericles' performance of, 220. *See also* charis; reciprocity

Bennett, S., 222n

Bloedrow, E. F., 181n

Bloom, A., 21n, 114n, 124n, 214n, 219n, 223, 224n

Boedeker, D., 29n

Bonner, R. J., 51n, 59n

Bourdieu, P., 4n

Bowen, A., 136n

Bowra, C. M., 26n, 33n, 40n, 149n

Brandwood, L., 152n, 186n

Brown, W., 194n

Browning, R., 9n

Brumbaugh, R., 119n

Brunt, P. A., 119n, 120n, 137n, 138n, 141, 142, 144n, 145n, 148n, 149n, 226n

Burkert, W., 29n

Burnyeat, M. F., 14n

Callicles, in the *Gorgias*: as lover, 193n; as touchstone, 163

Cartledge, P., 107n

Castoriadis, C., 8n, 61n, 169n

Castriota, D., 21n, 25n, 26n, 28n, 30n, 31n

Cave, allegory of the, 123, 216–17, 221–23

Cephalus, in the *Republic*, 212–216